HONORED
BUT
INVISIBLE

HONORED
BUT
INVISIBLE

An Inside Look
at Teaching in Community Colleges

W. NORTON GRUBB

with

HELENA WORTHEN
BARBARA BYRD
ELNORA WEBB
NORENA BADWAY
CHESTER CASE
STANFORD GOTO
JENNIFER CURRY VILLENEUVE

Routledge
New York and London

Published in 1999 by
Routledge
29 West 35th Street
New York, NY 10001

Published in Great Britain by
Routledge
11 New Fetter Lane
London EC4P 4EE

Printed in the United States of America on acid-free paper.

Library of Congress Cataloging-in-Publication Data

Grubb, W. Norton
    Honored but invisible : an inside look at teaching in community colleges / W. Norton Grubb and associates.
      p.   cm.
    Includes bibliographical references and index.
    ISBN 0-415-92164-3 (hb.) — ISBN 0-415-92165-1 (pbk.)
    1. College teaching—United States.   2. Community colleges—United States.   I. Title.
LB2331.G78   1999
378.1'2—DC21   98-35021

                                                                     CIP

We have a tradition that is honored, I suppose as much in the breach as not, but we do have a tradition as seeing ourselves as the teaching college. . . . But I think that, at least, the tradition is there and it can be called upon when the occasion warrants.

—A community college English instructor

Community colleges are invisible, right? I mean, many people don't see community colleges. They're not institutions like the university; they're looked on as kind of very low-status. Teachers in community colleges . . . really need to think how they feel about being at a non-prestigious institution where many of the students are underprepared. They're going to have to think about why they chose that piece of the vineyard.

—A remedial/developmental instructor

CONTENTS

ACKNOWLEDGMENTS

We argue throughout this book that teaching should be viewed as a collective activity, rather than as the individual and idiosyncratic effort that it usually is. It's fitting, therefore, that this book itself is a highly collective effort. Most obviously, we relied on observations of about 260 instructors from every imaginable field of study, and on interviews with virtually all of them. We also interviewed about sixty administrators, from every possible type of community college. These individuals were unfailingly helpful and generous with their time, providing insights into their teaching and their institutions that are available in no other way. What we report about teaching, and about the institutional responsibilities for improving instruction, we learned from them. This is really their book, and we dedicate it to the many excellent instructors in community colleges around the country who are working as hard as they can—often under trying circumstances—to expand the competencies of their varied students.

This book is collective in another sense: The observations and interviews were carried out collectively, and interpreting these voluminous materials and formulating arguments were joint efforts as well. The process began with a seminar that planned the research; in addition to the associates who participated in the book itself, Bill Charland, Larry Forman, of San Diego City College, and Jim Wilczak, of West Valley College, took part at this early stage. As we all continued to observe classes and interview faculty, we met periodically to make sense of what we were learning, and to add to the issues that seemed important. These meetings were crucial in shaping the arguments that this book presents.

Of those who continued to participate, Helena Worthen was the most active. She drew her dissertation from these observations and interviews (Worthen, 1997), an effort that won the 1998 award for best dissertation written at the School of Education, University of California, Berkeley. She wrote some of these results into a first draft of Chapter 4, on literacy practices. She also wrote a first draft of Chapter 5, on remedial education, participated extensively in the writing of Chapter 6, and made extensive comments on various other chapters, particularly the first three. Because of her unique background as both community college

teacher and researcher, with particular interests in part-time instructors, her contributions were always sharp and to the point, and I thank her for her commitment to this project.

Barbara Byrd took a particular interest in teaching in occupational education
and observed numerous classes in these areas as well as visiting several technical
institutes. She wrote an early draft of Chapter 3 and continued to participate in the
development of that chapter. Elnora Webb concentrated on observations and
interviews in colleges within the Bay Area; she wrote an early draft of Chapter 8
based on these results.

Norena Badway has been most concerned with various efforts to integrate academic and vocational education, and she contributed numerous observations
about these practices; in addition, she observed the co-op seminars at LaGuardia
Community College. Chet Case was particularly interested in learning communities and visited a number of colleges active in promoting this particular innovation. Stan Goto concentrated on examining remedial/developmental programs,
including the innovative program profiled at the end of Chapter 5; he has also
completed a dissertation on remediation (Goto, 1999), though not based on these
materials. Jennifer Curry Villeneuve visited a number of colleges, especially in
California; like many of us, she was particularly captivated by learning communities. All of these individuals contributed both to the collection of information
and to its subsequent analysis in long discussions in which we hashed out what it
all meant.

While this volume is principally based on the research we carried out, the work
has also been informed by our own experiences in community colleges. Helena
Worthen has been an instructor in several community colleges, including Laney,
Alameda, Merritt, and Vista, all in the Bay Area, as well as the University of San
Francisco and Dominican College in San Rafael. She has been active in commu-
nity college unions, particularly advocating for part-time instructors through a
newsletter she edited. She now works for UNITE! (Union of Needle Trades,
Industrial, and Textile Employees) in Philadelphia. Barbara Byrd was an instruc-
tor and department chair in the labor studies program at San Francisco City
College; she now teaches at the Labor Education and Research Center at the
University of Oregon, Portland. Elnora Webb has been working as a consultant to
several colleges and is now completing a dissertation at the University of California, Berkeley, on community colleges. Chet Case has been an instructor, faculty
development coordinator, dean, and finally president of Los Medanos College in
Pittsburg, California. Stan Goto has been a remedial instructor at Contra Costa
College; he is now a postdoctoral fellow at the Community College Research
Center and at Teachers College, Columbia University. Jennifer Villeneuve has
worked extensively on special projects for colleges throughout California and is

now completing a dissertation on novel multimedia programs in community colleges. Finally, Norena Badway and I have presented numerous workshops for community college faculty and administrators on topics ranging from curriculum integration to tech prep to workforce development. We are currently engaged in creating a network of colleges to provide technical assistance in precisely the continuous and collaborative forms we outline in Chapter 8. This direct experience with community colleges has provided us with more personal information to complement what we have learned through research.

This work arose from early examinations of programs to integrate academic and vocational education, undertaken first with Eileen Kraskouskas and then with Norena Badway, as part of the National Center for Research in Vocational Education at University of California, Berkeley. We uncovered many creative practices, but also a puzzle: While we learned of many remarkable innovations, few of them had been extensively replicated. We then began to realize, partly by giving numerous workshops, that most colleges were not actively supporting teaching innovation in any form, and we undertook this research to understand why. The initial collection of information through observations and interviews was supported by the National Center for Research in Vocational Education (PR/Award no. V051A3003-98A), administered by the Office of Vocational and Adult Education, U.S. Department of Education. However, the contents do not necessarily represent the positions or policies of the Office of Vocational and Adult Education, U.S. Department of Education.

I also want to thank Paul Ryan, King's College, the Department of Economics and the Department of Education at Cambridge University, for providing a congenial place during a sabbatical in fall 1996, where a first draft of this book was written. Finally, I thank my wondrous wife, Erica, who edited a final version of the manuscript. Her efforts to improve my writing and other personal failings have been unstinting, if not always successful.

W. Norton Grubb
David Gardner Chair in Higher Education
University of California, Berkeley
June 1998

Introduction

WHO CARES FOR TEACHING IN COMMUNITY COLLEGES?
The Rationale and Methodology of Our Inquiry

Surely educational institutions should be primarily concerned with teaching and learning. At least in our society, schools and colleges have little formal role in business to distract them from teaching, and their political roles are also marginal except on certain hot issues (like affirmative action). Extracurricular activities may be important, but no one thinks well of institutions that become party or football schools. Our educational institutions are relatively specialized; presumably they can concentrate on teaching and learning in ways that families, workplaces, and community and political institutions no longer can.

Sometimes, however, teaching and learning seem the last concerns of schools and colleges. The lofty rhetoric—the notion of educating all Americans to the limits of their ability, the faith in education as the engine of economic growth and personal advancement, the recurring belief in equality of educational opportunity—has real consequences, particularly in stimulating public funding, but it says almost nothing about what goes on in classrooms. Local school board elections and political jousting in state capitals and Washington, D.C., are far from classroom practices. The administrators who represent schools and colleges to the outside world often speak in platitudes and the language of boosterism; their political and managerial roles often swamp their roles as educational leaders. All too often debates about education become mired in conflicts over *means*—funding, political control, personnel policies, the allocation of space and equipment. The *ends*, the learning of students and its facilitation by instructors, are forgotten.

In this book we intend to make visible instruction in an institution—the community college—where teaching is both particularly important and especially neglected. To pull teaching out from behind the closed doors of the classroom, we concentrate on describing and interpreting the teaching we have seen in about 260 classrooms, trying to find patterns in colleges that have greater variety than any other type of educational institution. Consistently we emphasize that while teaching is often thought to be an individual activity, it need not be seen that way. The ways instructors teach are profoundly influenced by the students who come to them, the resources at their disposal, their own education, their preparation specific to teaching, the networks of peers they create (or fail to create), and the culture and incentives of their colleges. Institutions can influence these conditions of teaching, though many do not. Indeed, a central conclusion of this book is that many community colleges *as institutions* pay little attention to teaching: They fail to use their institutional resources to enhance the quality of instruction, so that good teaching emerges only in isolated and idiosyncratic ways.

The institutional analysis of teaching is our response to a "great divide" within education, one that is partly responsible for proponents of community colleges continuing to trumpet their institutions as "teaching institutions" while doing little to improve the quality of instruction. On one hand, large social, political, economic, and cultural influences on education have dominated some perspectives. In the world of practice, this is where administrators and policy makers are most comfortable, and in research this is the arena of economists, historians, political scientists, and sociologists. On the other hand, classroom-level perspectives have been concerned with the interactions between instructors and students. Most teachers operate wholly within the classroom, and psychologists, some anthropologists, and students of teaching methods usually focus at this level. This divide, pervasive in both practice and research, has been everywhere counterproductive. It has led to the lack of support for instructors that we first identify in Chapter 1 when we describe the dominant approach to teacher development, trial and error. It has also led to the distance between administrators and instructors that we examine in Chapter 8. It underlies the neglect of instruction in state and federal policy, and the conventional but flawed analysis of funding that we correct in Chapter 9. The goal of bridging this divide stands behind much of our analysis.

While we have examined teaching specifically in community colleges, many of our conclusions are just as applicable to other institutions, particularly high schools and four-year colleges. The approaches to teaching that we clarify in Chapter 1, and the issues associated with different forms of "hybrid teaching" in Chapters 2 and 3, are present in every educational setting and have been debated from early childhood education through the Ph.D. level. The different conceptions of literacy in Chapter 4 and the issues of standards in Chapter 6 are nearly universal. High schools and four-year colleges have wrestled with the need for remediation, the subject of Chapter 5, just as community colleges have. The "great divide" between institutional influences and instruction is a serious problem at every other level of the educational system, too.[1] The absence of institutional mechanisms to enhance teaching is as prevalent in high schools, most four-year colleges, and research universities as it is in community colleges. The details of our analysis are specific to community colleges, then, but our central arguments are universal.

I. THE IMPORTANCE OF COMMUNITY COLLEGES

Comprehensive community colleges and technical institutes (or technical colleges) specializing in occupational preparation have become important institutions in the American landscape, and they play several unusual roles in postsecondary education. [2] Most obviously, enrollments have increased substantially in these institutions. In fall 1995, community colleges accounted for 37 percent of all enrollments in postsecondary education, up from 18 percent thirty years earlier; during this period community colleges were the fastest-growing segment of education. However, the total enrollment figures include college juniors and seniors plus graduate students, who by definition do not attend community colleges. For students attending college for the first time, 44 percent enrolled in community colleges in 1995—up from 17 percent in 1955. Thus, almost half of students entering postsecondary institutions do so through community colleges.[3]

Their importance is not simply a function of numbers, however. Because their tuition and fees are lower, and because they are generally commuter institutions that don't require students to leave home, they attract many students who cannot afford to attend four-year colleges or who are unwilling to leave their homes. Because they are open-access institutions—without an admissions process requiring academic qualifications—they have often been called "second-chance" institutions, providing a second crack at higher education for students whose motivation and performance in earlier schooling were inadequate to gain them admission to four-year colleges. For both reasons, community colleges have high proportions of lower-income and minority students. For example, 35 percent of white undergraduates are enrolled in community colleges, compared to 40 percent of black students and 54 percent of Latino students.[4]

The status of community colleges as "second-chance" institutions also rests on their importance for older students—not only those who failed to enroll earlier in their lives, but also those deciding to take a different course, women joining the workforce after a divorce or after their children are grown, individuals bounced out of promising careers through no fault of their own, and displaced workers affected by economic dislocations such as the decline of manufacturing (or timber or mining in specific regions) or the cyclical variations in defense and aerospace employment. As an economics instructor described the mix:

I find it [the community college] very rewarding, exciting, challenging. I tend to think it's probably one of the most important parts of higher education in that, as far as I'm concerned, it's the last real opportunity for many people in our community. You can be a high-school dropout, you can have all sorts of problems or issues of your past, and as long as the community college is there for you, there's still that hope. . . . Very, very difficult to quantify or measure or whatever, but I know it's there, I feel it's there, I sense it.

While "lifelong learning" and "flexible enrollment" have become buzzwords, the community colleges best exemplify this ideal, since 52 percent of their students are older than twenty-four.[5] These students violate many assumptions of traditional colleges; they are usually employed, and thereby undermine the separation of schooling from the outside world. "They're scheduling their classes around their work hours," as one instructor put it, and real work competes with their commitment to schoolwork. But older students can compensate for such problems by their maturity, their clearer sense of what they want from college ("They're coming for a specific reason"), their wider experiences that enrich the classroom. Almost universally instructors prefer teaching older students; as one mentioned,

The older students are more prepared to function as active students, in any context, large or small. . . . The older ones are generally more willing, and they're clear about why they're there. The younger ones are just not sure that they're even there.

Other community college students are new to this country—immigrants who use the community college as a low-cost place to learn English, to learn about the customs of a new country, and to find out how the mechanisms of mobility operate. It's hard to determine precisely how many immigrant or limited-English students there are in community colleges—they often enroll in regular courses or in remedial courses open to all students rather than English as a Second Language (ESL), and they are concentrated in urban community colleges on the coasts—but there is no doubt their numbers are large on many campuses.

Some students in community colleges are there for specific purposes, but others aren't sure what they want to do—they are using the community college to find out. These "undecided" students, or "experimenters" (Manski, 1989), leave high school without knowing what they want to do, or find themselves in dead-end jobs without a clue about what directions might be more productive. Guidance and counseling services in this country are hard to find, so they enroll in community colleges as a way of exploring their options. As a representative of this group described her situation:

> Well, it'll be nine years this August that I've been licensed [as a manicurist], which is the longest I've ever done anything, and I really do enjoy it. But I feel like there's . . . you can only go so far, and I would just like to have an opportunity someday to do something else. I just don't happen to know what it is right now.[6]

An instructor described such students in precisely the same terms:

> They want to do something, they want to succeed, but maybe they haven't exactly tapped into what it is yet.

These "experimenters" create some special pedagogical problems, particularly because their motivation is still uncrystallized. One instructor mentioned:

> It's almost like they come because they've made no decision about their future—not because they have made one but because they *haven't* made one. They enroll because of their quasicommitment to education.

Another complained, "I have some people who want to take the class for information, and don't intend to do any of the work." Many "experimenters," having attended low-quality high schools, have no sense of their abilities or what postsecondary education entails. As a remedial instructor described her students, writing about the obstacles they might need to overcome:

> Two thirds of my students in the very basic skills classes can barely write. But I'll get, "I don't really see anything that will hold me back." It's things like that are clueing me into the fact that the realness of this decision has not come to them.

But most instructors accept that helping such "lost souls" find their way into the world is an important (if underrated) function of the community college—"a wonderful, cheap opportunity to do it."

As the emergence of "experimenters" illustrates, the purposes of community colleges have shifted as the institutions have developed. The original purpose of the early "junior college"—allowing students to transfer to four-year colleges—is still alive and well, and (as we shall see) it remains the highest-status purpose in most institutions. But it's difficult to justify the community college solely by its transfer function. Many students don't intend to transfer, and by most estimates transfer rates are relatively low and have declined over time.[7] Other purposes have become just as important, though lower in status. The occupational purpose is among these. As we will clarify in Chapter 3, virtually all students attend for broadly occupational purposes, and fully 60 percent of those enrolled say that they are in occupational programs. Thus community colleges have become the most important locus of relatively job-specific occupational education, preparing individuals for the sub-baccalaureate labor market that includes about 60 percent of all workers (Grubb, 1996b). And the growing numbers of students who leave high school with low levels of academic preparation, or older students whose academic skills are rusty, mean that an increasing proportion of students needs remedial or developmental education.[8] The counterpart for limited-English students is ESL, somewhat different in its pedagogical requirements.

Still other purposes have emerged. In some communities, job training and welfare-to-work programs subcontract with community colleges to provide short-term skills training or remediation, and in other places community colleges are the administrators of adult education funds.[9] Some colleges have taken on roles in "workforce development," a vague phrase usually denoting training for the employees of specific firms. Others also play important roles in economic and community development, to strengthen the communities they work in (Grubb et al., 1997). In this book, however, we emphasize teaching in the core areas of academic preparation, occupational instruction, and remedial/developmental education and ignore short-term job training, workforce development, and community service. There's challenge enough in describing the range of teaching within core subjects, and examining other purposes would have taken us into an overwhelming variety of nontraditional settings.

The upshot for instructors of the diversification of community colleges is the enormous range of students. "We have everything here," declared a physics instructor. A basic reading instructor, when asked about her students, simply gave up: "The most common factor is that . . . ," she began, then paused. Finally she finished, "There's not one," mentioning in turn single mothers returning to work, young men in their twenties "who kind of did their own thing, and now they're ready to come back [to school]," welfare mothers, people switching careers, and traditional-age students.

The diversity of students and of purposes reflects two defining characteristics of community colleges. One is the commitment to a broad range of students, exemplified by the rhetoric about the "people's college" and "democracy's open door" (Griffith and Connor, 1994), the insistence on open access to all students who seek entry, and the support of virtually all instructors for this range of students. The inclusiveness of community colleges is part of what Cremin (1965) called the genius of American education, an inclusiveness manifest elsewhere in public support for four-year colleges, special education and mainstreaming for handicapped students, the funding of compensatory education, and bilingual education.

The inclusiveness of the comprehensive community college brings a range of pedagogical issues, as virtually all instructors recognize. The students who most need second-chance institutions are, by definition, less academically prepared than other postsecondary students, forcing instructors to find new ways to teach and requiring more remedial or developmental education; "the students need more nurturing," as one instructor put it. Indeed, the sheer range of students' motivations and skill levels is a problem. An auto instructor described the problem this way:

> We have this breadth—this senior gentleman here, he's got a master's degree in marketing, he's a very sharp guy, and then you get somebody that is remedial in every sense of the word, probably fifth-grade reading level. They're all out there in that classroom and you have to make it interesting for all of them—how do you keep this person from getting bored to death and at the same time not bury the one down here?

The "experimenters" often lack motivation, and attend classes more to find out about their interests than to learn a subject. Conversely, older students may be highly motivated—"They're clear about why they're here"—but are so constrained by job and family responsibilities that their schoolwork suffers. ESL students, individuals referred by job training programs, and welfare recipients all come with their own particular needs and learning problems. And so community colleges committed to diversity face both a greater variety of students and a greater number of pedagogical challenges than does any other institution: "We have everything here."

A second defining characteristic contributing to the inclusive and expanded functions of community colleges is a certain entrepreneurial spirit—a willingness to accept new roles, an eagerness to expand into new "markets." This makes colleges more responsive to local communities and to changing economic and demographic conditions than many other educational institutions. But like the commitment to diversity, this entrepreneurial spirit has its costs. It creates colleges that are sometimes fragmented and incoherent, and the commitment to expanding enrollments and revenues undermines institutional support for teaching in several ways (as we will see in Chapters 8 and 9). And so the very attributes that make community colleges distinctive also create pedagogical challenges that often go unrecognized and unresolved.

Despite the admirable features of community colleges, they—like the teaching within them—are nearly invisible. When Americans celebrate the quality of higher education, they are usually thinking about the Harvards and Stanfords and Berkeleys, not about community colleges. When they insist on providing access to postsecondary education, they focus on grants and loans that benefit students in four-year colleges and proprietary schools, not community colleges. As one instructor noted:

> Community colleges are invisible, right? I mean, many people don't see community colleges. They're not institutions like the university; they're looked on as kind of very low-status. Teachers in community colleges . . . really need to think how they feel about being at a nonprestigious institution where many of the students are under-prepared, and they're going to have to think about why they chose that piece of the vineyard.

Invisibility is unfortunate both because community colleges provide a great deal of access to postsecondary education and because they embody so many of the ideals Americans have always held for education. We hope in some small measure to make community colleges more visible by showing how they can be great in their own ways, by being everything a "teaching institution" should be.

II. THE IMPORTANCE OF TEACHING: THE MEANING OF A "TEACHING INSTITUTION"

Another defining element of the community college is its vision of itself as a "teaching college." The rhetoric about teaching is almost as pervasive as that about diversity; in the words of the Commission on the Future of the Community College:

> At the center of building community there is teaching. Teaching is the heartbeat of the educational enterprise. . . . Excellence in teaching is the means by which the vitality of the college is extended and a network of intellectual enrichment and cultural understanding is built. (1988, 9–10)

Cohen and Brawer's (1989) reference volume on the community college cites teaching as its *raison d'être*, quoting Albert Eels's comment that the community college is "a teaching institution *par excellence*" (p. 148). O'Banion et al.'s *Teaching and Learning in the Community College* (1994, vii) calls the institution a "learner-centered teaching college" and declares teaching and learning "a mandate for the 90s." The instructors we observed repeated this convention, though sometimes with hesitation; one said, "It's a teaching college, isn't it?" while another commented, "It's supposed to be a teaching college, but there's nothing for teachers here." The English instructor from whom we have taken part of our title expressed the problem succinctly:

I think we have a tradition that is honored, I suppose as much in the breach as not, but we do have a tradition as seeing ourselves as the teaching college. . . . At least, the tradition is there and it can be called upon when the occasion warrants.

When we scrutinize these statements, they prove to be comparisons between the community college and the large research university. They usually define the community college more as a "nonresearch institution" whose faculty is not distracted by research obligations than as a teaching institution emphasizing the improvement of instruction. As Cohen and Brawer noted, "College planners never envisioned these institutions as the homes of research scholars. . . . Classroom teaching was the hallmark" (p. 148). Virtually the only evidence that advocates offer for community colleges being teaching institutions is that they have smaller classes. But while smaller class size is important to the modal forms of instruction we examine in Chapters 2 and 3, it's quite possible to revert to conventional lecturing in small classes, as we show in Chapter 2.

In addition, proponents often claim that community college faculty have selected themselves into the institution because they are more interested in teaching than research, and tenure here does not depend on publishing. A typical example is a recent article by the president of Onondaga Community College claiming that "community colleges are equal to Harvard in the first two years," noting smaller class sizes, the lack of graduate student teaching assistants, and the faculty dedication to "teaching, not research" (Raisman, 1998). While it's true that community college faculty are less interested in research than their peers in four-year colleges, the inverse relationship between interest in research and teaching performance *assumed* by these advocates is questionable.[10] Given the hiring procedures of most community colleges and the lack of preparation in pedagogy (examined more carefully in Chapter 8), it's all too common to find instructors who speak the language of good teaching but who have paid little attention to their own practices. While tenure may not depend on publishing, it may not depend on teaching either (as we show in Chapter 8)—so again the community college seems less a teaching college than a nonresearch institution. And the dark side of being a teaching institution is that faculty have to teach much more—an average of sixteen classroom hours a week, 50 percent more than faculty in state colleges and more than twice that of faculty in research universities, with obvious effects on the time available to ruminate about what good teaching might be.[11] Thus the unending claims about community colleges as teaching institutions rely on certain conditions—the absence of research, a faculty drawn to teaching, small classes—that *could* enhance teaching but do not *necessarily* do so. The evidence that community colleges are teaching-oriented is simply missing.

One reason for the lack of evidence is that there have been almost no empirical investigations of teaching in community colleges.[12] There is, to be sure, a weighty literature about how faculty ought to teach, and how administrators ought to motivate their instructors. But this literature, by turns hortatory and celebratory, never asks what teaching looks like. In Cohen and Brawer's (1989) massive bibliography of the community college, for example, the chapter on teaching first reviews the claims for the college being a teaching institution, and then moves to a section in "Instructional Techniques" describing various methods—but with no analysis of how frequent these practices are or how teachers use them, nor any reference to empirical work (with one exception noted below). The massive *Handbook of Research on Teaching* includes a chapter on postsecondary education, but none of the literature reviewed is about community colleges (Dunkin and Barnes, 1986). Terry O'Banion and associates' *Teaching and Learning in the Community College* (1994) includes a chapter by Richardson and Elliott (1994) based on interviews with students about effective practices, and Matthews's (1994) chapter on learning communities is based on long experience, but there are no other reports from the classroom. Similarly, one might expect a book on remedial education like Roueche and Roueche's *Between a Rock and a Hard Place* (1993) to analyze different teaching strategies, since remedial/developmental education presents some of the most difficult pedagogical challenges around; but the reader can find only vague descriptions of instructional strategies (such as contextualized instruction and the importance of "learning to learn")—without any sense of what instructors actually do or whether they are effective. Griffith and Connor's celebration of the community college, *Democracy's Open Door* (1994), profiles some of the effective instructors "compelled to learn to teach in ways for which our professional training provided few models" (p. 49), but aside from referring to empathy for students, the authors never describe what these new ways of teaching look like.

The critics of community colleges are as much to blame as the advocates. McGrath and Spear's (1991) essay about the failure of the community college to establish an academic culture starts with two brief vignettes—one about a class where students come without their books, another reviewing a take-home exam on which most students received D's—but it isn't clear whether these vignettes describe common problems, their own experiences, or emerging issues. Throughout, the authors make generalizations—about faculty as upholders of academic tradition in contrast to counselors as advocates for students, about "traditional" teaching, about the differences between teaching in vocational courses and those for "professional, responsible, innovative careers," about the "cultural disarticulation" of underprepared students—that assume readers know and agree with them about the inner workings of colleges. The often-cited critics of the community college, including Brint and Karabel (1989), Pincus (1980), Zwerling (1976 and

1989), and Clark (1960) make literally no mention of teaching in any of their diatribes. They criticize community colleges for "cooling out" students by subtly lowering their ambitions, but aside from some ancient references to counseling practices, they provide no sense of how cooling out might take place.[13] The ethnographic writing about students in community colleges (London, 1978; Weis, 1985), also quite critical, reports the perceptions of faculty, but it does not explore classroom practices. We could go on and on; even where one expects some investigation of what teaching in community colleges is like, there is none.

One exception to this rule is Richardson, Fisk, and Okun's *Literacy in the Open-Access College* (1983), based on observations in a single community college in the Midwest.[14] They noted the dominance in academic courses of information transfer, with instructors intent on "getting through" a great deal of raw information, and discussions so highly structured that they were not real interchanges. In contrast, the vocational labs they described were equipment- and activity-dominated, with instructors playing a mostly advisory or guiding role, with more intrinsic motivation from the tasks themselves. The authors noted that a third typical course, in basic skills, was dominated by drill and recitation, and was highly teacher-directed. They concluded that most literacy instruction was guilty of what they called "bitting"—breaking reading and writing into small "bits" (like sentence completion exercises)—in contrast to the practices of "texting," where students read whole texts for information or interpretation.

A second partial exception is Seidman's *In the Words of the Faculty* (1985), which analyzed the dilemmas of community college teaching through interviews with seventy-six faculty members. He came to many of the same conclusions as we have, describing the unfortunate division between academic and occupational purposes, the incredible pressures on faculty, the special difficulties of teaching underprepared students, the unimaginative use of computers. He stressed, as we do, the complexity of teaching well, along with the tendency of many colleges to ignore teaching and learning.

There are a few smaller empirical pieces (like Richardson and Elliott, 1994, mentioned above), but that's about it. There's almost no information about what teaching looks like in the "teaching college." Teaching is invisible in several senses, then: Not only does it take place behind closed doors, out of sight of other instructors and administrators, but it has never been the subject of sustained description, or any analysis of what happens, or why it looks as it does. The lack of evidence has been a central motive for our writing. It's difficult to think about improving the quality of these institutions, enhancing their responses to the need for more remediation and ESL, or understanding how "cooling out" takes place without knowing more about what instructors do and what shapes their teaching.

In this volume we take seriously the claims of community colleges to be teaching institutions, as a springboard for our analysis. Because this phrase has been so devoid of content, we must first define what *we* mean by it. We assume that a teaching institution is one in which teaching is a collective and institutional responsibility, rather than an individual activity by isolated instructors. Such an institution devotes its resources first and foremost to improving the quality of instruction. Among its resources we count personnel practices, including the basic definition of an instructor's job; rewards, including pay but also status and institutional attention; support for innovation, staff development, teaching centers, equipment (including computers, new machines required in occupational classes, or science labs), and other means of improved instruction; and institutional culture, that ill-defined but critical element determining what is most valued in a particular college. We will work throughout this book to define these institutional effects, drawing them together in Chapters 8 and 9. The dean of instruction who declared that "institutions have very little leverage" on teaching was quite wrong, in our view: Institutions have a great deal of leverage, and those that use it consistently can improve instruction considerably. But most do not, and it's difficult to call them teaching colleges.

Another corollary of calling the community college a teaching institution is perhaps more difficult. This phrase assumes that the quality of teaching matters—that we can distinguish good teaching from mediocre and bad teaching, and that different approaches to teaching have different effects on students. On the one hand, this assumption seems obvious: The development of specialized educational institutions suggests that teaching must matter, and the oceans of ink spilled in arguing for one approach over another, or exhorting teachers how to become better, indicates that the assumption is widespread. The quality of teaching might also matter particularly to the academically underprepared students concentrated in community colleges. As we will see, many instructors and administrators feel that conventional didactic instruction is particularly inappropriate for nontraditional students, and they are searching for more participatory methods to motivate them. On the other hand, there is only scant evidence that different approaches to teaching affect what students learn, as we clarify in Chapter 1.

In our analysis, where we have observed classes but do not have information about student outcomes, the argument that teaching matters depends on different kinds of evidence. We have had to rely on variation in the competencies students acquire under different approaches to teaching; on our observations about student engagement and disengagement; on instructors' comments about what does and does not motivate students to learn; on our direct observation of classes with low standards and scant content, compared to those instructors with much higher standards for their students (especially in Chapter 6); and on patchy evidence about what effect mediocre teaching might have on dropout rates. Not surprisingly, given that we have written a book on teaching, we conclude that instruction matters a great deal. When we wind up in the last chapter considering the big issues facing community colleges—their promise as "teaching institutions," their success as "people's colleges"—we conclude that the quality of teaching is central to all of them. But this argument isn't obvious, and we note the necessity for *demonstrating* what is often simply *assumed*.

III. OUR METHODOLOGY FOR EXAMINING INSTRUCTION

In deciding to examine teaching in community colleges, we made the direct observation of classes and workshops our priority. This proved to be the right decision: While interviews with administrators and the instructors we observed were rich and informative, what happens in the classroom is often quite different from what instructors say goes on (as we clarify in Chapter 1). The activities of different classes, the patterns that dominate, the variations among teachers with different philosophies, the high levels of student engagement in the wonderful classes we observed and the deadliness of the really bad classes are all impossible to detect except by observing teaching directly.

When we observed classes, we used a protocol designed to capture as much as possible the composition of students, the physical arrangements, the dominant activities minute by minute, the nature of questions and responses (verbatim when possible), and all signs of engagement and disengagement. This protocol was shaped by the conceptions of teaching we present in Chapter 1. We did not record these classes on audiotape because the noise and bustle of most classrooms make such tapes almost impossible to transcribe; we did not videotape because of the intrusiveness and cost of doing so. After obtaining both institutional and instructor permission, we tried to observe between three and six hours for each instructor, which usually meant two or three classes of one and a half hours each, or two vocational workshops, which typically last three to four hours apiece.[15] In some cases—particularly in visiting distant colleges, where we had to let others set up our schedules—we saw only a single class, of between one and a half and three hours in duration. From those instructors that we saw in several courses, or teaching several different subjects, we saw remarkable consistency in teaching style; while everyone has good days and bad days, this consistency means that it is possible to capture a particular instructor's approach to teaching in a relatively brief period.[16]

Over time we became increasingly aware of important dimensions of teaching that escaped us earlier, and so we added to our observations. For example, we began to note the amount of indirect teaching in occupational classes about the "lore" of the workplace—interpersonal and power relations, tricks of the trade, differences between real work and classroom conditions—in addition to the cognitive and manipulative skills required. We began to see the amazing variety and sophistication of literacy practices in classrooms, even those (like occupational workshops) where literacy is not an obvious component. We began to understand the conditions under which students stay engaged in lectures, and when most of them tune out; we figured out that lectures are not all the same and not always deadly. The patterns of participation in "discussions"—which are sometimes real discussions and sometimes lectures in disguise (as we show in Chapter 2)—became increasingly obvious. The lack of much empirical literature on teaching in community colleges or other adult settings was a real handicap because we had little guidance about classroom patterns. Our research was learning by doing, and neither we, nor John Dewey, nor some of the instructors we observed think this is the best way.[17]

We then interviewed instructors for at least an hour each, asking them about their background, their preparation for teaching, their goals for students and philosophy of teaching, their conceptions of their students, their interactions with colleagues, and the role of administrators and their college in supporting teaching. We recorded these interviews, and so the quotations from instructors are taken from verbatim transcripts, though occasionally it was necessary to conduct interviews on the fly or over lunch. While we missed a few interviews because of scheduling problems, only two instructors declined to be interviewed. The vast majority of instructors were remarkably forthcoming and candid, because most are committed to teaching and therefore responsive to interviewers interested in what they do. Most instructors love to spin their stories; sadly enough, they rarely get to do so. Even when they were stumped—and many were taken aback by questions about good teaching and about the institutional resources available to enhance teaching—their answers were revealing.

But there proves to be a built-in bias in these interviews. A characteristic of good teachers—and we will present several conceptions of good teaching in the next chapter—is that they are concerned and thoughtful about pedagogy, and so their responses are more considered, more insightful, more revealing in every way. In contrast, mediocre instructors have often not thought about teaching at all, and so their answers are often flat and formulaic. Indeed, some of them don't even think that teaching is an issue; one of them, a full-time instructor for twenty years, went so far as to say, "I'm not a teacher." Our interpretations are inevitably skewed: We learned much more from those instructors who have been most active in reflecting about their teaching and changing their approaches, and this group tends to have moved away from conventional didactic lecturing toward approaches that are variously called "meaning-centered," or "student-centered," or "active" (as we outline in Chapter 1).

We also interviewed administrators in order to learn more about institutional practices and priorities. We tried to interview those administrators senior to the instructors we observed; for example, after we observed English instructors, we then interviewed the chair of the English department and the dean of instruction, and after observing automotive and business instructors, we interviewed the dean for occupational education. These interviews, also recorded and transcribed, were more mixed in their results. Some administrators are remarkably knowledgeable about teaching and the instructors under them, and candid about institutional problems; but the majority are (as we will see in Chapter 8) distressingly ignorant about what happens in classrooms. These interviews were most successful in describing the institutional procedures—for example, hiring, promotion, staff development, and funding changes—that are matters of record. They were less useful in eliciting opinion and speculation about what institutions ought to look like or how teaching might be enhanced. As in the case of instructors, the responses are biased in systematic ways: The administrators who have been most active in educational roles (rather than purely administrative functions) are also the most informative and insightful about teaching, and the least prone to repeating conventional mantras about the community college.

Finally, of course, we collected paper records: syllabuses for the courses we observed, tests and quizzes, reading lists, college catalogues, plans, institutional research about students, and anything else we could get our hands on. Unfortunately, community colleges do not conduct extensive institutional research, and so information about the effectiveness of different approaches to teaching or course-taking patterns—for example, the value of remedial classes for those judged to need remediation, or learning communities rather than independent classes—is rarely available. What is available is a tip-off to the priorities of colleges: a great deal of information to inform students about courses and programs, a little guidance to instructors about department or institutional goals, and a great deal of data on enrollments but not on outcomes.

We were unable to interview students. Our initial efforts to do so were met with a great deal of administrative resistance. Deans interpreted this request as evidence that we intended to *evaluate* instructors and the college, not merely *observe*. Approval to interview students would have required much more internal discussion, consent from many more sources—the academic senate, the unions, the president, even the board of trustees—and a great deal of delay, so we abandoned this component. While we were able to speak with students during breaks and after class, our information from students is incomplete and indirect. We did observe student behavior in class, and their patterns of engagement and disengagement are revealing. But such observations cannot substitute for student interpretations of the instruction they receive, and so a completely rounded view of instruction—with independent observations as well as interpretation by both instructors and students—will have to wait for another time.

We chose colleges to visit and classes to observe in various ways. We started observing in colleges in California, for obvious logistical reasons. We then expanded our observations to colleges in other states, because states have created very different systems of community colleges. Some (like New York's) have relatively high tuition, while others (like California's) are all but free; some (as in Wisconsin and North Carolina) are occupationally oriented, and others (like California's) are dominated by transfer. Some states, like Minnesota, have had both comprehensive community colleges and technical colleges, though the two systems recently merged—part of the process of specialized technical institutes giving way to comprehensive community colleges. Some systems (like those in Florida and Illinois) have relatively strong state administration and regulation, though most are weak, with state participation confined to funding patterns and to course and program approval (McDonnell and Zellman, 1993). By the end we had observed 257 classrooms in thirty-two colleges in eleven states.

Of the colleges we visited, twenty-four were chosen more or less at random, with no special reasons for visiting them. We visited eight other colleges for specific purposes. We visited five colleges to observe learning communities; we chose two because of their reputations for especially strong teaching; and we traveled to one college because of a distinctive developmental studies department. While the majority of colleges we visited were comprehensive community colleges, we also included three technical colleges or institutes to see how specialization might influence instruction. Finally, the majority of institutions were urban and suburban, though we also included several rural colleges, especially in Iowa and Wisconsin. Our selection was unavoidably unsystematic, though it did enable us to observe a wide range of colleges.[18] We list the institutions we visited, and the number of instructors we observed and administrators we interviewed, in Table A-1 of the Appendix. This is the only place where specific institutions are mentioned (except where their identities are already in print); henceforth we refer to all institutions and all instructors by pseudonyms.

We tried to avoid having administrators select the instructors we observed by getting a listing of all courses and making the choice ourselves; we wanted to observe a balanced array of academic, occupational, and remedial/developmental classes. However, while we observed a wide variety of classes—as Table A-2 reveals—we did not observe a random sample of classes. Because of our interests in literacy instruction, we observed more English classes than math classes. We observed a disproportionate number of psychology classes, because that is a social science that can be taught in several distinctive ways. In the occupational area we tended to concentrate on automotive, business, and drafting, as well as some locally oriented subjects (dairy herd management in Iowa, construction management in Seattle). While not random, the subjects we observed still cover a wide variety of those typical in community colleges.

In a few institutions we asked administrators to nominate especially effective instructors, and observed both the nominated individuals and others whom we chose. The results revealed how little administrators know about what happens in classrooms (as we clarify in Chapter 8), and so we did not continue this practice.

Our sample of institutions and instructors is biased, we suspect, in two ways important to our conclusions. First and most important, because we selected some institutions (eight of the thirty-two) for reasons related to innovative teaching, we think we observed a disproportionate number of good to excellent instructors—according to the varied criteria we set out in Chapter 1. Because we did not observe a random sample of instructors, we will not engage in many counting exercises in this book, except for a brief effort related specifically to literacy practices in Section IV of Chapter 4. We will not, for example, estimate what fraction of instructors is "good" or "bad," or what proportion follows meaning- and student-centered teaching practices rather than lecturing, or how many cite their institutions as supportive of teaching rather than unsupportive. Such statements would require a random sample, and they would obscure the patterns we emphasize: the distinct practices of certain instructors, the similarities as well as the differences between academic and occupational teaching, the variation in institutional practices related to teaching.

However, our bias in favor of good instructors is really a blessing. Good teaching is a joy to watch. The innovations are endless and surprising; the instructors themselves have usually thought long and hard about what they are doing, and their responses to even the most basic questions are often insightful and revealing. What we have learned came from many excellent community college instructors; their experiences provide guides for improving these institutions. In contrast, it's difficult to learn much from bad teaching. Mediocre classes are dreary in ways that soon become predictable, with practices—lectures that invite little reflection, questions that are not really questions, active participation by only a few students—that are time-worn and obvious. The classes are excruciating to sit through, and the faculty rarely have anything interesting to say about teaching or about innovation. To paraphrase Tolstoy, mediocre classes are all alike, but every wonderful class is wonderful in its own illuminating way.[19]

Second, we did not observe as many part-time instructors as a random sample would—a problem because, as we argue throughout (and as others have argued before, including Worthen, 1998), the expansion of part-time faculty creates serious pedagogical issues. One reason we undersampled part-time instructors is that they don't appear on lists of instructors—they are listed anonymously as "staff." They don't have offices and phone numbers and so are hard to contact for permission to observe. Many of them, the "freeway flyers," lead horrendously complex lives, commuting among several institutions to cobble together enough teaching to survive; they are paid only for instruction, and so are understandably reluctant to spend extra time with unknown researchers. Still, at least twenty-five instructors we observed were part-timers, and together with our personal experiences we were able to get a reasonable profile of their dilemmas—a subject to which we return in Section III of Chapter 9.

The results of these observations and interviews are wonderfully rich. By the end, we observed and interviewed 257 instructors in every imaginable subject, ranging from wonderful classes—fast-paced, innovative in their use of both in-class activities and assignments, highly engaging to students—to the absolute worst. We learned about the institutional practices in thirty-two colleges, varying widely in their characteristics and in the support they give instructors. No study of teaching can ever be complete, and so we hope that our work will stimulate others to analyze teaching in community colleges and understanding its influences.[20] Community colleges are important institutions where the quality of teaching is especially critical, and they deserve more attention than they have had.

IV. THE ORGANIZATION OF THIS BOOK

In the first chapter, we outline the different approaches to teaching that constitute the theoretical foundation for our inquiry. These approaches—articulated by many observers and theorists of education, as well as the instructors we interviewed—in turn generate *several* different conceptions of "good teaching." We also examine how instructors have developed their approaches to teaching. Their responses, particularly the frequency of trial and error or learning by doing, gave one of the first tip-offs that their institutions are doing little to help them. One purpose of this chapter is to illustrate the complexity of teaching—since different approaches contain many strands of assumptions and practices—and the variety of good teaching, but a second purpose is to provide the conceptions and vocabulary necessary for analyzing classroom practices.

From our observations, the most common classroom follows the pattern of lecture/discussion we examine in Chapter 2; in occupational classes, the analogue is the lecture/workshop, analyzed in Chapter 3. While each of these provides room for great variety in content and presentation, the real nature of a particular class is often invisible. Therefore we highlight the details of teacher questions, classroom interactions, and student engagement to clarify what goes on in many different classrooms. For occupational education, we spell out a number of differences from conventional academic teaching, including the common rhetorical claims that vocational teaching is exemplary because of its hands-on approach and frequent applications.

Because formal educational institutions have historically been preoccupied with literacy (Cook-Gumperz, 1986; Ong, 1982), we turn in Chapter 4 to the literacy practices that emerge in both academic and occupational classes. The results are surprising: Literacy practices are both more varied and more prevalent in subjects where one might not expect them (like many occupational areas). The ways instructors treat literacy varies, too, in ways that reveal once again the centrality of instructional approaches. Furthermore, different approaches to literacy practices often lead to differences in teaching remedial/developmental education, which we examine in Chapter 5. For remedial courses we stress again the variety of approaches, with pockets of real innovation coexisting with dreary methods based on "skills and drills," which interpret literacy as an individual skill.

In Chapter 6 we take up the issue of standards and content. Community colleges have always been subject to the charge that their standards are low—that they are merely "high schools with ashtrays." Some of these critiques confuse the need for remedial education, which is necessary in open-access institutions and which can be both demanding and sophisticated, with the very different problem of supposedly college-level courses that have been stripped of content. In fact, we did observe many classes with an appallingly low level of content, alongside many others of great sophistication. Maintaining standards proves to be a complex and multifaceted task, with many pedagogical and institutional factors contributing to the enormous variation in content.

Chapter 7 examines a number of innovations: attempts to develop more active or student-centered teaching; the use of "technology," or computers and distance learning; learning communities; and the integration of academic and occupational education. All of these show substantial promise and have led to some teaching that seems to be more engaging and effective. But none of them works automatically: When instructors change their practices without modifying their basic pedagogical approach, the result may be innovation in name only. And, as is always the case, institutional support is usually necessary and often missing.

In Chapters 8 and 9 we summarize the institutional effects on teaching that emerge throughout this book. Chapter 8 first examines the basic structure of the instructor's role, and then personnel practices, pre-service and in-service education, and the roles of administrators and institutional culture. While most community colleges fail to use their institutional resources to enhance the quality of instruction, a few do so, and we profile several that have every right to be called teaching colleges.

Chapter 9 is devoted to the effects of funding and policy (both state and federal) on teaching. Funding is at the same time the most obvious "solution" to various educational problems—usually cited as an absolute requirement for innovation—and one of the least-examined influences on pedagogy. In K–12 education, a long line of research has concluded that "resources make no difference," but this research is seriously flawed by neglecting the ways resources influence classrooms.[21] Instead of assuming that additional resources can automatically improve community colleges or, conversely, that resources make little difference to learning, we clarify the conditions under which resources could make a difference to the quality of instruction.

Finally, Chapter 10 takes up some of the largest issues facing community colleges. The purpose of the community college—the problem of "mission," or "mission drift," and the explosion of roles—remains a difficult one, with many critics continuing to lambaste the community college for allowing vocational and remedial roles to take over its academic function. There is great concern that community colleges do not serve their students well, especially those who are academically underprepared, low-income students, minority students, or older students—and that they "cool out" these students rather than enhancing their opportunities. The future of the community college is a subject of great worry for many instructors, since community colleges are being pressured to serve more students with fewer resources. And the role of teaching within the community college, and the meaning of a "teaching institution," remain unclear. In the final chapter we summarize the implications of our analysis of teaching in community colleges for each of these issues.

Throughout this book, we have faced a serious organizational problem. This is a book that ideally would be written in hypertext, giving the reader the ability to zoom around in nonlinear fashion. For example, we have alluded many times in this chapter to "good teaching" and "active pedagogy," but we cannot define these concepts fully until the next chapter. We refer throughout to innovative practices such as learning communities, though we delay discussing them until Chapter 7. Many advocates claim that community college problems cannot be resolved without better funding, yet we stave off the discussion of funding until the penultimate chapter, to incorporate as much of our prior analysis as possible. We see no elegant solution to this organizational problem, though we have tried to approximate hypertext with frequent notes and parenthetical references to other chapters. Any instance of teaching is a holistic event, with many different influences; but writing is partial, linear, and analytic, with one point following another despite their interdependence. There is nothing to be done about this disjunction except to keep it in mind.

The reader must remember two other complications. Community colleges are enormously varied—more varied than any other type of educational institution in this country. This means that no generalization is true for every community college, and no conclusion can possibly apply to all instructors or all colleges in the country. We have tried throughout to convey the complexity and variety of teaching practices, but it is also necessary to come to some conclusions, some judgments. There are inevitably exceptions to any statement we make, and readers should recognize this fact even where we don't have the space to clarify it.

Finally, our judgments are sometimes quite critical. We have seen a great variety of teaching, and some of it is terrible. We have been in dismal institutions that do little more than keep their doors open and churn out enrollments, that fail to support instructors in any way, and that treat their nontraditional students in the most rigid and conventional ways imaginable. But there is no reason to think that these poor practices are any more common in community colleges than they are in high schools, four-year colleges, or graduate schools. We have also seen wonderful teaching, innovative practices, and supportive institutions that truly deserve to be called teaching colleges. Our purpose is to understand this institution in order to improve it, to make it all that it can be. The basic structure of community colleges—their commitment to inclusion and to a variety of students, the concern with students embedded in the notion of a teaching college, the different purposes they embrace—is precisely right to serve their students well. The task that remains is to make good on their implicit promises so that every college is principally concerned with teaching and learning, as we hope all our educational institutions can be.

NOTES

1. There have been, however, some analyses in K–12 education that start to bridge this great divide. See especially Cuban, 1993; Cohen, McLaughlin, and Talbert, 1993; and Beardsley, 1990, for early childhood education.

2. As Appendix Table A-1 clarifies, three of the thirty-two institutions we examined are technical colleges or institutes. Overall, technical institutes account for only 3.3 percent of enrollments in two-year colleges and 1.4 percent of enrollments in higher education. Technical institutes as distinctive institutions appear to be dwindling: for example, the technical colleges and community colleges in Minnesota (including the two Minnesota institutions we visited) merged in 1995; the technical institutes in South Carolina recently became comprehensive community colleges; and many institutions called technical institutes—including Madison Area Technical College (WI) and Western Iowa Technical and Community College—have transfer components and are therefore more properly thought of as comprehensive community colleges.

The process of technical institutes becoming comprehensive community colleges reflects a long-standing American preference for comprehensive over specialized educational institutions, as well as a process of institutional drift as institutions try to move from the lower status of vocational institutions to the higher status of academic institutions; see McDonnell and Grubb, 1991.

3. Because students in two-year colleges are more likely to attend part time than their peers in four-year colleges, their fraction of full-time equivalent enrollments is somewhat lower—29 percent — than their fraction of overall enrollment (37 percent). NCES, 1997, Tables 173, 180, 200, and 206.

4. There is a long-running debate about whether community colleges attract students who would otherwise not go to postsecondary education at all, or whether they "cool out" individuals who otherwise would have gone to four-year colleges. For evidence that the former is dominant, see Grubb, 1996b,59–67.

5. It's important not to overstate the numbers of older students. Community college administrators tend to cite the average age of students (twenty-nine) as a mantra, as if it implies that most students are older. However, a few older students skew the average badly so that the *average* age, about twenty-nine, is much higher than the *median* age, which is about twenty-six. In addition, older students tend to take many fewer courses than traditional-age students do; the median age of part-time students is twenty-eight, compared to a median age of twenty-one among full-time students (drawing on 1992–93 NPSAS [National Postsecondary Student Aid Survey] data). As a result, the majority of courses are taken by traditional-age students. Traditional-age and full-time students tend to take courses during the day, while older and part-time students tend to enroll in the evenings; therefore particular classes are much more age-homogeneous than the institution as a whole. In effect, the community college is two institutions: a college for relatively full-time, traditional-age students by day, and a college for older, part-time students by night.

6. See Grubb, 1996b, 69–70. This analysis of experimenters is based on interviews with about forty community college students in California.

7. The magnitude of transfer rates is a subject of great controversy. The absolute rates depend on what data and definition are used; it's not hard to find transfer rates from different colleges that vary from 5 percent to 84 percent (Cohen, 1990), and estimates with different definitions using a consistent national data set vary from 20.2 percent to 39.8 percent (Grubb, 1992). In these last results, the proportion of students intending to transfer who succeeded in doing so was 33.9 percent—so by the often unreliable measure of student intentions, transfers appear low. For evidence that transfer rates have been declining, see Grubb, 1991.

8. There's a long-running debate about what to call this kind of education, with "remedial," "developmental," and "basic skills" all vying for attention; see Goto, 1995. As a compromise, we have decided to call this "remedial/developmental education."

9. The opportunities for doing so are even greater. For a proposal to create more coherent systems of occupationally oriented education, adult education, and job training using community colleges as critical linkages, see Grubb, 1996a, or Grubb, 1996b, Ch. 4.

10. See Astin, Korn, and Dey, 1991, especially Tables 4 and 5. Virtually all faculty in postsecondary education claim they are interested in being good teachers; the real difference is that only one quarter of community college instructors are interested in research, compared to about two thirds of those in four-year colleges. See also Boyer, 1989, Table 30.

11. In contrast, full-time faculty in comprehensive public universities average 10.9 hours and those in public research universities average 6.9. See Kirshstein, Matheson, Jing, and Pelavin Research Institute, 1997, Table 3.5.

12. By "empirical" we mean investigations that observe classes, ask instructors about their teaching, or ask students about the teaching they have experienced. Our study is empirical in the first two of these senses. We do not count as empirical any work that asks administrators about teaching—for example, Baker, Roueche, and Gillett-Karan's (1990) selection of 869 "award-winning" instructors as exemplary because their presidents have nominated them—because of evidence presented in Chapter 8 that most (but not all) administrators are simply ignorant of what goes on in classrooms. Similarly, Easton, Forrest, Goldman, and Lading (1985) studied "exemplary" teachers first recommended by administrators and then selected because their students had high average levels of achievement—a procedure likely to pick out instructors with middle-income students.

13. Many of these critics rely on Clark (1960a), who cited counselors (rather than instructors) as responsible for cooling out. He relied on interviewing counselors and reviewing counseling guides but did not observe counseling sessions directly. Given that his evidence comes from a single college in the 1950s, when counseling practices were quite different than they are today, it is irrelevant for drawing any conclusions about the present. See also note 4 in this chapter.

14. In addition, Roueche and Comstock (1981) carried out a parallel methodological and empirical study, though this was never published and has not been widely cited. It contains a number of useful observations about common classroom practices, as well as interviews with numerous instructors.

15. We first obtained permission from the institution to observe instructors, usually approaching the dean of instruction; in some cases this was simple to obtain, but in other cases the faculty senate, unions, or other administrators had to be consulted and the process took several months. We then contacted individual instructors to obtain permission to observe individual classes, selecting from college catalogues or lists of classes (rather than having administrators recommend which instructors to observe). While permission sometimes took a long time to arrange, we were turned down by only two instructors of the hundreds we approached.

16. We received some direct confirmation of this hypothesis: One of the instructors we observed for three hours had fortuitously been extensively observed, interviewed, and video-taped by one of our colleagues, Glynda Hull (as described in Hull, 1993b). The portrait of his instruction that emerged in our short observation was precisely the one that Hull's much more thorough evaluation had captured. The advantage of longer observation is that the external relations of the class—for example, the fact that students come to this class almost purely by chance, and that this instructor is preparing them for much lower-level jobs than they realize—can be uncovered, whereas our methods can determine only what happens within the classroom.

17. Dewey is often misquoted as advocating "learning *by* doing," but—given Dewey's antipathy to false dichotomies—this is not at all what he meant. In *Schools of Tomorrow* he and his wife explicitly stated, "Learning by doing does not, of course, mean the substitution of manual occupations or handwork for textbook studying" (Dewey and Dewey, 1915, 74), and they went on to clarify the complementarity between learning *and* doing.

18. It would be almost impossible to carry out the usual kind of reputation-based study—for example, choosing a sample of colleges with good reputations. Because community colleges are relentlessly local, almost no one has much direct experience in other colleges. Sometimes reputations are based on a president with a high profile, sometimes on sheer size, sometimes on their centrality in a particular community, and sometimes on transfer rates that in turn reflect the class status of students. None of these is a good indicator of instructional quality. In fact, we doubt that anyone in the country has direct information about more than a few colleges.

19. "Happy families are all alike; every unhappy family is unhappy in its own way." *Anna Karenina*, Part I, Chapter 1.

20. This kind of research could easily be carried out by faculty members themselves, as part of processes in which faculty members observe and learn from each other. This is consistent with the movement for "teachers as researchers"; see especially Palmer, 1993, and Boyer, 1990.

21. This research is summarized particularly in Hanushek, 1986 and 1989; see the statistical rejoinder by Hedges, Lane, and Greenwald, 1994. For our critique of this literature, see Chapter 9.

1

INSTRUCTORS' APPROACHES TO PEDAGOGY AND THE MULTIPLE CONCEPTIONS OF "GOOD TEACHING"

It's hard to talk about teaching. Teaching is so complex, with so many facets, that any particular description is inadequate. Community college instructors often refer to their teaching in brief comments—about their commitment to covering course material, their aversion to lecturing, their efforts to "get students to think for themselves," or the importance of hands-on projects in occupational courses—that hint at but don't fully convey what they do in the classroom. Others resort to metaphors, as many people describing teaching do; one described his class as a "sheepdog situation," in which he herded his "sheep," while others referred to "teaching from the sidelines" or described their roles as facilitators or mentors or coaches.

Many faculty find it difficult to answer questions about their teaching; they have neither the time nor the reasons to discuss teaching, and they lack colleagues with whom to do it.[1] One, a part-timer, said frankly, "I don't know if I'm a good teacher; I have no idea. And so I don't know if I'm really a good authority for any of the things I'm telling you." Some don't even think of themselves as teachers, even though they are nothing but; the head of a commercial art department, an instructor for twenty years, declared, "I'm not a teacher—I don't have lesson plans all written out or anything. I just react to what students are doing." Their inability to talk analytically about what is, after all, their life's work reflects in part a pragmatic view of what they need to do; as one admitted, "I don't think I have principles of pedagogy. It's more a matter of what seems to work and to capture interest."

Most postsecondary instructors have no formal preparation in teaching methods, and they tend to discount the study of pedagogy. Many emphasize mastery of content as the only prerequisite for good teaching. For example, one architecture instructor was asked whether teaching ability is a criterion for hiring. He replied:

> Not really. A person can come in and not have had any experience in teaching, and mostly it's based on their knowledge of the subject matter—because once they know the subject matter we can show them how to make up presentations and things like that.

Others stress desire and relations with students:

> I think a lot of people have not been trained to teach, but rather have a strong desire to teach. And therein lies, probably, the fact as to why many of them are successful—because they have a real desire to teach and understand the relationship with their students.

When community college instructors do reflect upon their teaching, however, their comments are consistent with long traditions of writing about pedagogy. Because of their lack of formal preparation, this consistency is due only in small part to learning about teaching from theorists. Instead, conceptions of teaching and learning have often been developed by researchers and theorists observing instruction closely, and then creating descriptive categories to codify their observations.[2] One instructor described the process in these terms:

> There's always been this way of teaching, and then we put names on it later, that you do what makes sense and is good, and then people say, "Oh, that's like Vygotsky."

Now, a description of *teaching* is not the same as a theory of *learning*, and therefore the correspondence between these descriptions and what students are learning can be superficial. Nonetheless, the consistency between the way instructors talk about their practice and the way researchers have written about teaching and learning allows us to use the extensive writing to clarify two (or three) distinct approaches to pedagogy. Each of these is braided with many strands of assumption and practice—many more than instructors usually articulate.

For our purposes, clear statements about approaches to teaching are crucial because we need ways to understand the different classrooms we observed. In addition, it's necessary to define what "good teaching" might be because even the simplest description of a classroom starts the process of judging how good it is. The two dominant approaches to teaching imply *at least* three conceptually distinct conceptions of good teaching—and so normative statements about instruction prove to be both complex and dependent on what approach to pedagogy an instructor takes.

In this chapter, we are concerned with approaches to pedagogy—with the *instructor's* methods and strategies, which usually (but not always) incorporate theories of student learning. In addition, we emphasize conceptions of *pedagogy* as distinct from *content*, with a focus on *how* instructors teach rather than *what* they teach. This distinction is to some extent artificial, since instructors embracing different pedagogies tend to emphasize different content. Nonetheless, the difference is still vital because virtually any subject can be taught using different approaches—with consequences for content, as we will see. Furthermore, as we mentioned above, many postsecondary instructors reject the importance of pedagogy at all, emphasizing that mastery of content is the only prerequisite for good teaching. Similarly, many staff development programs act as if only subject mastery is important, supporting trips to disciplinary conferences and further specialized study but not the examination of alternative pedagogies. But faculty who stress content often practice the most conventional teaching—the didactic approach, emphasizing lecture and information transfer—and so they have implicitly embraced a particular pedagogy (and rejected others) even as they dismiss the importance of teaching methods. The only solution to the problem of unwitting choice is to be as explicit as possible about approaches to teaching, their assumptions, and their consequences.

Once we describe how instructors conceive of teaching, we then examine how they have developed their approaches to teaching (in Section III). In the absence of any preparation for teaching, most instructors develop their methods through a lengthy process of trial and error, sometimes helped by discussions with their colleagues. But community colleges are not set up to encourage collegiality around teaching, and so teaching is often an isolated and idiosyncratic activity. It's not hard to see why community college instructors have such a difficult time discussing their teaching: Not only do they lack the time, the reasons, and the colleagues that would facilitate such discussions, they are all too often in institutions that simply ignore this dimension of their lives.

I. APPROACHES TO PEDAGOGY: THE MULTIPLE STRANDS OF TEACHING

In the vast literature about teaching, two major approaches to pedagogy (and possibly a third) have been "discovered" or conceptualized by many writers, in different vocabularies. Before we describe these approaches, we should first clarify that very few instructors follow one or another rigidly. Most take an eclectic or hybrid approach, using some elements from each. Indeed, many instructors consciously reject "pure" approaches; one stated simply, "I really like a mix" of lecturing and discussion. As an English instructor who embraced inductive or discovery methods, rather than lecturing, mentioned, "You can't do everything inductively. It would take too many lifetimes." Another complained about the debate over whole-language versus grammar-based teaching: "We're back to the same old thing—top-down or bottom-up—and that's ridiculous."[3] The modal class we examine in Chapter 2—the lecture/discussion—is a perfect example of a hybrid practice, as is the lecture/workshop approach to vocational instruction in Chapter 3. Each provides time for didactic and teacher-dominated presentation of knowledge and skills, as well as time for student interpretation and practice of that material, in the discussion or workshop.

The first and most common approach, now and in the past (Cuban, 1993), goes by many different labels—behaviorist, passive, teacher-centered, didactic, or simply "the conventional wisdom" (Knapp and Turnbull, 1990; Knapp, 1995). John Dewey (1938, Ch. 1) called it "traditional," contrasting it with the "progressive" practices often (and sometimes incorrectly) associated with him. Still others have called it "mimetic," because it emphasizes students copying the activities of the teacher (Jackson, 1986). Knowles et al. (1984) called this practice "pedagogy," stressing the Greek root meaning "children," and coined the term "andragogy" to refer to more adult-centered instruction. Barr and Tagg (1995) used the awkward terminology of "teaching" ("teacher-controlled" knowledge transfer in "bits") to refer to this practice, in contrast to "learning," which they offered as a new paradigm for undergraduate education. We sometimes call this dominant approach "skills and drills" because of its basic impulse to break complex practices (reading and writing, for example, or mathematical formulation and problem solving) into component skills and then to drill on these subskills (Grubb and Kalman, 1994). Others have similarly labeled this the "skills approach," or "drill and kill" to signify the tedium of rote memorization and drill. As one instructor described his approach:

> What I do is I just try to bombard students with various stimuli, recognizing that some are going to work for some, some are not. For example, I have available to my students two different study guides.... I use, maybe what I just want to say, a shotgun approach, hoping that at least parts of what I do will affect each and every student in one way or another.

Because the subskills are not especially interesting, this approach relies on a behaviorist theory of learning—on the extrinsic motivation provided by the rewards and punishment of grades, teacher approval and disapproval, and future consequences (like employment). The use of humor, a conventional bromide in discussions of good teaching, can be one of these extrinsic motivators. An instructor in this tradition mentioned, "Teaching has as much to do with entertainment as anything," and another described his approach to motivation this way:

> I think you have to be enthusiastic about your teaching . . . and you really have to care. . . . You visually stimulate them, you move around, whatever you can—joke. . . . And I think different colors, just a simple concept like different colors and an overhead, makes it more appealing to the eye. . . . Then I would start Xeroxing them [the overheads and lecture notes].

As we will see in Chapter 6, however, humor and other forms of extrinsic motivation are tricky: They may hold the attention of students, but they may also undermine the content of the classroom by replacing substance with what John Dewey called "agreeable diversions."

The decomposition of complex practices into subskills means that this approach follows part-to-whole instruction, emphasizing the teaching of component parts arrayed from simplest to more difficult.[4] Here's a description of part-to-whole instruction in biology:

> So we started with the chemical aspects of living things, and did a little chemistry, and then we did cells, and then the next logical step is to go to tissues.

This approach stresses mastering prerequisites before moving on—spelling and grammar before writing, arithmetic facts before any use of math, remediation before any serious occupational or college-level academic coursework. Richardson, Fisk, and Okun's [1983] portrayal of most community college instructors as "bitting," or breaking literacy practices into small "bits" for instructional purposes, also describes this central impulse. Often the purpose of skill building is ignored, leading to the common complaint, "Why do I need to know this?"

The goal of instruction is to move students from the simplest skill in a hierarchy to more difficult ones. Therefore "starting where the student is," or "individualizing instruction"—phrases that seem to indicate student-centeredness—means identifying the point in a hierarchy the student has already mastered, and moving up from there. Conventionally, students in community colleges are administered diagnostic tests and then assigned to appropriate levels, including the "right" remedial classes (as we examine in Section I of Chapter 5). The goal of any particular course is to progress a certain distance along this hierarchy. "Coverage"—

delivery of a certain body of content—is therefore important, and many instructors emphasize their responsibility to "cover the material." Here are two such
teachers, one in English and one in automotive, commenting on their goals:

> To make sure the student understands and covers the topic.

> Giving them accurate information, just trying to be on the cutting edge of this auto-
> motive stuff so that you're not teaching them about 1959 Buicks.... So I like to
> think I'm prepared....I figure if I can get the information, if I'm kind of up-to-date,
> I can relay the information.

While part-to-whole instruction assumes that skills and knowledge are arrayed
in a hierarchy, the materials of instruction are usually *made to fit* into a hierarchy
contrived for the purposes of instruction. Thus math texts have appropriate drills
and problems, basal readers have the right level of vocabulary and sentence construction, history and social studies texts are written to fit both the assumed reading level and conceptual sophistication of a particular class. Materials from the
"real world" outside the classroom are unlikely to fit. Therefore occupational
instructors complain that their students can't understand instruction manuals
written at the twelfth-grade level, or note that the messy problems arising in work
are not easily solved within conventional math courses; the readings that might
engage adult students are not necessarily consistent with their tested reading levels. As one remedial/developmental teacher complained about many community
college reading texts, "There's nothing to read in them"—they have been written
for low reading levels and in the process stripped of any content.

Within this tradition, the teacher is the primary source of authority and knowledge, so that many observers describe this approach as "teacher-centered." In a
particularly vivid metaphor, one electronics instructor described the instructor-
dominated classroom as a "sheepdog situation":

> It's like a sheepdog situation. The sheep wander one way, and the dog runs around
> and barks in that direction, and herds 'em back, and then some more sheep will run
> over here.... All you can hope to do is have the sheep through the gate by the time
> they get down to the lowlands. So it's the same thing out here. Different sheep, dif-
> ferent directions.

Lecture is one standard mode of the teacher-centered classroom, though we will
clarify that instructors can dominate the classroom in several different ways.
The role of students is limited to learning what the instructor teaches—a role
often described as "passive" (or sheeplike) since the students absorb whatever is

conveyed in lecture and drill. Metaphors of the student as a tabula rasa, or blank slate, on which the teacher inscribes knowledge or as an empty vessel filled up with knowledge by the teacher are equivalent ways of describing the dual responsibilities of teacher and student. However, students may aspire to high test performance *rather than* learning; then they often engage in what our colleague Judith Warren Little calls "studenting," or endless negotiation over the precise requirements of a course, the repeated question "Will this be on the test?," and the quest for a precise definition of a good paper ("You must have at least four references, and none of them can be an encyclopedia").

The conventional approach to teaching often embodies several assumptions about intelligence: that it is relatively fixed rather than malleable, and that it is single-dimensioned rather than multiple-dimensioned. The notion of relatively fixed intelligence or ability leads to an emphasis on screening mechanisms and prerequisites, with the aim of tracking students based on their perceived abilities. This also fits with the view that students who score poorly on diagnostic tests are deficient, lacking the skills and knowledge that would enable them to score at the right level. The language of deficiency is quite common in conventional instruction, particularly in remedial or developmental education (Rose, 1989; Goto, 1995; Hull and Rose, 1989; Grubb and Kalman, 1994). The assessment of deficiency then often slides over into assumptions that students are to blame for their deficiencies—that they are stupid, or that they come from intellectually impoverished families and communities—and this reasoning has been frequently applied to the "disadvantaged" students who have not done well in school.[5] We should stress right away that most community college instructors do *not* hold such views of their students; as we clarify below, most of them are respectful of students and their abilities, and take great pains to lay the blame for low achievement elsewhere, particularly on poor high schools and the "busied-up" conditions of their lives. But this kind of sympathy with students is not universal, and assumptions of deficiency often have negative consequences —particularly, as we will see in Chapter 5, in remedial education.

A second approach, much less common in American education, is one we sometimes call "meaning-making" because its central impulse is to enable students to create meaning or interpretation for themselves (Bruner, 1990). This has also been called "progressive," "constructivist," "student-centered," or "andragogy" (for adults, in contrast to "pedagogy," for children), or "learning" (contrasted with "teaching"). Others have labeled it "holistic" because of its whole-to-part practices (Tomlinson, 1989), or simply the alternative to conventional wisdom (Knapp et al., 1995; Knapp and Turnbull, 1990). Many refer to this as "active" instruction, because students must be active creators of knowledge rather than passive recipients from instructors; both passivity and "studenting" are anathema to instructors in this tradition. Rather than being the source of all knowledge, the instructor is more a guide to students as they create their own knowledge, relying on expertise from a variety of sources; the authority for interpreting a text is more likely to be shared between the instructor and the students, as we will see more clearly in Chapter 4. The metaphors describing this approach include instructors as coaches, facilitators, collaborators, mentors, or shepherds (not sheepdogs), or (in the current doggerel) "the guide on the side, not the sage on the stage"; at some point they step aside, or "fade," to allow students to work more independently. One such instructor described her role as "teaching from the sidelines":

> I operate a student-centered classroom, so that means a kind of teaching from the sidelines in the early part of the semester. I try to have people doing activities, reading; if I'm teaching a writing class, various activities in writing but sort of low-key, to give me a chance to see how people perform in all different situations.

Also invoked is the relationship between master and apprentice, in which the master gives apprentices a series of increasingly responsible tasks until they are independent workers; others have compared this approach with the "natural" teaching relationship of parent and child.[6] Some of these metaphors are awkward and romanticized—there are many authoritarian coaches and parents, and masters were just as likely to exploit their apprentices as to educate them—but they intend to differentiate a supportive and cooperative mode of teaching from a didactic and authoritarian style.

Moving toward more student-centered teaching does not mean that instructors abandon their role in structuring the class. For example, one English instructor who has moved away from a didactic approach acknowledged that he still structures the classroom:

> I've tried as much as possible to avoid lecturing, not only in terms of it as a pedagogical strategy but just as a relationship between the teacher and student . . . although there are times when it is appropriate. My own style is what I'd call a discussion/lecture. . . . The teacher really does decide what's going to be discussed [and] how much, and so it's a kind of manipulated situation. I try to avoid having that be artificial or, let's say, destructive to the in-class relationship.

Instructors in the constructivist tradition have clear pedagogical goals in mind, then, but they achieve those goals though discussion and interaction rather than lecture.

In this tradition, teaching is whole-to-part rather than part-to-whole, with the technical aspects of any particular practice (such as grammar, spelling, arithmetic rules, specific electrical components) taught explicitly only after students understand the larger problem, competency, or system within which these parts are embedded. Here, for example, is one instructor talking about her approach, where drill is subordinated to meaning-making:

> It's very student-centered—it focuses on what students need to be able to do to succeed.... They need to be able to write in ways that let their papers be read with respect.... [It's] more bottom-up than top-down, because I'm trying to get them to have the meaning—I try to have meaning drive what they're doing. Although we may need to do a drill, time is so precious that I'd rather have them do more writing and talking than doing worksheets. And I expect *them* to take responsibility for a lot of it themselves—I'm not the error police.

The stress on meaning might lead students to idiosyncratic interpretations, and we will describe classes in Chapters 2 and 6 where instructors seem to accept anything students say as valid. But skilled instructors in this tradition typically stress that the most powerful interpretations of events, texts, or responsibilities at work or in politics have been *socially* rather than individually developed, by communities including students in a class, readers in a particular historical period, workers in a specific company, or citizens at the local (or state, or national) level. They reflect a belief in knowledge as a social construction in their teaching practices—for example, the use of small groups, group projects, or (in occupational courses) work groups. When we return in Chapter 4 to literacy practices, a clear difference emerges between instructors who treat literacy as an individual skill, to be mastered by decomposition and drill, versus those who stress its social character in communicating with others.

Meaning-centered faculty are much less likely than conventional teachers to talk about coverage, or "learning the material," and more likely to discuss interpretive abilities.

> My role is not really [as much] to disseminate information as it is to present possible ways of thinking, strategizing, reading, writing, and then having interactive sessions to see, first of all, whether or not students understand them, and secondly, whether or not they're going to be able to make them [the ways of thinking] work for them.

The emphasis on discussion rather than lecture is one common method; another is project-based learning (including the projects in occupational workshops), which allows students to explore possibilities on their own. Instructors in this tradition are more likely to have students reading entire texts ("texting" rather than "bitting," in the language of Richardson, Fisk, and Okun, 1983), writing purposeful essays, confronting real problems in science and social science, or taking on real occupational tasks such as fixing cars or building houses.

Much more could be said about these two approaches to teaching. Because of its emphasis on coverage, "skills and drills" is generally more concerned with efficiency; for example, some remedial programs like to measure gains in grade equivalents per hundred hours of instruction. Meaning-making approaches, by contrast, generally worry more about depth of understanding rather than coverage or efficiency. The search for efficiency in education has a long history (Callahan, 1967), and it has become more important recently because of fiscal constraints. As we will see, particularly in Chapters 7 and 9, efficiency concerns often promote didactic instruction.

The didactic approach to teaching has also been called the "factory model" or "industrial model," since it tends to treat students as "raw material" to be "processed" by teachers into a "finished product." To continue the analogy with production, many critics have argued that the competencies best developed by "skills and drills," with its tendency to fragment knowledge and track students, may have been appropriate for Taylorist production, with its minute division of labor, its separation of management from labor, and its distinction between "academic" and "vocational" learning. However, with newer forms of production in which workers need a greater variety of abilities, including problem solving and communications skills, and where the separation of management from execution is no longer so sharp, many have argued that teaching should now emphasize the higher-order abilities stressed in the constructivist tradition (SCANS, 1991; Berryman and Bailey, 1994; Berryman, 1996; Stasz et al., 1993). Within community colleges, the view that work requires a greater range of capacities has led to integrating academic and occupational education (examined in Section IV of Chapter 7) as well as to other pedagogical reforms.

Finally, the structure of many educational institutions follows many of the practices of behaviorist and didactic instruction. The tendency to identify student abilities and then track students into different programs has virtually defined the community college, which is by construction the lowest "track" in postsecondary education. The usual ways of structuring courses, with classes of fixed length in teacher-centered classrooms, reflects conventional pedagogy. The practice of fragmenting knowledge has generated the disciplines, which shape the allegiance of most instructors as well as the status hierarchy of subjects, with occupational and remedial/developmental programs having the lowest status. We could multiply these examples endlessly; the point is that conventional approaches to teaching and the organizational practices of educational institutions, including community colleges, reflect each other.

There are, then, many ways to understand these two approaches to teaching, by turn psychological, economic, and organizational. Each approach combines multiple strands of assumption and practice, though both instructors and theorists usually refer to teaching in shorthand and dichotomous descriptions—teacher-centered versus student-centered, behaviorist versus constructivist, individual versus social, passive versus active—that describe only one or two of these strands. Despite the variation in vocabulary, it's important to recognize the underlying patterns. Otherwise the interactions in real classrooms—which are usually hybrids of many practices, coming thick and fast—are too complex to understand.

Because it doesn't follow consistent and recognizable practices, hybrid teaching varies enormously and is extremely difficult to analyze.[7] In examining literacy practices in Chapter 4, we address this problem by separating the social relationships of the classroom, the source of interpretive authority, and the level of technical explicitness; these distinctions make it possible to separate the "skills" dimensions of classes from their social and authority relationships, clarifying the forms that hybrid instruction takes. In addition, the effectiveness of hybrid instruction depends on the balance of different elements, and whether they reinforce or negate one another, as we clarify in Chapters 2, 6, and 7. But to disentangle what happens in specific classes, we need first to understand the different assumptions and practices that particular instructors are using.

A third approach to pedagogy has sometimes been mentioned by those providing advice to teachers, and a few instructors emphasize this kind of teaching. The approach we label "student support" assumes that if students are given enough encouragement, they will develop into autonomous individuals ("empowered," in the current jargon) who can learn anything they feel is necessary. For example, an instructor in a medical assisting program spent an entire class on personal stories about her own education; she spoke of her teaching almost entirely in the language of student support:

> [For motivating] students, you have to communicate to students that you really do care about them . . . so they feel they're in a supportive environment with someone who really treats them like a human being. . . . I don't care how much you have in the way of audiovisual materials or video presentations or quality textbooks, laboratory equipment—none of that can take the place of a truly caring, sensitive, motivated, and inspired teacher. So I use these other things to simply support my efforts as I try and demonstrate some sensitivity, some caring, and of course, at the same time sharing a body of knowledge that I think is important.

For her, various ways of "sharing a body of knowledge" (a content-oriented approach) are distinctly secondary to "truly caring." She never once talked about the competencies her students might acquire, but she did wax eloquent about the change from lacking self-esteem to being more self-confident—and therefore better able to perform in clinical settings as well as to handle personal problems.

Others writing about teaching have also articulated "student support" in slightly different vocabularies. Fenstermacher and Soltis (1992) include a "therapist" approach in which the teacher is "an empathetic person charged with helping individuals grow personally and reach a high level of self-actualization, understanding, and acceptance" (p. 4). At the college level, Dressel and Marcus (1982, 2) describe "student-centered affective teaching" focused on "the personal and social development of the student." In their celebration of the community college, Griffith and Connor (1994) emphasize teachers "becoming aware of students' lives," "learning to connect with them," "accepting them." Most of the "award-winning programs" profiled in Roueche and Roueche (1993), intended to enhance the success of low-achieving students, provided student services such as tutoring, mentoring, and counseling but left the basic teaching of remedial/developmental courses alone. These programs implicitly assumed that student support is sufficient for success, even if core teaching is poor. We suspect that many counselors also follow this approach; the director of career counseling at one college declared that self-esteem is more important than technical competence for achieving life goals, and she was proud of protecting her "troubled" and "fragile" students from demanding courses.

This approach describes a role for instructors (or student service personnel like counselors) in their personal relations with students. However, it is silent about every other element of teaching: how to present academic or occupational content, appropriate goals for learning, what assessments should be devised, the responsibilities of students. In our interpretation, "student support" in its extreme form is really an evasion of teaching responsibility rather than a distinctive approach, and we present several examples—particularly in Chapter 6, on the collapse of standards in certain classes—where it has been detrimental to learning.

However, "student support" is a reaction against one of the most damaging aspects of teacher-centered instruction, and moderate forms are pervasive. Conventional teaching, or "drill and kill," can be quite harsh to students. Teachers present material once and expect their students to master it; there are no alternative ways of teaching for students who don't learn well in this particular mode. For students who perform poorly, low marks on tests are palpable evidence of failure, reinforced by the disappointment or the ridicule of the teacher. A large testimonial literature about demeaning school experiences clarifies how horrible conventional instruction can be, particularly for the low academic achievers who are common in community colleges (e.g., Rose, 1989), and throughout this book we will describe the damage caused by demeaning instructors.

Because such punitive approaches are counterproductive, many instructors take great pains to provide more supportive classrooms and avoid punitive judgments. In our observations, this is also true of instructors in the didactic tradition, who often work hard to develop positive reinforcement (including tests with novel formats, described in Chapter 6) rather than negative sanctions, and of constructivist instructors, who avoid harsh treatment because they want learning to be intrinsically motivating. These instructors sometimes acknowledge that their responsibilities to educate students, which require them to be demanding, may conflict with simple notions of supporting students. As one described good teaching, it is

> caring about your students—and the part of teaching that I have difficulty with is the part of caring where it might mean telling them that "I don't think you can do this" or "I don't think this is the place for you." I have difficulty with the tough-love part of being an instructor.

But when the "caring" element of teaching is elevated to the principal concern of instructors, rather than embedded in other conceptions of instruction, the approach of "student support" is the result.

One dimension of student support has been almost universally adopted by community college instructors: a basic sympathy with their students, an unwillingness to label them as "deficient" or "not college material." As a dean mentioned, "There is real care on the part of the faculty, a faculty that is quite sensitive to the different students—the unique student, the language-poor students, the basic-skills student—and tries to create an environment where those students are acceptable, and we work with them." Even though there is a consensus that students have "gradually gotten worse" in terms of their preparation, instructors consistently blamed the sorry state of high schools (or the poor schools in their native countries) and the difficult conditions of their lives—"They tend to be overworked"—rather than students themselves. Often, they praise the motivation of their students under difficult conditions: "They want to reach very much what they are working toward, which is some kind of better life, better job—and often they have just the most appalling personal circumstances." One instructor who lamented the inability of students to complete homework contrasted their lives with those of "traditional" students (as most instructors themselves have been):

> The major issue I see with my students, and this is why I think they're having difficulty learning and concentrating, is students' lives are so incredibly complicated and busied-up compared to twenty-five years ago, twenty years ago. I mean, they're

trying to juggle their child care, their broken-down clunker that can barely get here, their husband who's pounding on their door threatening to shoot them, relatives who are moving in, taking people to the airport, caring for ill parents. I mean, they are just burdened. I went to school on a scholarship. My job was to go to school; that's all I did. And I know that's a pipe dream now—nobody does that. They're just incredibly stretched, and I think they're so stretched they can't . . . I mean, I notice myself personally, if I'm really stretched, it's hard for me to concentrate on anything. That's the biggest difference, is they're kids leading lives no one should have to lead.

And so an enormous reservoir of support for students underlies the actions of instructors—not all of them, but certainly the vast majority. This basic sympathy comes out in different ways—sometimes in student support, sometimes as dilution of standards (as we see in Chapter 6), sometimes as tough love. But it represents a distinctive feature of community college teaching, a genuine reflection of inclusiveness, a deep commitment to the ideals of the "people's college."

II. CONCEPTIONS OF "GOOD TEACHING"

Given these different approaches to teaching, there are many different conceptions of "good teaching." From the perspective of didactic or teacher-centered instruction, common precepts of good teaching include instructors who are knowledgeable and up-to-date about their fields; adequate coverage of certain skills and issues considered central to their subject; instructors who are well prepared for class and present material clearly, ordered from simple to more difficult, and who reinforce course material through repetition, worksheets, projects, and homework that reinforce the content. Such instructors should devise tests and other assessments that are closely related to the material they present, to check student comprehension and also to provide motivation. They should use humor, varied pacing, and different modes of presentation to enhance motivation; their own enthusiasm signals the importance of the subject. From within the teacher-centered tradition, therefore, instructors may range from poor to mediocre to excellent, depending on their handling of these recommendations.

Many precepts of conventional instruction are unexceptionable. No one could possibly be in favor of presentations that are incorrect or out-of-date or confused, tests or homework that are unrelated to the rest of the course, or instructors who seem bored with their subject. But the central concerns in meaning- and student-centered instruction lead to very different kinds of recommendations. Within this tradition, instructors should stress mastery of fundamental competencies—typically, practices that students will use outside the classroom, on the job or in their lives as citizens and family members, or that suffuse all of subsequent leaning and life (as many literacy practices do). Instructors should formulate activities so that students create as much of their own learning as possible, becoming autonomous learners rather than passive or dependent. These activities include Socratic questioning, group work in which students learn from one another, and independent study and projects; lecture is subordinated to student-generated learning. The content of courses should not be bound by conventional disciplinary and occupational divisions, but should instead (or in addition) be dictated by the goals of students. Instructors should know their students and their goals well, and modulate instruction to fit both their interests and their backgrounds (including levels of preparation).

Within this tradition, bad teachers are those who lecture in traditional fashion, of course, and who concentrate on conventional cognitive operations and the application of rules (grammar, arithmetic facts, inert facts and figures) and disciplinary boundaries. Bad teachers fail to relate their classes to the world outside the educational institution, neglect motivation, act in demeaning ways that cut off student participation, or fail to create opportunities for students to develop their own knowledge. The precepts related to meaning-making are criticisms of conventional teaching; for example, Bruner (1990, 84) has declared forthrightly that learning "is best when it is participatory, proactive, communal, collaborative, and given over to constructing meanings rather than receiving them." As we will see later in this chapter, many experienced teachers have moved away from didactic approaches and are critical of their colleagues who continue to teach in teacher-directed ways.

But instructors can be bad teachers *within* the student-centered tradition, as we will show throughout. For example, teachers may devise small-group work with the intention that students explore their own interpretations, but they may structure the group's work so that it is purely fact-oriented. Discussions intended to be student-centered can quickly become teacher-dominated. The projects intended to allow students to learn on their own may be so constrained, so poorly explained, or so simple or beyond the abilities of students that they yield nothing in the way of learning. Like the precepts related to didactic instruction, recommendations for good teaching in the meaning-centered approach specify certain practices and goals for instructors, but in the crucible of the classroom individual instructors can follow them well or badly.

Still a third conception of good teaching springs from the common observation that almost no one teaches with only one approach (recall the comment "I really like a mix"). From this perspective, stringent adherence to one pedagogical approach would be undesirable and ineffective (illustrated by the remark, "You can't do everything inductively"). Instructors often articulate the need for hybrid approaches:

> A good teacher is prepared, is knowledgeable about the content area and its applica-
> tions and its theoretical implications. I think a good teacher more and more tries to
> get the students to do as much for themselves as they can ... that's a fine line you
> walk between trying to help people be efficient in how they learn things, yet making
> them go out and figure things out for themselves. . . . My goals for my students are . . .
> to meet the stated objectives of the course: When they leave here they should under-
> stand and be able to apply the implications of the material they're dealing with at a
> broader level.

This instructor began with a conventional statement about content knowledge, shifted to more constructivist ideas ("making them go out and figure things out for themselves"), and ended up with dual goals, for students both to under-stand the material and to be able to apply it "at a broader level." From this stand-point, good teaching involves an appropriate mix of practices, some didactic and discipline-centered, and some constructivist and student-centered—"a fine line you walk."

But *how* ought these two approaches be combined? We will describe different hybrid approaches, particularly in Chapters 2 and 3 on modal approaches to academic and vocational teaching. Some appear to work, in the sense of engaging students and enhancing content, while others do not because they are con-tradictory or because instructors don't fully understand the purpose of a practice they are using (see Section I of Chapter 7 in particular). However, there are sev-eral common precepts about hybrid instruction, particularly in the advice literature on teaching adults.[9] Instructors ought to clarify applications of their material by importing reading, problems, and applications from the "real world" outside the classroom, providing relevance to what otherwise might be lifeless academic content. For example, here's one computer instructor discussing his treatment of drill:

> When it is a drill you make it clear that yes, this is a drill, yes, this is boring, and then
> you try to link it to something real and practical so they say, "Okay, I understand why
> this has relevance." Maybe you come up with a practical example, maybe you have a
> contest or something to motivate them into treating a drill as a little more interesting
> than it might otherwise be. I'm very big on simulations.

Many instructors recommend that courses incorporate goals related to the needs of students, particularly (in community colleges) their progress toward employ-ment.

Another common recommendation is that instructors use a variety of ap-proaches—for example, lecture, small-group discussions, and project-based work—because students learn in different ways, or have different "learning styles."[10] Sometimes instructors recognize that both teacher-centered and student-centered exercises are necessary, and some methods are better suited for certain competencies than others. For example, a physics instructor mentioned, "If you want to teach techniques and methods, then this [discovery] format probably is not as good." Similarly, a remedial/developmental instructor noted the need for two different types of writing:

> For about half of my assignments, I give a very structured assignment, where I say exactly what I want . . . because I want them to be exposed to all the [different types of] writing. But then I also give them some assignments [where] each person is gonna have to develop his or her own purpose, because, like, when they go into sociology, and they have to write a research paper for sociology, their teacher is usually not gonna spend three weeks going over the assignment like she would in an English class.

A biology instructor was adamant about the importance of both content ("facts") and process ("biological thinking"), insisting that neither should give way to the other. She criticized some science courses as including only facts and passing this off as science, and noted that because of weak science teaching in high schools, "students think that learning a format is learning, but this isn't right . . . they have no understanding of what it means to know something, that facts don't equal knowledge." Instead, she tried to get them to develop a reasonable hypothesis, judgment, or interpretation rather than the "right" answer. In essence, this teacher voiced the perspective that the competencies emphasized by didactic instruction and those emphasized in meaning-making complement one another. As Resnick (1989, 2) put it, knowledge begets knowledge: "Those who are knowledge-rich reason more profoundly. They also elaborate as they study and thereby learn more effectively." Thus a certain store of information is necessary in order to reason and interpret; in turn, these interpretations generate the constructs that help individuals organize and absorb further knowledge and content. From this perspective, teachers need to provide their students with the facts, figures, skills, and discipline-based content that are prerequisites for interpretation; they need also to guide or stimulate students to explore interpretations for themselves, so that they may have their own reasons to learn further content. A sociology instructor who described his teaching as "eclectic" spoke about it this way:

> Occasionally there are times when there is specific content that needs to be covered, and I just have to kind of do it. I don't like it as well. I'd rather have the students develop the concepts themselves. Then they own it, you know.

Sometimes the recommendation of multiple approaches seems to be the counsel of moderation: In teaching as in other activities, one ought to avoid extremes. (This is also a Deweyan position, though community college instructors usually don't articulate views positions in theoretical ways.)[11] Extreme positions on pedagogy—for example, the position that instructors ought never use drill of any kind, or ought never teach grammar or spelling—have been widely ridiculed. Similarly, teachers who never depart from the textbook or who spend all their time lecturing are also lampooned. Indeed, among many instructors a conventional wisdom about the ineffectiveness of lecture has developed. They articulate their dissatisfaction with lecture—it's "hard to motivate students in lecture"; "they all throw the notes out as soon as they get their grade, and they don't remember"— and they talk frequently about trying harder not to lecture. Many disparage their colleagues who continue to lecture:

> In the math department we still have 60 percent of the department that just lectures. They don't do feedback, they don't do groups, you know. They just lecture and students get through it.

They sometimes use the language of cognitive apprenticeship, like the instructor who mentioned "teaching from the sidelines"; another, a culinary arts instructor who self-consciously balances practice with lecture, said, "I feel I'm more of a coach than a teacher," where a "teacher" refers to a standard lecturer. Even those instructors whose classes are quite didactic denounce lecture. One nursing instructor operating a textbook-driven class mentioned that she was "trying to do as little formal lecturing as possible, and really activate the learning," when in fact students were rigidly limited to the content of handouts. There remains a great deal of lecture, and periods of lecture are the foundation of the lecture/discussion classes we examine in Chapter 2, but opinion seems to have turned against straight lecture.

Finally, almost universally, instructors believe that they should know and support their students, even if the teacher remains the central authority; an older model of the teacher as authoritarian figure is almost completely out of favor. As with a synthesis of didactic and constructivist learning, there is widespread recognition that the emotional or personal dimensions of learning (emphasized particularly in student support) and the cognitive dimensions reinforce each other: Students need self-confidence and support to approach new cognitive tasks, and success in learning in turn reinforces the confidence to attempt yet further learning. In this sense one element of student support has become all but universal.

There are, of course, many other conceptions of good teaching. Almost every book on adult education and on postsecondary teaching contains recommendations, usually drawn from the experience of veteran educators. A widely read example in higher education is a list of "seven principles for good practice in undergraduate education" (Chickering and Gamson, 1991): good teaching (1) encourages faculty-student contact; (2) encourages cooperation among students; (3) encourages active learning; (4) gives prompt feedback; (5) emphasizes time on task; (6) communicates high expectations; and (7) respects diverse talents and ways of learning. The fourth, fifth, and sixth are rooted in assumptions underlying behaviorist and didactic instruction; the second, third, and seventh are part of the meaning-centered tradition; the first is an expression of student support, as well as student-centeredness more generally. We suspect that most lists of recommendations borrow from different traditions—implicitly expressing the view that good teaching requires varied approaches to instruction.

If the approaches to teaching we have presented are so fundamental, one might expect more evidence about their effectiveness. However, there is very little—if by "evidence" we mean statistical evidence about learning outcomes. What evidence exists supports the superiority of meaning-centered and constructivist methods, but there isn't much of it.[12] One reason is that researchers have conceptualized teaching in different ways, so that empirical results are not often consistent with one another. A deeper problem is that different approaches measure outcomes differently: Those advocating skills and drills can rely on existing multiple-choice exams, but advocates of constructivist and meaning-centered instruction generally despise such measures and have worked to devise alternative and "authentic" assessments.[13] A third reason is that it is technically difficult, particularly in noncompulsory institutions such as community colleges, to carry out evaluations of instruction.[14] A final explanation is the dearth of research about community colleges in general, and the lack of institutional research. There are, then, good reasons for the lack of empirical evidence about teaching effectiveness, though the consequence is to leave us without clear empirical justification for one approach over another.

In the absence of hard data, other kinds of justification become more important.[15] Throughout this book we will describe the judgments that instructors—and, less often, administrators—make about pedagogy. Sometimes instructors' goals determine what they do. If teamwork and cooperation are important outcomes (in business or social work, for example), then instructors are more likely to use small groups and cooperative learning methods; preparation for an external, fact-oriented test—a licensing exam, for example, or the GED—may lead to didactic instruction and a concern with coverage. Often instructors have been led over time to certain practices by a rough sense of their effectiveness in *their* classes with *their* students. Many have shifted, largely by trial and error, away from conventional lecturing to more student-centered and constructivist methods (as we show in the next section). In our observations of classes, we often judge effectiveness by the participation of students; while engagement does not necessarily imply that students are learning, particularly if they are engaged by an amusing discussion or activity that's off the subject, it's hard to imagine that learning can take place when students are disengaged.

It is, then, possible to say a great deal about teaching without data on outcomes. Indeed, it's *necessary* to make such judgments: If educators wait for evidence about different approaches, it becomes impossible to provide any recommendations for either instructors or institutions about the quality of teaching.

III. THE ORIGINS OF INSTRUCTIONAL APPROACHES: TRIAL AND ERROR AS TEACHER TRAINING

How do instructors develop their approaches to teaching? They have not, with very few exceptions, graduated from teacher training programs; they are hired for their subject matter expertise, with master's degrees or doctorates in academic subjects, or with experience in occupational areas. Without preparation in teaching, and with only a few colleges providing any support during the early years of teaching (as we will see in Chapter 8), instructors are basically on their own; "they just throw you right in," as one remarked. As a result, they develop their approaches to teaching in highly individualistic ways, though two patterns dominate: trial and error, and discussion with peers.

By a large margin, most instructors credit trial and error for their current practices. As one instructor commented when he noted the lack of staff development in his institution:

> I thought that was the way it was at all community colleges. It's just trial and error, you know. If a person is an accountant or if a person is a lawyer, we just bring 'em in and let them teach.

As another described how he developed his approach to teaching,

> Well, trial and error, I guess. I mean, part of it was the struggle . . . my own struggle to figure out how to become a good teacher — and I think I'm still in that process. Sometimes I think I'm pretty effective, and other times I just want to start over again, you know, I just . . . this isn't working, I need to do something different.

This example illustrates several common elements in the "struggle": It's a long process, and instructors who have gone through it usually remain unsatisfied with their teaching and continue to search for improvement. But above all it is an individual's *own* struggle, without much help. This teacher mentioned some role of colleagues and feedback from students, but these were clearly secondary to his own experimentation. Very often, instructors who have shifted to constructivist teaching or hybrid methods report going through the process of trial and error. As one business instructor, notable for the variety of practices he used within a single classroom, told us:

> I have to admit, I've made it up. A lot of times students are very shocked at the way I do things in my class.... In my management class, I tell the students early in the semester that the class is theirs, not mine. I'm simply the facilitator; they are the individuals responsible for the direction of the class.... So I simply learned [to teach] by doing—and that's not always the best way. I tell students that—that's not always the best way, but that's how I've taught myself to teach.

This is an instructor in the constructivist mold ("I'm just the facilitator"), but he rediscovered its principles for himself by "making it up," "learning by doing."

Many instructors describe an odyssey in which they first started with conventional teacher-centered practices, found them ineffective, and then moved through trial and error to more student- and meaning-centered practices, or to some version of hybrid teaching. (Never did an instructor describe a journey in the opposite direction, from constructivist practices back to more didactic and teacher-centered practices.) But the problem with trial and error as a method of teacher training—apart from the fact that it is inefficient and time-consuming—is that only some faculty begin this odyssey. As one dean of instruction mentioned,

> Most community college instructors don't go through a teacher training program in order to become instructors. They get a master's degree and that's it. Hence the skills that are needed to be a successful teacher acquired by most community college faculty will be a trial-and-error approach.... Many of the faculty are still teaching with the same paradigms that were successful when we had a different student population.... Given the heterogeneity of our student population in terms of just their cultural background, and with the learning styles that these students bring to the college campus, it becomes to me somewhat overwhelming for a teacher to assume that I can still use the traditional lecture/demonstration and be successful. I think the future rests in the faculty's ability to develop alternative teaching styles, to address the various learning styles of students that are here.

Evidently the trial-and-error method of teacher preparation is inadequate to the task: Too many instructors remain mired in "traditional lecture/demonstration" and haven't yet started moving toward "alternative teaching styles." This dean acknowledged the institution's responsibility to these instructors—"my number one task is to provide those faculty with the resources that they need to get over that hump"—but his college provided very little staff development or other institutional support for teaching, and he also claimed that "institutions have very little leverage" on teaching. The result is that there's very little—in this college, and indeed in most colleges, as we will see in Chapter 8—to speed up the process of improving teaching.

Second to trial and error, instructors report that discussions with their peers are important influences. As one commented:

> Instructors tend to be experimenters who pick up from their immediate colleagues, or respond according to their conceptions of what's important in teaching. They don't read the literature!

Many have stories of outstanding teachers that they have had, or colleagues and mentors in their early years of teaching. A nursing instructor noted:

> In my doctoral program, I had some excellent professors and I was just really struck with how much of a difference it can make. . . . The other thing is I think just watching the way that different people teach exposes you to different instructional styles, whether it be small groups or group or individual presentations in the class.

One computer instructor noted that her teaching practices came from

> a combination of a lot of things—it's learning things from my colleagues, a lot of tips from . . . the old-timers, the ones that've been here twenty and twenty-five years, like the idea of using transparencies . . . using the computers, the overhead, doing this thing with the outline.

Sometimes the examples have been negative as well as positive. An electrical instructor related his preparation:

> I just observed what they [other instructors] were doing in the classrooms, even in other areas because while I was going here [as a student] . . . and I saw what poor teaching is all about. . . . I've been with two outstanding instructors. One was my supervisor at the naval shipyard, and he taught in the adult ed. in a technical pro-

gram there. The other was my department chairperson, who has since retired. He could have mentored this whole campus as to how to instruct a class.

Even among those who acknowledge the influence of mentors and peers, however, there's a central role for trial and error. One instructor, in an institution where learning communities have promoted greater discussions among faculty, described his peers in the following way:

> I would say that the primary way I think that people learn about it is through talking with other instructors. I mean, there's always dialogue—I mean, we're always exchanging ideas about something that works really well or something that totally flops. But I think that a lot of it is sort of working with your students and finding out what works and what doesn't.

Another, a political science instructor with a self-consciously hybrid approach, described the influence of classroom experience on any philosophical position:

> Over the years, every time I think I've got some great philosophical insight, then something happens in the class that shows me that I haven't succeeded yet.... You know, obviously it's [good teaching] knowing the material and knowing the subject and knowing the discipline, and—you can't fool students just by pretending like you know something if you don't know it. Second, it's sort of respecting the students in the sense of not thinking of them as empty vessels that you're gonna fill up with knowledge, but as human beings with their own concerns . . . where they actually can come to some of their own conclusions as opposed to just parroting back the books.... But, you know, those are just kind of general—those are all not as much of a philosophy as just a pragmatic way of trying to get things across.

Discussion with colleagues can therefore stimulate new ideas, but the crucible of the classroom—trial and error with different methods—is the ultimate test. The implication is that if instructors are not willing to experiment—or if they are so overburdened by the press of multiple classes and multiple assignments (described in Chapter 8) that they cannot experiment—then the process of improving their teaching never gets started.

A very few instructors mentioned that their disciplines influenced their approaches to teaching. Several English instructors cited the writing process approach. One early childhood instructor noted the influence of early childhood practice:

My early childhood experience has interested me in learning to learn, and that process. How is it people construct knowledge? And watching that from infancy and childhood, into adolescence, and watching how people learn and grow, has made me realize that our students here still need a lot of concrete experience—whether they're academic or vocational or professional career track. They need learning that is in context, that is applicable, that is relevant, that is somehow tied into what they already know, that, like children who need to mess and fuss, they need to mess and fuss with information also.... And I think that's what my early childhood background helped me to see, is that not all students construct knowledge in the same way.

A business instructor mentioned that teaching should be "client-centered," a phrase taken from business, because "we're dealing with clients, we're dealing with consumers in the classroom." An arts instructor attributed his notions of teaching to the nature of artistic efforts:

A good teacher stimulates and motivates, and has an open mind, and listens, and is willing to be flexible.... I think a teacher's a facilitator. Not one that knows the answers or all the answers, but maybe can help a student in some direction to discover [his own answer].... I think if you're gonna be an artist, you have to have an open mind. And there is no right and wrong way. You can't be real judgmental of your work while you're doing it—you'll kill it.

An instructor in women's studies noted that feminist pedagogy (e.g., Noddings, 1992) stimulated her student-centered teaching:

A lot of women's studies or feminist pedagogy is focused upon student-centered learning—where there's sort of an equal emphasis for everyone in the classroom, and you sort of individualize the instruction.

Several occupational instructors noted the similarities between teaching and the conditions of production. A construction instructor put it this way:

Teaching—I don't think it is separate from construction, because if you're a foreman you're teaching all the time, if you're a superintendent you're teaching the foreman, and so you're a teacher whether you want to be or not.

In Chapter 3 we will examine other cases where instructors deliberately modeled their classrooms on production, sometimes leading to authoritarian workshops and sometimes to classes suffused with the ethic of the caring occupations.

But examples where instructors were able to draw on their disciplines for intellectual support were relatively few. We observed many teacher-centered business instructors, and early childhood instructors often took teacher-centered approaches despite the child-centered orientation of their field. Some faculty who have moved toward constructivist teaching may be able to find justification from their disciplines, but other influences have been more powerful.

The dominance of trial and error—"sink or swim" is the other common metaphor—as the dominant method of learning about teaching illustrates a point we will make repeatedly throughout this book. With some notable exceptions that we describe in Chapter 8, most community colleges do little systematically to help their instructors improve their teaching. As a result, teaching looks like an individual activity, varying enormously from person to person without apparent rationale, and justifying the old saw that "good teachers are born, not made." But this isn't *necessarily* so; it *is* so because community colleges, like so many educational institutions, have failed to assume much institutional responsibility for the quality of instruction.

IV. THE COMMUNITIES OF INSTRUCTORS: THE CONSTRUCTION OF THEIR ROLES

As many instructors describe them, mentors and colleagues can be powerful forces for improving teaching. But here too there is a substantial problem, partly systemic, partly individual: The isolation of most community college instructors inhibits the interaction with their peers that might provide them with new ideas about teaching, suggestions about teaching problems, and support for their experiments. Thus, instructors—particularly those whose teaching is most in need of improvement—don't have much access to colleagues from whom they might learn about teaching.

A defining aspect of instructors' lives in community colleges is their isolation. Except in a small number of exemplary institutions, most instructors speak of their lives and work as individual, isolated, lonely. A teacher's job is a series of classes, with the door metaphorically if not literally closed. Some faculty view isolation as an inherent part of teaching: "Teaching is a very individualistic endeavor, and people are often secretive and unwilling to seek out or utilize a different approach." Another described her institution (a technical college) in these terms: "From the day I entered this place to right now, you sort of figure out how you're gonna teach something yourself." An auto instructor noted that his disconnection from the rest of the institution came both from the general isolation of teachers and the special status problems of occupational instructors, compounded by their physical isolation from the rest of the campus: "I'm an independent contractor—

no one gives a shit what I do as long as enrollments are up." One instructor contrasted the reality of isolation with the rhetoric about the community college as a
teaching institution:

> We face here what I call the community college paradox. . . . It's that the community
> college touts itself as being the teaching institution in higher education. It's the one
> that's not burdened, if you will, by the research assignment for the teacher. . . . What
> you would expect, I think, is communities of teachers who are developing their skills
> as teachers, and that there'd be a lot of institutional attention to that very goal. . . .
> But instead what you find in the community college is . . . teachers who are just phe-
> nomenally isolated. They have their classes, they have class autonomy. . . . For the
> classroom there's nothing that's forced on us, so if you happen to be interested in col-
> legiality, and if you happen to believe that developing your craft as a teacher requires
> you be in the classroom all the time, you're going against the system. Because there's
> this irony: It's a teaching institution, but there's almost nothing for the teacher. . . . So
> I've felt really isolated.

A partial exception to the profound isolation of instructors is the department
in which they teach. Many instructors have considerable interaction with others
in their department, from whom they get teaching ideas. But departments in
community colleges are not usually large or cohesive enough to form a real
community except in the subjects with substantial enrollments, such as English,
math, and business. A social science department is likely to have one econo-
mist, one sociologist, a political scientist, and an anthropologist, without much
in common. A typical college will have one or two historians and a number of
part-timers to teach various foreign languages. Occupational departments are
equally fragmented because each occupational area has at most two or three
instructors (perhaps with some part-timers who are not around much), and
automotive instructors may not think they have much in common with instructors from drafting or electronics. Even occupations that appear to outsiders to be related may not be. Take one automotive instructor's description of
his situation:

> I don't get involved usually with any committees or anything like that. I'm trying to
> do this job here. . . . The only people I really talk to—I mean I say hi to other faculty,
> English faculty. I mean I know who they are. The only ones I talk to are the other
> automotive faculty. I don't even talk to the body shop people 'cause I don't know
> what I would ask them. So if I need any help or advice or whatever, I talk to [two
> other automotive instructors] or whatever, and that's the only people I talk to.

Even within departments, there is enormous variation in how instructors use them to discuss teaching. Without a collegial culture, departments are not much more than places where instructors get their mail and their assignments. As one English teacher—an individual who had sought out a learning community—mentioned:

> As a big division, we tend to be kind of wrapped up in our individual work. . . . If I didn't have that kind of opportunity [for interaction within a learning community], I think I would feel very, very isolated. I'm not sure what collegiality would be based on.

This last comment—"I'm not sure what collegiality would be based on"—is especially telling: In the absence of any sense of teaching as a shared activity, the very notion of collegiality lacks any meaning. Similarly, the auto instructor quoted above indicated how little real contact he had even within his three-person unit:

> We don't do any team teaching around here that I'm aware of, okay? I just do my own thing. I can pretty much teach what I want to teach here and I don't think anybody would know. The administration wouldn't. . . . And like what goes on in [another instructor's] class, you kind of know because you hear students talk about it and sometimes I hear him talk about it and I do the same thing. And I kind of know what goes on in there. But it's really none of my business and he's doing a good job. I mean I just know he is. He's conscientious. So we kind of leave each other alone.

This passage expresses the ignorance within many colleges. The administration doesn't know what goes on in classrooms, and while this instructor claims to "kind of know" his colleague's classes, he gets most of his information from other students. Valuable though they may be, departments are far from a solution to the isolation of teaching.

Furthermore, we found no evidence that other collectives of faculty, particularly academic senates or unions, have any influence on teaching. Most of these bodies spend their time in disputes about governance, funding, salaries, the division of prerogatives—that is, the *means* of education rather than the *ends*. In some colleges unions are particularly counterproductive since they focus only on wages and working conditions and create an adversarial climate in which faculty and administrators cannot find common cause. Sometimes they even forbid the kinds of peer observation and mentoring that might improve the quality of teaching; in several colleges, peer evaluation procedures had been halted by union opposition

("The evaluations here are done strictly by the managers"). And so these kinds of faculty representation have been largely unsuccessful in making teaching public and visible. As a vice president for instruction noted:

> The faculty unions deals with working conditions; I don't think that's the decision-making body for academic issues. We've tried to create something, but those issues need clarity.

In the absence of any *institutional* commitment to creating collegiality, a few instructors do so in small groups. A few participate in learning communities, which we describe in Chapters 5 and 7. A very few participate in networks of instructors from other institutions, like the math instructor (mentioned in Chapter 7, Section II) who participated in a National Science Foundation (NSF) colloquium about innovative uses of computers. But teacher associations for community colleges are small and weak, particularly compared to their K–12 counterparts, and for occupational subjects such associations are generally missing.[16]

Furthermore, the networks of colleagues that instructors do create—the communities of practice that influence their teaching—are limited in an interesting but ultimately damaging way. The most active and innovative instructors create their own communities of like-minded individuals, both inside and outside their college. As one instructor who had participated extensively in learning communities mentioned, "There's a few people on the faculty that are really interested [in teaching]. We kind of find each other." But those most in need of improvement— teaching the kind of "distressed" and "collapsed" classes we document in Chapter 6, where content has been undermined by their teaching—tend to isolate themselves from their peers and their institution.

The best way to see how instructors create their communities differently is to contrast individuals within the same institution. In the exemplary college we call Metropolis Community College, profiled in Section V of Chapter 8, there was virtually unanimous support for the institution as a teaching institution, "a *great* place to be a teacher." But one sociology instructor, who taught in a rigid and didactic manner quite at odds with other instructors in his learning community, complained that the college wasn't supportive of academic instruction since he (unlike his colleagues) perceived it to be vocationally oriented. He criticized learning communities for tracking students, contrary to his colleagues who saw them as ways of allowing students to learn from one another, and he had decided to stop teaching in learning communities and revert to individual teaching.

In a different case, one urban community college was perceived by virtually all the faculty as unsupportive of teaching, without staff development, administrative support for teaching, or any interaction among faculty. But even there, a microbiology instructor—one who worked hard to get his students to think as scientists would, nudging them to develop their own answers rather than asking him—had developed a program with other faculty on his multicampus college and had visited a distant community college to look at an environmental program. He acknowledged that such collaboration "is dependent on the aggressiveness of the faculty" and was quite rare in his institution, but his example confirms that active instructors can create communities even when institutional conditions are quite hostile.

In another institution, one with middling institutional support for teaching, a number of instructors were notable for their efforts to collaborate with others. These include the math instructor who mentioned that those interested in teaching "find each other"; a physics instructor who team-taught and had extensive connections outside the college with a FIPSE (Fund for the Improvement of Postsecondary Education) project, an NSF project to get community college physics instructors together, and an innovation called workshop physics; an instructor of theater history who managed to sit in on a number of other classes; a construction instructor with a great deal of contact with other colleagues; several English instructors who had teamed up with each other and with outside colleagues to develop innovative computer-based approaches to writing. But an architectural history instructor, whose classes were remarkable for their lack of content and student engagement, was hostile to the college's staff development activities, cynical about the administration's ability to support teaching ("This evaluation thing, I mean, I don't think that it's gonna do anybody any good"), and ignorant about student resources on campus, such as tutoring services ("They seem to be working primarily with handicapped people"). This instructor taught full time at this college and part time at another, so there was little time for him to participate with his colleagues. Similarly, an anthropology instructor whose class collapsed (see Section I of Chapter 2) complained that the institution cared about "teaching and student satisfaction," not about the disciplinary content and coverage that she valued:

> There's no one who really looks at the content of my teaching or who's currently interested in what I'm doing researchwise. It amazes me. Here at [this college] the emphasis is on teaching and on student satisfaction. And people who come to evaluate me have evaluated me on my lecture technique, and they are not anthropologists. So I could be saying things that absolutely were wrong and they would not know the difference.

But students were learning very little of what she tried to cover. She could certainly have benefited from the experiences of other instructors in her college, many of them quite dedicated to their disciplines and coverage, but she had isolated herself from the institution. She did not take part in staff development, noting that there were no institutional requirements to participate, and did not even work with the other anthropologist on the campus because he came from another school of thought—so "we [faculty] just work pretty much independently."

In yet another college we were unable to assess the institution's commitment to teaching because the faculty were so divided about the college. On closer examination, the most effective instructors had gone out of their way to create contacts around the institution, while those with more pedestrian teaching were the most disaffected. A culinary arts instructor with low student engagement, in a program that might be closed because of systematic enrollment problems, complained about other instructors and administrators alike ("The administrators mainly just talk to themselves"). Her interactions were entirely within her department, and she admitted, "I'd be lucky if I could name ten faculty members." An economics instructor, teaching through straight lecture with "applications" drawn from his family rather than economic or student issues, complained about the lack of staff development and collegiality on the campus: "Most of us are pretty independent." An anthropology instructor, again teaching in a conventional lecture style punctuated with simple fill-in-the-blank questions, no longer did any experimental or collaborative teaching ("When I taught high school we used to do all sorts of weird stuff, but here not at all") and was particularly bitter about the administration ("This place is strictly body count, and the dean will give you some bullshit—his role is quieting intrafaculty fights").

On the other hand, a nursing instructor with a high level of engagement in her class noted the team teaching and extension interaction among the nursing faculty, and cited many examples of administrative support for teaching, including staff development, classroom assessment workshops, and an instructional resource center. A dental assisting instructor, who used a variety of teaching methods and generated a high level of engagement, had created links with the rest of the campus (the library, the child care program, the culinary arts department to discuss nutrition, the business department) to enrich her program. She described the administration as supportive of teaching through computer-based methods, classroom assessment, and some staff development. An early-childhood teacher, who used student teaching experiences as a springboard for a fluid discussion about workplace conditions, ethical issues, and effects on children, claimed that "[this college] is a very social college" and described many examples of collaboration: "There's a lot that the college has and it's available—it's a matter of whether you have the time to go." There were several more examples in this college. In virtually every case, instructors who were more student- and project-centered had actively sought collaboration across campus and viewed the institution as supportive of teaching, while the more rigid and didactic instructors uniformly viewed teaching as isolated and the institution as unsupportive. As far as we could determine by interviewing faculty, there is no single "truth" about this college: Instructors interpret the institution differently because they construct their experiences differently.

Finally, we kept a running list of instructors who struck us as especially effective—with high levels of student engagement, active student participation, and relatively sophisticated content—and those who were particularly ineffective, including those whose classes collapsed (described in Chapter 4).[17] The same pattern turned up in these extreme cases. The effective instructors were almost universally linked with other faculty, often in learning communities, while really bad teachers were generally alienated from their peers. They were sometimes burned out, or isolated in tiny one- or two-person programs, or hostile to the college's nontraditional students and out of step with the orthodoxy of student support, but they were uniformly distant from other faculty and hostile to the administration.

The link between approaches to teaching and the tendency of instructors to create communities of like-minded faculty—or remain isolated and alienated—is certainly complex. Faculty who teach in meaning-centered and constructivist ways tend to view learning as a social enterprise, in which individuals create meaning within a community —a group of students and teachers within a single classroom, for example, or a group of teachers within a college. It's quite consistent for them to reach out to other faculty and administrators, to create a community of practice for themselves. Those teaching in behaviorist ways are more likely to see learning as an individual activity, one where the students absorb what teachers and texts present them; it's also consistent for them to treat teaching itself as an individual activity (as most educational institutions do). In addition, there are more obvious connections: Faculty may teach poorly because they have no help with their instruction, or they may isolate themselves so that others can't discover how ineffective they are, or they may become so alienated for personal reasons that they neglect both their classes and their colleagues.

The isolation of instructors in community colleges is a problem for several reasons, then.[18] It contributes to the invisibility of teaching: without contact among colleagues, there are few discussions about instruction, no forums where the special pedagogical problems of community college can be debated and resolved, and no ways to bring problems to the attention of administrators. In an institution where learning from peers is one of the few ways of improving teaching, isolation means that new instructors, or experienced instructors who come across a new challenge, or those who (like the English instructor we describe in Chapter 2) fear that "I'm not doing it correctly" have nowhere to turn for help. And, as we will see in subsequent chapters, the novel practices that spring up can't influence other instructors if there is no contact among them, and innovation then remains limited and idiosyncratic. If there's no learning among instructors, it's hard to be a real teaching college.

The special isolation of the most ineffective instructors is particularly disheartening. Because (aside from trial and error) instructors learn most often about teaching from their colleagues, these individuals have cut themselves off from their only sources of support and improvement. Their actions make the usual institutional mechanisms of improving teaching—ongoing workshops, instructional centers, departmental and administrator encouragement—ineffective, even as their isolation makes it difficult for others to understand what their teaching is like. In this way of constructing an educational institution, a college has virtually no way to improve the quality of the worst teaching.

V. THE INDIVIDUAL AND THE INSTITUTIONAL

As community college instructors articulate their approaches to instruction, they replicate the broad spectrum that others have noted over many years of commentary about teaching and learning. Many of them, particularly those wedded to their disciplines, are most concerned about coverage and content. Both their own descriptions and their actions in the classroom reveal practices that have been variously called teacher-centered, didactic, behaviorist, or skills-oriented. Many others have moved away from these traditional teaching practices and articulate a commitment to teaching that is more constructivist (or "active") in its conception of how students learn, more student-centered, more concerned with students creating their own understandings than with coverage of facts and skills. And a few instructors—a very few, in our estimation—think that being supportive of students is the only prerequisite for good teaching. While we think that student support is an inadequate conception of instruction, its central insight—that students must feel supported by their instructors and classmates, that humiliation is poor pedagogy—is widely shared. The vast majority of community college instructors are highly sympathetic to their students; they can clearly articulate how difficult their lives are and how poor their prior schooling has been.

We suspect that there has been some change in the attitudes toward teaching over the last ten or fifteen years. After some experimental teaching in the 1960s and early 1970s and then a subsiding of innovation in the 1970s and 1980s, many instructors are now eager to declare that conventional lecture is inadequate, particularly for the academically underprepared students entering community colleges. But many of those who say they embrace student-centered or hybrid methods teach in quite conventional teacher-centered ways—or, confronted with the conditions of the community college classroom, they revert to drill, to lecture, or to discussions that are essentially lectures in disguise. In the next several chapters we examine the kinds of teaching that take place in community college classrooms, to illustrate what really happens and to clarify how complex teaching really is—and how important it is, therefore, for institutions to support their faculty as they struggle to improve their own approaches to teaching.

Moreover, the odyssey from didactic methods toward more meaning- and student-centered approaches is often idiosyncratic, shaped by *individual* dissatisfaction with what conventional lecture can accomplish. Less often, faculty mention the effects of peers and mentors in stimulating their thinking about teaching, and describe a process where faculty committed to teaching "kind of find each other." But this process too is idiosyncratic, since community colleges have structured the demands of teaching and the interactions among faculty so that isolation is common and collegiality is difficult. So neither of the major forms of teacher training—trial and error, and the counsel of peers—is effective for a large number of faculty members. Community colleges have structured the requirements for instructors and the conditions of their lives so that their preparation for teaching is unsystematic.

These twin conclusions—the individual nature of teaching in community colleges, and the lack of institutional support for teaching—are themes that we will develop throughout this book. Of course, community colleges need not be this way. We will mention throughout the institutional practices that could support good teaching (variously defined), and in Chapter 8 we will profile several colleges that have devoted virtually all their institutional resources to the improvement of teaching. Unless educational institutions make teaching a priority, instructors follow a wild variety of practices and good teachers are viewed as "born, not made"—because there are no systematic influences to help them.

NOTES

1. On their communities of practice, see especially Chapter 7, Chapter 3 for occupational instructors, and Chapter 5 for remedial/developmental instructors.

2. This is a major claim that merits greater investigation, though a few examples may help. Both John Dewey's writing about teaching and, much more recently, Jerome Bruner's wonderful writing (especially Bruner, 1990 and 1996) are based on observation over long periods of time. The recent work of cognitive scientists is usually based on careful observation of teaching and learning. The conceptions of teaching in this chapter were based on observations in remedial/developmental education (Grubb and Kalman, 1994), and the very similar analysis in Knapp and Turnbull (1990) was based on observations in K–6 classes. When conceptions of teaching are not based on observations of teaching—for example, the "teaching as leadership"

conception in Baker, Roueche, and Gillet-Karam (1990), based on a "path-goal" concept of four types of leadership—they can be awkward to apply.

3. In K–12 education, the "reading wars" over phonics versus whole language have recently been adjudicated by a panel of the National Research Council. The final recommendations are a hybrid, insisting on deriving meaning from print as well as direct teaching of "sound-symbol relationships" (i.e., phonics). See Snow, Burns, and Griffin, 1998.

4. This in turn assumes that the ordering of difficulty is unambiguous—though students may vary in the tasks they find more difficult (Bruner, 1990). See also Resnick, 1987, who notes that the notion of "higher-order skills" implies that certain "lower-order" or "basic" skills need to be learned first—whereas certain reasoning and problem solving abilities can be integrated into classrooms from the beginning.

5. For the various ways of assigning blame for the poor performance of low-income and minority students, see Cuban and Tyack, 1989.

6. On "coaching," see Collins, Brown, and Newman, 1989, who also invoke an idealized master-apprenticeship relationship in describing good teaching as a process of cognitive apprenticeship.

7. In the large literature around teaching, there are few references to hybrid teaching. For two exceptions see Cuban, 1993, who notes that hybrid teaching practices are often signs of innovation, and Grubb and Kalman, 1994, who note that eclectic practices can be so contradictory as to be ineffective. Recently there has been increased commentary recognizing that hybrid instruction may be the best approach; this has been particularly frequent in discussions about grammar-based versus whole language approaches to teaching literacy.

8. This comment about self-esteem clarifies the connection between student support and the debate in K–12 education about self-esteem. See especially Kohn, 1994.

9. For examples of this literature, see for example Balmuth, 1985; Solorzano, Stecher, and Perez, 1989; Kazemek, 1988; Fueyo, 1988; Fingeret and Jurmo, 1989; Salvatori and Hull, 1990; and Sticht, 1988. Like most of the writing on teaching in community colleges, this literature tends to be based on the experience of its authors, not on any wider empirical investigation.

10. Instructors often use the idea of "learning styles" to describe the preferences of students for text versus video versus aural sources of information; this is quite different from the approaches to thinking styles developed by Sternberg (1990 and 1988b), who focuses instead on differences in metacognitive approaches among students.

11. John Dewey counseled that educators ought to avoid false and counterproductive dichotomies—for example, the distinctions between play and work, between the abstract and the applied, the academic and the vocational. In a succinct statement on the two approaches to pedagogy in the very beginning of *Experience and Education* (1938), he decried the tendency of educators to think in "either-ors," and then went on to describe traditional versus progressive education as an example. But the problem for Dewey was not simply to replace traditional education with progressive practices: "The problem is not even recognized, to say nothing of being solved, when it is assumed that it suffices to reject the ideas and practices of the old education and then go to the opposite extreme" (p. 22). Instead, a new philosophy of education could be constructed from a combination of the two, "in the idea that there is an intimate and necessary relationship between the processes of actual experience and education" (p. 20)—or, to put it simplistically, by combining doing and learning. Dewey was not often specific about how this was to be accomplished—he was not a writer of how-to manuals, after all—but he consistently promoted a synthesis of traditional and progressive practices.

12. In the field of writing, a meta-analysis has concluded that the presentational (or didactic) mode and the conventional teaching of grammar are the least effective (Hillocks, 1986); similarly, the National Assessment of Educational Progress concluded that writing proficiency is positively related to teachers' use of the writing process (Appleby et al., 1994) rather than grammar-based instruction. Knapp and his colleagues (Knapp, Shields, and Turnbull, 1992; Knapp et al., 1995) examined math and English scores in elementary classrooms with high proportions of low-income students and found that classrooms with larger numbers of "alternative" practices—which they defined almost precisely as we describe meaning-making—led to significantly higher scores. Some specific practices in the meaning- and student-centered tradition have been found to be more effective, including cooperative learning (Slavin, 1980; Walberg, 1986) and reciprocal teaching (Palincsar and Brown, 1984; Brown and Palincsar, 1989; Brown and Campione, 1994). In the community college realm, there is some evidence that interdisciplinary learning communities are effective in increasing retention, grades, and subsequent success in courses (McGregor, 1991; Tinto, Love, and Russo, undated; Gudan, Clack, Tang, and Dixon, 1991).

13. See, for example, the vituperative debate between McKenna, Miller, and Robinson (1990) and Edelsky (1990) about evaluating whole-language approaches.

14. The evidence about K–12 instruction usually compares pretests and posttests in experimental situations, or in quasi-experimental conditions where attrition is not a problem because attendance is compulsory. However, in the community college setting, where students can "vote with their feet," one consequence of low-quality or demeaning instruction is that students simply drop out, so that posttests would be inadequate measures of effectiveness. However, students drop out for many different reasons, and these would have to be determined before including persistence as a measure of effectiveness. Students also self-select themselves into different types of courses, and so selection bias is a serious evaluation problem.

15. See also Resnick, 1987, 34: "If we were to demand solid empirical evidence . . . we would be condemned at this time to inaction." We note that the evidence available is almost entirely about K–12 education, not about community colleges or higher education (except for the evidence about learning communities). While Chickering and Gamson (1991) claim that their "seven principles" for good undergraduate teaching are based on different kinds of research, the evidence comes largely from four-year rather than two-year colleges, as well as from the K–12 literature. Some of this research involves student ratings of instructors rather than information about what they have learned, and is therefore suspect.

16. The Community College Humanities Association, with 1,200 members, publishes a journal, the *Community College Humanist*. The American Mathematics Association of Two-Year Colleges, with 2,800 members, and the Community College Association of Instruction and Technology, with 350 members, both publish newsletters. Otherwise there appear to be no national associations of community college teachers that might provide forums for discussions of teaching—nothing comparable to the National Council of Teachers of English, for example, of the National Council for the Teaching of Mathematics, both of which have been quite active in K–12 instruction. Occupational instructors are particularly poorly represented; the American Vocational Association, which acts more as a lobbying group than as a substantive forum, generally represents secondary rather than postsecondary instructors, and the National Council on Occupational Education represents administrators rather than instructors.

17. There are not many of these memorable instructors—perhaps a dozen especially effective and another dozen dreadful instructors. Among those of us working on this research, there was

a high rate of agreement about these individuals—though because we did not have random samples we did not carry out formal statistical analyses.

18. The issue of collegiality has been extensively examined in K–12 education, and it proves to be crucial to the ability to innovate—because innovations require support from other instructors, and tend to wither away if instructors must develop them independently. Some schools have moved toward a model in which teachers form a collective with responsibility not only for improved teaching, but also for many administrative and managerial tasks, breaking down the conventional separation of teaching and administration. See especially Little, 1987 and 1996; Darling-Hammond and McLaughlin, 1995; Lieberman, 1995.

2

THE MODAL CLASSROOM
The Varieties of Lecture/Discussion

The variety of classroom practices is bewildering. Even in the 257 classes we observed, in only a tiny slice of the 994 community colleges across the country, we saw everything from a conventional lecture with eighty students to an intense discussion about Muslim history in a seminar of four students, from conventional classrooms with seats arranged in neat rows to vocational workshops in dairy barns and automotive shops, from remedial classes struggling with basic punctuation to the most sophisticated discussions of microeconomics, calculus, and the physics of heat transfer.

Still, one kind of teaching is prevalent: the lecture/discussion, a hybrid approach in which the instructor devotes some time to lecture and structures some time for discussion. (The analogue in many occupational courses is the lecture/workshop, the subject of Chapter 3.) This basic format is possible because most community college classes have between ten and thirty students, a size that permits discussion and is too intimate for straight lecture.[1] In addition, as we saw in the previous chapter, many instructors dislike straight lecture and combine it with other activities. Several instructors acknowledged how common this format is. One instructor described his basic approach as "lecture and discussion— isn't this what we all do?" Another said his method is "probably the same one most everyone uses, which is lecture/discussion: I pose questions and try to get answers."

But the lecture/discussion is more complex than just "posing questions." It encompasses a huge variety, from classes dominated by discussion to those in which lecture predominates and in which the discussion is so teacher-directed and formulaic that it merely extends the lecture. Nothing is as it seems: Lectures can turn into discussion, and what appear to be discussion-based classes can be lectures in disguise. In teaching, God is in the details: in the kinds of questions posed, in the role of the instructor relative to students, in the myriad interactions that pass by almost too fast to notice.

We also discovered a variant of the lecture/discussion that we call the textbook-driven class, in which the instructor and students follow a textbook closely, often slavishly. This form clarifies that didactic instruction may be less *teacher*-centered than *textbook*-centered, where the teacher is the dispenser of the text rather than the central authority. There are some advantages to the textbook-centered class, particularly in forcing students to read, and it certainly ensures coverage and orderliness. However, these classes provide the most extreme examples of passive learning—contrary to the practices of those who believe in more meaning-centered approaches.

Students behave in different ways in these classes, and their reactions provide important clues about their engagement and learning. From seeing students with different instructors, we think that student behavior is largely the result of each instructor socializing students anew, in each class, to a particular kind of teaching and a particular student role. The skill of instructors in establishing patterns of questions and interactions, and in communicating what content is important, determines how engaged students are and how much they can learn from the class. This is one of many reasons to conclude that teaching matters—and that the role of community colleges in helping instructors master their own teaching can make all the difference.

I. THE BASIC STRUCTURE OF LECTURE/DISCUSSION

The common form of lecture/discussion usually begins with lecture intended to convey particular facts or specific procedures (like mathematical operations). The discussion portion then provides some room for student interpretation or clarification. Sometimes instructors present material for a relatively large chunk of time, perhaps twenty to thirty minutes, and then break for questions; in other cases instructors intersperse lecture with a few questions and then move on to further lecture. Here's a good example:

> A transfer class in physical geography, with about twenty-two students at the outset (and another eighteen or so arriving within ten minutes), is arranged in conventional rows. It begins with the instructor noting the weather (dense fog known as tule fog) and explaining its origins. She then begins the day's lesson, on igneous rocks, starting with a brief review from the previous class in which she makes a series of factual statements, pausing for students to complete her sentences with the appropriate word or phrase. Then she begins lecturing on new

material, writing on an overhead projector as she goes along; as she lectures she picks up various rocks to demonstrate their properties. Most students have their textbooks open to a particular chapter. After about ten minutes she throws a question out to the class: "Can you think of a rock that was primarily calcium carbonate?" A student answers correctly; then another student raises her hand and asks, "What causes the different colors in marble?" The instructor gives a long, clear answer, though speaking too fast for students to take notes.

The instructor continues with lecture and questions, and then leads students through an exercise in drawing the earth's surface and the geological features underground; she builds up a diagram on the overhead using three colors while most students follow her, drawing a similar diagram in their notebooks. She builds up the features of this diagram through a series of questions—"What affects the earth's surface?" "What goes on underground?" She then holds up an inflatable globe and asks, "What helps us know anything about the structure of the earth? How do we know? No one has dug a hole." She uses a slide of a cutaway model of the earth and asks, "How did they get this picture?" In their responses students refer to a twenty-page photocopied handout with the cutaway image in the middle of one of the pages; they use the text and handouts to explain the methods of uncovering hidden features of the earth.

Occasionally students raise their hands and ask questions for clarification, for example: "Why wouldn't the core be molten as well?" The instructor turns this question back to the class, waits until she hears the answer, "Pressure," then moves on. She begins to explain the concepts of geological time and its record in rocks of different ages. A student asks, "What process do they use to determine age?" The instructor responds, "It's all part of the fascinating story of the 1960s, which I'm going to get into tomorrow—the theory that all the continents were once together." The class breaks up slightly before the hour as the instructor appeals for the attendance sheet.

There was a high level of engagement in this class: Most students were following the instructor, drawing in their notebooks the diagram she developed on the board, taking notes and responding to questions. They had done the reading, and they had ready answers to her questions. The class covered what the instructor intended, about igneous rocks, and there were bridges at the beginning and the end to prior and subsequent classes. The instructor's use of questions helps keep students engaged, and the frequency of student questions suggested that they had been encouraged to ask such questions. None of the questions dwelt on course requirements—not once did a student ask, "Will this be on the exam?" The questions were also related to the topic of the day, so that the class was on task for virtually the whole hour. And all of this was accomplished in a large class, one that reached forty students at its zenith.

The interactions in this class are sometimes called "Socratic" by instructors because content is partly developed through questions that students answer, based on previous lectures and reading. Several features are typical of the lecture/discussion format, at least in the hands of competent teachers. The instructor varied her presentation, moving among topics and activities—for example, moving from facts about rocks to diagramming the structure of the earth. The latter exercise required students to participate more actively, and shifted students from one form of representation (written language) to another (schematic diagrams).[2] The instructor made substantial use of supporting materials, including globes, maps, and rocks observed for their physical properties. The instructor outlined her presentation on an overhead as she went along, clarifying her organization.

We suspect that most observers would consider this a good class—on-task, covering a good deal of content, with students highly engaged and discussion supporting the course material. But, we should point out, the content of the class was almost entirely teacher- (or text-) directed. The discussion was largely in service of lecture, of conveying facts about igneous rocks and the origin of the earth's surface features, rather than opening up new areas for discussion or questioning fundamental assumptions. There was little student-to-student interaction; in this class, as in many others, the teacher and the text were the source of all knowledge. There were some metacognitive questions, about how geographers have inferred the structure of the earth when they cannot directly see it, but they were comparatively rare. Such classes are essentially lectures, though the relatively small size allows the instructor to scan the class constantly for comprehension, to ask questions to see whether students are following, and to permit students to raise their own concerns.

The lecture-discussion format also lends itself to more constructivist and less fact-oriented classes. Consider the following Growth and Development class, a psychology course attended by both transfer-oriented students and occupational students in early childhood and elementary education:

> The class, with about twenty-two students, starts with the instructor outlining the topics for the day's class and circulating handouts. She then reviews the stage of middle childhood, presenting definitions and conceptions drawn from the handout, the text, and prior classes; this is a short lecture, using the overhead projector and verbal clues ("Here

are the main concepts I want you to think about") to clarify the central ideas. She then asks, "How many of you had chores?" This open-ended question prompts many responses; for most of them she has a follow-up question or substantive comment. The instructor then summarizes the implications of these responses for the developmental tasks in early childhood, including socialization to work and responsibility. She then continues her lecture, illustrating points from developmental theory from applications in elementary teaching and parenting.

She then shifts to a different activity: "What I am going to do is take you back to grade school. . . . How many of you liked math?" As the class groans at a slide with conventional arithmetic problems, she arranges the class into groups to work on some math games, commenting, "If you were children, I would work with you on the directions of what to do, but as adults, I assume you will figure it out." The students do indeed construct the rules of the game for themselves, and play it; after twenty-five minutes the instructor reconvenes the class to discuss the implications of games and game playing as pedagogical devices, the value of rules, and the pedagogical strategy of using games rather than drill to teach math to young children.

The instructor then transitions into another aspect of middle childhood with a cartoon, discusses teasing briefly, and initiates a discussion based in part on students' experiences.

Within a ninety-minute class, this instructor has engaged in three short periods of lecture, each followed by discussion—both whole-class discussion and small-group discussion based on an exercise (the math games). The first discussion, about the chores individuals have, is based on students' experiences and is genuinely open-ended. The second, proceeding from the math games, draws upon their own experiences in elementary schools and on the insight generated by a brief class "project," and it provides various insights about both development and pedagogy. The third discussion, about teasing, is similarly dependent on the students' experiences while remaining germane to the topic of child development. The class has been carefully structured by the instructor in order to get through three topics and three related discussions and exercises—this is not a free-for-all, or an unplanned class—but the student contributions are less predictable, less structured with "right" answers, than in the physical geography class. It helps that the subject (child development and education) is one where every student has relevant experience—as is true of many occupational classes, but which may not be true in academic classes such as physical geography, math, or literature.

This instructor used one unusual but illustrative device to stimulate discussion:

When she initiated discussion the first time ("How many of you had chores?"), she tossed a fuzzy ball into the classroom, which was then passed among students who talked. In part this is a motivational device: "It can sometimes wake up students—literally. It's like, 'Oh, it might come to me.'" But it also serves to enhance class participation. Students can signal other students for the ball, or they can "pass"—literally pass the ball on to someone else—if they don't want to participate, but the physical passing of the ball means that a large number of students participate. As the instructor explained it:

> In the process of passing, if . . . they're given the ball and they're not ready, or they're too uncomfortable—they didn't raise their hand, but they got it anyway—they can say, "Pass." But most of the time they don't. But it always gives them that choice, and it's like, "You still are given the opportunity; you're invited to participate; you're respected for not participating—but you're included and you're important here." So it's a very nonthreatening way to invite some of the people who are reluctant to speak up in a large group.

The passing of the ball symbolizes the engagement that discussion can create: Participation is widespread, though uncoerced, and is a central feature of learning rather than peripheral to the lecture component. Other skillful instructors prompt such discussion without a physical symbol like the ball, but they take similar care in the way they construct questions, in the rhythms of lecture and discussion, and in the combination of whole-class and small-group activities.

Veering toward Lecture

Lively as it can be, the lecture/discussion can turn deadly in the hands of other, less skilled instructors. A number of common practices have the effect of converting the class from one in which discussion plays an important role to one in which the teacher, and "teacher talk," dominates everything else.[3] None of these practices seems particularly harmful, but collectively they can generate classes that become entirely didactic. And by discouraging student participation, they often undermine the content of the class even though instructors intend to enhance content and coverage through lecture:

   • More often than we like to remember, classes begin by reviewing a quiz or test. Now, review allows a quiz allows to be educational, rather than simply providing a grade; students can ask questions, seek further clarification, and challenge the instructor's interpretation. But most quizzes that we observed are multiple-choice exams of fact, not assessments of problem solving or interpretive abilities where substantive disagreements might arise.[4] A quiz is therefore a teacher-directed event in which students are being judged, and reviewing a quiz is entirely teacher- and fact-centered. The questions from students are invariably short and ask why a particular answer is right; many ask about the "curve," partial credit, and other issues of grading. Invariably, some students have done poorly, and so the beginning of class is a deflating event for them. Occasionally instructors make matters worse by adding nasty comments; as one history teacher remarked at the outset, "Let me say that the test broke down into the good, the not-so-good, the bad, and the ugly. That will keep you awake for the rest of the class, won't it?" Instructors who are more student-centered tend not to give such quizzes, as we will see in Chapter 6; when they do, they seem to review them toward the end of the class. They also try to find something more substantive to begin a class, something related more to content than to grading; for example, the physical geography teacher described above started with a pertinent observation about the weather, reinforcing links between everyday life and the class.

• Most questions instructors pose take the form, familiar from K–12 education, of inquiry, response, and evaluation (IRE). The instructor asks a question that has a factual answer (like "Can you think of a rock that was primarily calcium carbonate?"), gets a correct student response (often by waiting through incorrect answers before the correct one emerges), and then praises the correct answer or corrects a wrong one. This might be termed "fill-in-the-blank" teaching, because the format is so close to workbook exercises that require students to fill in blanks in sentences. The student role is limited to finding the right answer; there's no real discussion, only simple responses to predictable questions.[5]

Instructors often describe their questioning as "Socratic." More often than not, however, they are actually practicing this kind of fill-in-the-blank questioning: The instructor pauses in a statement, waits for a student to fill in the blank with the correct phrase, and moves on. In contrast, Socrates's dialogues depended on large, open-ended questions by which he led his respondents to complex moral positions—a far cry from fill-in-the-blank questioning.

Sometimes the interaction between instructor and student is so formulaic that it appears to be a form of call-and-response, the singsong catechism often seen in church. For example, here is a segment of a political science class:

Instructor: "What's the most prevalent way of participating in a democracy?"
Students (chorus): "Voting."
Instructor: "Voting is fundamental to a democracy; but how much power do voters have? How is the president elected?"
Students (chorus): "Electoral college."
Instructor: "How are U.S. senators elected?"

Students (chorus): "By state."
Instructor: "Who elected senators in the past?" After a pause: "State
    legislatures."

His questioning is a way of drawing students into the class, of getting them out
of a purely passive role, and of affirming their knowledge, but it is confined to
low-level facts that the class has already mastered, and it remains a teacher-driven
exercise. In this interchange, the one genuine question that could elicit serious
debate—"How much power do voters have?"—is treated as a rhetorical question,
and the instructor moves quickly to a factual question ("How is the president
elected?"). The pattern of call-and-response in church is a way for a congregation
to reinforce a generally accepted theology; it's not very different in the classroom.
    • In a contrary pattern, instructors often throw out large and difficult questions
without sufficient preparation; then, when students cannot answer, the instructors answer themselves. Very often this happens in the midst of a lecture, and complex questions put to an entire class tend to go unanswered. For example, a
sociology instructor lectured about the categories of status, class, race, and caste,
stopping his lecture to ask, "What are examples of *class* divisions? What are examples of *caste* divisions?" Receiving no responses to these complex and controversial
questions, he simply gave his own answers—rather than explaining the controversy over such categories—and continued lecturing.
    In a more extended example based on a project, students in a cultural anthro-
pology course had made mud bricks in a prior class.

Instructor: "Now before we go on to the test, I would like to ask for
    your reflections, if you can remember the mud work exercise. How
    many people found it an interesting exercise? Did anybody get any-
    thing out of it besides dirty? Did anyone think about how an arche-
    ologist might have produced the exercise? Do you have any
    comments about it?"
Student 1 responds with a comment about requiring teamwork. The
instructor stresses the importance of teamwork both in various tribal
cultures and in anthropological work; then, having not gotten the
answer she was seeking, she asks: "What else did we learn besides
camaraderie?"
Student 2: "Experimental."
Instructor: "Experimental archeology, right. And that would be based
    on what other kind of archeology?"
Student 3: "How the hell do we even know how to make mud bricks?"

The class is suspended in silence for about five seconds, and then the instructor recognizes another student.

Student 4: "Reconstructive."

Instructor: "Reconstructive, um, archeology. Reconstructive archeology. Well, that's an interesting term, but I had in mind ethnoarcheology, which would show us how people today were working with those materials and living in mud brick houses make their bricks. Archeologists watch them and then they try to recreate it in an experimental form. So we have a little of ethnoarcheology and experimental archeology [in the brick-making exercise]."

In this interaction, the instructor got one right but unexpected answer about teamwork; an incorrect answer (about "experimental archeology"); another response indicating deep hostility to the whole exercise, which she ignored; and finally a single-word answer, "Reconstructive," that provided an opening for her to state what she had in mind.[6] She had not clarified the purpose of the brick-making exercise, and she provided no forum—for example, no chance for students to discuss this question in small groups, or for them to return to the text—to work out an answer. Despite the apparent discussion lasting perhaps ten minutes, in the end she simply told students the right answer she had in mind all along: ethnoarcheology, not "experimental archeology."

• Instructors often fail to pace their questions consistent with students' ability to respond. One example, exceedingly common in "discussions," came in the political science class mentioned above: When students didn't answer the question about who elected U.S. senators, the instructor answered his own question. Yet another example came in the anthropology class. The instructor, trying to stimulate discussion about brick making, asked four different questions, three of them (whether it was interesting, what students got out of it, whether they had any comments) open-ended, and another (how an archeologist might have interpreted the exercise) more specific and course-oriented. Students had begun to answer the first two questions when the instructor hit them with the third, very different question. By the time she paused, there were too many questions in the air for them to respond. The instructor most wanted to examine the question about how an anthropologist might respond, but rather than asking it directly and providing some context for students to answer it, she embedded it in other confusing questions, the responses to which she ignored.

Of course, the practices that convert discussion back into lecture are subtle. Many of them—such as reviewing quizzes or asking questions to check on student comprehension—have their own pedagogical rationale. But when a class is dominated by such practices, discussion is converted into formulaic responses and simple reinforcement of lecture. Unfortunately for community college instructors, there's no one around to counsel them about these techniques of discussion—no preparation in teaching methods, few discussions among colleagues, and little classroom observation by sympathetic peers who might provide feedback.

The Form and Reality of the Seminar

In constructing discussions, many instructors have a vision of a seminar, where instructors do not lecture and where students come in with reading completed and have a spontaneous, high-level, far-ranging discussion in which they probe the reading in greater depth, make comparisons with other reading and other experiences, and learn from one another as well as from texts and the instructor. Such idealized seminars are difficult to pull off at any level of education—certainly complaints about students not doing the reading are staples of graduate teaching—but they are especially difficult in community colleges. Students there have often not done the reading, sometimes because of the complexity of their lives, sometimes because they don't see the point. Often they come to college used to passive roles for students, and instructors need to socialize them to a more active role (as we explore later in this chapter). They are often unfamiliar with other literature and historical events. And the community of learners necessary for a seminar to work well is difficult to construct in a community college, where students take individual courses rather than programs and rarely see each other outside of class.[7] As the anthropology teacher complained,

> The assignments are to come to class prepared to discuss them. While I'll often do a little bit of a lecture, I like to have a discussion, and I find that was problematic because I find that on most class days most of the students have not read the material. And the only way that I can counteract that is to give pop quizzes, and I don't like to—I don't think that's an ideal way to function, but I'm more and more convinced that maybe I'm going to have to go that way.

But resorting to pop quizzes to enforce reading requirements is antithetical to the interpretive questions and student-centeredness of the seminar format.

If an instructor cannot create the conditions of a seminar, the discussion that follows is often frustrating. The instructor poses questions while students provide answers only reluctantly, usually in a few words, and the instructor ends up stating conclusions of her own. This is particularly frequent in English classes concerned with interpretation of literature. Here's an example from an English 1 class, a basic transfer course in literature and composition:

In a class of twenty students, the instructor begins by collecting papers, though only half the class hands them in. She then launches into a ten-minute lecture about Hilda Doolittle (the first author in an anthology of women's poetry), then discusses the imagist poets, Doolittle's reliance on Greek myths, and some facts about her life: "She knew everyone—she was psychoanalyzed by Freud and sang with Paul Robeson."

Next she asks, "When you think of Victorian poetry, what do you think of?" Different students respond: "Lace," "fussy things," "houses with gingerbread." The instructor then recites "Rose Aylmer" as an example of Victorian verse and asks, "What was becoming available at that time?" When students don't respond, she says, "Electricity, cameras." Her purpose is to clarify the shift from images in print (especially poetry) to images in photographs, then film, and now video, but this introduction generates no discussion.

The instructor, ready to turn to Doolittle's poetry after this introduction, asks if anyone would like to read—"Or shall I?" She then reads "The Sea Rose," after which she brings up Julia Kristeva, the French feminist—"Some of you might want to look her up"—and then reads "The Sea Rose" a second time. She asks what *acrid* means, and sends students to dictionaries when she gets no responses; she also asks what *onomatopoetic* means. The interchanges with students are short:

Instructor: "Does the poem rhyme?"
Student 1: "No, other than the repetition of the word *rose.*"
Instructor: "If the sand is crisp, and it's blowing in the wind, what does that mean?"
Student 2: "Sharp."
Student 3: "I also think of crust."
Student 4: "Yeah, that's what I was thinking."

The instructor then reads another poem aloud, "The Helmsman." She asked for a definition of *helmsman,* receives a dictionary version of the definition, and accepts it (even though the poem uses the word in a different sense). Then she asks for an interpretation.

Instructor: "'We parted green from green'—what does that mean?"
Student: "We left the green ocean for the green land."
Instructor: "Okay."

In the context of the poem, the image probably refers to parting bushes to make their way on land; when a second student makes a second inappropriate (to the observer) interpretation, she responds, "Good, that too, both correct."

Later she asks, "Do you like these poems? Yes? No? Are they hard to understand?" When she receives no responses, she responds, "Well, you don't have to like them. Just know of their existence out there in the world."

This is a class that aspired to be a seminar: several poems were reviewed and placed in their historical context, Greek mythology was invoked, other individuals and movements were brought in—Freud, Robeson, the imagists, Kristeva—and the instructor invited interpretations of specific passages and personal reactions to the poems. But students were unfamiliar with the historical and biographical references and could not connect them to the poems being reviewed; they either failed to react or responded in short phrases. The instructor didn't exploit opportunities to have students participate—she herself read the poems, for example, even after inviting students to do so—and she wound up answering most of her own questions. Many questions were about vocabulary or were quite simple ("Does the poem rhyme?"). A number of opportunities for extended discussion arose—for example, images in poetry versus film, the differing interpretations of "parting green from green," the esthetic issues in rhyming and nonrhyming poetry, various feminist interpretations that the instructor raised—but were not followed up. The overall result was that "teacher talk" dominated this classroom because of scant student performance. The instructor intended to have "conversation, as much as possible"—though she acknowledged that "it's often one-sided," a recognition that her intentions are often frustrated. It is certainly possible to have active discussions in community colleges, and we will present some excellent examples later. For the moment, however, our point is that classes that appear to be discussions with a minimum of lecture can easily turn into teacher-centered exercises.

The agonizing efforts to elicit student contributions sometimes produce classes that are, measured by both student reactions and the instructor's admission, failures. Here is another English 1 class, this time in composition:

The instructor opens by answering some questions about the next writing assignment. She then tells students to get out a piece of paper for a quiz on a short story by Nathaniel Hawthorne, "Young Goodman Brown": "Make sure your name is in the upper right-hand corner. Your packet should not be anywhere within view." The first five questions are purely factual, but the sixth involves some interpretation: "How is Goodman Brown different at the end of the story from the way he was at the beginning?" Two extra-credit questions refer to earlier lectures:

"Tell me what an ellipsis is" and "What is the difference between paraphrasing and summarizing?" About half of the students appear not to be writing.

After they hand in whatever they have written, the instructor asks for the citations about Hawthorne they were supposed to bring in and reminds them about the correct form of the citation, but doesn't appear to get many submissions. She then asks students to define *ellipsis,* and one does.

She asks students to arrange desks in a circle for a discussion; the result is a U-shaped arrangement with the instructor's chair at the opening of the U. She asks students about their experience finding references on Hawthorne; one student volunteered that she "just found it" on the shelf, prompting a brief lecture about the value of standard bibliographic sources. Much shuffling, coughing, talking, and working on other assignments takes place, perhaps because relatively few students have done the assignment.

The instructor then turns to "Young Goodman Brown" and asks students for their reactions. Getting no volunteers, she calls on a student who declares the story "pretty weird," a response that the instructor elaborates by asking whether the events in the story were real or dreamed. A student then asks, "I was wondering if he [the main character] was schizophrenic or not." While it isn't clear whether this is a serious or sarcastic question, the instructor responds. Then she raises a question from the quiz about how the character changed from the beginning to the end; after an uneasy silence, because few students have read it, she admonishes them that they need to finish the story because it is required for the final paper. One student volunteers that the ending was sad, another that the main character became pessimistic; a third says that she didn't understand it, while others confess they haven't read it. One student then says she couldn't "relate to the story," recalling personal experiences of hypocrisy where people were not who they appeared to be. Still another says that the story is like a parable; picking up on this, the instructor defines the term and explains how the sermon genre is important in American literature. She then goes on to review the remaining quiz questions; students are more responsive to the factual questions than the interpretive ones. With widespread restlessness, the instructor reviews the next assignment again and ends the class.

In her interview, this instructor acknowledged her deep frustration :

> Mondays are very bad. Monday I often find myself doing a solo or trying to do some
> group thing that might teach them something. And I've even asked them why ...
> why don't they do the reading? The answers are very interesting to me. They're not
> convincing, but I think they're convincing to them. They say they don't have the
> time. There's so much work, they're taking other classes. . . . And so I keep thinking,
> what's gonna happen when they get a life? When they get a real assignment? My
> assignments probably don't take them more than half an hour or an hour at the most
> to read ... and I've jumped up and down, and I've coaxed and I've cajoled ... and
> I've decided just not to get mad anymore. It doesn't work, anyway. That makes 'em
> terrified for the rest of the period. . . . It's sometimes very clear to me I haven't taught
> a damn thing, you know. . . . I don't think they care very much about this class. . . .
> Sometimes when I go in there, I feel sorry for them, you know. I wanna ... I wanna
> help them, but ... but it's almost as if they can't make the connection. And I don't
> know if, you know, I—I'm simply not the right teacher, or I'm not doing it correctly.

Now, this is not an atypical class, nor an atypical teacher. She was not by any means
a bad teacher: she was well prepared in her subject; she had sixteen years of experience teaching; she was devoted to getting her students to read and write well; she
understood (even if she failed to convey it to students) that the "real assignments"
students face when they "get a life" are even more difficult than what she asked; she
sympathized with the "busied-up" conditions of their lives. But she made a series
of small decisions that placed students on the defensive, restricted their participation, and undermined her intentions of making students independent ("I want
them to get it so that they don't need me anymore"). She started the class with a
quiz based largely on facts, putting them on the defensive. She provided no mechanism—no small-group discussions, no early presentation of the large questions—to facilitate the interpretations she wanted students to make. Even near the
end of the semester, she had failed to motivate students to do the reading. She
chose a story with no obvious connection to the lives of students and made no
effort to relate either the story or composition to student's interests or to "getting a
life." Unlike the instructors we describe later in this chapter, she had not socialized
students to the kinds of learning she wanted to go on, and she blamed students
themselves—the complexity of their lives, their lack of preparation, their immatu-
rity—for what was, when all is said and done, a disastrous class.

This instructor worried that "I'm not doing it correctly," and she had tried
various ways to improve her teaching. Unfortunately, she taught in a community
college where there is almost no institutional attention to teaching. The hiring and

selection procedures include almost nothing about teaching ability; staff development is random and unfocused; evaluation criteria for departments focus almost exclusively on enrollments. The dean of instruction has a counseling background, and while he supports innovations such as learning communities initiated by teachers and supported by outside funding, he speaks of innovations almost solely in terms of the difficulties they create for scheduling and funding. The administrators "make no effort at all that I know of" to improve teaching, according to an occupational instructor nominated as one of the best in the college. This English instructor knows that her teaching is inadequate and is clearly anguished about it, but there is nowhere in her institution to go for help, no collegiality, no administrative help. As she said about both faculty and administration: "I don't think people are interested in their jobs. . . . I think we have people who are tired, burned out, stale."

Of course, not all lecture/discussions are disastrous, and not all of them turn into lecture or teacher-dominated sessions. But this particular form always has the potential for veering into lecture and for generating meaningless discussions. To prevent that, instructors need great control over what they do—over the sequence of the class, over the balance of teacher talk and student talk, over the questions they pose and their reactions to students, over the kinds of material they select and what they make of it. Many instructors lack this control. Their preparation has not taught them anything about pedagogy—indeed, their own experiences and expectations (about seminars, for example) may have come from very different settings—and few of them have ever explored pedagogy in any formal or informal way. Worst of all, for many instructors such as the English teacher we have just described, their institutions do nothing to help them gain such control.

II. THE VARIETIES OF LECTURE

Even though a lecture/discussion can segue into lecture with disastrous results, and even though dislike of lecture has become an orthodoxy among many community college instructors (as we saw in Chapter 1), we think it wrong to condemn all lecture. Like discussion, lecture can be handled well or badly; good lectures can be as engaging, as instructive, and (under special conditions) as interpretive and meaning-centered as any other approach to teaching. While lecture is, by its nature, teacher-centered and didactic, and therefore inappropriate for many educational goals, it can still be a powerful aspect of community college teaching.

Here is a class dominated by the instructor's presentation of relatively difficult material, but where the engagement of students is high and their understanding of a complex subject (microeconomics) is relatively sophisticated:

The instructor, in a class of twelve students in a Midwest community college, begins by reminding the students of the previous lecture and asking a student to summarize it. Then he presents different conceptions of cost, using diagrams to represent various cost functions. When he asks what the isocost function represents, one student gives a simple answer—"the slope"—but another gives a fuller explanation; this triggers a further question from a third student, which the instructor uses to clarify different aspects of production, drawing on agricultural examples. The instructor also asks a series of counterfactual questions—"Wages are going up. What will happen to that point? Will the isocost change?"—as a way of checking their comprehension. He then presents the concepts of long-run and short-run costs and cost functions. Throughout this section of the lecture, students are taking notes and keep their textbooks open to the relevant chapter, though this lecture does not follow the text.

The instructor then shifts to market structures, an application of economic theory. He presents the first of four kinds of market structures, perfect competition, with an agricultural example that appears familiar to these rural students. He clarifies the necessary assumptions and poses questions to specific students; he approves each answer and elaborates it somewhat. When one students gives an incomplete answer, he encourages her to explore and elaborate her answer until she gets it right, rather than simply asking for other volunteers. He moves swiftly among applications of economic theory, the further development of cost functions, and geometric diagrams on the board; occasionally he circulates to check whether students are getting the diagrams correctly.[8] The class ends with the instructor mentioning what will happen in the next class and what chapter of the text to read.

This was a "real" lecture—not a regurgitation of the textbook, as we will see in the textbook-driven class described in Section III, but a synthesis of textbook theory and applications that the instructor developed. The class was entirely teacher- and subject-centered, though it was not straight lecture. The instructor used a variety of questions to clarify material, encouraged students to participate (for example, by having a student summarize the prior class), and pressed students to improve their responses. Engagement was high, students were uniformly taking notes and replicating diagrams, and their responses—fluid and complete, rather than forced and schematic—indicated that they were following what the instructor presented. This was in every way a successful lecture, one that followed the precepts of "good teaching" in the teacher-directed mode outlined in Chapter 1.

On the other hand, there are plenty of poor lectures, too, and they tend to violate these precepts. One clear example was a lecture in architectural history in a Western community college with one of the highest reputations in the state. The instructor presented a lecture about eighteenth-century architecture that consisted of names and dates and presented almost none of the stylistic and historical issues important in architectural history. He shifted erratically from a comparison of Greek and Roman architecture to the problem of literacy in the United States, a quiz about when women in the United States and Switzerland got the vote, and various other unrelated topics. He then announced, "Now I'm going to show you a bunch of slides of houses. There's nothing really much to look at," and began showing the slides, which are typical in art history classes (often called "Darkness at Noon" by students) and which provide the material on which a skillful instructor can invite comment. But his narration of the slides lacked any real content—he commented that certain houses were "charming" without any explanation, and several times mentioned that "those drapes have got to go." The instructor was poorly prepared—he lacked his notes, the projector had not been set up ahead of time—and the transitions in the beginning, middle, and end of the class were extremely awkward; he even undermined the entire section based on slides when he said, "There's nothing much to look at." (Indeed there wasn't, because the instructor said nothing of interest about the slides.) Students were confused about assignments, and they voted with their feet, leaving the irrelevant slide show in large numbers; one student seated behind the observers said to another, "I've never actually sat through the slides." It's hard to imagine what even the most assiduous student could have learned from this class. In contrast to the economics class we profiled above, this class violated every maxim for good teaching in a didactic style.

One way to examine any example of lecture as a pedagogical technique is to ask how it relies on information transfer as a theory of learning—how a student is supposed to learn from lecture. By far the most common approach is the fact-intensive presentation—the description of mathematical procedures, or historical names and dates, or common business practices, or the physics of cooling systems. Instructors using this approach seem to assume that students will learn material simply by being exposed to it and that lecture is simply an efficient way to cover large amounts of material. But this method raises the problem of how students are supposed to retain these facts—how they can relate new information to prior knowledge, how they can organize this information, how they might apply it—since (from a constructivist perspective) presentation does not guarantee that information will be transferred to the learner. In many classes, as in the physical geography class at the beginning of this chapter, instructors write phrases on the blackboard or overhead projector, or circulate outlines. They also give many verbal clues about the most important material, like one comment in an American Indian history class (described below): "Put it down so you know it." Other instructors phrase it more threateningly: "This might be on the exam."

While such written and verbal reinforcement may be good practice, in many classes these outlines substitute for anything that students might generate. Students write down only what the instructor outlines or writes on the board, or (especially when there is an outline handed out) take no notes at all. In effect, this substitutes a *teacher*-generated summary for a *student*-generated summary, and the important competence of extracting the main points from a body of information is undeveloped. As one instructor complained:

> I always hope that the outline will teach them how to read and organize the material. But I have to say that sometimes I feel that the students use it as a crutch, and often use the outline to avoid studying or organizing the material. And when I stop giving them the outline I find that the grades drop. I really find that a lot of the students are handicapped in that not only do they have poor reading skills but they don't know how to outline. They don't know how to organize and integrate material. So it's a real frustrating problem, and as much as I want to digress from the text, I sometimes find that I can't.

In addition, the practice of putting important material on the board, or on outlines, often leads to compressing complex information into small phrases or slogans, an example of the "bitting" that Richardson, Fisk, and Okun (1983) criticize. Sometimes instructors provide their own instruction in "study skills," including note taking, and many community colleges include these in remedial courses. But these are not simple skills (as we will see in Chapter 4) and they are not quickly mastered, since they require the ability to interpret what the main and subordinate points are, a facility with language and its subtle clues, and sometimes a prior familiarity with the issues involved in a subject. In the absence of such capacities, even the most straightforward purpose of lecture is undermined.

A very different approach is for instructors to encourage (and in some cases model) the construction of knowledge at the same time that they cover new material, through what we might call the synthetic and interpretive lecture. In this format, skilled instructors convert lecture into more meaning-centered teaching by drawing together material from many sources, illustrating the conflicts in interpretations, and modeling the process of constructing different arguments. While the synthetic lecture doesn't give students practice in synthesizing for themselves, it can at least show them that such interpretation is appropriate and illustrate how others do it. The economics class described above is a good example, synthesizing textbook theory about cost functions with applications in different market structures. Another (somewhat less successful) case was an American Indian history class, where the instructor introduced the subject of the class—the Roanoke colony in Virginia—and then rapidly introduced the notion of cant (specifically the practice of misleading the Indians); a book called *The Cant of Civilization*; the Spanish Inquisition and the role of Pope Alexander VI; the settling of Brazil by the Portuguese; and a Swiss jurist, Vattel, who wrote about rights to land in ways contrary to the practices of American settlers. His intention was to present a synthetic lecture, moving beyond the text to bring in many influences on the early settlements. However, he moved too quickly, and then returned to the real subject of the class: "Here we go, traditional history, 1607, Jamestown. Put it down so you know it." In this case, many problems of the seminar format were present: students didn't appear to understand the references, many were restless during this blitz of points, and—perhaps because the instructor did not clue them by writing any phrases on the board or by verbal asides (like "put it down so you know it")—students took no notes during this segment.

The difficulties of synthetic lectures are similar to the difficulties of seminars. If students don't understand references to other events and writing—and there is little check by any of these instructors to see if they do—then what could be a synthetic lecture becomes instead a list of meaningless facts, dropped by the instructor but not retained by students. Community college students are particularly unlikely to have the fund of references that synthetic lectures require. They have typically not done well in their prior schooling; many of them have been in high schools where they were taught next to nothing; and they come from backgrounds—especially lower-income families where parents have little education themselves—where they are unlikely to have picked up this kind of material.[9] As a result, we saw numerous lectures where references seemed to pass right over students, despite the possibilities for synthetic and interpretive lecture in skilled hands.

Evidently, then, lectures—and the lecture components of lecture/discussion classes—come in a variety of styles. Some are deadly, and the conditions necessary for certain kinds of lecture (especially the synthetic lecture) are often not met in community colleges. Nonetheless, blanket condemnation of lecture is inappropriate, particularly since virtually every instructor has to rely on lecture to some extent. Some instructors organize their material carefully, provide examples that are familiar to most students and appropriate to the subject, pace the class well, and use questions to check comprehension and elaborate the lecture. Others present material that is so vapid, disorganized, full of unrelated facts, and unrelieved by any applications that it's hard to imagine what a student could learn. The difference between approaches to lecture depends on myriad small details of planning, presentation, questioning style, and attitude toward both the content and students. A skillful instructor must be able to control these details, or else student attention quickly wanders away, as was evident in the architectural history class. And when colleges lack any institutional resources to help their instructors gain that control, the result is that the lecture components of lecture/discussion classes are less successful than they could be.

From Lecture to Discussion

Just as the lecture/discussion can easily turn into a teacher-centered presentation, what appears to be a lecture can become a discussion. For example, in one class in computer information sciences (CIS) with fifty students, the instructor nonetheless managed to develop a free-flowing discussion. Here's a part of it:

> The class takes place in a tiered lecture hall. The instructor starts, "What are we going to cover today?" A chorus of replies: "Chapter 5." He then moves into some statements about fifth-generation programming languages and structural versus procedural languages, using references from *Star Trek* and other sources students know. The he asks, "What were the three most important things we talked about in the last class?" When diffuse murmurs result, he says, "Okay, I changed my mind, get out a piece of paper and write it down." After four to five minutes he says, "I don't want your name on the piece of paper—pass it to someone next to you." Then students read out some of the responses. He jogs their memories by asking, "What was on your test?" and a number of students respond, "American Standard Code II." He writes this on the board, continues to prod students for other responses, and develops a series of points through this call-and-response technique. In addition, students raise their hands with questions; in many cases they are answered by other students, sometimes individually and sometimes in chorus.
>
> At one point a student complains, "Bill, this chapter seems to talk about things without really explaining things." The instructor responds by giving them a handout, thirteen photocopied pages describing different programming languages. Several students exclaim, "It's Greek!" Then the instructor starts moving through the handout, explaining the "Greek" components (mathematical notation) and continuing to elicit responses to questions he and other students pose.

In this class, what could have been a conventional lecture—because of the size of the class and the content (the characteristics of programming languages)—has been converted into a lecture/discussion. The instructor has used a few methods to facilitate the discussion, which he apparently learned from the classroom assessment techniques developed by Pat Cross and her colleagues (Cross and Angelo, 1993; Cross and Steadman, 1996). He interspersed didactic material in little segments, illustrating it with computer applications familiar to all students— unlike, for example, the references to Greek architecture or to the feminist critic Kristeva in the history and English classes we examined earlier. He included call-and-response questions to review certain material, and asked other open-ended questions. Because it is difficult to elicit answers to open-ended questions in a class of fifty students, he had students write down their reactions before contributing them. He had learned all students' names and could call on them, both for comprehension and for their specific contributions. He circulated constantly, and genuinely listened to and responded to questions from everywhere in the class. Clearly he had established an informal climate in this class, and students were comfortable both with asking questions and with responding. One could argue, of course, that the time spent in various interchanges could be more productively spent in covering more material; but given the widespread participation of students, this class was clearly more engaging to students than a conventional lecture could be.

While lecture/discussion is certainly the most common approach to teaching in community colleges, it takes many different forms.[10] The numerous classes that become completely teacher-directed, with student contributions forced and clipped, provide one direction; the discussion-oriented class, even under the conditions of lecture, is a quite different direction. The details of pacing, the specific balance between lecture and discussion, the style and intent of the lecture components, and the nature of the questions and of interchanges during discussion are all responsible for the character of any particular class. And while some of these elements are obvious and covered in the standard bromides about good teaching, others are not. The question we will return to again and again is whether instructors have the understanding and control over these elements to be good teachers, and whether they get any help from their colleges in mastering the art of teaching.

III. THE TEXTBOOK-DRIVEN CLASS

When classes are dominated by instructors and "teacher talk," it is common to describe the classroom as teacher-centered. However, one common variant of the lecture/discussion clarifies that the real source of authority may be the textbook, with the teacher simply the presenter. The textbook-driven class can be found in both occupational and academic subjects, and in all regions of the country; small segments of many classes can be textbook-oriented. However, this approach to teaching seems to be most prominent in colleges where students and instructors are homogeneous in both background and language (as in the Midwest). In such classes, students and instructors alike appear well socialized to the distant authority of the textbook. Students displayed none of the restlessness and disengagement typical of teacher-dominated classes—they are "raised to be mannerly," one instructor mentioned—and some instructors (and administrators) did not recognize that any other approach to teaching could be possible. In this sense the textbook-driven approach "works": There is an equilibrium in the class, where teacher expectations match student expectations and behavior.[11] However, the consequences for learning are distinctly mixed.

Here's an example of such a class:

About twenty students in a word processing class are seated at computer terminals, arranged so that most students face the instructor in the center front of the room. The instructor reviews a quiz; one student wants to know about calculating the percent increase, and the instructor responds, "Did you use the formula?" Students do not press for any further explanation.

The instructor then begins reading from the word processing manual, in a loud, clear voice: "It tells you to enter the text. . . . " She continually directs students to the page she's on: "Go to page 415," "Go to page 419." When a response from the class is required, there's a kind of hum while they say the answer—usually just one word. She consistently refers to the authors of the textbook as "they," and to the commands in the text with this phrase: "They want you to . . . " The instructor follows the manual to the letter; when a student wants to know if she should print out what she has typed, the teacher consults the manual to see if "they" want students to print it. Consistently, the exercises in the text are taken as given, rather than choices to be made by an individual; for example, when she refers to some text that is left-justified only, she says, "Did you notice that it doesn't have full justification?" and then "Wouldn't it look a lot better if we could even it up?"—but there is no discussion about the purposes of justification or the conditions under which it might be appropriate. Then the instructor moves the class into the lab component, where they will practice certain commands: "The first exercise you have to do is number five, so let's take a look at number five, that's on page 230." All exercises come straight from the textbook. The students work on these exercises for the remainder of the class while the instructor circulates.

Many elements of this class are typical of the textbook-driven approach. The entire content came from the text, with the instructor literally reading the textbook. All exercises and quizzes came from the text. Questions to students were simple and factual, and could usually be answered with a single word or short phrase from the text. There was virtually no choice for students or the instructor, and the text was consulted even on questions—whether to print a document out or not—where, one might think, a student could exercise just a mote of discretion. The text was the real authority, and it's difficult to see what the instructor added to it. She marched students through the textbook in a particular time, but otherwise played no role. And there was no way to challenge the text; in contrast to English or history instructors who stress that students must come up with their own interpretations, or occupational instructors who stress that texts may become obsolete, the text-centered approach treats the textbook as gospel to be taken literally.

This instructor's comments about teaching were revealing:

> The students, I find, will learn or pick it up so much closer if you stick with the textbook. . . . They're the type of students that, you know, they want things to go in a step-by-step order, and they pick up things a lot quicker that way.

She then told a story about the problems students had when the text taught Paradox 4.5 while their computers had Paradox 5.0: "Oh, they had a terrible time dealing with that." She attributed the proclivity for "sticking with the textbook" to the students themselves, as if this were innate. Instead, we suspect that students "want things to go in a step-by-step order" because this was the only approach allowed by this instructor—and, possibly, by most of the instructors they have had in this homogeneous community. Her story also revealed a fatal flaw in her teaching: If students find themselves on the job with a word processing program that varies from the manual, they may have a "terrible time" there, too. They have learned the details of one program, not the general elements of word processing.[12]

We saw many other extreme examples of textbook-centered instruction: a philosophy course where philosophers were labeled with slogans summarizing their views, such as "voluntary/involuntary acts," "culpable ignorance," "pragmatism," "existentialism" ("This is just a big fancy word that comes out of the word 'to exist'"); an anatomy and physiology course where students had a sixty-page "charley" of study questions (named after the printer who used to reproduce them) and where the instructor declared, "I lecture to these." In such classes students are particularly passive. Questions are almost always teacher-initiated and designed to be answered in one or two words. Students sometimes ask questions for clarification, but—mimicking the questions the instructor asks—these too are likely to be answered very briefly; never do students raise a new interpretation or challenge what the text says.

Within such classes, even exercises intended to enhance student participation become textbook-directed. For example, in the philosophy class mentioned above, the instructor broke the class into small groups—a practice intended to facilitate student discussion of complex issues—but he simply had the students read the text to each other. Similarly, two nursing instructors broke their class of thirty-three into small groups, "teaching each other the material." First students in these groups simply read to each other definitions of terms (like "blunted affect") from a nine-page handout and wrote them down; then the instructor asked the groups to come to a consensus about multiple-choice questions (for example, what would be the proper treatment for a schizophrenic) that turned out to have "correct" answers. The groups therefore served as vehicles for repeating the text rather than for genuine discussion.

Of the instructors who taught in this mode, only one seemed to recognize its limitations. Indeed, he showed how a textbook-driven approach might be made student-centered:

> The instructor in an environmental science course starts by reviewing some "critical-thinking" questions from the textbook; as in most text-centered classrooms, all students have large textbooks open on their desks. But he diverges from the text, asking if the class has any HVAC (heating, ventilation, air-conditioning) students in it, and discusses the environmental effects of Freon, the regulation of Freon, supply and demand, and the development of black markets. The instructor asks, "How many of you are directly involved in farming?" A discussion ensues about the pollution issues in farming, the alternatives to regulation, and political perspectives on pollution. Then, in shifting to the text, the instructor turns the class to Chapter 10 and says to a student, "Walk us through the textbook." This converts the usual "textbook march" into a more student-driven activity, and he intersperses progress through the chapter with various questions, most of them close to the backgrounds of the students.

This instructor later commented on the textbook-centered approach:

> You probably noticed today, we were going through the textbook. I hate that. . . . I'm not big on going through textbooks. But I have to. If I don't. . . . I had one section [where I didn't], and it was miserable. The test scores were just . . . because if I

don't go through it with them, they don't read it. . . . Their willingness to read is poor. . . . I detest that [going through the textbook]; I try not to do that in every class. I try to get right to the critical thinking, right to the analysis, right to the opinion, right to the discussion stage, the anarchy stage, [but] I have to do it [go through the textbook].

In practice, of course, this individual has managed to move away from the textbook-centered approach: His questions were not taken from the text, discussion was more open-ended, and he gave *students* the responsibility for moving the class through the text. But he still felt constrained to follow this approach partly because of his perception that his students would otherwise not read at all, and partly (we suspect) because this approach to teaching is so common that both students and faculty have come to expect it.

There are, of course, some advantages to this approach. In contrast to some instructors, who seem to direct students *away* from texts as sources of learning (see Chapter 6, on ways of undermining "standards"), this approach does make sure that texts are central. The "textbook march" also assures coverage, since a prescribed amount of time is allocated to each chapter. But this variant of lecture-discussion permits little real participation by students in what they learn, and little chance for instructors to elaborate the content of the classroom; teachers don't *teach* as much as they simply *manage* the text. Like most forms of "skills and drills," the textbook-centered approach assumes that students are motivated; classes themselves are predictable and dull. And because the text is so central and unquestioned, there is no room for developing the critical faculties, the flexibility in thinking about issues, and the ability to judge sources of information and weigh contrasting points of view that are so important to other approaches to teaching, to many employers, and to those concerned about an active citizenry.

IV. THE ROLES OF STUDENTS: SOCIALIZING STUDENTS TO THEIR RESPONSIBILITIES

In observing classes, we noted the behavior of students—how they responded, what activities they initiated, what other things they might be doing—as well as the pedagogy of the instructor. Student reactions are crucial because their level of engagement and the nature of their questions affect what they are likely to learn. The quality of student participation is not, we think, a characteristic of students themselves. Like the extent of student engagement, it is *created* by instructors who, deliberately or inadvertently, socialize students to certain patterns of involvement. This is an important argument for supporting the improvement of teaching in community colleges: Behavior that is often taken to be fixed, a predetermined characteristic of students, can be changed in the hands of a skilled instructor.

One hallmark of didactic instruction is that a minority of the class participates—perhaps one quarter to one third. In community colleges, where students attend voluntarily and are more mature than high-school students, there is very little of the frank hostility and overt outbursts that one often sees in high schools; direct challenges to the instructor, like the comment, in the anthropology class described above ("How the hell do we even know how to make mud bricks?"), are rare.[13] But there are high levels of inattention, marked by students reading newspapers or doing other assignments; low rates of participation and responses to IRE questions, with a few students doing the majority of the talking; and a great deal of "voting with their feet"—students coming late, leaving early (as in the architectural history class), or simply not attending, prompting the plaintive instructor question, "Where is everyone today?"

Students are particularly disengaged by straight lecture unless it is of the rare synthetic variety. The architectural history class described above provides a common example. In it, a class of thirty-two students was converted into a de facto lecture because of the instructor's style; only a minority of students were following the instructor or taking notes, and many students simply left. In contrast, in lecture-oriented classes punctuated by discussion, attention is much higher. The physical geography and Growth and Development classes we described in Section I were ones where discussion was frequent and genuine enough that students were highly engaged. The economics class that we presented as an example of high-quality lecture had the same character. Finally, in many occupational classes that we examine in the next chapter, students sat attentively through the lecture component because they knew the following workshop would require them to use the knowledge covered in the lecture. Engagement during lecture is not a simple issue, and motivation can come from many different sources. But instructors need to create this motivation, and conventional lecture is not the way to do it.

Student interest almost always picks up when instructors begin asking evaluative or interpretive questions ("Why do you think something is important?") rather than factual questions. Here's an example from a remedial writing class of about twenty-eight students:

> The instructor is teaching about writing resumes, as part of the process of job application. This is a textbook-driven lecture with a few personal asides from his experience applying for jobs. He then displays a transparency, "Important Resume Tips," and reads through the tips; when he asks if there are any questions, students simply stare at him quietly. He writes on the board, "Cover letter: sales tool," and asks, "Do you

remember what the cover letter does—the three things?" About one fourth of the class is taking notes while he pulls the answers out of students. He continues with relatively trivial factual questions, all drawn from the text—for example, what things to avoid in an introductory letter.

Then he asks, "What do you do when the application asks for your desired position and salary?" He gives his own position on this, and then asks students what they have done. The class perks up a bit as a real discussion starts to emerge. Then the instructor goes on to cover five more important tips, and the class continues with the instructor asking a series of textbook questions and providing his own answers to them. About one quarter to one third of the class is following the lecture and taking notes.

In this class, a discussion emerged when the instructor asked students about their own experiences, and some students who had not been paying attention started to waken from their slumber. But the instructor then cut off discussion by returning to his agenda (five more important tips!), and student engagement subsided. In many classes, we could see student attention flow as instructors turned to more interpretive questions, or questions related to student experiences, but it invariably ebbed when teachers cut off discussion by answering their own questions or returning to lecture. Students themselves often articulate their dislike of lecture. As two students in a community college that makes extensive use of learning communities commented:

> *Student 1*: Talking gets a lot more people involved in discussions instead of, like, teachers standing up there doing lecture. I get—I tend to lose my attention when there's lecture. I don't pay attention as much as I do to my peers.

> *Student 2*: I agree with you because, like, when the teacher's lecturing, I don't know—you don't get as much involvement from other people because as you sit there taking notes, you're really learning what the teachers want you to learn. [In group work] you get to learn from your peers instead of just your teacher. . . . I consider myself an introvert, and I can't really adapt to that big of a seminar [more than fifteen students]. . . . But in this class I've learned that students can be teachers and teachers can be students.

Another hallmark of classrooms is that when students do participate, the quality of their participation varies widely. In some classes the questions that students pose, and the responses that they give to questions, are germane and sophisticated.

For example, in the Growth and Development class, students played a cooperative game and then extracted generalizations about rules, cooperation, and the role of play in early childhood development. In the economics class described above, student were prompted by the instructor's questions to apply economic theory to various familiar settings. These are indicators of students behaving "actively" rather than "passively"—struggling to make sense for themselves of the material, to raise genuinely interpretive questions.

In other classes, however, the questions are procedural—"How long do our essays have to be?" or (about an oral presentation) "Does it have to be exactly nine minutes? Should there be time for questions?"—or they simply ask the instructor to clarify facts like "What causes the different colors in marble?" In certain classes students simply express their opinions without any evidence or reference to other material (like the text); examples include the student declaring "Young Goodman Brown" to be "pretty weird" and another who "couldn't relate to the story." And in some classes students tell little "stories" from their own experiences that are not especially germane. In a biology class where the instructor had just pointed out the necessity of warming air before it enters the lungs, one student then contributed a personal story: "We learned the importance of [warming air before breathing] this winter when my friend . . ."; later another student contributed, "I've had motion sickness," and told about a trip during which she became sick. These are student contributions, to be sure, and instructors may even take them as evidence of engagement, but they are peripheral to the subject and suggest how little learning is taking place.

The quality of student participation is determined in part by instructors as they respond to students. For example, the English instructor who accepted statements about a story being "pretty weird" or something that a student "couldn't relate to" made an implicit decision not to press the students for reasons. The anthropology instructor accepted incomplete one-word responses to her questions ("experimental," "reconstructive") rather than encouraging students to elaborate. In contrast, the economics instructor described above pressed his students when they gave incomplete answers, forcing them to elaborate their thinking. Instructors who ask questions that can be answer by one word or short phrases, or who create call-and-response dialogues, have implicitly decided that the important content of the class is confined to brief facts. In contrast, instructors who pose larger, interpretive questions and who press students to answer them fully instead of accepting cursory responses are asking students to participate in very different ways.

Other, more direct evidence for thinking that instructors shape student participation comes from learning communities, where we observed the same students with different instructors. Student behavior in these classes differed remarkably from teacher to teacher. For example, in one learning community pairing a biology instructor and an English instructor, the students in the biology class confined themselves to procedural questions and simple questions of fact—for example, "When you're deaf, what do you lack?"—as well as personal stories. The biology instructor herself provided a model for simple factual questions, asking questions like "What cultures have spicy foods?" One student persisted in asking more analytic questions, but the biology teacher gave her short, formulaic answers. For example, when the student asked, "Why does the brain 'require' a horizon?" the instructor replied, "Because it's wired that way," and moved back to the lecture. Perhaps even worse, the English instructor of this pair contributed only simple questions, like "Is sugar a preservative?" and "When you fly, why do your ears hurt?" In this class, students had been "taught" through the examples of both instructors to ask simple fact-oriented questions. The instructor discouraged complex and analytic questions, yet allowed students to contribute their personal "stories." The class was full of student discussion, but it was random, personal, and off the day's topic.

In contrast, in a class with the English instructor, the same students participated very differently. When the instructor asked at the outset, "Where would you like to start discussing the book?" a student replied that she wanted to discuss "what it means to be an artist, open to using your senses," a sophisticated question that was especially germane to the text (Diane Ackerman's *Natural History of the Senses*). The instructor posed numerous questions of interpretation, and students responded with references to the text. When one student began a personal story about how she used to wear makeup, the instructor reminded them of an earlier reading about how male colleagues respond to women and then returned the student to the text by asking, "How do these things you're saying grow out of Ackerman's book?" Students initiated interpretive discussions of their own. For example, one student stated, "I have a gripe," and then read a passage in which there were too many metaphors for her taste, while another provided examples of the author being "too cute"—both aesthetic responses to the text. This class was in many ways a model of what many instructors think of a seminar, with close interpretation of the text and a combination of both meaning-centered and aesthetic responses. The instructor skillfully guided students away from purely personal stories, or got them to relate these stories to the text and the class topic. In every way the discussions in the two classes were different in character and content, even though the students were the same.

Similarly, a learning community in another community college joined an English instructor (for remedial purposes), a sociology instructor, and an instructor teaching Introduction to Human Services. The class consisted of older welfare recipients (all black and Latino) who wanted to enter social welfare occupations. The English class was a model of what a seminar might be: The instructor posed a series of interpretive questions about the day's story—Tony Morrison's "Tar Baby," chosen from an anthology of fiction about black women because, as the Asian-American instructor explained, "I thought they would be interested in that." The students explored the characterization of the protagonist, relating her to their own lives ("This was the sixties, when we [black people] were finding our real selves") and exploring the pros and cons of working within the system. Building on the earlier student-initiated debate, the instructor than asked, "What were Kiswana's [the protagonist's] counterarguments?" in response to students' charges that the character in the story was working too much within the system. The students contributed a series of points, again searching through the story to back up their views. Participation was widespread and unforced, and the level of engagement with interpretive questions focused on the text was impressive—particularly because these students came from a group (welfare mothers) that is not conventionally thought to be highly literate.

In contrast, the companion sociology class was agonizing to watch. The instructor presented the conceptions of class, socioeconomic status, income, occupation, and education, arguing to students that the United States is a caste society (following the arguments of Ogbu, 1978). He threw out several complex questions that students had a difficult time answering; the level of participation was much lower, and students did not make any connections between the course material and their own lives (as they had in the English class). The instructor asked students to find some examples of caste status in a reading about a black immigrant. Though the students were quite capable of doing so—they had, after all, done a skillful job in the English class earlier in the day—they did very little of it in this class, offering instead personal examples from their experiences. The students throughout the class were confused because the instructor presented an *interpretation* by Ogbu, that blacks have a castelike status in this country, as a *fact*. But because this "fact" was contrary to their experiences and their aspirations—they were enrolled in this college to escape from poverty and welfare—they consistently came up with interesting but "incorrect" examples of caste status (like black groups treating other blacks as castes, and examples of castelike status among poor whites), and their confusion reduced their willingness to participate further. In the hands of this teacher, a group who had earlier in the day been active, meaning-centered, highly literate individuals were converted into confused, halting, and resistant students. An observer viewing only the sociology class might conclude, quite incorrectly, that these students were "illiterate," incapable of drawing conclusions from text, and uninterested in participating.

Still another example arose in a learning community with both remedial English and remedial math, along with a third course in introductory biology. The

English course, taught by an instructor who had written a text for whole-language instruction in community colleges and was committed to active involvement of students, was marked by widespread participation. The math class, taught by a beginning instructor unsure of her abilities and relying on conventional demonstration of arithmetic procedures, was listless and unengaged.[14] Even though the same group of students was involved, and faced remedial work in both subjects, their responses were completely different.

There aren't many examples of the same group of students acting differently with different instructors, because most learning communities try to include instructors with relatively similar approaches to teaching. (Indeed, the sociology instructor in the learning community for social welfare occupations had declared that he would no longer participate, to the relief of the other instructors.) But there are enough examples so that we are relatively confident of the implication: Instructors create the kind of class they want by their approaches to the content, the kinds of questions they encourage and discourage, and the way they manage the flow of the classroom.

The process of socializing students is not, we think, a simple or quick one. It starts at the beginning of the semester, and it continues throughout the semester in the kinds of questions an instructor asks, the encouragement and discouragement of different interactions, the treatment of both individual students and the class as a whole.[15] Several such practices are obvious from the classes we observed:

• Instructors themselves model the questions that students then ask. Instructors who are didactic and fact-oriented tend to ask simple IRE questions. Their students then ask questions to clarify facts and to ask about procedures ("Will it be on the test?"), the kind of behavior we have labeled "studenting."

• Some instructors tolerate—and thereby implicitly reinforce—certain questions that serve little instructional purpose. For example, the biology instructor who accepted personal stories about breathing cold air and motion sickness both allowed students to interrupt the flow of her lecture and legitimated these kinds of contributions. In contrast, the English teacher directed students to relate their personal observations to the text being discussed ("How do these things you're saying grow out of Ackerman's book?"). Similarly, in a microbiology lab, the instructor answered a series of factual questions about the lab exercise. Then, when he felt that he was answering too many questions, he commented, "A scientist has to think systematically; always think before you ask," and he urged them to read their lab notebooks before starting the exercise. He discouraged a series of questions about his own children and redirected students back to the task at hand by asking rhetorically, "Would that help you do your work?"

• Instructors can squelch students and make them passive and unengaged, as the "kind of military" sociology instructor described above did to the most active students in the class. Another example came in a graphic arts class where the instructor introduced student presentations by calling on a student, saying in a sarcastic tone, "Let's get JoAnn down here so she can share in this *enlightening* experience." Several students, apparently burned in prior classes, did not participate from the start; a student who failed to deliver the correct response was harshly corrected and failed to participate thereafter. When students were presenting their projects (designs for corporate logos), the instructor kept cutting off presenters with harsh comments; typically, when a presenter was interrupted, he or she did not restart the presentation. Student presentations of their own work are usually a stimulus to lively discussion, but this instructor managed to dampen every contribution by his interruptions and critical evaluations. Particularly with students who are not especially self-confident—and insecurity is very common among community college students—harsh and negative reactions can eliminate participation almost immediately.

• In the rare cases of team teaching, the teacher who is not at the moment the central instructor also models questions for students, for better or worse. In the English/biology pair described above, the English teacher asked a series of quite irrelevant questions ("When you fly, why do your ears hurt?"), reinforcing the student habit of asking unrelated personal questions. However, in other learning communities, teachers provide very different models. For example, in another English-biology pair, the English teacher consistently asked a series of metacognitive questions—"How do you know that?" "How did you infer that from the laboratory evidence?"—using these questions to model scientific inquiry rather than to satisfy her own curiosity.

Many students come to community college poorly prepared for the active discussion that some instructors want. Many of them have been in high schools where didactic teaching predominates; they are unlikely to have been in the college-prep tracks or advanced-placement courses where more student-centered teaching takes place.[16] Many immigrant students have been reared in education systems with especially rigid approaches—the schools of many Asian countries, for example, or Muslim countries. And many students are unsure of their abilities and uneasy about participating. At the outset, then, instructors who want their students to play a more active role must prepare them to do so.

Thoughtful instructors can articulate the process they use to move students from fear and passivity to more active participation. The early parts of a semester often require drawing them into the educational enterprise. For example, one instructor, part of an innovative learning community for Latino students, divided the semester into thirds:

I operate a student-centered classroom, so that means a kind of teaching from the sidelines in the early part of the semester. I kind of try to have people doing activities which I direct, but sort of low-key, to give me a chance to see how people perform in all different situations. I try to watch what works for different folks and what gives different people problems. Then toward the middle third of the semester, I try to begin giving information in whatever ways I've seen people's interest. Like this semester I have one student who is particularly interested in myth, the Indian guy. So I did a lot of stuff to kind of relate this European and Native American tradition. . . . Then by the last third of the semester I really move back into the early format, but this time folks are much more independent. They have much more—they have the tools and then it's mostly just fine-tuning. . . .

Everybody is so different, you can't assume they're like you; you can't assume they're like each other. So you really have to spend that first month doing what I call four for nothing. You're just beating, you're just finding the rhythm, one, two, three, four, go; one, two, three, seeing what they do. Then after you kind of know how people do things, then you can begin to teach what they are interested in, what they need, what makes sense to them.

Another instructor described her process for making students more responsible for their own education, in effect creating a social contract:

The first day of school, I assume that learning is the number one thing for them. Now, for most eighteen-year-olds anywhere, that's not true; they don't yet realize that that's what they're there for. But I make that assumption, and because I'm making that assumption, they give me that back. . . . I've got an example: In one class, I have eight out of twenty students [who] have their drafts . . . about three more had either been sick or had come by to talk to me. They were all kind of drifting out, so I had to talk with them. I told them [how] I saw my role; I said, "I'm here because I want you to succeed in writing, and I expect that you're here because you want to do the same," and I said, "Here are the things that I mean to try to meet my end of the deal. . . . You all haven't met your end of the deal. It's really your decision. . . . You cannot depend on me to force you to do the things that you need to [do]; to be successful, that's what you've got to learn to do on your own."

There are many more examples; the tactics that good teachers use to convert students into more independent and active learners are endlessly varied. But the process doesn't happen by itself: it takes care and planning, and control over the elements of instruction that encourage student participation. In its absence, students behave in ways that are counterproductive. They fail to do assignments; they operate in "lecture mode," failing to retain information for very long; they spend endless amounts of time quibbling about the requirements of classes; they fill up class time with irrelevant personal stories and unrelated questions. These ways of undermining learning, while they are often deeply bred into students by years of K–12 education, are not really the fault of students. They result from instructors who, either because they believe in passive roles for students or because they lack control over crucial elements of teaching, wind up creating classes in which student participation is ineffective.

V. THE INSTITUTIONAL ELEMENTS OF LECTURE/DISCUSSION

The frequency of lecture/discussion seems an obvious response to the conditions of community college teaching. With only a few exceptions, community colleges do not have large classes, and it is faintly ridiculous to lecture to ten to twenty-five students. In addition, most instructors condemn straight lecturing, as we saw in Chapter 1. On the other hand, the conditions for small seminars are lacking in community colleges: students are not well prepared for synthetic discussion, and it's hard to get them to do the reading. The lecture/discussion is the obvious compromise, providing elasticity for a variety of approaches.

But in practice, the lecture-discussion often drifts toward the kind of didactic, teacher-centered lecture that many instructors say they dislike. When questions to students become simple or fact-oriented, then no real discussion takes place. When instructors cut off students, answer their own questions, or disparage the contributions students may make, then student participation withers. Because students have often come from high schools (or foreign countries) where didactic instruction has been the norm, many are initially quite passive; if instructors don't consciously prepare them for more active participation, then discussions are labored and awkward, with long silences and instructors themselves filling in the gaps.

The requirements for creating a good class—one with an appropriate balance of lecture and discussion, where the lecture components are carefully prepared and well structured, where discussion is lively and contributes to the content of the course, where the lecture and discussion components are consistent with each other—are therefore substantial. While many instructors have control of the complex elements necessary to make such a class work, many more do not, and the results range from mediocre to abysmal. Students may be passing these classes and moving up to higher levels of the educational "pipeline," but it's hard to believe they are learning much.

For these instructors, the question we raise persistently is whether there is anything—in their preparation for teaching, in their networks of peers, in mentoring early in their teaching careers, in staff development, in the culture of the institution that sponsors their teaching—that would give them that control, that could enable them to improve their teaching. All too often, as we will see in Chapter 8, there is nothing to help them; as one instructor put it, "It's a teaching institution, but there's almost nothing for the teacher." Under these conditions, the community college fails to live up to its promise as a teaching institution.

NOTES

1. The way many classes get to be this size is instructive. Many colleges have enrollment limits—larger (perhaps forty to forty-five) for social science, smaller (perhaps twenty-five to thirty) for English classes where considerable writing is expected, sometimes smaller still for vocational classes, especially where equipment or safety considerations limit class sizes. But depending on the conditions of the class—its difficulty, the nature of the teacher—up to half of the students may drop it within the first month, and nonattendance levels are high. Therefore a class with an initial enrollment of forty-five may have only twenty-five enrolled by midsemester, and only fifteen to twenty students on any particular day.

2. On the different forms of representation, which are in effect different types of literacies, see Chapter 4, especially Section III.

3. On the predominance of "teacher talk" in high-school classrooms, see Sirotnick, 1983.

4. This is not uniformly true; for the variety of novel assessments devised by community college instructors, see Chapter 6.

5. In a survey of college classes, Barnes (1994) notes that the overwhelming proportion of questions are of the lowest cognitive level, requiring simple recall.

6. These kinds of overt challenges to the authority of the instructor are rare; they virtually always stop a class dead in its tracks. The question is testimony to the extent to which this instructor has lost this class, in this case by failing to explain the point of the entire brick-making exercise. We return to the problem of collapsed classes in Chapter 6.

7. Instructors often reinforce the isolation among students by their conceptions of literacy and their teaching practices. See Chapter 4, on the literacy practices within classrooms and the difference between social versus individual conceptions of literacy. See also Chapters 5 and 7, on the use of learning communities.

8. The diagrams in economics are other forms of representation; see note 2 in this chapter. New students have great difficulty "reading" these diagrams, and one of the tasks of an economics teacher is to move students from simple and literal interpretations of such diagrams to more facile and sophisticated interpretations.

9. In more formal terms introduced by Bourdieu (1977), they lack the "cultural capital" necessary for successful school performance. The complaint by McGrath and Spear (1991) that community college students are "culturally disarticulated" seems to encompass both their weakness at conventional academic analysis—for example, identifying main and subordinate points, comparing and contrasting—and their lack of historical, literary, and cultural references.

10. See also Astin, Korn, and Dey, 1991, Table 4, based on questionnaires to faculty; they report that class discussions are the first and lecturing the second most common teaching practices. Surprisingly, there are no real differences between faculty in two- and four-year colleges in these responses. But given the tendency for discussion to become teacher-dominated, we don't think these questionnaire responses are particularly valid indications of what takes place in classrooms.

11. The notion of an equilibrium in the classroom has been suggested by Joe Harkin, who is carrying out a roughly parallel analysis of teaching in the further education colleges of the United Kingdom. For preliminary results, see Harkin and Davis, 1996a and 1996b.

12. See also the discussion of the "skills" approach versus the "systems" approach to occupational teaching, in Chapter 3, Section III.

13. In Chapter 6 we describe classes with overt challenges as "distressed." Classes marked by inattention—"collapsed classes"—are much more common. Both of these types have little content.

14. We describe a segment of her class in Chapter 5, Section II.

15. The logistics of observing classes prohibited us from seeing this process unfold. The right way to see this would be to observe a number of classes over time, starting from the beginning of the semester. However, we were unable to view classes over time. In addition, it is difficult to observe classes near the beginning of the semester because the process of getting institutional permission to observe typically could not start until the third or fourth week of the semester (since the start of the semester is too busy) and takes several weeks. Typically, therefore, we observed classes after the process of socializing students had already been substantially completed.

16. A staple of the literature on high schools is that didactic instruction is more prevalent in the lower tracks, with more meaning- and student-centered instruction in the upper levels of the college prep tracks; see, for example, Goodlad, 1984; Sirotnick, 1983; and Oakes, 1985.

3

LECTURE/WORKSHOP AND "HANDS-ON" LEARNING

The Complexities of Occupational Instruction

Occupational education is central to most community colleges. About 60 percent of all students declare they are there for occupational purposes, including an especially large fraction of part-time and older students—re-entry students returning to higher education after raising children, or dislocated workers trying to find another career after the collapse of a local industry.[1] Virtually all students, even "academic" or transfer students, are there for broadly occupational purposes, as many instructors note: "They're already somebody but they want a decent job, you know—the American dream." Instructors note a variety of student purposes—transferring to a four-year college, becoming better parents, increasing their self-esteem—but in the end their responsibility is "to help students to get a job; that's what they're coming here for." And so occupational instructors often feel they have a central role within the college; as an HVAC instructor noted,

> I think that we're doing the student more justice than [academic instructors] are because they can teach English and math and all this stuff but that doesn't get them any jobs. At least what we're teaching them, it gives them something they can then can fall back on. Even if they don't use it right now, five years down the road, if they need to get a job, they'll be able to get a job in this field. . . . The community colleges, the way they're designed [here], do more to aid the socially disadvantaged people than any other institution. They do more to help the student.

In this age of angst about our economic future and of efforts to rev up a high-skill, high-wage economy, the occupational role of community colleges is crucial.

Despite the centrality of broadly vocational purposes, the occupational side of the community college has been widely neglected. In most states transfer and academic education have been the most prestigious missions. Colleges are generally administered by individuals from the academic side. Their internal governing groups, like faculty senates and unions, are usually dominated by academic instructors. And community colleges (like most other educational institutions) are funded and structured with academic classes in mind, requiring little more than a teacher, a chalkboard, some seats, and books. From the outside, critics have blamed trends in vocational enrollments for problems ranging from low transfer rates to a debased academic culture (e.g., Brint and Karabel, 1989; Pincus, 1980; Zwerling, 1976; McGrath and Spear, 1991). Many of these criticisms are based on outmoded information: The greatest economic benefits of community college come from completing occupational programs and finding related employment, not from completing academic programs (Grubb, 1996b, Ch. 3), and transfer rates are now as high from occupational programs (in subjects like business, health, technical and computer fields) as they are from academic programs (Palmer, 1986–87; Grubb, 1991). But the legacy of these attacks is a continuing ambivalence about the role of occupational education.

The attacks on occupational education have also been counterproductive for reasons more closely connected to teaching. The nature of instruction in occupational subjects has been almost completely invisible. The national associations, which don't pay much attention to instruction anyway, tend to ignore occupational education. There are very few teacher associations or occupational groups where instructors might discuss their teaching.[2] Aside from some easy references to the superiority of hands-on learning and project-based instruction, there's been almost no discussion in this country about vocational teaching (Achtenhagen and Grubb, 1999). The empirical literature on teaching in community colleges, sparse enough to begin with, has emphasized reading, writing, and remediation rather than occupational teaching,[3] and the how-to literature about adult education has nothing about the special conditions of vocational instruction.[4]

The neglect of occupational teaching is deplorable partly because it is valuable in its own right—after all, between four million and five million students a year take these courses—and partly because many people, including academic faculty, could learn a great deal from it. In some dimensions, of course, occupational classes aren't much different from academic classes, as we explore in Sections I and III. Occupational courses have lectures, too, and some subjects—most business classes, many health-related subjects (like mental health or basic physiology), real estate courses—require no more than a teacher, a chalkboard, and books. A construction management instructor acknowledged that his course was "academic," principally concerned with "disseminating information," and (as any academic teacher concerned with coverage would) he complained that the "material is so voluminous."

But for many fields, occupational teaching turns out to be rich and complex, more so than teaching in academic subjects. In most occupations there are many competencies to master, including manual and visual abilities, problem solving, and interpersonal skills as well as conventional linguistic and mathematical abilities. The literacy practices are varied and sophisticated, though quite different from those in academic classes (as we will examine more carefully in Chapter 4); mathematics is also more applied, and demanding more because it requires sequences of applications rather than difficult procedures (Forman and Steen, 1995). Occupational instruction provides opportunities for both "doing" and "learning," as we clarify in Section I; the workshops or labs in most occupational programs, the locus of hands-on teaching, are unexpectedly sophisticated educational settings, described in Section II.

However, the flip side of this complexity is that occupational instructors must master a range of teaching methods. While some do, others fall back on the same kind of skills-oriented teaching that we have seen in academic instruction, as we see in Section III. And, unlike academic faculty, occupational instructors must also balance the demands of both students and employers—and the influences of the workplace prove to be multiple and conflicting, as we clarify in Section IV. The profound differences mean that occupational instructors have to balance even more elements, more demands and pressures, than do academic instructors. Yet, as we clarify at the end of the chapter, they have even less institutional support than do academic instructors.

In this chapter, therefore, we begin to remedy the neglect of occupational teaching by examining its most important features. In doing so, we draw upon a staggering variety of occupational programs. (We will also return to occupational teaching in other parts of this book, especially Chapter 4 on literacy practices and Chapter 7 on innovative efforts to integrate academic and vocational education.) The most familiar subjects include business, computer and information science (CIS) or information technology (IT), nursing and other health occupations, early childhood education, electronics, drafting, various construction trades, and automotive and diesel mechanics—all mainstays of community colleges. But we also came across many unusual subjects: arborism, dairy herd management, construction management, band instrument repair, electron microscopy. The programs are as varied as the economy itself, and they change as the economy changes. These are unusual subjects only to those who don't live in rural areas, or haven't thought about how many band instruments are dropped or what it takes to erect large buildings, or haven't followed the technical advances in medical and automotive occupations. The variety makes it difficult to examine their pedagogy: The dairy barn is so different from the business classroom and the "equipment"—very large cows—so dissimilar to personal computers that it is hard to imagine both within the same sphere of instruction. But this simply means that the competencies in occupational instruction are more varied than they are in academic education. The tools and objects of occupational instruction—cows and electron microscopes, medical instruments and auto diagnostic stations—are also more complicated.

In the end, the purpose of exploring the special characteristics of occupational pedagogy is to understand the institutional conditions necessary if community colleges are to fulfill their many purposes. Like high schools, on one hand, and four-year colleges, on the other, community colleges have become inescapably occupational institutions, both in explicit forms—in the programs preparing students for employment in business and agriculture, in cosmetology and electronics—and in the less obvious forms of preparing all students to enter the economic mainstream. If institutional conditions are inadequate for occupational instruction, then reforms are necessary before two-year institutions can call themselves teaching colleges.

I. THE MODAL APPROACH TO OCCUPATIONAL INSTRUCTION: THE STRUCTURE OF LECTURE/WORKSHOP

The dominant approach in occupational teaching is the lecture/workshop. In the lecture component, instructors present the "theory," the academic underpinnings, the necessary facts: information about how hydraulic systems work, what different accounting systems are like, what diseases are likely to strike dairy cows and how they can be cured, or what conventions are used in drafting either on drawing boards or in computer-assisted drafting (CAD). Then the workshop or lab component provides the applications and practice of material presented in lectures, often in worklike settings created within the college, but sometimes in real work settings—for example, when a construction program builds a house, or a culinary arts program runs a restaurant, or a dairy program manages a herd of cows.

The lecture/workshop is a good example of hybrid teaching, with one component allowing for didactic instruction while the workshop component focuses on more student- and project-centered instruction. The combination also exemplifies the Deweyan precept of "learning *and* doing": it is not, in most cases, repetitive practice in manipulative skills (as one sometimes sees in short-term job training), nor is it all "theory" (or "learning"), but rather an amalgamation of the two.[5] For example, a construction program incorporated an "installation class" covering the fundamentals of building before students went out and constructed a house. As the instructor described the combination, "They learn from the books, that's true, but they get the hands-on." Another occupational instructor, in early childhood education, was similarly explicit about the combination:

> I really try to think in a two-hour class of some way to balance. I think the instructor should really dominate just a portion of that, and there should be a balance with some student-initiated [activities]. As to what those activities are, most of them have been gleaned from other presentations and from classes. I've kept real big files of things that may work. Some of it is just trial and error; you know, let's try this to try to illustrate this particular topic. Sometimes I'll have them take the perspective of children.

Almost always, lecture precedes workshop, an arrangement suggesting that practice rests on a foundation of knowledge. But instructors vary in the extent to which they explicitly think of their teaching in this way. Some are quite clear that the conceptual material presented in lecture is fundamental to practice. For example, the construction instructor commented that the hardest thing about teaching was conveying to students

> that there's more to it than the hands-on. It's the planning, the thinking, the organizing, the layout, the design. Otherwise they're not going to get the good jobs out on the street, and they're gonna be a gofer and they're gonna be a helper if they can't do the head work.

Many occupational instructors who have embraced the integration of academic material into their programs, or who participate in linked courses combining both academic and occupational coursework (explored in Chapter 7), are similarly explicit about the knowledge base that underlies practice. More often, however, occupational instructors are wedded to the practice of their craft, just as many academic instructors are wedded to their disciplines. Therefore the workshop component is the heart of their programs, even if it comes after the classroom. Practice drives the entire program, including lecture—in contrast to the lecture/discussion in many academic classes, where discussion is peripheral to or subsumed by lecture. As one welding instructor noted:

> With this population I'm teaching, they're really into hands-on. Putting them into a classroom, they get kind of agitated, so I use a varied presentation all the time. . . . It's very important for these people to always have it visually related, because that's the mode they're coming from—visual and hands-on and such.

A variant of the lecture/workshop takes place when students return to the classroom in order to discuss what has taken place in the workshop—a trio of lecture/workshop/discussion. For example, one commercial baking class included an early morning lecture about the different mixtures and leavenings used in commercial baking. Next students moved into the adjacent kitchen (set up like a bakery) to make a variety of breads and muffins, and then reconvened in the classroom to discuss the morning's results, including the mistakes that turned out too liquid, too dry, or too misshapen for commercial purposes. Similarly, a class in commercial banking started with a lecture, moved into a simulation of a bank with tellers facing "customers," and then reconvened in the classroom to discuss the problems students encountered. In a class preparing students to be recreation directors, a student lectured about the rules and purposes of a particular game; the class then went to the "workshop"—the gym—to play the game, and finally reconvened to discuss what they had learned about the effect of rules, the rhythms of play engendered by those particular rules, and the balance of competitive and cooperative elements in this and other games. In these examples, reconvening after the workshop is central. The purpose is not really to make muffins or play games, but rather to understand the elements of baking and game playing, and discussion is necessary to extract "learning" from "doing." In other vocational classes the discussion necessary to explore the implications of practice takes place within the workshop itself, as instructors circulate and work with individuals or small groups of students.

The lecture component of lecture/workshops displays the same variety as do lectures in academic classes. Some are as didactic, as teacher-driven, and as decontextualized as any academic lecture. For example, in one welding metallurgy class, the instructor simply reviewed the facts about welding compounds ("What is an alloy?") and elements from the periodic table ("What is the symbol for manganese? What are the weight and properties?") without any discussion about the use of different alloys or any other references to practice. This was a good example of a textbook-driven lecture, as are many other occupational classes with thick textbooks.

Another didactic example came in a drafting class, with students sitting at computers running a CAD program. The instructor's computer was attached to a projecting mechanism so that all students could see the commands he entered. After drawing several two-dimensional shapes, he led students through the commands for dimensioning (labeling diagrams with their dimensions), following the textbook. Although this was presumably a hands-on class—students were operating computers—it was essentially a lecture in which taking notes was replaced by replicating verbatim the instructor's commands.[6] It's quite possible for a class to be hands-on and yet to be as didactic, passive (on the student's part), decontextualized, and skills-oriented as any grammar or multiplication drill.

More often, however, the lecture component includes some discussion, with the instructor posing questions to check comprehension and students asking questions for clarification. Sometimes, as in academic classes, this takes the form of call-and-response, particularly when instructors are reviewing material they think basic. For example, this electronics instructor is reviewing facts before shifting to a presentation of possible problems:

Instructor: "What is flux?"

Student 1: "Lines of magnetism."

Instructor: "Yes, but it's a force; that's what I want you to remember.
   What can I do with that magnetism?"

Student 2: "Make electricity."

Instructor: "How?"

Student 3: "Coil the wire."

Instructor: "What do I do then?" [He continues with this line of questioning. After a presentation on the workings of a hydrostatic
   pump:] "What would cause a catastrophic failure on this system?
   Where is it gonna come from?"

Student 4: [Gives an example of an individual mixing up lines while
   changing them.]

Instructor: "Right. What should you do before you replace a line?" [He
   answers his own question.] "What other things could cause catastrophic failure?"

Student 1: "Run low on oil?"

Instructor: "Right. What happens if I plug this filter? . . . "

Many questions in occupational classrooms ask about simple facts ("What is an alloy?" "What is flux?"), just as in most academic classrooms. However, occupational instructors tend to shift to more demanding questions, particularly to diagnostic questions, which require knowledge of how a component works rather than simple recall ("What happens if I plug this filter?"). A typical progression might go like this:

What is this? (referring to pictures in a text, or to an actual engine part)

What does it do? ("Tell me how a brake circuit works.")

What happens if you do X to it? ("What happens if we reverse these two lines?"
"What happens if I plug this filter?")

What would cause it to do Y? ("What would cause a catastrophic failure in this system?")

What if you see Z happen? What might cause that? ("What does it mean if I get a voltage reading of 9.8?" "The car you brought in today has vibration; what might cause that?")

In this way occupational instructors move from simple recall to causal analysis to counterfactual analysis to problem solving, often within a very brief span of time.

Classroom discussions tend to be instructor-driven: Students ask questions for clarification, but they rarely ask questions that go beyond the immediate topic or application. Instructors typically respond to student questions immediately and directly, based either on textbook material or on their own experience, but they rarely challenge students to come up with their own answers and elaborations. The following interchange in an electron microscopy class was typical:

> Student: "Why do they use a ruby on the end?"
> Instructor: "It's like a ball and socket: it has to fit precisely and roll smoothly."
> Student: "Why not a synthetic diamond?"
> Instructor: "Synthetic diamonds aren't hard enough."

Instructors take their role as experts for granted, as do students—indeed, the prior experience of many instructors coming from industry gives them a stature that academic instructors lack. But in this process, occupational instructors often miss opportunities to force students to think for themselves. "Showing and telling" is usually didactic, rather than forcing students to formulate the knowledge necessary for successful work.

In some classrooms, there are demonstrations of materials, tools, or equipment, so that students can see and feel the objects they will work with later in workshop—visual and manipulative skills are engaged from the outset.[7] For example, in a diesel engine repair class the instructor brought in a pair of two-lobe helical gears; he demonstrated the symmetry of the gears, passed them around for students to manipulate, and asked a series of questions about how the gears might fit with the rest of an engine. Of course, the manipulative elements within classrooms are limited by the size of what can be handled. An electron microscopy instructor, obviously unable to bring the huge and immobile electron microscopes into class, instead had her students go through a visualization exercise ("You can see the column; you can see the fluorescent screen . . . visualize what those striations look like when it's really saturated"). In these cases the boundary between the classroom and the workshop becomes blurred.

While the lecture component of occupational classes displays the same range that academic classes do, there are some noticeable differences. The most obvious is that lectures tend to discuss applications, ostensibly from practice. To be sure, the applications vary depending on the instructor's background; those who have not recently been in the trade, or who have never worked extensively in the area they are teaching, either fail to use examples or use applications that are contrived or outdated. Business classes and CIS classes seem particularly prone to being taught by instructors without real experience, and here the examples are often contrived. For instance, one business instructor used numerous examples from his family (as if running a family were like operating a business), and another generated "applications" from within the community college itself. Most often, however, the applications discussed in class come from the work experience of the instructor, as well as that of students. One instructor described his lecture as a "precept-and-example-type thing":

> I will take something out of the text that was part of the assigned reading, we will talk about it in the text form, and then I will try to give them something that I have experienced that will coincide with what they have read. It's kind of a real-world experience that I can add to it. And sometimes there are others in the class [who], maybe through their construction background, will contribute something, too, along the same line of thinking.

This introduces practical knowledge (as distinct from textbook knowledge) and occupational "lore" into the classroom. Students are particularly attentive to this information because it seems especially relevant to their occupational futures.

Students often have their own experiences to contribute, either from everyday life or from their work lives. For example, a marketing instructor in (you guessed it) Marketing 101 developed a great deal of information through questions to students immersed in consumer culture: convenience shopping versus specialty shopping, marketing niches and targeting strategies, the new product cycle from introduction to competition to stability. Since occupational students are often employed in jobs related to their occupational subjects (albeit at lower levels than they hope to obtain), occupational instructors can draw on a range of work experiences within their classroom discussions. Lectures in occupational subjects can therefore organize and codify experience that students already have—a characteristic that is not true of algebra, Shakespeare, or biology. One cabinet-making instructor described his classroom as a "one-room schoolhouse" because of the mixtures of ages and experiences. He paired younger students with more experienced students to convey their more developed skills and attitudes to work. Indeed, while many instructors describe the age range of students as a distinctive feature of community colleges, occupational instructors are virtually the only ones who use this diversity in the classroom.

In our observations, students were more attentive to lectures in occupational classes than they were in academic classes. The lecture in virtually every case was followed by a workshop that applied the content of the lecture. Unlike discussions, where students can "hide" by failing to participate, the workshop is an exposed setting where ignorance and inattention to lecture are quickly revealed. Indeed, many lectures are so explicitly connected to the workshop that follows—they often provide the instructions for projects and exercises, including health and safety warnings—that students would be foolish not to pay attention. In this sense the lecture in occupational classes contains a built-in motivation that is unlike anything in academic instruction.

On the whole, therefore, the lectures in occupational classes we observed were more successful than most academic lectures. They developed more work-related applications, they drew on students' experiences, and students were generally more engaged. But some lectures we observed were so contrived in the applications developed, so lacking in any occupational relevance, or so teacher-directed (even in hands-on settings) that they could not possibly be opportunities for learning. The question is whether community colleges provide their occupational instructors with sufficient preparation and support so that they can deliver the lectures best suited to their subjects and their students—or whether the institutions leave them to develop their approaches individually, by trial and error.

II. THE WORKSHOP COMPONENT: THE MEANING OF "HANDS-ON" INSTRUCTION

Legions of vocational teachers have asserted the virtue of "hands-on" instruction. But what is the special value of hands-on instruction? Why is having students work on engines, bake cakes, or construct houses more educational than having them conduct science labs or look up primary sources in history or social studies? And do the benefits of hands-on instruction extend to all occupational applications—even, for example, to the CAD class where students were merely copying the instructor's commands?

To the casual observer, workshops seem remarkably similar. Typically, students work on specific projects—sometimes individually, often in small groups—while the instructor circulates to answer questions, check on the progress of work, correct errors, and otherwise monitor performance on these projects. Projects may be simplified versions of production, or slowed down for instruction, but they are still tasks recognizable from real work: automotive students are fixing engines or brakes; drafting students are drawing objects, either on boards or on computer-based systems; electronics students are building circuits and diagnosing them; culinary arts students are cooking and baking; construction students are likely to be completing parts of an actual house. Sometimes instructors may interrupt a workshop to give mini-lectures, or show the class a particularly interesting problem that has come up, or to give the entire class a necessary corrective. And these workshops are hands-on in obvious ways, with students building or fixing things, using sophisticated tools and equipment, evidently using their hands in ways different from simply writing in academic classes.

However, there is a great deal more going on than meets the eye, and hands-on instruction covers a variety of conceptually distinct elements. Instructors use the term "hands-on" in various ways, some of them inappropriate. For example, a business instructor showed us a student exercise by saying "I also use this, which is a managerial grid, hands-on"; the exercise was a fill-in-the-blank worksheet like those forced on generations of students in grammar and arithmetic drills, and "hands-on" instruction referred to everything except lecture. Another business instructor declared that his students "need more direct hands-on teamwork and people work, rather than computer work"; in other words, "hands-on" referred to all personal interaction, as distinct from lecture and individual work. Similarly, a child development instructor asserted that she tried to provide "some hands-on discussion kinds of things." These examples suggests that any student activity may count as "hands-on." But group work and worksheets are not necessarily student-centered or constructivist, and to label discussion as "hands-on" seems to miss the point of the metaphor.

In other cases, references to "hands-on" instruction express a primacy of workshops over classrooms, a distrust of classroom learning, an anti-intellectualism that is hostile toward the academic world and its central competencies (including basic literacy and numeracy). For example, one instructor described his students this way:

> The learners we have here are very hands-on—papers, books, they don't care for that kind of stuff. Some of them probably weren't scholarly-oriented. A lot of these guys, you know, working with books and reading, that's maybe not their niche in life. But I'm not gonna say that they're not as intelligent as other people.

Similarly, a business instructor said, "We need some theory but we need some hands-on practicality." The point of his comment was that only the "hands-on practicality" was important. In such cases, praise of hands-on instruction may be a code indicating a deep hostility to academic learning.

When occupational instructors talk about their workshops as "hands-on" instruction, they tend to conflate several conceptually distinct virtues. It's worth disentangling these elements because they clarify the distinctiveness of occupational teaching. (One of them, the ability of the workshop to mimic the conditions of real work, we postpone until Section IV, on the multiple influences of external employment.) Furthermore, these elements are not always present, and some workshops have so few educational features that they are just as tedious as any skills-and-drills class could be. As in every other subject, good vocational teaching requires control over many elements of instruction.

Showing and Doing

The workshop equivalent of didactic lecture is showing, where an instructor demonstrates how to change a brake pad, inject a cow, wire an assembly, or adjust an electron microscope. Showing is a teacher-dominated activity, normally followed by doing, by the student mimicking what the instructor has just shown.[8] As one construction instructor mentioned, "This is how things in the trade have been taught in the trades since the dark ages—explaining, showing, doing. It gives me a laugh that Bill Clinton has just discovered this." The student activity, the doing, is the heart of the workshop, the essence of what hands-on activity means.

Sometimes there is only one right way to carry out a task, particularly in regulated occupations (like construction trades) or in practices related to health and safety, as in health occupations and automotive trades. In these cases student "doing" is entirely mimetic. Often, however, an instructor may present several ways of carrying out an operation, reflecting individual styles of working. As a construction instructor mentioned, the hardest thing to teach students is "pride in what they do by themselves, getting out there and thinking for themselves, leading instead of following ... they don't learn by following, not all the time." In another example, an auto instructor showed students several ways of repairing piston rings. At the same time, he stressed that an engine imposes its own limits: While there may be several different approaches, in the end the engine has to run correctly.

In other classes, instructors deny students access to alternative ways of carrying out tasks. For example, the CAD instructor who led his students through a series of commands on his computer cautioned students *against* using the text as a reference. In response to a student question, he said, "When you get to the advanced class I'll tell you how to work with PFP files; for now I don't want you messing in there [in that particular chapter]." He also failed to mention the help menus within the CAD program, a serious omission because help files are always up-to-date while both manuals and instructors may be outdated. Consistent with the role of the teacher as sole authority, this instructor had cut off his students from two of the three sources of information—including both sources that students could use on their own. In teaching workshops, therefore, instructors make a series of implicit decisions about what students should and shouldn't do, expanding or contracting student initiative accordingly.

Developing Noncognitive Abilities

Most occupational classes involve competencies in addition to verbal and mathematical abilities. Most of the time, they involve manipulative skills, or (in the vocabulary of Gardner, 1983) kinesthetic intelligence: the ability to machine parts, to use tools in construction and automotive trades, or to carry out medical procedures in health occupations. Often visual ability is required, as in drafting classes, in carpentry, in many other construction trades, and automotive classes, where students have to imagine how parts fit together in three dimensions. Auditory abilities (or musical "intelligences") are more rare, though well-tuned cars sound a particular way, and medical procedures often require recognizing the distinctive sounds of the heart and respiratory system.

Instructors vary in the extent to which they make explicit the teaching of noncognitive abilities. In the traditional crafts and trades, instructors spend a good deal of time showing hand skills and the proper use of tools; the initial stages of a program involve substantial practice in manipulative abilities, a vocational example of "skills and drills." Culinary instructors will point out the appropriate look and texture of food in different stages of preparation. Instructors in areas involving three-dimensional construction will often spend time on the process of visualization; as one automotive instructor said to his students, to get them to "read" their texts (the "auto encyclopedia") in a different way:

> If you buy an English 1A text, they may be complex and abstract but there are only a few concepts. But the auto encyclopedia has vaster quantities of information; it requires physics, engineering, et cetera. We have a heck of a problem here trying to get you to visualize things, in your mind's eye. . . . Your visual skills are the most important skill you have.

And vocational instructors often spend considerable time teaching the distinctive literacy practices of their occupations, the ways in which work is described in diagrams, maps, and specialized symbols—as we will examine more clearly in Chapter 4.

However, in other cases instructors fail to teach noncognitive abilities explicitly. Many drafting instructors teach CAD as a series of computer commands necessary to reproduce objects in three dimensions, ignoring the visual process of moving between two and three dimensions. An employer complained about the consequence for employees:

> You're seeing a subtle revolution in the drafting field. It used to be that your drafter was probably a person who could visualize; they have a real conceptual mind. ... Today you've got computer people doing this; you're dumping out your frustrated artists and really bringing in the computer hackers.... The difference is that the CAD operator cannot think conceptually and does not have design skills. (Grubb, 1996b, 27)

In other cases instructors ignore noncognitive abilities because they believe they cannot be taught. For example, one burned-out auto instructor used to screen students with a test of mechanical aptitude; when the college told him the test violated affirmative action regulations, he gave up teaching his students since they didn't have the appropriate aptitudes: "As long as they're working on something, I leave them alone."

Occupational instructors face at least two problems in teaching the range of competencies required in most jobs. The cognitive, manipulative, and visual skills required in successful work are sometimes unrecognized, even by experts themselves.[9] These abilities are often described, by instructors and employers alike, as innate or intrinsic—aptitudes that individuals either have or don't have but that are not amenable to instruction. When instructors don't teach these competencies explicitly—for example, when they fail to teach the literacy practices necessary for the occupation, as we will see in Chapter 4—then students who lack such abilities may fail or drop out. Then the course becomes a filter allowing only those students with these "innate" skills to succeed, rather than a truly educative enterprise.

In addition, there has been little discussion about how best to develop these work-related noncognitive abilities. Academic instructors who worry about reading and writing, for example, or mathematical competencies can find a vast literature, colleagues, and professional associations who debate endlessly how to develop these abilities. But occupational instructors can rely on almost nothing except the craft lore they bring to their teaching: there's very little written about how to teach manual and visual competencies, there have not been extensive debates about teaching strategies, and most instructors have no colleagues or professional associations to talk with except those in their immediate department.[10] Even more than their academic peers, occupational instructors are left to their own "natural" teaching proclivities in developing approaches to instruction.

Developing Teamwork and Communications Skills

Teamwork and communications skills are still other competencies that have been celebrated as part of the high-skills workplace. As the Secretary's Commission on Achieving Necessary Skills (SCANS) said:

> Very few of us will work totally by ourselves. . . . Today's worker has to listen and speak well enough to explain schedules and procedures, communicate with customers, work in teams, understand customer concerns, describe complex systems and procedures, probe for hidden meanings, teach others, and solve problems. (1991, xviii–xix)

In vocational workshops, the practice of having students work on projects in teams is widespread (sometimes as a solution to the lack of equipment). In forming teams, instructors sometimes deliberately group more experienced students with less experienced individuals, like the cabinetmaking instructor who described his classroom as a "one-room schoolhouse" because of the amount of peer teaching. Similarly, a welding instructor mentioned the value of having older, experienced students contribute stories from their job experience, reinforcing those of the instructor himself.

Like problem solving in workshops, teams are ways of preparing students for the conditions of real work. As one auto instructor commented,

> Five other students helped him put the wheels back on because he was behind. They all pitched in. That's the way it should be; they're all aware of what each other is doing. The concept I hold is, you don't have to like one another, but you have to work together.

Teamwork also helps develop communications among members of the team directly, by experience. Other communications skills—particularly those necessary in interacting with customers—are taught by directive and example, as instructors tell stories of their own practice. For example, one instructor in a building inspection program told of defusing a potential conflict by writing a conciliatory letter to a wealthy client: "Communication is the key to survival in this job. When people get fired, it is not for the lack of knowledge, but for not getting along with people." An auto instructor talked about the "five o'clock surprise" when a customer walks in and finds out that the car isn't ready or that it will cost more than expected: "The solution to this is communication. Explain the choices.

Let the customer choose. Have him sign that he wants you to do the work." This particular instructor physically enacted the various roles—customer, mechanic, boss—at the front of the workshop; if his students couldn't experience the "five o'clock surprise" directly, they could at least envision what it might be like

Of course, teamwork doesn't always work well. Sometimes members of a team are reduced to watching the others, or spend more time wandering around than working. For example, in a construction class building a house, the instructor allowed students to find their own work to do (rather than assigning them tasks); several lost souls drifted without any task or purpose. Like the academic classroom, the space and freedom of a workshop allows students to get physically as well as mentally "lost"—though the most careful instructors monitor workshops carefully to make sure that the benefits of teamwork are realized.

Teaching Problem Solving

A recent appreciation of demands in the flexible workplace has led to a new emphasis on problem solving in all of education (e.g., SCANS, 1991). Workshops and their project-based activities provide opportunities for problem solving that are different from (and often superior to) the classroom. Often, activities are based on real problems. For example, many auto programs have customers bring in their nonoperating cars, and students first diagnose the problem before they learn to fix it. In one class, for example, students had learned the general functioning of brakes; then teams had to find the problem on several cars with failing brakes. The student teams tended to generate hypotheses and test them one by one. In circulating among students, the instructor showed students how to narrow the range of plausible alternatives to speed up the process, but he still allowed them to try out alternatives on their own. Similarly, electronics workshops often start with problems—like circuits that don't work—where again students have to sift through several alternatives to determine the error. This kind of problem solving is very much preparation for the job; as one electronics instructor remarked,

> They've got to survive out there. They accept the job as being a service, maintenance, or installation technician, or a troubleshooter. They aren't gonna go out and troubleshoot the same job every day, or troubleshoot the same problem. . . . So you have the book and you have independent thinking.

The point of teaching "independent thinking" is to cope with problems on the job, usually less predictable than "textbook" examples:

[In the classroom] they have the formulas, they have the component in front of 'em. In engineering, that's basically selected from the specifications for parts that the engineer has chosen from catalogs or off the stock shelf . . . and then when manufacturing creates them, they all come out within the ball park. But that's not what happens when they get out in the field and all these things have been overheated, sent up to the North Pole, rusted out in fields for six weeks—and then they [students] have to go to all three places to try to fix one of those circuit boards, and every one of those circuit boards is acting differently.

On occasion, instructors have students create the problems. An auto instructor described his procedure:

I have the students decide how to create problems with the car, based on the component that we're working with—have them bug the car. And before they bug the car, they have to come to me and explain what problems they're trying to put in the car, and what the result of that problem's gonna be, if customers complain, what would result from that problem. And then, is it solvable? The class is broken up into four teams of people, so team one bugs this car and teams two, three, and four try to diagnose the problem. And I keep track of their time as to how fast they diagnose the problem. Then I have them work up a lab sheet, and I question them to make sure they're all participating.

Both "bugging the cars" and fixing the problems have their own value, and the problems are similar to ones that customers might come in with.

The pedagogy of problem solving is tricky, however, just as it is in academic classrooms. The best instructors make sure that the problems are accessible—"solvable," as the auto instructor noted; they provide their students with alternative approaches and enable them to understand the logic behind different approaches. In contrast, an electronics instructor gave students circuits with multiple problems, allowing them to flail away while he made sarcastic corrections when they identified improbable causes. He also complicated simple problems before students had fully grasped the solution, so students were always confused and behind on the next problem. After students had tried unsuccessfully for some time, he stepped in and unraveled the problem step by step, a didactic procedure that made a mockery of students' earlier efforts. Students in this class appeared frustrated and impatient; the instructor's initial structuring of problems was too complicated, and his interactions with students were demoralizing rather than supportive. Instructors who are unconscious of the pedagogical elements in workshops can thereby destroy their educational value.

Student Engagement and the "Tactile" Student

The rhythm of workshops is crucial to involving students actively. Students move around purposefully and independently, talking informally about work problems with each other and with instructors—a very different feel from academic classrooms where students sit in silence, or have reluctant contributions dragged out of them. Students may be able to hang back in a lecture or discussion, but in the workshop their nonparticipation is obvious. As a banking instructor mentioned,

> From a lecture standpoint there is not that much involvement from anyone other than me. But from a lab standpoint you got to actually do it. You balance or you don't; you either count or you don't.

Several instructors noted that some students might be reluctant to ask questions in lectures, but the combination of informality and pressure in the workshop—the necessity of working on a project—causes them to open up. A CIS instructor described it this way:

> A lot of people don't know things but are afraid to ask. . . . What we find out is that when we go over it in the lab, and we say do it and there's nobody to help them . . . we get the immediate feedback once they get in the lab, but over here [in the classroom] I can only prompt the students.

The greater motivation of the workshop is often related to the types of students who select occupational programs. Here is the description by an instructor in construction management who, like his students, spent most of his life in the trades:

> These students, they're very much like me, they have to take it, they have to feel it, and they've got to do like this, and they have to weigh it and everything else. They've got to smell it—very tactile people in vocational education. And they can grasp ideas, grasp abstract ideas, so long as you give it to them and then you have to apply it immediately, the algebraic equation for this concrete admixture or such. Okay, now here, immediately do that and then here is the presentation. Here's the concrete.

An instructor in a John Deere–sponsored program in farm machinery echoed the same idea:

> If we want to talk about something and we don't have it [in the workshop]—the learners we have here are very hands-on, you know, they gotta see the stuff and want

to work with it. Papers, books, they don't care for that sort of stuff. If we just talk about is, they're not going to remember it.

For these "tactile" or "hands-on" students, then, abstract ideas cannot be absorbed unless there is a concrete component, a physical manifestation:

> When I'm on a roll on a material [in a materials course], I'm talking, talking, talking, and people of a second language, number one, can't process that much; other people just don't relate to words that well. . . . So it's got to be—the oral word has got to be tied to the written word. . . . They have to absorb it on their own time, and then none of the words are any good without something to touch or move or twist, weigh it and feel it and stuff like that.

Sometimes the workshop is not just a way of reinforcing theory, but a form of compensation for students who don't learn well in the classroom, who "don't relate to words that well." As one electrical instructor mentioned, "Many of them, they lack basic educational skills. So that's why I place great emphasis on hands-on."

Comments about vocational students being "tactile" or "hands-on," lacking basic educational skills and "unable to relate to words that well," are reminiscent of a century-long discussion in this country in which some students have been labeled "manually-minded" or "concrete," unfit for academic studies and able to succeed only in vocational programs teaching them manual skills. However, a more positive interpretation is that occupational instructors embrace a wider range of abilities and understand the importance of many different abilities or "intelligences." For many purposes, cognitive abilities are just not adequate. As Isadora Duncan, who translated kinesthetic intelligence into great art, expressed it: "If I could tell you what it is, I would not have danced it" (Gardner, 1983, 224). On the job, cognitive abilities are not enough, as an electronics instructor remarked:

> Where you find individuals that lack dexterity or the hands-on, then they place a lot of emphasis on the technical information. Whereas employers are not concerned with your knowledge of technical information. They're concerned with your ability to perform the work. Like I tell students, you don't need to know anything about how electricity is generated and all that to wire a house . . . . What you do need to know is what conductors connect together, okay, and what the codes are, how should you space your outlets, what size wire to use where. And you can wire a house as good as anyone that's been doing it for fifty years.

Under these work conditions, theory—or theory by itself, theory as a *substitute* for technical skills—is simply not valued by employers. Manipulative skills are not second-class competencies, therefore; they are the only abilities worth having.

To be sure, this view—that classroom theory is irrelevant, that "you don't need to know anything about how electricity is generated to wire a house"—is part of a debate within vocational education between narrow conceptions that emphasize technical or manual skills only versus broader conceptions insisting on theoretical foundations as well. This debate manifests itself in different approaches to vocational instruction (in Section III of this chapter) and in efforts to integrate academic and occupational education (in Section IV of Chapter 7). For broader conceptions of occupational teaching, noncognitive skills are necessary *in addition* to cognitive abilities, and all of them reinforce the others: "The oral word has got to be tied to the written word . . . and then none of the words are any good without something to touch or move or twist." This is the vocational equivalent of whole language: Oral instruction in lecture, written instruction through the enormous textbooks and manuals common to occupational classes, and practice in workshops are all necessary for effective learning and performance.

One-on-One Instruction and the Use of Errors

Like their academic peers, occupational instructors value the chance for one-on-one instruction, and occupational projects lend themselves to such teaching. As instructors circulate, they typically spend extensive periods with individuals (or small groups), discussing their progress, their solutions, their thought processes, the alternatives they might pursue. One-on-one instruction allows faculty to tailor their teaching to the varieties of students. One auto instructor noted the problems with the lack of tracking in community colleges, and gave one-on-one instruction as his solution:

> They're all out there in the classroom and you got to make it interesting for all of 'em . . . what level do you throw this out at? How do you keep this person from getting bored to death and at the same time not bury the one down here? . . . I don't know what the answer is—the lab thing lets you pull away and go one-on-one with this.

Because the results of learning in workshops are externalized, embodied in objects of activities that are visible, errors become visible too. One air-conditioning/refrigeration instructor described the process of diagnosing and correcting errors:

> After we've done the lecture and after we've done the demonstration, then they go out on their work station and do the job and we usually circulate through the lab and

if they're doing something wrong we tell 'em about it . . . usually you correct them right away, particularly if it's any kind of a safety violation. . . . You interact more closely with the students, rather than just sitting and talking to 'em, because I sit and talk to them all day, too, but I don't know if they are getting anything or not. If they are understanding it, at least this way [from the workshop] I can see what they know they're doing.

An auto instructor commented on the differences between mistakes in the classroom and mistakes in the lab:

Vocational, even though it's getting higher technology, is still a hands-on type of program. . . . The students learn by mistakes—okay, everybody learns by mistakes— [but] in the lecture you can go and over and over, the students are having trouble being motivated by that . . . because they've not experienced those mistakes. . . . In the lab they make their mistakes and then you can correct them and then many times they're under the same type of pressure of a shop and they remember those mistakes and then they usually don't make them again.

In addition, vocational instructors generally expect that students learn as much from errors as they do from any other form of instruction—"They remember those mistakes and then they usually don't make them again." The process of circulating among students is intended to detect mistakes, discuss them, and correct them, and the debriefing or discussion sessions *after* the workshop are explicitly devoted to reviewing errors and problems that arose during the workshop.

Occupational workshops usually contain materials and projects that impose their own kinds of corrections on students. If a circuit is not properly wired, it won't perform; if an auto part is not correctly installed, it won't function as intended, or the motor won't run; if baking conventions are ignored, the results turn out soggy and inedible. The corrections come, at least some of the time, from the task or project itself and not from the instructor; the instructor need not constantly personify authority or expertise. Thus the physical representation of "learning" in physical objects and visible procedures make the detection of these errors and their correction easier than in the academic classroom.

Drawbacks to "Hands-on" Instruction

While there are many pedagogical benefits of workshops, there are potential liabilities, too. Project-based work and practice can take over a class, so that it is left without any general learning; the purpose in such a workshop may be practice to gain automaticity and speed in low-level manipulative skills. However, this approach, common in short-term job training programs preparing individuals for assembly-line work, is rare in community colleges.[11] Instead, the classroom/workshop format is explicitly dedicated to learning *and* doing, or combining theory and practice.

A more common problem is that, just as academic instructors often answer their own questions, occupational instructors sometimes solve problems for their students rather than allowing them to develop their own solutions. This is exemplified by the following auto class:

> The instructor goes up to a pair of students and watches as they try without success to loosen a brake drum. He asks, "Is that drum loose?" When the student replies that it is not, the instructor says, "Don't beat on it. I'll be right back." He comes back with two bolts and penetrating oil, which he then applies to the car. He loosens the drum, says, "Presto!," and walks away without any elaboration. One student remarks to the other, "I didn't know you could do that. Good thing we had him."

Some instructors justified this practice on the grounds that trial and error might be dangerous or expensive. But others had devised ways to allow students to develop their own solutions without endangering themselves. An electronics instructor contrasted his own practice with how he was taught on the job:

> Well, the hard thing is to show [a student] why it would work without actually telling him flat out why. He needs to *see* why it doesn't work. It doesn't do me or him any good to sit there and tell him exactly what the circuit does. I guess that's the way I was taught: If it was out on the job, they [the supervisors] would come up and tell you how to do it. And I didn't like that, because it was just like, do this. And what did I learn out of that? I really didn't learn much until I sat down and worked with the circuits afterwards. I don't know how the rest of the instructors feel, but I don't believe that just by telling somebody how to do it is a good way for them to teach.

But instructor impatience, or authority, often truncates this kind of learning and doing, usually without instructors being aware of it.

The final drawback was evident, unfortunately, in most workshops we observed. The workshop is an amazingly variegated environment: Several groups of students are working on different projects, with the instructor (and sometimes an assistant) providing individual help as well as mini-lectures to the entire class. There's too much information swirling around to retain easily. Yet students rarely take notes during workshops. They listen intently, and in many cases practice immediately what they've heard, but it seemed to us that a great deal of information was lost. A few instructors realize this and have tried (without much success) to get students to take notes; as one automotive instructor commented,

> I don't know how to get these guys to take notes. I give them a clipboard every semester, I tell them, "Here's your clipboard; you use it. And the reason you're given this is because you now have a writing surface to take notes during the demonstration." . . . But in the lab, they don't take notes . . . as much as we remind them [to] "write it down." There are times I'll stop and say, "This is important—write it down." And none of them has anything to write on. And they lose out.

The lack of note taking exemplifies the separation between the classroom and the workshop. The occupational classroom is, as we will document more carefully in Chapter 4, a place of extensive and sophisticated literacy practices, where textbooks, manuals, and professional journals serve as sources of information and students produce a stream of memos, work orders, and conventional papers. But the workshop is largely an oral, manual, and visual culture, in which the literacy practices that aid learning are much less common. In more integrated programs, this division would be softened by incorporating literacy practices into the workshop as well as the classroom.

In sum, the workshop is a pedagogically sophisticated place, and hands-on instruction incorporates more than meets the eye. But this complexity has its own costs. The instructional benefits of workshops emerge only when they are appropriately developed, and "hands-on" instruction can backfire when instructors fail to understand the pedagogical principles underlying their practices. And, as in academic classrooms, there are many elements of teaching to control and balance—but little help from colleges in helping occupational instructors master the demands of their work.

III. DISTINCT APPROACHES TO OCCUPATIONAL INSTRUCTION: "SKILLS" VERSUS "SYSTEMS" METHODS

While many occupational classrooms and workshops look superficially similar, there prove to be distinct differences in pedagogical approaches. Many occupational instructors take what we call a skills approach, while others embrace a systems approach. The division has much in common with skills and drills, emphasizing subskills and part-to-whole instruction, versus meaning-making or holistic instruction.[12]

The difference was nicely illustrated by an auto instructor. In the approach he has refused to take, time is divided into small units like academic classes—"kow-towing to the academics"—where each unit is devoted to a particular subskill. This instructor considers the skills approach to be a failure. His tactic has been to have longer classes where students work on real projects—cars with different problems—where students learn by having them "get on the cars and mess around." In this problem-driven approach, technical skills are learned by develop-ing solutions to larger problems—whole-to-part instruction rather than part-to-whole. While he describes the workshop as "messing around" with the cars, he structures the problems—the cars that come in—so that students rotate through all important automotive systems. He described an effort to "get away from the shop environment":

> We wanted to get away from the manual training, specifics, narrowly focused, "here's how a pump works" environment to "let's look at the hydraulics fundamentals involved here, let's look at pneumatics, let's look at applied physics, let's look at applied mathematics"—not just cars, but the entire concept of hydraulics. It's a little bit like any liberal arts graduate . . . those young, supple minds, they can hand them a book on irrigation and they can teach themselves.

Teaching students how systems operate is especially important in auto repair and other occupations where there are many different models. As another instruc-tor described the problem:

> I try to teach them how things work, you know, the theory behind—like how an automatic transmission works. You know, on the American road there's probably seventy to eighty different transmissions. You would have to be a repair shop doing transmissions day in and day out for about five or six years before you could be com-fortable doing all of those. There's no way I could teach the students to do that. But if I can teach them the basic fundamentals for how any transmission works, how the fluid dynamics works, then when they do get whatever job they're going to get, they will then be prepared to get specific training.

Other instructors noted that a systems approach is necessary for problem solving and troubleshooting. As an air-conditioning/refrigeration instructor noted:

> What I generally do is I take the first couple of months of school, I spend a lot of time lecturing and a lot of time going over how the system works and properties of ther-modynamics and stuff like that, 'cause if they don't understand that, then they can't understand why the system works, and I always say that if you can't understand how it works, you can't troubleshoot it.

Instructors who focus on problem solving are trying to get students to understand an overall system that has malfunctioned, and then to think about which parts are most likely to have failed—again, whole-to-part instruction.

The alternative is to teach a series of independent skills. As one drafting instructor noted, "Drafting is a kind of skills class; I think teachers call it motor skills, where you learn by doing." But teaching drafting as a motor skill neglects the process of visualization and the central problems of moving from three to two dimensions. In classes taught this way, the result is often a copying exercise where students use boards or CAD to copy drawings, rather than thinking about the process of two-dimensional representation. Similarly, a construction instructor described the process he followed in his class, engaged in building house:

> We start with concrete . . . we start with the footings . . . we pour the walls using foam form blocks, then we pour the floor . . . we go through a rough framing . . . we start with floor framing . . . then we do the walls; we lay out and install rafters or trusses, depending on the roof system . . . we do all the sheathing, and we do all the finished roofing as far as the shingles, then we go as far as putting soffits and fascias on, and we put siding and windows in, and hang all the exterior doors.

So a house is a series of independent tasks that take place one after the other, instead of a unit where different systems interact. This approach may work—it does get the house built, and it is particularly suited to preparing the specialized trades (roughing-out carpenters, finish carpenters, plumbers, electricians, dry-wallers, etc.)—but it neglects those issues of coordination and design, all left to the architect, that might prevent construction problems from arising.

The difference between the skills and systems approaches is particularly evident with computer-based technology. Some instructors teach such technology as a series of computer commands, rather than having students think about what the computer is supposed to accomplish. In addition to the CAD classes taught this way, a good example is the word processing class described in Chapter 2. Teaching secretaries what commands to use to set margins, rather than having them think about what margins are appropriate, reduces them to individuals who can only follow orders without exercising independent judgment about creating a text. The skills approach can lead to serious error because there is so little thought involved. In one computer class, the instructor taught the commands to develop spread-sheets. But she had them start programming before they understood the problem—"First put in the data, then see what calculations you have to make"—and some students set up spreadsheets with too few cells. Because the instructor had them think about spreadsheets as computer commands, rather than a way of facilitating mathematical calculations, most students made an elementary arithmetical error in their spreadsheets when the sum of ratios across a row did not equal the ratio of sums—but neither they nor the instructor understood why. There are several reasons for the widespread use of skills approaches in computer-based classes. Many instructors teach in this mode anyway, and it may seem natural to teach a series of computer commands rather than a systems approach because of the way manuals and texts are written. Finally, as we will argue in Chapter 7 as well, there has been little attention to the pedagogy of computer instruction.

The skills approach has a long history in this country. It follows the approach of competency-based teaching in vocational education. This, and the related DACUM (Developing a Curriculum) process of curriculum development, typically starts with a "skills audit," identifying the skills necessary in specific (and usually entry-level) jobs, and then generates a long list of skills to be taught. While such skills can be taught through systems approaches, it is often easier simply to cover the skills one after the other. In some cases, industry associations and certification mechanisms stress part-to-whole approaches; an example includes the competencies defined by the National Automotive Technician Education Foundation (NATEF), which has developed a curriculum and a process of certifying both instructors and auto programs. In other cases, however, an industry association has championed a systems approach. As a computer instructor noted,

> The data processing management association has done some really nice work on designing [an] ideal curriculum for the information systems industry, and what you'll see is the structure's very different from what we do now. What we do now is very much a tool-based [approach]—now you're gonna learn how to use a compiler, now you're gonna learn a specific language—whereas the emphasis really should be project-based: we're gonna accomplish a real-world task and we might have to use eight or nine tools to do it. But the innovative people who are doing this are making the argument that for the students it's actually better to learn it the breadth way first than the depth way first.

While we were unable to review industry certification procedures, we suspect that they can have powerful and unintended effects on pedagogy.

Aside from the potential influence of external standards, it remains unclear why instructors have adopted the approach they use. Some seem to conceive of work as problem solving and troubleshooting, and they are likely to develop a systems approach. Others confine their teaching to narrowly defined skills, as if they view their students as future workers with little autonomy on the job; in that case, we suspect, their students are trained only for entry-level jobs, and they are poorly prepared for changing jobs or thinking about work in a broader context. And of course many instructors draw on both the skills and the systems approaches, presenting the necessary skills together with a broader understanding of the purposes (or systems) into which technical skills fit. But the differences are, as far as we could determine, individual and idiosyncratic.

Furthermore, there are no sustained discussions about how best to teach a subject, such as auto repair, drafting, or electronics. Associations of occupational instructors are weak—much weaker than they are in academic subjects such as English or math—and they are usually too preoccupied with keeping up-to-date and maintaining funding to discuss pedagogical issues. National associations have rarely addressed pedagogy, and even less often the pedagogy of vocational subjects. As we will see in greater detail in Chapter 8, most community colleges do little to engage faculty in sustained examinations of their teaching practices—and in any event, occupational faculty have relatively low participation levels. Like most academic instruction, occupational teaching has become an isolated and idiosyncratic activity, and under these conditions it's not surprising to find a wide variety of approaches.

IV. THE INFLUENCES OF THE WORKPLACE

Occupational instruction differs from academic instruction in part because it serves two masters: the students, and the employer or the workplace. The workplace makes itself felt in many different ways. Most obviously, activities within workshops often mirror work, albeit at a slower pace and with tasks defined more by pedagogical goals than by production concerns. In addition, the presence of employers creates a set of external demands and standards to which instructors must respond.

The effects of these influences on learning are complex and sometimes contentious. Occupational instructors generally feel that they are serving students better if they pay attention to employer demands—"We're doing the student more justice"—and it's clear that occupational faculty are connected to the labor market better than are academic faculty.[13] From an academic perspective, on the other hand, external demands are usually suspect. As an economics instructor commented about advisory committees, "The local business community literally tells them what curriculum they want. I was just appalled to hear that." But however one comes down on this long-running debate about the purposes of education, there are many more subtle aspects of the workplace that find their way into occupational teaching, and they complicate the goals of instruction in ways quite different from academic teaching.

External Standards and Demands

All occupations are subject to external standards of performance, since competence on the job—outside the college—is the ultimate arbiter of success. External standards are expressed in various ways. Most often, occupational instructors have come out of practice, and they bring with them conceptions of what well-trained workers should be able to do. Many instructors have operated their own companies or run their own shops; they have therefore been employers looking for certain characteristics in potential employees. They often tell their students stories about the standards required for employment. The electricity instructor who told his students, "I would fire the shit out of you," because they were not using drawing to think about electrical circuits, was conveying the competencies necessary for continued employment, as well as the autocracy of the workplace.

Several institutional mechanisms bring the standards of the workplace into occupational classes. Virtually every occupational program has an advisory committee of local employers, who provide advice about changes in employment and technology. Many instructors mentioned their value in keeping programs up-to-date and adding various academic competencies to their programs. As a vice president for instruction noted:

> The thing that amazed me, which I was very pleased by, and I think was a little more than the faculty thought it would be, was the high level that the advisory committees wanted them to have in reading . . . and in writing and in math.

Others mentioned the value of advisory committees in keeping up-to-date on technical issues. As the chair of a dental assisting program explained:

> They provide me with constant feedback on what the office needs are in an employee, what kind of skills they're looking for. . . . They also provide me with information on new equipment, new materials, besides what I observe when the students are placed in individual offices.

In one college, advisory committees had counseled that students needed to combine manufacturing skills with business understandings, because these functions are no longer separate; this led to a "product-based curriculum interaction project" to develop these cross-functional skills. However, advisory committees work unevenly. Many committees don't meet very often, and seem to exist for public relations purposes only. Even when colleges claim to have active advisory committees, employers often perceive them to be paper exercises (Grubb, 1996b, Ch. 6); most of the contacts between colleges are employers are instructor-initiated, not institutional, and low-intensity linkages are more common that those requiring significant planning and preparation (Brewer and Gray, 1997). Like any other institutional practice, therefore, advisory committees and other linkages to employers work only to the extent that programs make good use of them. But even when they become symbolic, they are mechanisms of contact with the external world that academic programs lack.

The final mechanism of external control comes from licensing requirements. A surprising array of occupations require occupational licensing, including all health occupations, early childhood teaching, cosmetology, construction supervision, aircraft maintenance, and welding. Certain craft workers, including carpenters and bricklayers, are not licensed but have to practice according to building codes. In addition, several occupations have developed voluntary standards that, according to some occupational instructors, are becoming the norm for good practice: NATEF for auto mechanics, the American Welding Society for welders, the regulations of the American National Standards Institute and the American Society of Test Materials for construction managers. In these occupations, instructors must construct a curriculum to cover the elements specified by the national standards (or that might be covered in a licensing exam), and their comments are peppered with references to these external requirements.[14]

Even though the external pressures of the workplace are uneven, occupational instructors are, much more than academic instructors, oriented to the world outside the community college (Brewer and Gray, 1997). They are more likely to mention national debates about the future of the country, the SCANS report, and other concerns about the quality of the workforce. Their basic allegiances are to norms and standards external to education, not (as for academic instructors) to disciplines within education. This creates a division of loyalty; as a division head for applied technology described this dilemma,

> We really have two professions. If you talk with my faculty and you ask 'em "What is your profession?" they're gonna tell you they're welding instructors. But many faculty in the technical areas forget about the fact that, in addition to the technical specialty, we're also educators. And my faculty are more prone to undertake professional development activities that relate directly to their specialty than they are to the teaching profession. . . . So one of my jobs has been to encourage faculty to address the needs of issues other than their teaching specialty—that is, the issues of teaching, the teaching/learning process, teaching methodology . . . and not just teaching the mechanics of electronics.

This division creates a special problem for occupational teaching: Unless a college has powerful institutional mechanisms for improving teaching, occupational instructors are all too likely to go their own ways and fail to examine their roles as educators.

Developing the Conditions of Real Work

Unlike the classroom, the workshop can mimic real work, and thereby prepare students for practices on the job. As one auto instructor expressed this:

> Sometimes I think the class is like work; it's like I'm the supervisor, the dispatcher, and I'll assign different cars to different types of students. Sometimes they'll have their own choices. And other times, they have no choice; they have to do what I say. I'm their supervisor, and if they have a problem with it, we can talk about it.

A different auto instructor made an explicit link between the conditions of his classroom and the auto shop he used to run:

> We literally . . . taught them [new hires] on the job when they came in working for us, so in that regard we were teaching them with the business checkbook being their grade book . . . and that's the way I tell my students, "That's how you're going to learn from me. You should treat me as your employer, instead of a teacher kind of thing, because ultimately that's what I'm trying to do, is get you employed."

When a class cannot be engaged in real work, including co-op education and school-based enterprises (Stern et al., 1994), instructors make their workshops as worklike as possible, even though they cannot have the most up-to-date equipment and do not replicate the pace of production.

The pedagogical advantages of doing so are varied. In addition to developing the kinesthetic, visual, interpersonal, and other noncognitive abilities that students will need at work, realistic workshops incorporate the culture of the workplace— the authority relations of work, the role of the client (or the patient, in health occupations, or the child, in early childhood programs), the differences between textbook conditions in the classroom and real conditions on the job, ethical dilemmas, and workplace norms. These lessons are delivered by the way instructors structure workshops, to mimic the conditions of work, but they also come through the personal experiences of instructors and the stories they tell. Because most occupational instructors have worked in the occupations to which their students aspire, they are role models in the most direct sense (unlike academic teachers, since few community college students want to become English teachers or historians). Their status as role models invests the stories they tell about their own practice with a special power, disproportionate to the attention instructors pay to them. These are tales about what work is "really like," told by an individual of real stature in students' eyes. They are, as Bruner (1996) emphasizes, visions of the world in which students can find themselves, narratives in which students can understand the relationship of school to future performance. While these narratives are quite different from formal instruction though textbooks and workshops—oral rather than written, idiosyncratic rather than general—they are usually complementary, providing particular examples, embroidery on standard practice, hints about competencies (including the many interpersonal issues arising at work), and correctives about the complexity of the "real world."[15] Invariably, a class becomes more attentive when an instructor begins one of these stories, and they often provoke a barrage of questions about how the instructor handled various problems.

We can only begin to illustrate the variety of lessons about workplace norms. Sometimes instructors try to clarify the difference between the textbook approaches of school-based learning and the conditions of the real world. As an auto instructor stated,

> I just think that is a real plus for them to have an instructor that not only owned and operated a shop but also was the service manager at a very busy dealership, so I can give them an insight into what it's really gonna be like. . . . I can sit down and go through the book with them and you know, lecture and discuss the chapters in the book . . . but then when we work in the lab . . . some of the jobs students do aren't gonna go right. . . . I try to bring up real-life situations—what will happen between a customer and a repair shop.

Similarly, a baking instructor tried to clarify to students how different conditions are in real life:

> What I try to do is during the lab time, any kind of situation that comes up, I will tell them how this differs from what it would be in real life. If you ruin this in real life, you get one shot. Here you can ruin it a couple of times and hopefully you get it by the end of the second or third time. . . . Out there, I know what I used to do is if they ruined it more than once, they paid for it. That gets their attention.

Often instructors convey information about the social relations of the workplace—about the kind of deference due bosses or clients, or the "five o'clock surprise" that happens when customers haven't been prepared for the amount of the bill. Some crucial lessons are conveyed in the relationships of the workshop itself. Often, particularly where instructors re-create the workplace, the instructor takes on the role of boss rather than teacher, and—particularly in male-dominated occupations—his actions mirror the relatively authoritarian relations of the workplace: "They have to do what I say—I'm their supervisor." In such classes, the directives from instructors are often simple, blunt commands—"Get it done!" for example, instead of the inverted request "Would you please do this now?" more typical of teacherly behavior. In one electricity class, for example, the instructor interrupted the class with the following outburst, talking first to a small group of students and then convening the entire class:

> Man, you know what really gets me . . . *Stop! Stop! Stop!* You know, you guys could not work for me 'cause I would fire the shit out of you, okay? And the reason being because you guys would have me in the poorhouse, because you've never drawn, I don't see anyone with a drawing of what you're trying to do, okay? And let's say that I was out there and I had a twenty-thousand-dollar piece of equipment, okay, and I told you to go and hook it up—and you just go out there and you're hooking the thing up and it walks off the roof when you're putting the power to it, okay? That's gonna come out of my pocket . . . because you just decided to go out there and just start hooking things up without nothing to go by.

This is not the measured, judicious correction of a teacher embracing "student support"; it is the correction of a boss, angry because thoughtless behavior of his employees is likely to cost him money.

For instructors in the caring occupations, usually dominated by female students and taught by women, the concerned role of the student-centered teacher replicates the concern for the patient, client, or small child typical of health workers, social workers, and early childhood educators. In these cases the social relations of the classroom mirror the social relations of workplaces, and students are learning indirectly about appropriate forms of behavior. Sometimes the lessons about social relations are unconscious and indirect. An instructor in a health records course provided examples that portrayed doctors as arrogant men from whom patients and nurses, all women, need protection. In this view, the role of medical coding was an ethical one—to protect patients and their health, where inaccuracy might hurt the patient.

Sometimes instructors convey how an individual participates in a larger organizational and economic structure. An instructor in band repair described his class in these terms:

> We try to teach them what to expect, what's expected of them, and how income is made. . . . We try to cover it pretty thoroughly as to what actual working conditions are like, and how they fit into it, and the whole scheme of the music business and how the repair part fits into the whole chain of events and helps the company [stay in business]. Other than just repairing the instruments, we teach customer recruiting,

retention, many other workplace basics such as inventory control, shop needs, and we have a class called shop management practices.

This all-encompassing view is a good illustration of teaching about "all aspects of the industry," an approach to broadening vocational instruction embedded in federal legislation for vocational education (Andrew, 1996).

However, we found instructors almost uniformly oblivious to their implicit teaching in two areas. The first involves gender relations. Gender segregation is more prevalent, and is diminishing more slowly, at the sub-baccalaureate level than in professional and managerial occupations (Blau and Ferber, 1992). Therefore many occupational classes are almost completely gender-segregated. Health occupations, dental assisting, secretarial programs (as well as related CIS courses, like word processing), and early childhood education are dominated by women; automotive and agricultural equipment programs, electronics, welding, machining, HVAC, the building trades, and many farming programs are almost entirely male. With few exceptions, occupational instructors made almost no comments about gender segregation, either about the negative consequences (especially for women) or about how students might prepare themselves for the gender relations of the workplace. Many occupational classes display a great deal of stereotypical behavior. While male instructors are uniformly solicitous of female students, male-dominated classes are often preserves of "male" behavior, with many jibes, some roughhousing, and a few dirty jokes. In contrast, classes dominated by women are often suffused with the ethic of caring that is stereotypically female. The gender segregation typical of the workplace is immediately visible in these programs, but—in contrast to the constant barrage of messages about the real world of work—the silence about gender issues is profound.

Similarly, occupational instructors say almost nothing about unions, worker rights and representation, and other aspects of power relationships at work. While instructors often explicitly replicate the relationships of the workplaces, we never observed them discussing the limits of authoritarian relations, cases when workers ought to challenge their bosses, or what workers' right are (or ought to be). Nor, in our interviews, did instructors mention unions, or workers' issues more generally, as subjects of concern or teaching. The reasons are manifold, we think, and not as simple as the hegemony of capitalist relations. Some instructors have run small businesses and take the political stance of employers. Some are so intent on teaching a craft that the critiques implicit in political issues may seem counterproductive. Others think it inappropriate to discuss political issues. For example, a welding instructor in an antiunion region discussed with us the fact that his students had been hired to replace striking workers, but while he was sympathetic to the strikers, he felt he should not discuss the issue in class. And some distrust unions for their own reasons, as did a black electronics instructor who castigated unions for creating barriers to black workers.

If students learn as much from what is not taught as from what is explicitly taught, then they must be learning not to question the gender roles and the authority relations of the workplace.[16] Implicitly instructors emphasize the role of occupational education as a means of conveying the expectations of employers. They are preparing workers to function in an accepting mold—"punctuality, being there, doing the very best they can, willing to learn"—not workers as citizens who might have something to say about the conditions of their work. In so doing, they are also neglecting the potential of community colleges for political educa- tion as well—an issue to which we return in Section IV of Chapter 7, on ways of integrating academic and occupational education.

The efforts to mimic work in workshops involve an old dilemma: How work- like must vocational education be? If work-related competencies can be taught only in worklike settings, perhaps work itself is the only appropriate education, in apprenticeships or cooperative education. But if employment is flawed as a form of education—because the incentives to extract work from apprentices overrides the concern to educate them, or because the conditions of production do not allow time for instruction, or because hierarchical relations at work are antitheti- cal to instruction, or because invisible aspects of production cannot be learned by mimicry—then formal schooling becomes the locus of instruction, with a combi- nation of classroom and workshop. Unfortunately, the *balance* of worklike and school-like elements in workshops is rarely discussed. None of the occupational instructors we interviewed indicated how they tried to create a balance. Instead, like so many aspects of vocational teaching, this balance emerges class by class, depending on the equipment and space available and on the instructor's own inclinations in teaching.

Work-Based Learning

A potential advantage of occupational education is that it can bring the workplace directly into education by incorporating work experience, cooperative education, and school-based enterprises. The advantages of work-based learning have been articulated in this country at least since the early 1900s, when cooperative educa- tion began. More recently its proponents have promoted school-to-work pro- grams, prompted by the success of the German dual system and stimulated by federal funding in the School-to-Work Opportunities Act of 1994.

Within community colleges, work-based learning is widespread—about 90 percent of community colleges report that they provide some kind of work expe- rience—but it reaches only a small percent of students in most institutions (Stern et al., 1995; Bragg, Hamm, and Trinkle, 1995). In the colleges we observed, work experience is quite patchy. One learning community combined remedial reading and writing with an auto repair course, and also required work experience with local dealers. In the Midwest, several colleges have agricultural equipment maintenance programs supported partly by John Deere, and students work for local dealers during vacations and summers. Even in occupational education, work experience is available to relatively few students.

The potential value of work-based learning is exemplified by the LaGuardia Community College program, which is mandatory even for transfer students (Grubb and Badway, 1998). Students are required to have three nine-week periods of work experience. Each period includes a co-op seminar, where students meet once a week to discuss issues in work placements and the relationships between their work and learning in college-based courses. When these seminars run as intended, they provide forums for the Deweyan ideal of combining learning and doing (Heinemann, 1983). For example, in one seminar attached to a business program, students described the different accounting systems they encountered at work placements and related the modifications to the requirements of their employers; the instructor then used these experiences to reinforce the general rules of accounting and the variations allowed in good practice.

But even here, where the college has intentionally structured the co-op seminar to allow student evaluation of their experiences, didactic and teacher-centered impulses are hard to control. Many co-op seminars became forums for didactic instruction, veering away from student-centered discussion just as the lecture/discussion classes described in Chapter 2 often did. Elsewhere, investigators have found that work-based placements differ greatly. Some provide substantial and varied opportunities for learning, while others are unplanned, limited in the competencies they teach students, and dominated by the didactic procedures of "show and tell."[17] In a lesson that repeats itself over and over, educational institutions have to work hard, with careful selection of instructors and staff development, to prevent instructors from backsliding into teacher-directed instruction.

By and large, then, community colleges have not exploited the teaching advantages of work experience.[18] Very few have set up extensive programs except in a few areas such as nursing. From a pedagogical standpoint, however, work-based learning provides yet another opportunity to integrate learning and doing.

V. THE INSTITUTIONAL PROBLEMS OF OCCUPATIONAL EDUCATION

In many ways, then, the pedagogy of occupational instruction is quite different from that of academic instruction. Workshops look very different from academic

classrooms, with a great many activities taking place simultaneously; the influences of the workplace are powerful and varied. But occupational education also
differs from the academic side because of certain institutional practices and cultural norms. These problems—of low status, isolation, inadequate funding, and
the unavoidable problems of keeping up with changing technology and work conditions—undermine occupational instruction and prevent the academic side
from learning about its pedagogical advantages.

Complaints about the low status of vocational education are common among
occupational instructors. "The administration is not committed to vo-tech ed" is a
common complaint. "The faculty as well as the administration do not know what
I do back here," lamented a welding instructor whose workshop was physically
separate from the rest of the college. Some of this low status is blamed on simple
ignorance. One instructor in electronics complained, "The administrators come
from an academic setting and so they're unaware.... Most academicians do not
understand the world of meaningful work." Anger about their low status is sometimes compounded because many occupational instructors feel that their hands-
on teaching is superior. As a vice president for instruction in a technical college
argued, "We may not have the degrees, but we actually know about teaching people so they can really learn."

For occupational programs, their low status—together with special funding
problems we examine subsequently—means that they are always threatened with
being cut to make room for academic programs or for remedial education. One
institution we observed, for example, began as a technical high school, became an
occupationally oriented community college, and then added high-profile transfer
programs while occupational programs were allowed to decline—a good example
of "institutional drift" away from vocational purposes.[19] The remaining occupational faculty were quite bitter, of course; as one complained, "The administration
in [this] district is not committed to vocational-technical education. The district
was renowned and at one time was rated one of the top three technical institutes in
America." Of course, decisions to open and close programs depend on student
enrollment and employer demand as well as status considerations. But this particular college served large numbers of poorly prepared low-income black and
Latino students in a city with a dreadful public school system, and almost no one
transferred to four-year colleges; the institution apparently sacrificed occupational programs in favor of "academic" programs that led nowhere.

The low status of occupational education is intertwined with its isolation on
campuses. The most obvious reflection of that isolation is physical location.
Vocational workshops are usually located on the periphery of the campus, partly
because of their space requirements, partly to move the noise and debris of workshops away from other classrooms. Often facilities are far away from the cam-

pus—an airplane hangar at a regional airport, a dairy barn in the midst of the fields, or a construction site where students are building a house. At another college the segregation was vertical rather than horizontal, but it achieved the same symbolic effect:

> The staff here is a divided staff and the administration saw to that. . . . Look at the way this campus is built. All the vocational courses are down in the basement. Everything above us is academic, liberal arts.

The physical isolation of vocational programs hampers the integration of both faculty and students into the life of the campus, to be sure, but isolation is more than physical. As we saw Chapter 1, community college instructors have the greatest contact with colleagues within their departments. But occupational departments are tiny—often two or three people, or a couple of full-time instructors and several part-timers—and so occupational instructors are typically not in contact with a significant number of other faculty. They have fewer reasons than their academic colleagues for working with other instructors outside their departments— less reason to participate, for example, in committees about general education requirements, or Writing Across the Curriculum, or transfer procedures. Because of the time demands of their teaching and their sense of being peripheral, and perhaps because of insecurity about their verbal abilities in competition with English and philosophy instructors, occupational faculty participate less in the governance of most colleges. An occupational dean noted,

> It really works against occupational faculty. [They] don't have the time to be involved in shared governance. So it gets populated by philosophy teachers and history teachers and social sciences teachers and English teachers, and as a result, a lot of occupational issues don't get properly considered in that environment.

We suspect that occupational students are also more segregated on community college campuses. In contrast to transfer students and to "experimenters," who typically take a variety of courses, vocational students have chosen a field; their occupational coursework and workshops are likely to take up all their time. As one student remarked, "I don't really feel that this is a college. For me it's just a culinary arts program—the program here is, like, so different from any other part of the college."[20] We suspect, then, that occupational students are more likely than transfer students to be relatively invisible, just as their instructors are.

The isolation of occupational education may be caused in part by its low status, but lower participation by occupational instructors in college affairs in turn contributes to their peripheral status. The debates within most colleges are largely academic and transfer issues; colleges are usually run by administrators and presidents who come from the academic side. The national associations are largely occupied by academic concerns. Long after the community college has become a predominantly occupational institution, it continues to be governed by academic norms that do little to enhance the quality of occupational teaching.

The Special Funding Problems of Occupational Programs

While complaints about funding are ubiquitous, occupational programs face two fiscal problems that academic programs do not, and which contribute to their marginal status in many colleges. The first involves current funding, supporting recurring expenditures such as instructor time and materials. Because most community colleges are funded on the basis of enrollments (usually full-time equivalent students, or FTEs),[21] administrators have become skilled at "profit maximizing"—that is, understanding which programs take in more revenue (in the form of state aid and tuition) than they cost in instructor time and materials. Fiscal motives therefore dictate that classes costing more than the revenue they generate should be cut. As one instructor mentioned "Every course is a profit center—not every program, not every area, *every course*." Obviously, courses with high enrollments and low costs—like social science courses of forty students, or remedial English taught in large labs with part-time (and low-paid) instructors— are favored over those with low enrollments and high costs, including most occupational courses, especially those with expensive workshops. As an instructor in criminal procedures laid out the economics:

> It comes down to a matter of dollars and cents and ADA. . . . When we start balancing how we are funded by our ADA, the number of students in the class and what it costs, for example, to have a classroom when I teach forty students as compared to a vocational classroom where they need specialized kind of equipment like our dental assistant program or nursing program or auto repair programs that need tremendous floor space, academic administrators, start balancing those things, it's so easy to go with the numbers and the bodies because that generates the ADA. It costs a lot to put on a vocational program. . . . So a college president has to make a decision: Are we going to offer more classes in English composition or are we going to offer a new program in robotics, for example? Well, it's a no-brainer as far as the costs are concerned.

In a few states, the fiscal pressure against vocational programs is balanced by weighted funding, where students in certain vocational programs generate more revenue than academic students. But these are exceptions: In most states, and for most occupational programs, state funding mechanisms are devised with academic programs in mind, and the smaller class sizes and higher costs of occupational workshops make them easy targets.[22]

The problems of current expenses are compounded by the treatment of capital expenses. Educational institutions are typically funded in ways that seem to have English and math classes in mind, where the only equipment necessary is a blackboard and chalk. Capital expenditures—whether computers for writing or CAD classes, or science labs, or auto diagnostic stations, or CNC machining equipment—are typically supported from separate capital accounts on the basis of special requests. The funds available are never enough, particularly when the costs of up-to-date equipment have skyrocketed; virtually all instructors complained about the costs of equipment for their programs. Furthermore, the process of requesting funds is itself a time-consuming and divisive activity. As an automotive instructor described it,

> It's a real interesting process that's used to determine that. It's vicious. There's great competition among departments in the college and in T & I [trade and industry]— they give us a chunk of money and let us decide how to allocate it. It does pit departments against each other, but we try to take turns.

Another illustrated the bind his air-conditioning/refrigeration program is in. The Environmental Protection Agency (EPA) directed him to replace CFCs (chlorofluorocarbons) with more modern refrigerants, but the administration had not come up with the money to do so even though "the EPA is not going to go away, and neither is the Clean Air Act":

> They forget what it's like to be in a classroom, to use 1966 equipment, and, you know, have them [the EPA] come down here. For example, refrigerant when I came here was $37 a bottle, and now we're paying $360 for the same amount and our budget is still the same. And they say, well, I'm always bitching, and that's basically what I'm doing because there's no money. We get by, but I mean we beg, borrow, and steal to do it.

The problems are even worse in other occupational areas: electron microscopy, auto repair with expensive computerized diagnostic stations, machining programs that should be using CNC machines, agricultural equipment programs that need access to enormous combines and reapers, dairy programs that need a herd of cows. None of these fits into the funding structure of an educational institution—especially not community colleges, with their relatively limited resources (discussed in Chapter 9).

The "solutions" to the lack of capital funding are varied. Many programs are simply out of date. Their computers are four or five years old, or they train students on conventional lathes and milling machines instead of computer-driven equipment. In other cases instructors "beg, borrow, and steal" to keep programs up-to-date; they spend a great deal of time writing grant proposals for equipment or canvassing local employers for cast-off equipment and donations of materials. In a few cases cooperative agreements have been developed that benefit both educational programs and employers. For example, partnerships with John Deere provide some agricultural mechanics programs with expensive machines, and co-op programs allow students to work with up-to-date equipment on the job. But these stable and institutionalized arrangements are comparatively rare; most occupational instructors have to spend substantial amounts of time scrounging resources to keep their workshops going.

The need to "beg, borrow, and steal" for equipment and materials is only the most obvious of the extra demands on occupational instructors. Another, mentioned by virtually every occupational instructor we interviewed, is the requirement of keeping up with changing technologies and work conditions. In contrast, English, math, and most other academic subjects don't change much, at least not at the community college level; one instructor noted wryly that Shakespeare hasn't changed much in four hundred years, while technology has. Occupational instructors typically keep up by reading technical journals, visiting with employers (particularly if they have internship programs), and sometimes by being employed in their fields during the summer. A few continue to operate their own businesses on the side. Some don't keep up at all, and then one can see occupational classes that are out-of-date. The time required to keep up is not figured into the obligations of instructors, and the difference between those instructors in ever-changing occupational fields and those in static academic disciplines is striking.

The special funding and time problems of occupational instructors are *institutional* problems. They are caused by the disjunction of having high-cost, equipment-intensive programs located in educational institutions whose funding mechanisms are designed for conventional academic programs. Of course, decisions about such expenditures should be made rationally; perhaps training on CNC machines, electron microscopes, or agricultural equipment should be done on the job because it is too expensive for community colleges to have such equipment simply for training purposes. But there is no forum for such discussions: State legislatures don't think about such details, even though they provide the (inadequate) funding for capital outlays, and there are few forums in which employers and policy makers discuss training needs. Instead, such issues fall to individual colleges to work out, and then—because colleges typically do not do anything *as institutions* to alleviate the problem of capital costs—individual instructors bear responsibility for the age-old problem of keeping up to date. This means that the least powerful participants are responsible for resolving what is, after all, an institutional and social problem. The resolutions are therefore uneven: While some occupational instructors work hard to stay up-to-date, elsewhere occupational programs are behind the times.

The special institutional problems facing occupational instructors create a paradox. On the one hand, occupational teaching is rich and complex. It incorporates a greater variety of competencies than academic instruction, and it takes place in more varied settings, including workshops with a bewildering variety of activities as well as classrooms, workplaces as well as colleges. Instructors must serve employers as well as students, and sometimes the job demands are powerful. Precisely because of the richness of occupational education, instructors face a great variety of pedagogical decisions usually unappreciated by their academic peers. On the other hand, community colleges do little as institutions to help occupational instructors. With a few exceptions, they don't require any special background in teaching methods or provide any special help for new instructors.[23] Because they are governed by academic norms and funding mechanisms, they actually make life particularly difficult for occupational instructors.

As a result, the quality of instruction depends on individual instructors. Those who are closely connected to the world of employment, who have developed their own systemic views of their subject, and who have carefully considered how different instructional elements fit together are among the best instructors we observed. But others waste the pedagogical opportunities created by hands-on workshops, providing their students with skills that are out-of-date, overly narrow, or delivered in dictatorial and demeaning ways. Once again the quality of teaching is individual and idiosyncratic, rather than the institutional responsibility of a teaching college.

NOTES

1. For data on academic versus occupational intentions, see Tuma, 1993, Table 2.1, using 1989–90 NPSAS data. Of course, students in occupational programs also take academic courses, particularly in English and math, and many of them are also in remedial/development courses; as a result, the proportion of courses that are occupational is smaller than the proportion of students who claim to be occupational.

2. During 1996 and 1997 the American Association of Community Colleges *Journal* published sixty articles; two were on tech prep, a program to smooth the transition from high school to community college; six were on workforce development and economic development, concentrating on the training of incumbent workers; two were general articles on changes in workplaces and the new skills required; but *none* was about conventional occupational programs. Similarly, the League for Innovation in the Community College has had an annual conference called Workforce 2000, though this is dominated by customized training and economic development, not "regular" occupational programs. The main association for vocational education, the

American Vocational Association, is dominated by secondary concerns, and its attention to post-secondary issues is weak. An analogous group for community colleges, the National Council for Occupational Education, is quite small and generally concerned more with funding and administrative issues than with teaching.

3. Richardson, Fisk, and Okun (1983, 52–57) devoted a small section of their book on community college teaching to occupational instructors, pointing out the dominance of equipment- and project-dominated teaching and the relatively greater levels of interaction in vocational labs. And five of the instructors profiled in Seidman, 1985, are from the occupational side, illustrating the different roles and lower status of vocational instructors compared to their peers. There is very little empirical literature on teaching in vocational education in English; see Achtenhagen and Grubb, 1999, for a review.

4. See, for example, the adult education literature reviewed in Grubb and Kalman, 1994. There is not an extensive how-to literature on teaching specifically in community colleges, and none of it covers vocational instruction. On teaching in occupational education in the British further education colleges, see Curzon, 1980, and Kerry and Tollitt-Evans, 1992; the latter is focused on instructors coming from industry.

5. About the tendency to misquote Dewey as advocating learning by doing, see note 17 in the Introduction.

6. This class also illustrates how an occupational class can easily become decontextualized: The class was dimensioning simple geometric shapes, rather than parts that might be included in a real blueprint. The final exam required students to draw an object on their computers, copying from a photocopy the instructor handed out rather than rendering an actual object; the instructor had no idea what part the students were copying.

7. See also the discussion of lecture/demonstration followed by lab, by a small engine instructor, in Seidman, 1985, 189ff.

8. See for example, Bruner's (1996) analysis of four modes of learning. The first two—showing and telling—fall in the didactic and teacher-centered tradition.

9. Butler and Evans (1992) provide an excellent example of welding instructors who stress the planning and feedback processes necessary in expert practice, but who teach welding as a series of manipulative skills. See also Hutchins, 1996, who stresses that experts may have lost conscious knowledge of the intermediate steps necessary for beginners and students.

10. For a review of what little is known about the teaching of non-cognitive competencies, see Achtenhagen and Grubb, 1999.

11. We observed only one such class, one that gave students practice on ten-key calculators so they could operate check verification machines; this class was part of a job training program for welfare recipients rather than part of the regular certificate and associate's degree programs of the college. This is also the class profiled in Hull, 1993a.

12. The differences between "skills" and "systems" approaches also emerges in research on troubleshooting in programming, electronics, and military applications (Gott, 1988, 1995; Perez, 1991). One way to teach troubleshooting is a procedural one, where students learn a series of specific skills and procedures to follow. But, particularly in complex systems, deeper and more abstract knowledge of a system—including mental models, or "device knowledge" and "strategic control knowledge"—are necessary for expert practice.

13. See also Brewer and Gray, 1997.

14. Licensing requirements are surveyed in Wills and Lurie (1993), though this compendium gives no information about how widespread the practices are.

15. See especially Bruner, 1996, on the power of narrative. He points out that most schools

treat the arts of narrative—song, dance, theater, etc.—as secondary to logical-scientific ways of organizing experience. Our point is that in certain settings, including many occupational classes, the two are complementary rather than antagonistic.

16. There is a large literature in critical pedagogy complaining about the inattention of vocational education to power relations at work, and suggesting that it should instead explicitly incorporate a critical approach following the model of Paolo Freire (e.g., Simon, Dippo, and Schenke, 1991; Lakes, 1994). Quite apart from the difficulty of getting vocational instructors to accept such a critical stance, there are many pedagogical issues in such teaching that critical pedagogy has failed to address.

17. See, e.g., Moore, 1981; Stasz and Kaganoff, 1997; Villeneuve and Grubb, 1996; for Australia see Harris and Volet, 1997, and Billett, 1993. On the lack of research about the pedagogy of work-based learning, see Achtenhagen and Grubb, 1999.

18. There are also powerful institutional advantages to work-based learning as employers come to know community colleges better; see Grubb, 1996b, Ch. 3, or Villeneuve and Grubb, 1996, on the Cincinnati co-op programs and the interaction they promote between colleges and employers.

19. An advantage of technical institutes is that occupational education is not a low status enterprise. However, technical institutes are dwindling in numbers; "institutional drift" occurs when area vocational schools become technical institutes and then develop into comprehensive community colleges, eliminating specialized vocational institutions in this country (McDonnell and Grubb, 1991).

20. This quote is taken from interviews with community college students in California, reported in Grubb, 1996b, Ch. 2.

21. Fiscal patterns vary from state to state; see McDonnell and Zellman, 1993; Fountain and Tollefson, 1989; and Honeyman, Williamson, and Wattenbarger, 1991. Based on a survey in 1990, McDonnell and Zellman report that at least twenty states consider enrollment directly in setting funding (see their Table 3.5). Of the remaining states, many of which use some kind of negotiated funding, it is likely that enrollments affect funding though not in a linear way.

22. Only eight states vary funding according to the costs of programs, though a few other states may do so through negotiated funding; see McDonnell and Zellman, 1993, Table 3.5.

23. In the colleges we visited, the Iowa colleges have requirements described in Chapter 8; the California community colleges used to have a two-course requirement for occupational instructors, particularly aimed at those coming from business and industry. In addition, one technical college sponsored a "Critical Literacy Seminar," designed "to build a supportive teaching community where successes, problems, and issues of our everyday classroom lives are shared." The topics included work on writing-to-learn, learning styles, reading instruction. collaborative learning, designing sequences of materials, and performance assessments. Valuable as these subjects are, we note that none of them are topics specific to occupational teaching like the special role of workshops, the teaching of noncognitive competencies, or balancing the demands of employer versus student needs

4

LITERACY PRACTICES
IN THE CLASSROOM
The Foundation of Schooling

Literacy is a central concern of formal schooling in virtually all cultures.[1] In this country, for example, the first legislation providing for public schooling was the "Old Deluder" law: "It being the chief purposes of that old Deluder, Satan, to keep men from the knowledge of Scriptures," all communities in Massachusetts were required to establish schools so that children could read the Bible (Spring, 1986, 3). The early grades were called "grammar" schools and taught the most basic literacies, the three R's. We still think of basic education as reading, writing, and simple math. An educated person is said to be "well-read," while an uneducated person is "illiterate," meaning unable to read but implying uncouth, unsocialized, perhaps even dangerous. The literacy "crisis" of the 1980s publicized estimates that as many as a third of Americans were "functionally illiterate," and they were blamed for the drop in American competitiveness (Kozol, 1985). The "literacy crisis" has passed, replaced by a "skills crisis" in which workers are said to lack a variety of higher-order skills to participate in high-productivity workplaces (SCANS, 1991). Still, a preoccupation with literacy as the foundation of other learning is evident.

The levels of literacy among students, and the ways of enhancing literacy, are particularly central in community colleges. By design, community colleges are open-access institutions. They accept students who by conventional measures— grades, SAT scores—have not performed well in conventional school tasks. So we heard, over and over, instructors commenting that their students are not good readers or writers, do not read, and can't be counted on to do the reading. One aviation instructor commented,

140

> I think it was more that 75 percent were not able to read the [existing] textbook.
> They would not read the textbook at all because they didn't have time because when
> they got out of class, they had to go to that job; in a few cases, even problems with
> plain old reading.

The problems with reading and writing were often cited to justify some pedagogical compromise, like the reduction of anthropology to slogans described in Chapter 2 or the replacement of philosophical debate by short phrases (Kant = "categorical imperative"). The widespread recognition of many community college students as "illiterate" has fueled the enormous growth in remedial or developmental education, a subject we postpone until Chapter 5.

Instructors' comments about students are worth examining more carefully because they reveal attitudes toward students and conceptions of what colleges can do for these "weak" or "underprepared" students. Some instructors—relatively few, we should emphasize—simply believe that these students shouldn't be in college. One business math instructor responded to a question of how he handled diverse levels of preparation by recalling students who got stuck converting fractions to decimals:

> If they can't do that, they don't belong in college, right? This is supposedly a college,
> not a junior high—my feeling, okay? So how do I handle the diversity of students?
> Typically, there isn't any diversity after about four weeks.

Some faculty are simply baffled, apparently feeling that they face a hopeless task for which they are completely unprepared; as one commented:

> These students are the most needy, the most undereducated, and often limited by
> disabilities. It's not uncommon to find a student who has allegedly studied something like parts of speech for several weeks who still identifies *a* as a verb. What to do
> with these students in a postindustrial world is a real quandary.

We might ask what learning parts of speech has to do with the elevated demands of a postindustrial world, but in any event this teacher has no idea what to do.

Many instructors, sympathetic and struggling to explain the problem of low-performing students, have located the source of the problem outside students themselves—in the economy and culture, in the schools from which they came, or in their impoverished experiences:

> Our students used to be much better in the beginning ... and they've gradually gotten worse. One [reason] is the economy. Most of our students are working, so they

have limited time. The other thing is probably television. They have a much shorter attention span, and I suspect they don't do much reading on their own.

> We've got a lot of quote "privileged" unquote students here whose parents are lawyers and doctors and airline pilots, and they come in and they can't read or write. They say, "That's okay, my dad's rich, I'm going to be rich." That's a terrible attitude to have, because the way the world is going, they're not likely to be rich if they can't write a paragraph that other people can understand.

And some instructors are really complaining about the approach that has dominated their students' earlier schooling, the conception of knowledge as unquestioned facts:

> It isn't that they're not teachable, it isn't that they can't get it . . . but many of them don't know what a generalization is, or what a false conclusion is, or that if it's written in a book it doesn't mean it's true.

> They're so used to reading and accepting everything somebody says. If it's in print, it's true. Really, that's what they think. Why do they trust the text? When you go to school, you have a book and that's the authority, that and the teacher.

> Why are students so weak? They have no understanding of what it means to know something, that facts don't equal knowledge. This starts very early in the home, pretty much takes place in early childhood. They're illiterate—but science illiterate. They know nothing about atoms, what an organism is, they're not experienced with living things, they place no value on living things.

And many complain about students' lack of autonomy, reflecting passive approaches to teaching and learning:

> Apparently the majority of them have never learned to do anything on their own— with a microscope, with a lab experiment, with a field investigation, with a library. They want me to tell them what to know, and they'll tell me back.

These instructors are more concerned with overcoming the weaknesses they perceive in their students' grasp of literacy. These instructors best exemplify the premise that the community college should be a place where good students are *created* rather than *selected*. One economics instructor—an individual who provides his students with two levels of study guides as well as a computer tutorial—expressed the hope in these terms:

> We give great numbers of people what I call their last chance, their last hope, and sometimes it happens in an econ class, it may happen in a philosophy class, it may happen in an ESL class, it may happen in an auto body class. Part of it is just being there.

The success of instructors in this "last chance" role depends on what they do in the classroom, on their doing something other than replicating the mistakes of students' past schooling. This in turn requires that they *not* use the class to filter out weak students, nor throw up their hands at the problem. Rather, they must develop methods of enabling their students to master the literacy practices they will require in the future. But this proves to be incredibly complex, both in the "regular" courses we examine in this chapter and in the remedial or developmental classes we examine in Chapter 5. In the first place, literacy itself takes many forms within community colleges, particularly given the variety of purposes and backgrounds that students lug in. Even in reading and writing, the most familiar forms of literacy, there's no consensus about what instructors should do. And beyond the three R's, there's little recognition that virtually all classes—including most occupational classes—involve sophisticated and varied forms of literacy. There's often little explicit attention to these different literacies. In such cases, when instructors assume that students are following a lesson, classes may serve more as filters than as sites of real education.

And there's little agreement about who should teach the various kinds of literacies, and how. Academic subject specialists often slough off this burden onto English and math teachers, who resent others not sharing some of it. Occupational instructors complain about how academic faculty approach basic literacies, while they feel unprepared to teach some competencies directly. And—as we will see in the next chapter—the tactic of simply sending students to remedial education is as common as it is ineffective. There isn't, in most colleges, any forum for these issues about literacy to be discussed and resolved. There are some exceptions, including some discussions in English departments or developmental studies departments, and some discussion in learning communities like those we mention in the next chapter and in Chapter 7.[2] But in most colleges, there is no ongoing, cross-departmental debate about what students should master, despite the presence of complex literacy practices in virtually all classrooms. In the process, approaches to teaching literacy—in many ways the most fundamental responsibility of schooling—wind up being developed by individual instructors with idiosyncratic notions and personal solutions to widespread teaching issues.

I. LITERACY AS SKILL AND LITERACY AS SOCIAL PRACTICE

Language and literacy are always contentious areas. The inability of national committees to develop standards for K–12 English, the debates over the extent of illiteracy, and the interminable wrangling over phonics versus whole language are just a few of the current debates. Even when we confine literacy to its most familiar forms—reading and writing—powerful differences in approaches emerge. Within community colleges these differences are not always acknowledged, though they surface in inconsistencies in courses within departments—even in different versions of courses with the same name and number. Said one dean of instruction:

> When you look at [English] 101, you go, "Are all of you doing what 101 is supposed to be doing?" Well, first of all, what is 101 supposed to do? And they'll probably say, "Well, it's English comp." And you go, "Oh, okay, what do you teach in English comp?" If you have ten sections, you're gonna have ten different answers. If you're lucky enough to have an instructor who seems to pass all his students, you're gonna get through that. Or you hit some instructor who is probably teaching nothing but Shakespeare instead of any composition—you'll be at a total loss.

In this institution as in many others, English 101 was a "gatekeeper," a barrier to progressing through the college for many students who wanted to do something other than study English all their lives but still had not mastered the conventions of reading and writing well enough. Yet each section was different, so the individual approaches to teaching in each section—that is, the variety of approaches to literacy—determined who would succeed and who would fail.

But what do these courses look like? And why are they so often barriers? To analyze the various literacy-related classes we saw (including the remedial/developmental classes examined in Chapter 5), we need to describe different ways people think about literacy and how it should be taught. Often literacy is viewed as a *skill*: A student has a particular facility with reading or writing, and the task of the class is to increase that skill. But this conception focuses on the individual, whereas reading and writing are presumably intended for communication with others and are therefore social rather than individual activities. In addition, the conception of literacy as a skill presumes that the goal is simply to move up a well-defined ladder of competencies, and as such it provides no way to understand the value of literacy or the purposes that cause students to want to become more competent (as distinct from institutions requiring them to pass English 101).

A different approach to literacy views it as a *social practice*, particularly since the classroom is more than a student and a book.[3] It always includes an instructor (or two or three, in some learning communities), many students, many texts, and sometimes (particularly in the occupational classes we describe in the next section) a great variety of unfamiliar texts and writing activities.[4] The relationships among these elements can be configured in many ways—other than instructors lecturing to students—to teach students how to extract information and meaning from a text, and to use writing to communicate to others. The literacy practices of the classroom are therefore part of a pedagogical repertoire. In an institution that calls itself a teaching college, the ability to recognize and implement a range of literacy practices would be part of every instructor's pedagogical technique.

To illustrate the difference between literacy as a skill and literacy as a social practice, we can examine the activity of note taking. This is a conventional feature of college classrooms, a necessary "study skill" requiring the student to write in order to extract meaning from a lecture, film, lab demonstration, or workshop. Good note taking means that the student can reconstruct the class later, rethink it, continue to learn from it; poor note taking requires the students to rely solely on the limited power of memory.[5] Even in occupational classes where, for example, students are learning to disassemble machinery and reconstruct it, and where the pieces spread out on workbenches serve as a record of the work process, student notes can record instructor comments, trials and false starts, and the methods of appropriate reconstruction. (See the end of Section IV of Chapter 3, on the difficulty occupational instructors have in getting their students to take notes in workshops.)

Our understanding of note taking changes substantially when we conceive of it first as a skill and then as a social practice. The handbook *Rules of Thumb: A Guide for Writers* (Silverman, Hughes, and Wienbroer, 1990, 52–53), often used in study skills or remedial classes, devotes one and a quarter pages to note taking. It gives these instructions to students about how to take notes:

Listen for lead-in phrases.

Use one or two words.

Leave plenty of white space.

While your memory is fresh, re-read and fill in your notes.

Mark all the important points.

This is note taking as a skill. The individual student is addressed, and the instructions are technical—concerned with the form of the text being created or the process by which it is created. All instructions refer to actions. Based on these actions, a student could be said to be a good or indifferent note taker, and an observer could judge a student's note-taking skills.

However, the conception of note taking as a technical skill neglects the learning that may be taking place. Is a student merely copying the lecture, extracting individual facts from it, or developing some other, more complex understanding—perhaps even a disagreement? And how is the instructor shaping the classroom practices to facilitate (or inhibit) note taking? By concentrating only on the process of note taking—on note taking as a *skill*—we miss its real value in learning. Here, for example, are four very different classes in which students are taking notes from a lecture. The differences result from instructors' implicit decisions about what is important and what students should learn—differences that cannot be described simply by noting whether students "use one or two words" or "leave plenty of white space":

A guest speaker is lecturing to a transfer-level political science class on economic development in the Pacific Rim. The lecture is not clearly structured and the speaker is moving too fast for these students. Some students cover pages with writing; others take down an occasional item; many try for a while, then give up. Under these conditions, it is difficult to extract the main points, and there is too much arcane and unfamiliar material for students to follow. A few students have extensive notes from which they can study, but the rest have no means to capture what is being said.

An instructor in child development is lecturing to a class. She has put her lecture onto overheads, and projects them on a screen. Each overhead has only four or five lines of text; she covers all but one line of text at a time with pieces of paper, reads that line, and pauses while the students copy it down. The topics "covered" in about half an hour include types of day care programs, forms of assessment, and the physical development of children—a set of topics that might very well take several classes each. In the last topic, under "Gross Motor Skills," the overhead shows: "a) Flexability [sic] b) Agility c) Force." She says very little in addition to what is on the overhead. The students are all taking "good notes"—at least they have copied precisely what is on the overheads, leaving nothing out (and adding nothing, because there is nothing to add). In her interview, the instructors says that putting one line of text up at a time helps the students focus.

A microbiology instructor is lecturing to a class on the human immune system. He writes an outline of his lecture on the board as he progresses, eventually filling four boards with small, clear writing, but he is not dependent on his outline; he turns away from the board and steps close to the students to speak his lecture. The students alternate between taking notes, asking for clarification, and making comments. Many questions arise from the personal experiences of students: "My older daughter came down with flu but my son didn't." The instructor sweeps comments and questions into his lecture without missing a beat. Indeed, there is so much commentary from the class that the effect is almost like a solo voice rising above a chorus. Although students all write what is written on the board, they also write other comments as well, including what other students say. Students look over each other's notes while they listen, ask each other questions, comment among each other, and still take their own notes.

An instructor in U.S. history begins by asking the students what is in the newspaper that day. He then launches into personal recollections of World War II. His personal associations constitute the only thread of the class, which moves tangentially from one anecdote to another. The instructor makes no reference to any text. Occasionally students call out questions or the instructor asks them for comments. There is very little note taking going on; given the lack of logical structure, taking notes would be hard to do. In his interview, the instructor tells us that he views students as both naive and conservative and therefore wants to teach them that history is both "continuing and full of dislocations— not always progress." But he does not make this goal—the "dislocation" of the narrative—explicit in the wandering way he presents information in class.

Note taking has a different meaning in each of these four instances. What students can learn through note taking has been structured by the instructor in every case, but it varies enormously. In the first example, only students who followed the content of the lecture could take adequate notes. The rest could not keep up, and their notes would not be worth much as a resource for writing a paper or studying. The effect of the lecture was to sort prepared students from the unprepared, the "good" note takers from the rest—though the quality of note taking in this case was not a technical skill but rather reflected the way the lecture was presented. The social effect was competitive; if this lecture was required information for the course, it sorted students as effectively as a test.

In the second case, all students undoubtedly were "good" note takers, copying every word that appeared on the overhead. The social effect of the class was equalizing, not competitive, since every student succeeded in learning the same information. But the offering was minimal, and precious minutes slipped by in the service of providing time to copy down the "lecture." No interpretations or comments arose from either the instructor or the students, so the limited text on the screen had an absolute authority, unelaborated and uncontradicted.

In the third example, the running commentary by the students seemed to influence the lecture. Although a detailed outline was written on the board, which students could copy, the students and the instructor expanded the lecture as it went along, satisfying individual needs for clarification and engaging in some discussion while still proceeding with the overall plan. Everyone could take adequate notes, but students were also recording the elaborations made in discussion by other students and by the instructor in response to questions. They also looked at each other's notes and commented on them, pointing out what might have been missed or overlooked; that is, they gave each other technical information about how to take notes for this class. Note taking in this class was a cooperative rather than a filtering activity. There also seemed to be the possibility of challenging, or at least shaping, the lecture through student participation.

In the fourth example, the anecdotal ramblings of the instructor created a situation in which note taking was impossible. No one could produce a set of notes that would help them learn from the course. By default, other sources of information (like the textbook) must supply the material to be learned. The social effect of the class was neither cooperative nor competitive; it was simply empty for all students. Both badly presented, incoherent classes and overly difficult classes are inaccessible to students, and neither can be rescued by technical skill in note taking.

The social dimensions of each class varied markedly. In the political science class, students were on their own. They might later be able to share their notes, but in the first instance the practices of this class reinforced the success of some and the failure of others.[6] The students in the child development class were on their own, too, with no interaction among them. Only in the microbiology class was there some sense that learning is a collective endeavor. The student who asked a question for clarification, contributed an elaboration, or corrected or added to a neighbor's notes benefited others in the class as well. This class was a social experience in which learning was something students did together.

In addition, these four classes varied in the authority behind the information being conveyed and written down. The guest lecturer was the authority in the political science class, inviting no contribution from students at all and moving too fast for questions. The child development instructor also presented an authoritative lecture, inviting no question or interpretation. The other two classes invited participation by students, including disagreement and elaboration; in this sense, the interpretation of the subject was to some extent shared between instructor and students. However, because there was so little content in the history class, the collaboration could not contribute much to learning. Such classes may have an egalitarian aura, a sense that instructors and students are on the same footing, but the content has vanished.

Thus the actions of instructors and the implicit decisions they have made about teaching and literacy have shaped both the note taking of these lecture-oriented classrooms and what students can learn from this familiar practice. As we examine the variety of such practices, we will continue to emphasize the social dimensions of the classes we observed, as well as the issues of whose authority is involved. And we will continue to ask whether literacy practices constrain or open up opportunities for learning, a central question given the promise of the community college as an open-access teaching institution.

II. CONCEPTIONS OF LITERACY PRACTICE: FROM ACADEMIC TO OCCUPATIONAL

By now, the variation in approaches to literacy practices should be evident. In one pattern, particularly evident in literature, history, and political science, the instructor invites students to contribute their own interpretation of a poem or story, historical event, or current debate; there may be no single authoritative interpretation of what a text means or says. Writing in such classes provides students opportunities to present their arguments. They may bolster their views well or badly, with details that are more or less convincing, but there is no question that both reading and writing are practices that are simultaneously *social* and *interpretive*. They exist within a community of individuals, including the community of students in a particular classroom, potentially arguing with one another about the meaning of a story by Nathaniel Hawthorne or a passage involving the identity of black women. Most seminars and the synthetic lecture format we described in Chapter 2 take this form. Specific instances may succeed or fail— for example, the English seminar described in Section I of Chapter 2, which became a mere listing of literary movements and figures, or the anthropology class described in Chapter 2, which degenerated from understanding brick making into a recitation of anthropological vocabulary—but the intention to construct a class around social and interpretive practices is clear.

In a different pattern, lectures and readings are viewed as facts to be mastered by students, and writing is used to reinforce these facts. Common examples ask students to identify the main points in a reading (a favorite exercise in remedial/developmental classes as well) or to respond to the fact-oriented questions at the end of textbook chapters. The political science and child development lectures described in the previous section were instances of this approach. Many conventional lectures, the lecture/discussion that degenerates into lecture, and the lecture component of lecture/workshops are common examples we have already described. In these cases the lecturer, or the text, is the authority: "When you go to school, you have a book and that's the authority, that and the teacher." When learning takes the form of skills or facts to be mastered by individual students, questions and contributions not directed at clarification may be ignored—exemplified by the biology teacher described in Section IV of Chapter 2, who deflected questions that opened up new issues. There may be a tendency for science classes and occupational lectures to stress individual and authoritative approaches, but this is not necessarily the case; the microbiology class described in the previous section, the child development class examined in Section I of Chapter 2, and the biology instructor complaining about her students ("They have no understanding of what it means to know something; that facts don't equal knowledge") are counterexamples. Individual versus social conceptions of learning can be found in all disciplines, as can both authoritative and interpretive approaches.

However, when we move away from familiar academic disciplines, the conceptions of literacy and the uses of text are even more varied. These differences are *not* those of sophistication or level of difficulty: The texts in occupational classes are often written at a higher level of difficulty, with more complex and specialized vocabulary, than many academic texts. Writing is in many ways more demanding, since the work of others, the satisfaction of customers, and the health and safety of the workplace may depend on the precision of writing on the job—certainly a more urgent task than comparing and contrasting themes in literature.

Instead, the *kinds* of literacy practices differ between academic and occupational classes. Occupational instructors are primarily concerned with effective communication and clarity, not formal correctness. A cosmetology instructor told us, "We teach them: write as you speak, then go back and reread it and have someone else read it, to make sure it's clear." Standard English is not essential: Working-class English is often evident (sometimes shared between teacher and student), and foreign students are allowed to talk in their native languages among themselves in the interests of clarity. In academic classes, however, the correctness of grammar and presentation at the level of words and sentences is more highly valued. Even in those classes in which reading and writing are not the subject matter, students are graded on their ability to spell, write sentences, and prepare papers that meet traditional standards of presentation; communication is secondary. In academic classes, standard English is the only language typically allowed. Often middle-class teachers speak standard English while their students speak a variety of working-class English, black English, or the accented English of non-native speakers. "Correct" speaking patterns are among the implicit lessons of these classes.

In addition, academic and occupational classes differ in the conventions of authority, or who has the power to interpret a text and how that power is shared. In academic classes, the instructor often represents the discipline, modeling its typical patterns of inquiry and interpretation. The source of authority varies. In some disciplines (literature, drama, and history are good examples) debates over interpretation are common, and an "authoritative" interpretation is one with persuasive power. In science, hypothesis formulation and experimentation constitute the dominant form of inquiry. In the social sciences, argument usually builds on some combination of example and theory, and skillful instructors (like the economics instructor of Chapter 2) model such an approach. However, community college instructors have rarely had firsthand experience of new developments in a discipline—the consequence of being instructors in teaching institutions. Sometimes, therefore, the textbook is the source of information and authority, and this leads to textbook-driven instruction. In other cases, including some of the clearest examples of bad teaching, an instructor violates the interpretive conventions of a discipline. This occurs, for example, when a biology instructor treats science as facts rather than a method of inquiry, when a literature teacher treats a plot as facts rather than as a story with deeper meaning, when the psychology instructor mentioned in Chapter 6 converted an introductory class into pop psychology, or when the anthropology instructor in Chapter 2 reduced her discipline to a few slogans. Many examples of low standards in Chapter 6 are cases where instructors have given up the disciplinary approaches to inquiry and interpretation.

In occupational classes the instructor often models the social relations of the workplace rather than representing the conventions of a discipline, and therefore assumes authority not only for the text but also for the workshop. One instructor mentioned, "I act like the boss and they act like employees; after all, being a boss or supervisor is mostly teaching, anyway." (This was particularly true in classes that were dealer- or manufacturer-sponsored, as in the John Deere agricultural implements programs or Chrysler or Toyota automotive classes.) While this practice may mimic the authority relations of many workplaces, the dangers of this employer-centered perspective were apparent in several classes. In one, students were told that "OSHA inspectors have bad personalities; everybody hates them." In many cases, conflicts of interest between employers and workers were ignored or dismissed in a way that might reduce the likelihood of students expressing their legal rights (about safety hazards or labor standards, for example) in their future workplaces.

For some purposes, texts or manuals are authoritative. They often provide the definitive information on specifications, parts, procedures, building codes and other legal requirements, and the details of many models of cars or types of machine that no one person could possibly hold in memory. Instructors who claim that "everything you need to know is in this text" or warn that "the main thing is you know where it's at in your service manual" reflect this view of a text as an authoritative reference for certain types of information. Students are often encouraged to use texts (manuals, rate books, indexes, code systems) as the guarantors of their own authority in the workplace for which they are preparing. They are learning to be able to say, to a future customer or a supervisor, "I am correct because it says so right here in the manual."

However, for purposes other than serving as repositories of fact, the textbook is often superseded or extended by experience, either from the instructor or from the workshop. For example, the instructor who had written the "bible" of his occupation spent classroom time illustrating written material with examples from his own experience. In addition, textbooks and manuals get out-of-date, and again the experience and authority of an instructor generally override the text. An instructor in dairy herd management taught students to be skeptical of printed material, and told them:

> Carpentry and construction and other programs have set rules and regulation, inspection guidelines and so forth that they have to meet, whereas in the dairy business we basically have no rules or regulations when it comes to feeding the cows, breeding the cows, or any of the other management in getting milk out of the cows. It's economics all the way.

Texts in his field "go obsolete in a year," so he told his students, "Don't believe the text, listen to me." When he warned students to read labels, he nonetheless cautioned them,

> Never choose something that is lab-tested over something that has been tested on Joe's farm. If it has been tested on Joe's farm, it will work.

So the real world has too much variation to be tested adequately in any lab. Similarly, an instructor in a John Deere-sponsored class explained,

> There's no actual formal book that we have that we can say, "We'll do Chapter 1 today, and then we'll do Chapter 2." It's stuff that—I guess, being that I've worked at a dealership, I know some of the things that they're gonna need to know . . . when they get out to the dealership.

Therefore the locus of authority shifts between the instructor (based on his experience) and the text, with the balance between the two varying from class to class. However, the authority to interpret a text almost never shifts to the student. We saw no examples of students being encouraged to consider the history of a text, changing interpretations of a text, or (more importantly) disputes about a text, and we saw numerous classes in which instructors backed away from this kind of instruction. This is unfortunate since the professional discourse of an occupation includes the struggle over authority. When a text is an Occupational Safety and Health Act regulation, or a reading about ethics in biotechnology, or a manual that determines the rates of pay for different repairs, the history of disputes is important information for a student who will be entering a workplace and will have to judge a changing work environment.

Academic and occupational classes also vary in the types of texts that they use. The ability to draw information from a text or to write effectively is strongly related to understanding the type of text, or text structure, that is being used or produced. Isolating the formal aspects of text structure enables students to know what to expect and how to proceed when something they should expect is missing. In academic classes, the standard texts are typically narrative, the conventional storytelling form of fiction or exposition, the explanatory forms that dominate the sciences and social sciences. These are rarely taught explicitly; when instructors "go through the text," they usually do so in terms of content, not the text structure itself. Even though students in English classes are taught the technical forms of essays and research papers, they are not taught the text structures of the books they read, or how to use an index or a table of contents.[7]

In occupational classes, however, many more types of texts are present, including conventional textbooks, instruction manuals, reference books of many kinds, invoices, spreadsheets, lab reports, police and medical reports, rate guides, software documentation, blueprints, wiring diagrams, and maps. These are quite different from conventional academic texts; extracting information from them can be difficult but is usually essential to accomplishing a task. As an instructor in an aviation maintenance program responded to persistent student questions about whether they had to memorize something, "No—the FAA, United Airlines don't want you to memorize it, but you have to reference it." In occupational classes, students are explicitly taught to read and write the specialized texts they have to use; they practice how to extract the relevant information from bulky rate books, parts manuals, and other reference books. These are typically unique to a field or task, so a student learns the efficient use of a single type of manual, not manuals in general.

For example, students in an auto program were being taught to estimate the number of hours a job would require by using a flat-rate manual. This manual required understanding multilevel indexing, where a task is indexed under make, model, year, system, and item. Tasks combined with each other must be looked up in different parts of the manual and added up in different ways. During this class students were flipping back and forth through the manual, jotting down fractions of hours and adding them up; they were learning the text structure of the manual. Similarly, in an engines and fuels class, the instructor was showing students how to use a manual while students took notes on his instructions. As he asked them how to take a certain measurement, he cautioned, "You always have to look in the manual." Previously, the instructor had assumed that students from academic classes would have the skills necessary to use the manuals easily, but he discovered that not to be true:

> Most of the people don't come into our program with the kind of skills that you could expect in a political science class or something, where you come and you listen to a lecture and you read the book and then you can answer the question. No way.

It's unclear that any academic class would have prepared students for these manuals, but in any event this instructor had begun to teach the text structure of manuals explicitly. Similarly, an instructor in a CIS course spent the first week teaching students how to use the textbook, approaching it as a book that students would refer to constantly and needed to use efficiently.

The discourses of academic and occupational fields—the specialized language used in an area of study, with its characteristic vocabulary, conventions, and speech patterns—also differ substantially. People typically learn a specific discourse by participation, since its fine points are not often consciously known by those who speak it and cannot therefore be taught explicitly (Kramsch, 1993). In community colleges, academic classes rarely engaged students in the entire discourse of their fields—anthropology, art history, economics, biology—because at a community college these classes are usually introductory. In addition, they are often taught as general education courses rather than as courses for potential practitioners of the field. Very few instructors think that their students will become anthropologists, biologists, or economists, and therefore they don't "need" such technical detail. As one anthropology professor told his students, "You should be able to hang names on theories and have a general understanding of the theory—but I'm not trying to turn you into an anthropologist in one semester." A math instructor mentioned to us, "I'm not under the illusion that I'm creating statisticians at all. It's more of an appreciation." Indeed, we were struck by how often an academic instructor would disparage long words or say "You don't need to know that term" or "Don't bother about that." This was an indication of a course whose content was negotiated down (see Chapter 6 on standards), where everyday English substituted for technical terms and students were discouraged from engaging in the full discourse of the field.

However, occupational classes took a distinctly different approach. Students were expected to "talk the talk and walk the walk." They actually rehearsed in class the vocabulary, verbal practices, and register of the field they were studying. In many occupational classes, students actively participated in all areas of that field. For example, in an electron microscopy class students not only prepared lab reports and read texts but also wrote a newsletter, read professional journals, and attended conferences. In a child development class students not only read texts and kept journals but lobbied with state legislators for enforcement of fair labor standards in child care facilities. These "extracurricular activities" are much more common in occupational programs than in academic classes, and virtually all of them involve a wide range of literacy practices.

Finally, classes vary in their use of social arrangements, particularly small groups—and these variations highlight different conceptions of literacy. Organizing small groups in the best academic classes (especially history, philosophy, or literature classes) is usually intended to make texts more accessible and to encourage a variety of interpretations. Time spent in small groups is then followed by whole-class discussion comparing different interpretations. A typical example was a philosophy instructor who used small groups to let younger students discuss with older students issues "like who I am, what is the meaning of life, and is there a God." However, in most occupational areas—as well as in many science classes— the idea of competing interpretations is not common; instead texts are supposed to be precise and unambiguous.[8] With this assumption, science classes tend to use small groups to develop the correct interpretations of texts, as do many vocational classes. In addition, occupational classes use small groups to solve problems as a team, to rehearse rote learning, and to accomplish tasks that require the cooperation of several individuals, not to contrast different interpretations of a text. For example, a business calculus class paired students to work at computers to understand the solution to a problem that had already been solved by the computer program. There were no student-initiated questions, interpretations, or elaborations, as there would have been in an English or philosophy class, but merely an effort to understand the prepared solution.

The gulf between conceptions of literacy in academic versus occupational courses is not always recognized. Most of the time it makes no difference: Academic and occupational instructors go their own ways, and the isolation of instructors in their own departments and specialties means that there's little reason to debate the details of what literacy means. However, when academic and occupational instructors try to work together, then the differences become obvious. Increasingly this happens because of the widespread recognition that all occupational students need adequate levels of reading and writing, that the days are long gone when craft workers could get by on manual skills alone. But when occupational instructors turn to the academic side for such instruction, the difference in what reading and writing mean become apparent. As a dean of occupational instruction mentioned:

> Reading and writing are key, especially in the technical fields, because you can't survive in the job market without being able to read, write, speak, and present your ideas. . . . But when students get into a developmental reading or writing course, they see little application to their technical specialty.

Others said:

> That's where we lose our students—in basic skills, because they don't see the benefit of being there.

> My students say they don't want any damn English class.

These are partly complaints about the legacy of high-school English and math, where community college students have struggled and found themselves belittled, but they are also disagreements about the kinds of reading and writing that are necessary. On differences in reading, one auto instructor remarked:

> The automotive technology field is getting to be a much more cerebral, thinking-type field. In the olden days it used to be something you could just learn by doing. Nowadays it's something you have to learn by reading the books . . . but they can't read the textbooks, so we said they need to have an English class. But all the English department had to offer was a class in which students read short fiction, narratives, and essays such as newspaper editorials.

The nature of writing differs as well:

> Over in building inspection technology, we want the guys—and they are very much in a guy world over there—to be able to write their reports and do the checklist and turn it in, and you [English teachers] want us to read *Hamlet.*

An occupational instructor described the frustration of trying to coordinate academic and vocational courses:

> We have made overtures to the humanities division . . . to come up with a vocational writing class. Also I have talked with other humanities division members about this

once, and they were more entrenched in the tradition of all the reasons why it wouldn't work. . . . It wouldn't work because of this, it won't work because of that.

One humanities instructor acknowledged that the distrust of academic instructors by vocational instructors was grounded in real experience:

> [In the 1970s and '80s] we didn't have a way to have the technical/professional/vocational trades folk enter into the humanities, to see its value. And at the same time, the humanities side never had anything but disparaging words with respect to the skill and intelligence, if you will, that it takes to deal with a circuit board or to weld something or to draft and visually prepare to make or build something.

When an academic department standardizes content in the name of consistency, this may interfere with efforts to modify courses for occupational purposes. One English instructor taught a class within an automotive program to improve the reading and writing abilities of these students. (Automotive manuals are often written at a thirteenth- or fourteenth-grade level, parts manuals and instruction manuals for computerized diagnostic equipment are equally complex, and technicians have to complete a great deal of precise paperwork.) But the English department had not agreed to let her change the course outline; therefore students' grades had to be based 75 percent on standardized tests of grammar and 25 percent on paragraph writing. The instructor had to spend time on pronoun-antecedent agreement, faulty modification, and comma splices, and she had to use the six standardized tests that every other English teacher on campus gave. Although this instructor had managed to make the paragraphs in such tests deal with automotive content ("Explain the effects of misadjusting a carburetor"), the course outline was so rigid that she had little leeway in terms of subject matter. She found herself torn between remedying the poor showing her automotive students made on standard grammar tests and exploring their potential as writers:

> We stereotypically think of these students as not being academic, not intellectual. And to find that they are, in many ways, better writers . . . surprised me. Now, they're not better test takers. They're worse test takers. But they're much better writers. And that threw me for a loop.

But these barriers are endlessly frustrating, since the occupational side recognizes the need for certain "academic" skills—that is, certain forms of literacy—but they cannot get the right kind of cooperation from the academic side. As another instructor summed it up pithily:

If ac and voc don't start talking to each other, we're all gonna die.

We will return to the efforts to integrate academic and occupational education in Chapter 7, when we examine innovations in community college teaching. Some instructors have developed powerful ways of integrating related subjects in ways that respond to requirements in the workplace as well as the broader educational purposes of students. But such innovations are uncommon because the barriers to them are formidable—among them unacknowledged differences in what subjects require of reading and writing. In the absence of any forum to explore these differences, they manifest themselves as disagreements reflecting status and power differentials, as conflicts over "higher" and "lower" uses of literacy, as academics' "disparaging words" about the vocational side. A more fruitful discussion would acknowledge the variety of literacy practices, recognizing that all of them may be taught well or badly.

III. LITERACY PRACTICES BEYOND READING AND WRITING: THE PROBLEM OF EXPLICIT INSTRUCTION

So far we have examined only the most familiar kinds of literacy, reading and writing. These involve the interpretation and production of communications that rely on a symbolic system. In English these symbols are letters, and their meaning is not immediately apparent in the way that images or pictographs are; they have to be defined or explained, which is the process of teaching. But while symbols are arbitrary because they are not representational, they are precise because they have been defined in specific ways. Communities of practice (like English teachers, business managers, or automotive mechanics) use them in particular ways, too, so there are correct and incorrect uses. When literacy is defined in this way, then it extends well beyond reading and writing. It encompasses math, where numbers, signs of operation, algebraic notation, and various geometries represent mathematical concepts in specific symbols; computer codes, where various operations are represented by mnemonics (in some computer languages) or other symbols or specific ways of using familiar language (like GO TO statements); symbols for chemical elements, chemical bonds, and molecular structures; diagrams, maps, blueprints, musical notation, two-dimensional drawings, electrical diagrams, and diagrams for refrigerant flows. These symbols are contained not only in the familiar textbooks and readings, but also in manuals, legal documents, indexes, recipes, instructions from supervisor to worker or explanations from worker to customer, and virtually anything a student or instructor might write or draw.

This expanded conception of literacy makes visible the variety of literacy practices within community colleges. Obviously English classes depend on conventional reading and writing, as do social science and science classes; science classes develop their own special symbols; math classes use familiar mathematical notation; and economics classes have a particular form of symbolic representation in the demand and supply diagrams of microeconomic theory, and the IS-LM diagrams of macro theory. Occupational classes often use special forms of representation unfamiliar to the academic side. Here, for example, are some sketches of the different forms of literacy we observed:

A cabinetry instructor explains that students in his program begin with a blueprint reading and a drafting class—"the communications systems of the trade," he calls them.

A CIS instructor, when asked about whether he gives writing assignments to his class, pauses to think and then asks, "In English or programming code?" While he gives few assignments that require writing in conventional English, he acknowledges that industry is demanding "that we pay great attention to communication skills."

A building trades class in measurements and plane surveying is studying the plans for a new freeway interchange. The point of the class is to learn to read and produce maps of construction sites. Students are explaining to each other the meanings of symbols used in map production—sine, delta—and how to use a certain kind of calculator.

In an upholstery class, one student is being taught how to read a ruler, while another is learning how to measure along a curved surface using a tape measure.

In the corner of an aviation program's computer lab, students copy the following from a blackboard:
SPAVA/OVDPA 270003/TM1133/FLDRGD/TPBe90/SK012BKN020
This is a weather report. The instructor explains it symbol by symbol; for example, one set of symbols represents wind velocity. Students ask about the need to know all this, and the instructor concedes that many people make up their own abbreviations; he adds, "Therefore you have to learn all the basic ones and guess the rest."

The purpose of expanding the conception of literacy beyond conventional reading and writing is not merely to be inclusive. The more specialized forms of literacy in occupational courses create the same kinds of cognitive demands and pedagogical problems as the teaching of reading and writing. We are concerned with teaching strategies and the ways instructors handle different forms of literacy because they affect the opportunities for students to learn. Students who are being tested on conclusions they must draw from a diagram of economic demand and supply, or students assigned to find the error in a roof framing diagram, must successfully "read" these diagrams every bit as much as a student tested on a specific chapter must read the textbook. Students who can adequately extract information from a blueprint or electrical diagram or who can successfully represent information in a particular symbol system will do well in their courses and then—if their classes are appropriately designed—in subsequent classes, on the job, or in their roles as citizens or parents or community members.

In general, the way that students learn to "read" a code, diagram, notation, or any other form of symbolic system is the same. The symbol system is explained to them verbally, the relationship between a concept and its representation is clarified, and students practice with it until they become facile. This is the way children learn to read, though for most of us the technical features of reading—the letters and their sounds, the fact that text is read from left to right, what spaces between words and punctuation and paragraphs mean—have been learned so long ago that we have forgotten them. But for unprepared readers, these and other aspects of text that show up in classrooms—for example, line breaks in poetry, tables of contents, indexes, bibliographic entries—all have to be made explicit. What varies from class to class is not only the use of particular symbol systems but, more fundamentally, the extent to which instructors teach these kinds of literacy explicitly, rather than leaving them implicit for students to infer, learn from other students, or pick up on their own.

We found enormous variation in the extent to which symbol systems are explicitly taught.[9] One math instructor made this complaint about his peers:

> I have a pet peeve about math teachers in general: They are very sloppy in how they do their stuff. An example is the minus sign. Say you had that sign, and a four. Some people would say negative four. Some people would say minus four. And there is a third meaning, the opposite of four, the additive inverse. There are three different meanings for the same symbol. And my point is it's much like in English. If you were learning English as a foreign language, and one day somebody says to you *to-two-too*, three words that sound exactly the same, meaning entirely different things, it must drive them nuts. Why do people have so much trouble with that symbol? Because it means three different things. Nobody ever points that out to them. So early in my class, I stand up there and I make this distinction.

The failure to make explicit the technical features of a symbol system is a striking feature of many classes. Sometimes the technical feature is as simple as the organization of an index; students who have not used books with indexes don't know how an index is arranged. Sometimes it is as complicated as exposition, a text structure that takes varied forms in the sciences and social sciences; a sonnet, a memo, a five-paragraph essay, an academic research paper, an invoice, and a telephone directory are other distinctive text structures that can be found in community colleges. Most classes use several different kinds of text structures. For example, students in a psychology class may read a sermon, a political speech, and a conventional expository text; faced with an unfamiliar text structure to read, they are likely to be lost unless the technical features are made explicit. Their writing assignment is usually some kind of essay, and unless they know (or are explicitly taught) the technical features of the essay, they will not know how to produce it.

In the academic transfer or liberal arts classes we observed, students were rarely taught the technical dimensions of what they were supposed to read. In math classes, students were expected to know mathematical notation; in economics and statistics classes, they were usually expected to know Cartesian coordinate diagrams and Greek letter symbols, though instructors spent considerable time on the specialized diagrams that illustrate micro and macro theory. Some students were competent and even fluent at these prerequisites; students familiar with geometric displays and (in economics) demand and supply analysis could "read" diagrams as if they were paragraphs. However, learning the basic notation system (the graphing of functions in two dimensions) was not part of the content of the class. Failure to make the technical features of texts explicit closes off access to the information embedded in a text, and it constrains learning not on the basis of a student's willingness or ability to grasp content but on his or her ability to guess the meaning of a form untaught and therefore opaque.

The failure of academic teachers to make the technical aspects of literacy explicit is sometimes part of their conception of what it means to be a "college" teacher: If students are unprepared to read and write at the college level, they must go elsewhere, for example to a remedial/developmental class. This kind of tough attitude toward teaching reading and writing was expressed by an English instructor who said of his English 1 class,

> The buck stops here. I'm not going to lower my standards. I'm the bad guy. No one has ever been willing to say before, "You're simply not doing the work."

In other cases instructors are simply unaware that their students are unable to read and write with facility. This is particularly true for new instructors who, because of the complete lack of preparation for teaching in most colleges, come into the class-room without knowing anything about community college students. As one veteran instructor said of them,

> We see a lot of new teachers come in and they're appalled—"My goodness, you should see these terrible essays I'm getting." ... Young teachers really need to think how they feel about being at a nonprestigious institution where many of the students are underprepared, and they're going to have to think about why they chose that piece of the vineyard.

To be sure, some instructors do recognize these problems and manage to redress them in class, leading to the forms of "disguised remediation" we document in Section III of Chapter 5. In other cases of learning communities, an academic class is paired with a remedial course for precisely this kind of explicit instruction. Often students are sent to remedial classes or learning labs, a solution that generally separates instruction in reading and writing (or math) from instruction in different content areas, a problem we also examine in the next chapter. But if instructors fail to recognize the problem, students are likely to remain lost because they have not mastered the conventions of text.

A different pattern often emerges in occupational classes. These instructors usually spend considerable time on the symbol systems that are critical to that occupation—as in the vignettes we gave above of the different literacies in occupational classes, from blueprint reading to computer code to the conventions of CAD to the specialized language of weather reports. Sometimes an entire class is devoted to learning a notational system; teaching is explicit and focused on making new symbols or representations comprehensible. Students engage in a certain amount of drill, and their tests are often concerned with successful "reading" of specialized representations. Projects in the workshop provide other forums for explicit teaching and practice. Indeed, it would be unthinkable to separate these symbol systems from the content of occupational classes and teach them in separate "remedial" classes; this is done only with the three R's.

On occasion, occupational instructors spend time on explicit teaching of reading and writing. The CIS instructor mentioned above, who spent the first week teaching students how to read a relatively conventional textbook, was one example. However, it's more common for occupational instructors to refrain from teaching reading, writing, and math, since that kind of literacy is presumed to be the province of specialists. Instead, students are simply told to "get into the text-book and read," without any other help or oversight. One auto instructor said to his class in a threatening voice, "I don't know if you're reading *Auto Mechanic* at the library like I suggested." Another revealed, "I told them to read the textbook, but I wasn't going to lecture on it, just test on it. Some found out the hard way." If a student cannot read a text, the instructor might find a technological fix; for example, one instructor reshaped her teaching so that reading became unnecessary, and another got the library to tape-record an entire manual for a student who then went around the shop with earphones, listening to the tape. More commonly, they refer students to a learning center or to a remedial program. One instructor in child development said that her students had a hard time reading the textbook, but she didn't try to teach them how to read. Instead, she designed her lectures to "expand" the textbook, to explain it in different words and different contexts. If her students seemed to be having trouble reading, she sent them to a reading specialist "if that's a problem they're having." An instructor in electronics expressed a similar point of view:

> You simply present and encourage [reading], and you hope they absorb it, and if they don't, they have antibodies against it—you couldn't teach them to bury a fence post in a hole without getting it crooked.

A student who has not mastered reading is certainly not going to improve in this setting or master the occupational content, since all he or she will get is encouragement rather than instruction—and perhaps a negative attitude toward his or her potential. In fact, the dropout rate in this program was 90 percent, a rate that the instructor justified by comparing it to dropping out from the Air Force training glorified in *Top Gun*.

The tendency to refer students elsewhere is also connected to a vision of reading and writing as grammar and spelling, which English teachers are presumed to know but that occupational instructors often find discomfiting. Although students may need sophisticated communication skills to talk with and write to a variety of customers, suppliers, fellow workers, and government regulators, occupational instructors often think that literacy is to be gained through lessons in grammar and spelling. One occupational dean described instructors in these terms:

> Not that they can't have students write papers in classes, and so on, but they don't necessarily feel themselves competent as they grade for spelling, punctuation, grammar, syntax, you know, and their question is, "I'm a welding instructor—do I have to have a second specialty in English?"

The tendency for occupational instructors not to teach the conventional literacies compounds the problem, described in the previous section, of occupational faculty trying to collaborate with academic faculty to improve the reading, writing, and math of their students, but too often winding up frustrated when their conceptions of literacy fail to mesh.

By now we can see the complexity of literacy in the community college. Literacy may start with the three R's, but it quickly expands to a range of symbol systems that must be explicitly taught. Literacy may seem familiar and obvious, particularly to those of us who participate in the culture of books, but disagreements abound about what literacy really is, and therefore about how to teach it. But in most colleges there is no forum for any extended discussion of core teaching issues, no workshops or planning meetings or curriculum sessions where conceptions of literacy can be discussed. There is no venue where the similarities in various literacy practices can be recognized, as well as the deep differences in the use of conventional reading and writing, where the issues of explicit teaching versus referral to remedial courses versus assumed competency can be explored. When these issues emerge, they erupt as conflict—when one department imposes its conceptions on another, when one instructor criticizes another's version of a course, or when occupational and academic instructors do battle over teaching issues that they might have in common. Such conflicts are often ways of asserting power and drawing lines, rather than resolving the underlying issues. And so, by and large, the important decisions about teaching literacy practices get decided behind the scenes, in individual classrooms, in idiosyncratic conceptions of literacy and individual solutions to the difficult problems of teaching.

IV. THE FREQUENCY OF LITERACY PRACTICES AND THE FOCUS OF INSTRUCTION

By this point we have developed three distinct ways of describing the uses of literacy in classrooms:

• The *social* dimension ranges from instructors who treat literacy as a skill to be acquired by an individual to those who consider literacy to be social practice embodying different kinds of communication with others and appropriately taught through cooperative social interactions within the class.

• The *interpretive* dimension ranges from instructors who locate the authority for interpretation in a single authoritative source, usually the instructor or the text, and those who distribute the authority for interpretation among a number of sources, including students as well as the instructor or participants in disciplinary or political debates.

• The *technical* dimension ranges from explicit instruction in the arbitrary but codified rules for representation in symbols, whether of language or music, mathematics or electronic circuits, to a lack of instruction, where instructors tacitly assume that students have mastered these technical dimensions.

These three dimensions enable us to distinguish among different kinds of classes, and then to classify them into several categories. For example:

> In an auto class, the instructor teaches the text structure of a repair manual explicitly. The students work in pairs or teams to find information in the text, identify the source of a problem, or fill out a repair order. The instructor is the only one to determine what a good repair order should look like and what information it should contain.

We would call this a socially cooperative, technically explicit, authoritative class.

> A psychology instructor expects students to read certain chapters from the textbook without being told how the book is organized; then they are tested on the chapters without having discussed them in class with other students. The instructor is the only one who decides whether answers are right or wrong.

We would call this class individual and technically tacit, with an interpretively authoritative treatment of literacy practices, since there has been no sharing of access to reading and writing and no explicit teaching of the technical aspects of text.

> A remedial/developmental composition class reviews how to organize a paragraph students were assigned to write, with students in small groups discussing their paragraphs as they develop them. The instructor encourages students to understand the poem upon which the paragraphs are commenting in a variety of ways, situating it historically and culturally in terms of their individual experiences.

We would call this class technically explicit (because students are being told explicitly how to organize the paragraph), socially cooperative (because they are learning from each other), and interpretively distributed, because the authority to interpret the poem is distributed among the students.

Using the more conventional terms in which teachers and commentators discuss teaching (and which are presented in Chapter 2), the second class was clearly a conventional didactic, teacher-centered class; the third class was a constructivist, meaning- and student-centered class. However, the three dimensions of literacy practices mean that we cannot simply sort classes into didactic or constructivist. In the first class, for example, the class was didactic and top-down as far as the text is concerned; students did not get to invent their own interpretations of the repair manual. Yet there were significant differences between the psychology class and the auto class, which was also didactic, because the auto instructor explicitly taught the technical aspects of the text—where certain information was located in the book, how to fill in blanks in the repair order, how to present the repair order to a customer—while the psychology instructor assumed that students could read the text on their own, without explicit instruction or discussion.

The most common configuration in all categories of classrooms except remedial classes was tacit, individual, and authoritative, accounting for 41 percent of the classes we observed.[10] In these cases, students were not being explicitly taught how to read or write the relevant texts, were not being encouraged to engage with each other to make a text more accessible by discussing it, and were not being encouraged to develop their own interpretations of a text. This is the standard didactic classroom, where students who are unfamiliar with the forms of literacy being used receive no help from the instructor in how to read or write (though they may be sent to a tutoring center or remedial class). To make the simplest statement about the literacy practices in community colleges, students in two fifths of all classes are not encouraged to develop their own interpretations of texts, are not encouraged to share information or rehearse with each other the development of their literacy skills, and receive little or no instruction in understanding the technical features of complicated text structures.

Classes of this type have two central problems: how to convey material to students without enabling them to get information on their own (because the technical aspects of texts are not taught explicitly), and how to get students to grasp an interpretation without enabling them to develop it themselves. Instructors had different strategies for handling these problems. One was simply to lecture, let students take notes, assign reading and writing, test or grade students on it, and let the students' grades fall where they may; these instructors tended to grade on a curve. In such classes, students' success depended heavily on the abilities that they brought with them to the classroom, and these instructors were often ones who complained about underprepared students. (This was the strategy of the instructor who noted that "typically, there isn't any diversity after four weeks" in his classes.) A second strategy was to simplify the material to a level where students were able to memorize it. Instructors in these classes prepared basic outlines (like that in the child development class described in Section I above) or summaries of textbooks, accompanied lectures with overhead projections with only a few words on them, required little in the way of note taking, and gave simple multiple-choice tests. A final strategy was to enrich the classroom with a variety of materials, but without ever letting go of the instructor's prerogative to determine their meaning. In these classes students not only listened to lectures, took notes, and did the usual reading; they also viewed videos or film, saw slide shows, heard guest speakers, went on field trips, and spent time in computer labs working on computerized tutorials. While didactic, these classes were clearly enriched experiences for the students. However, the first two strategies represent different ways in which instructors have given up on teaching—either leaving large portions of the class behind or giving everyone in the class very little to learn. The most common approach to literacy, therefore, has some evident pitfalls.

Of all classes, 74 percent follow an authoritative approach to interpretation, regardless of their approach on technical and social dimensions. Either the instructor or the text is the central authority, and students are being asked to accept this authority rather than to create their own understandings or to participate in their own education. Arguably, some subjects require such an approach, particularly occupational subjects where there is a standard practice or orthodoxy, and in fact 82 percent of occupational classes were authoritative, compared to 66 percent of academic or transfer classes. But there is no logical necessity for some subjects to take an authoritative approach. The issue within the classroom is whether or not instructors invite students to weigh alternatives to their interpretation of the text or of practice. Skillful instructors do this as a way of leading students to understand the reasons behind a particular understanding or procedure, even in cases where one interpretation dominates all others.

These authoritative classes are not always the extremely teacher-centered, didactic classrooms that many instructors belittle as "just lecturing." Many are examples of hybrid teaching: Instructors have incorporated some small-group work and other forms of more cooperative learning, or they have leavened their delivery of content with some explicit instruction in reading and writing or the other literacies that may come up, so that students are less likely to be left behind.[11] But whatever other student-centered practices they may incorporate, instructors in this majority of classes have not ceded any authority to students, and so the maxim that adults should participate in their own education—often expressed as the need for "active" learning—is consistently violated.

An issue in authoritative classes is that, for various reasons we explore more fully in Chapter 6, they may fall apart. Of all the classes we coded, about one quarter (62 out of 250) seemed to be troubled in ways that we call "distressed" or "collapsed." In some cases students were simply not cooperative or respectful; they came late, talked in class, slept or read newspapers, and otherwise failed to participate. In other classes the trouble was overt: Students were gratuitously disputatious, and instructors resorted to getting angry at them, perhaps insulting them in some way or asserting procedural authority ("Take out your pencil and paper") in order to stop a discussion that had gotten out of control. Almost all of these empty classes (55 of the 62) were those in which instructors were attempting to hold onto the authority to decide what texts meant, rather than encouraging students to develop their own ability to interpret texts. As common as authoritative approaches are, they contain the germ of their own undoing: Adult students in particular may resist the passive role they are assigned in these classes.[12]

At the other extreme, 17 percent of all classes followed the pattern of explicit, cooperative, and distributed approaches to literacy.[13] In these cases, instructors are providing students with explicit instruction in the literacy practices they are expected to improve; they assume that literacy is a social and communicative competence developed through cooperative practices in classrooms; and they invite students to participate in interpreting the materials used in these subjects. These are the clearest examples of the student- and meaning-centered classes described by instructors in Chapter 1, the practices to which many instructors say they aspire. They have the added benefit that instructors are being explicit about the technical aspects of the texts they are using, something particularly important for underprepared students.[14] These are also the practices that, instructors report, they develop after years of experience, through the processes of trial and error and learning from colleagues that we documented earlier.

When we look at the literacy practices in community college classrooms carefully, then, we find a number of troubling patterns. One is the disjunction between how instructors say they want to teach and how they actually teach. While many instructors (and orthodoxy in adult education) hold that students must take charge of their own education, the overwhelming majority of classes are taught so that the instructor or the text is in charge—so that students are *not* being invited to become independent readers, able on their own to make sense of the many standard and nonstandard texts.[15]

Other troubling patterns emerge because of the isolation of community college instructors—the lack of adequate discussion and professional development that would allow them to develop a critical understanding of teaching and the institutional conditions and relentless schedules that influence how they teach. While didactic practice and lecturing are widely criticized (as we saw in Chapter 1), a more nuanced view of pedagogy as it emerges in literacy practices is not widely shared. There is, for example, little recognition among instructors that many classroom problems are actually reading problems. We found little recognition among instructors (except some occupational instructors) of the need to teach new and unfamiliar text structures explicitly, rather than assuming students could transfer conventional narrative or expository forms to new applications. Incompatible approaches to literacy coexist in neighboring classes—yet with little recognition of the two approaches and little discussion between adherents of the two. Particularly in occupational classes, we found little appreciation of how much reading—of symbolic systems such as maps, blueprints, diagrams, weather codes, and technical notation, as well as of words—takes place, even though occupational instructors are generally more careful than academic instructors to teach such literacy practices explicitly. But since they view reading and writing as the domain of specialists, they are likely not to teach these kinds of literacies explicitly, even though their subjects require such competencies, often at highly sophisticated levels.

The conflicts that sometimes emerge—between occupational and academic instructors when they try to integrate their content, as well as among instructors in various subjects related to literacy—are testimony to the lack of discussion within most colleges.[16] These conflicts are not usually productive, because they do not continue long enough for the participants to understand what conceptions of literacy are at issue and how different perspectives can be bridged. Instead, they often result in decisions that simply reinforce the battle lines. Occupational instructors continue to think of their academic peers as impossible without reforming them, or those teaching literacy as social practice deride drills in grammar and spelling without changing the minds of more conventional English teachers.

In most colleges it would take a significant shift of institutional resources to produce enough time and space in the daily work of instructors to enable them to reflect on their practices, the opportunities they afford their students to learn, and the compatibility of practices among instructors. However, an institution that calls itself a teaching college must be prepared above all else to address the literacy practices that are the core of formal schooling. We return to this subject in Chapter 8, when we examine how most colleges structure the positions of instructors and use their institutional resources to influence teaching.

NOTES

1. For the argument that literacy is the foundation of formal schooling in many cultures, see Cook-Gumperz, 1986; see also the illustrations in Gardner, 1983.

2. See especially the description of the developmental studies department in North County Community College in Chapter 5, Section IV.

3. When the classroom is a student and a book, as it sometimes is in remedial education using programmed texts, or with computer-based remedial programs, literacy is always being viewed as an individual skill.

4. Our conception of literacy practice is derived from sociocultural theorists such as Scribner, 1984, Scribner and Cole, 1981, Hull, 1993a, Street, 1984, Myers, 1996, Heath, 1983, and Rose, 1989. For a more detailed analysis of this literature and its value in identifying literacy practices, see Worthen, 1997, Ch. 3.

5. See especially Ong, 1982, on the powerful transformations in shifting from purely oral practice to literate practice.

6. The normal relationships in a community college, dominated by nonresident students with erratic schedules and few courses in common, discourage this kind of sharing. Indeed, one of the

clearest advantages to students of the learning communities described in Chapters 5 and 7 is that they facilitate such exchanges.

7. There were a few exceptions, however. In a Muslim world history class, students explained the structure of their arguments in oral presentations, clarifying that they had been taught expository text structures and could reproduce them in their own writing.

8. The one important exception is the problem of datedness, an issue in both science and occupational areas, modifying the idea that a text is always authoritative.

9. Explicitness is a dimension of teaching that has rarely been mentioned. One exception is Delpit, 1986. She has pointed out that when teachers fail to make certain aspects of standard English explicit, including conventions of grammar and punctuation in writing, children who speak black English are likely to be barred from learning standard English. Her argument is essentially one for a hybrid approach, in which teachers working from a constructivist tradition should remember the importance of explicit teaching of standard pronunciation and grammar to students who otherwise have no access to these aspects of language.

10. These include 46 percent of occupational classes and 47 percent of academic or liberal arts classes. A relatively low proportion of remedial classes (12.5 percent) fall in this category, because they are more likely to be explicit about the technical aspects of literacy; 88 percent of remedial classes are explicit, while only 36 percent of other classes were. Of the 285 classes we observed (see Table A-1), we were able to include 250 in this analysis; the remainder lacked sufficient information to classify. These results are more carefully presented in Worthen, 1997, Ch. 6, especially Figure 1, from which all these percentages can be derived.

11. Of all classes we categorized, 74 percent were authoritative. However, 12.4 percent were authoritative/cooperative/explicit, 10 percent were authoritative/cooperative/tacit, and 11.2 percent were authoritative/individual/explicit—all forms of hybrid instruction—while the remaining 41 percent within the authoritative/individual/tacit category best illustrate the extreme kind of didactic, teacher-centered, behaviorist teaching.

12. We suspect that this same problem underlies much of the overt difficulty in many high schools. Community colleges experience less of this because students are there voluntarily. In addition, in some regions of the country—particularly the Midwest—students seemed to be so well socialized to this passive role that signs of rebellion and "distressed" classes are almost nonexistent.

13. These include 34 percent of remedial/developmental classes but only 15 percent of other classes, buttressing our contention in Chapter 5 that remedial classes include both the best and the worst teaching we observed.

14. Classes that are cooperative and distributed comprise 23 percent of all classes, and they might be said to be student- and meaning-centered. However, in fourteen of these fifty-seven classes instructors were not being explicit about the literacy practices they expected of students; if students do not enter the class well prepared, then instructors are expecting them to interpret materials that they do not fully understand.

15. We note that the rhetoric about lifelong learning, sometimes vapid, often refers to pedagogical practices intended to create autonomous learners. But without the approach to interpretation we call distributed, this cannot take place—and indeed it fails to take place in 75 percent of the classrooms we observed.

16. It doesn't help that in many community colleges there may be as many as four departments closely connected to reading and writing: a reading department, a writing department, a remedial or developmental education division, and an ESL department. See, for example, Section V of Chapter 5 for the divisions among instructors in the institution we call North County Community College.

5

REMEDIAL/DEVELOPMENTAL EDUCATION

The Best and the Worst

Remedial/developmental education is one of the most controversial aspects of higher education.[1] Virtually all two- and four-year colleges provide some form of remedial education, though the amount is especially high in community colleges. Estimates of the proportion of coursework devoted to remedial education have ranged from 25 percent to nearly 80 percent.[2] Many observers blame the deteriorating conditions of urban schools, exacerbated by increases in the number of children born into poverty. Large numbers of immigrants also contribute to expanding enrollments, even though many of these students would be served better in programs aimed at second-language learners.[3] No one thinks that the need for remedial education will wither away soon.

As large as remedial education has become, its very presence in postsecondary education is controversial. Periodically, both two- and four-year colleges—or the legislators responsible for public funding—propose eliminating it entirely and handing these responsibilities to adult education or voluntary programs. The efforts in 1998 by Mayor Rudolph Giuliani of New York to eliminate remediation from all colleges in the City University of New York system is merely the most contentious episode in a long-running controversy, often pitting budget cutters and those upholding academic standards against faculty arguing for underserved and underprepared students. Even as it survives and expands, remediation is a low-status activity, the custodial or housekeeping department of college-level instruction (Traub, 1994). Prestigious upper-division institutions try to make it invisible, isolating it in tutorial centers or shifting it entirely out of four-year institutions into adjacent community colleges or adult education programs. Within community colleges, remediation is usually organized as an activity separate from the core

purposes, isolated in a jigsaw puzzle of developmental reading and writing departments and tutorial programs.[4] And so a central questions is whether remedial education should be maintained within any institution that calls itself a college.

These opposing points of view are, not surprisingly, evident among community college faculty as well. Though most instructors are quite sympathetic to their
students, a few seem to think the task of teaching underprepared students is hopeless. As one instructor lamented, speaking in the language of student deficit:

> These students are the most needy, the most undereducated, and often limited by
> disabilities. It's not uncommon to find a student who has allegedly studied some-
> thing like parts of speech for several weeks who still identifies *a* as a verb. What to do
> with these students in a postindustrial world is a real quandary.

Others described students as being "not college material," or viewed their primary
role as gatekeepers, performing quality control in a flawed production system that
had let too many unqualified students pass too far down the line. "The buck stops
here; I am the bad guy," said one English 1 instructor, cheerfully acknowledging
that he failed a high percentage of his students. Others saved themselves from
boredom by putting technology between themselves and their students. As one
instructor told us:

> I didn't want to be a junior-high-school or high-school teacher, dealing with gram-
> mar, dealing with basic sentences and paragraph-level writing skills. . . . But the thing
> is, using the computer, it's the technology and the potential of this technology . . .
> What I'm doing is putting the computer between me and the student in terms of
> these kinds of basic repetitive activities that are so necessary for these students, who
> either have not had exposure to instruction in their basic language skills, or else they
> had it in ways that just didn't take.

On the other hand, some administrators and instructors see the task of remediation as the heart of what they are there to do, given the role of community
colleges as open-access institutions. The head of a developmental-studies department reflected on the purpose of her department: "You have to go back to the mission of the community college, and the mission is to take students where they are
and bring them up to the freshman level if you can." One instructor, in a state that
prohibits students from taking transfer-level courses until they have passed basic
skills requirements, said:

> I want my students to feel that they have a voice and that voice fits into the institu-
> tion. Students who are in our classes have expressed the desire to move into higher

education in a more formal way. And that requires that they meet the demands of formal education.

Her view of how this was to be accomplished combined the practical and the religious:

> I'm a Methodist, and Methodists believe this: that we are going on to perfection. You just keep going on and getting better and better. That's what developmental studies is—it's the most Methodist of all disciplines.

For an instructor with this perspective, bridging the gap between the competencies students bring with them and those they need do well in the classroom and in society is crucial to making them useful members of society. Another instructor, in an automotive program where students needed basic reading, invoked a more familiar cost-benefit argument:

> We as a people living together, we got three choices. We either educate these people so that they can go to work and get a good job and become productive citizens and in turn educate other people ... and keep the cycle going, or we can pay to keep them on welfare, or we can pay to lock them up. Either way, we're going to pay. The cheapest deal is education. The most expensive deal is the big house, forty thousand a year.

Another occupational instructor reinterpreted the meaning of "underprepared" in describing his students:

> A lot of time, instructors in different curriculums will say, "Well, Joe Blow should not have been in my class; he should be in pot walloping or basket weaving or something." My contention is that in my class, I will bend over backward to help them.... I will tell the student when they first come to class, "I don't care what area we are in, if you take me out of my environment and put me in your area, I would be all thumbs until I caught on. It's not that I don't have the intelligence to do it." It's the same way in the classroom.

The contrast between dismissing some students as "not college material" and finding a religious or social motive for basic skills instruction is one of the central debates within the open-access college. But it's not openly debated, as least not in the realm of practice; it's yet another issue that—with a few notable exceptions, like the innovative efforts described in Section IV—most institutions leave to individual instructors. As usual when institutions do this, we saw a great range in remedial classes. We found both the best and the worst teaching—the most inspired student- and meaning-centered approaches and the most deadly drill-and-kill classes. These different approaches often embody different conceptions of literacy as well as conceptions of learning, replicating the distinctions between literacy as a skill and literacy as a social practice that we examined in Chapter 4.

We also found remediation in some surprising places. We have taken the following as our definition of remedial/developmental education: "a class or activity intended to meet the needs of students who initially do not have the skills, experience, or orientation necessary to perform at a level that the institution or instructor recognizes as 'regular' for those students."[5] When the *institution* defines the skills necessary for "regular" or college-level instruction, it usually does so with standardized tests and the procedures we describe in Section I. The college then assigns students to courses formally considered remedial, examined in Section II. But when *instructors* recognize the need for remediation, even in courses that are not formally remedial, these activities take place in other guises, as we show in Section III. Sometimes this happens when an instructor finds herself with large numbers of students unprepared for college-level work—for the reading and interpretation of literary texts that dominate most English courses—and simply converts a transfer class into a remedial course. Sometimes support courses—like technical math or business English—become remedial/developmental courses rather than sophisticated approaches integrating academic and occupational content. In yet other classes, instructors manage to address heterogeneous skill levels by weaving remedial activities and content into both academic and occupational classes. In such cases it becomes clear that the intellectual challenges of remediation, to both students and instructors, are comparable to those of teaching higher up the academic ladder. While the status of remediation is low and its claim on resources is uncertain, as an intellectual task it is no less difficult and absorbing than the other forms of teaching.

When critics bemoan the "dumbing down" of higher education, they usually refer to academic courses in which the content has been negotiated away, as we describe in Chapter 6, or to courses that have been converted into remediation, as we describe in Section III of this chapter.[6] But they are not usually referring to remedial courses that have been carefully structured to redress the problems of underprepared students. Once we recognize the distinction between an unsystematic collapse of student and instructor expectations and a rigorous course of remediation, then we can see that developmental education is one of the most difficult teaching challenges and needs to be rescued from its second-class status.

I. SORTING INTO REMEDIAL PROGRAMS: THE POWER OF STANDARDIZED TESTING

In most community colleges, entrance into the official world of remediation is governed by tests, usually given upon enrollment. These tests—usually standardized multiple-choice tests such as the TABE, ABLE, CASAS, ASSET, or COMPASS tests produced by American College Testing (ACT)—sort students according to their scores on reading, writing, and math components. In addition to these standardized tests, a few colleges create their own assessment tests. Often these are wholistically graded writing samples, in which students are given a simple statement (a "prompt") and then write for twenty to thirty minutes. These short essays are graded by faculty from developmental or English departments. Such tests are arguably more appropriate assessments than standardized tests, since they are created by instructors who will teach the students sorted by such writing samples; they can be tailored precisely to the competencies instructors are looking for in college-level classes.[7] But such time-consuming procedures are rare compared to standardized tests, which are cheap, quick, and widely accepted.

The ways tests are used vary widely, and their ability to influence students' careers is enormous. In many colleges, students who score below certain thresholds on these tests are simply directed toward remediation. While some students badly need such programs, the courses may take them six months, a year, or longer to complete. Faculty sometimes complain of "permanent" remedial students who never complete remedial coursework, never get to start college-level classes, and make little progress toward their academic or vocational goals. For low-income students, those who have work or family responsibilities, or those who may be on time-limited financial aid (as welfare has become), the requirement to take extra courses is especially perilous. These students are caught in a dilemma: They may need remediation and may not be able to finish their college programs without such classes; but the extra time required, the drudgery of many courses (described in Section II), and the lack of any connection to their academic or vocational ambitions may knock them out of college altogether.[8]

There are other ways of using diagnostic tests. In California, because of a challenge from the Mexican-American Legal Defense and Education Fund (MALDEF), tests may be used for advisory purposes only, but not to require remedial coursework.[9] In Texas the TASP must be taken before the tenth hour of classes; those who score below a certain level are allowed to take remedial courses concurrently with transfer courses, but if they fail a remedial course they are dropped from all transfer courses, losing credit for those courses even if they have been doing well. Sometimes entrance tests are used for other directive purposes.

At one college, the TABE was used to determine whether students could enroll at all: "If they don't test at tenth grade [level], they go to a neighboring adult education program." Given the low quality, unsystematic pedagogy, and short duration of most adult education, such a decision—essentially an entrance exam, contrary to the image of the community college as an open-access institution—is likely to push some students out of postsecondary education altogether. And sometimes entrance exams are used to direct students into one program over another. Certain high-demand health programs, particularly in nursing, often have such entrance requirements. In one college an elite program in agricultural machinery, sponsored by John Deere, used a test as an initial filter:

> We give them the ASSET tests. If they don't score well, we'll have them take the [remedial] academic class, and then if they still don't score well, we'll steer them into the diesel program.

But never did we uncover a procedure where test scores were combined with more deliberation—for example, counseling or (particularly for "experimenters") a longer process of exploring alternatives within the college—to decide whether remedial coursework is appropriate.[10]

In using these initial tests, colleges assume that they are valid measures of the ability to do college-level work, or to benefit from an agricultural machinery program instead of diesel repair, for example. But the value of these tests is the subject of much confusion. Administrators at several colleges indicated that they had carried out informal studies of validity and found no correlation between ASSET reading scores and subsequent student grades in transfer-level courses; one remedial instructor mentioned that the TASP "has no predictive validity; it only tells whether or not the student is ready for college-level work." But a test without predictive validity cannot be used to measure the need for remediation, and colleges have rarely carried out the analyses necessary to validate such tests. Administrators at two colleges confided that the validity of these tests as predictors of academic success was spotty—for example, they were predictive for psychology but not for sociology—suggesting that the classroom practices of different courses rather than student ability might influence their validity.

Although standardized placement tests are virtually universal, instructors remain ambivalent about them. While conceding that "they do tell you something," faculty readily admit that they are not sure precisely what tests measure. Tests seem to assess a combination of test-taking skills, command over standard English (a feature that is especially unfair to non-native speakers), and knowledge of the technical features of both written English and arithmetic procedures, but they cannot distinguish among different kinds of errors.[11] And they certainly cannot diagnose the specific language and mathematical skills that specialized classes, such as occupational classes, need. For example, one automotive instructor complained not about problems in reading and writing but about more technical uses of language and math:

> What it really is, we can't use slang like we used to. We have to change our act in automotive. I don't mean foul words, just automotive language. . . . You know, if I said in the past "O_2," I have to say now "oxygen sensor."

A different math-related difficulty would not require traditional remediation:

> We'd tell them to go out and get the VIN number off the car, the vehicle identification number. I'd ask for the eight digits. And they keep coming back with the wrong one. And I found out that the Vietnamese kids were reading from right to left.

For such instructors, the diagnostic value of conventional entrance tests is quite limited.[12] And when specialized tests are used, with more precise diagnoses, the college may not be able to respond. One college gave a special workplace readiness test but found it didn't have any way of teaching listening skills:

> [According to this test] the jobs request that students be at a 7 for listening skills, but we have tested these students and they're really only at a 3, so even though you have English Comp 1, 2, and 3, it doesn't mean that they have listening skills. . . . So you haven't overeducated them—you've educated them to have a certain set of skills, but not the right skills.

But the main criticism from instructors is that these entrance tests, unlike locally developed writing samples, cannot improve teaching. Because they are proprietary and confidential, many instructors have no idea what they test and cannot judge their appropriateness for initial placement. Since the detailed results are secret, instructors cannot use the information generated by them to tailor instruction—for example, by creating remedial programs that address the particular problems students have. Instead, the tests are used to dump students into all-purpose remedial courses that may or may not address the competencies that students lack. Not one college we visited reported using a second round of standardized tests to check for improvement in scores following remediation, even though such a follow-up test is offered by at least one test purveyor.[13] And so colleges assume both that standardized tests can predict the ability to do well in

Table 5.1

Five-Year Outcomes for Degree-seeking Students Entering Fall 1989, Miami-Dade Community College

Needing remediation in:		Did not complete remedial coursework	Completed all remedial courses
No areas	N	(not applicable—	2,581
(N=2,581)	Graduated	no remediation	45%
	Still enrolled	needed)	14%
One area	N	638	1,097
(N=1,735)	Graduated	7%	28%
	Still enrolled	10%	24%
Two areas	N	633	485
(N=1,118)	Graduated	5%	16%
	Still enrolled	12%	34%
Three areas	N	672	218
(N=890)	Graduated	2%	9%
	Still enrolled	11%	40%

Source: Morris,1994, Table 6. "Still enrolled" includes only those with a GPA of 2.00 and above.

"college-level" courses and that their remedial courses improve the performance of students—without checking on either assumption. It is likely that these diagnostic tests are both overinclusive and underinclusive: They direct into remediation many students who won't benefit from remediation, at least for their purposes, but they also fail to diagnose the needs of other students whose problems are not measured well by standardized tests.

It's inappropriate, however, to conclude that just because conventional tests are not carefully validated, they consistently misdirect students into remedial education. At Miami-Dade Community College, which has been much more careful than most colleges about evaluating its remedial program, the results indicate that students who are diagnosed by conventional tests as needing remediation but do not complete the appropriate courses are less likely to complete programs or pass the state's CLAST (a rising junior exam required for entry into four-year college). As Table 5.1 indicates, students diagnosed as having one deficiency increased their chances of completing an associate's degree from 7 percent to 28 percent if they completed the appropriate remedial course; students with two deficiencies who completed the necessary courses increased their chances from 5 percent to 16 percent. But at the same time, 63 percent of students judged to have one deficiency and 76 percent of those with two failed to complete the appropriate remedial courses. Furthermore, even those who completed remedial coursework were more likely to be still enrolled five years after entering, and this longer period is both costly (in time, money, and energy) and likely to decrease their long-run chances of completing. These developmental programs have clear value, therefore, but they have substantial costs as well, and both underinclusion and overinclusion are detrimental to student progress.

Conventional testing as a mechanism of diagnosing the need for remediation is, we think, a subject that merits more discussion. In an institution committed to the progress of its students, the assignment issue—the ways of assigning students to courses such as remediation that may benefit them, but may also impede their progress or even direct them out of postsecondary education altogether—would be part of an active debate about how best to educate underprepared students.[14] We suspect that the successful resolution of this discussion would establish decision mechanisms more elaborate than simple multiple-choice tests, for example by involving counselors and by encouraging and training faculty to advise. Such discussions could also link debates about remedial instruction itself—the subject of the next two sections—with debates about the most appropriate diagnostic methods, rather than leaving them independent as conventional practice now does.

II. THE "EMPIRE OF REMEDIATION": THE VARIETY OF PRACTICE

Once students are diagnosed as lacking the competencies necessary for regular courses—or, to be more exact, once they fall below some score on a diagnostic test—then they are directed to courses labeled remedial or developmental. The "remedial" label implies that such courses remedy a lack of skills, and the pejorative connotations—blaming students for their "deficiencies"—have caused many to avoid this term. The alternative label, "developmental," stresses the further development of competencies that students bring to college, and avoids the negative implications of remediation (Goto, 1995). But what counts, after all, are the practices within classrooms, and the labels matter much less than the ways instructors approach their task.[15]

Formal approaches to remediation show up under many different course names. The most obvious are the stand-alone classes in reading, writing, math, and study skills designated in the college catalogues as remedial, developmental, or basic. Usually they carry no college credit, and they are articulated in a sequence of two or three courses leading up to the first college-level course. A second type of remedial course is the stand-alone support class linked to occupational areas, often with content appropriate to related occupations, and sometimes modified to meet occupational demands ("They'll have to do this kind of thing on the job"). These include courses called applied math, technical math, business English, essentials of communication, and other similar titles; one college has designated sections of remedial courses as "especially appropriate for" certain occupational students. In addition, as we clarify in Section IV, learning communities often include remedial language or math courses. While these tend to have conventional titles, they can be linked to the other courses in the learning community, with their content modified accordingly. Finally, most colleges have learning labs where students can come, either on their own or directed by counselors or instructors, to work on particular skills. These typically have self-paced workbooks and computer programs that are among the most extreme forms of skills-oriented teaching, and they assume that students are both motivated and capable of working on their own.[16]

Because of the variety of remedial efforts, which fall under various course titles, it's difficult to estimate how much formal developmental education there is within individual colleges. Administrators in our sample admitted that the proportion of students in remediation ranged up to 72 percent in math and 30 percent in reading at any one time. The magnitude of remediation may be a function of how conventional courses are structured and funded. One automotive instructor pointed out a tension between introductory college-level courses and remedial ones: If the resources of the college were spent on improving the quality of instruction, the need for remediation would be less.

> We have two kinds of classes at this college, vocational and remedial. The truly college stuff, you're looking at 10 percent. Innovative money generally goes toward remedial. But if you put a lot of money in remedial, you starve the basic instruction. My thing is, is you do a hundred percent, all-out job on the basics, you'll have some remedial, but it will be less. But if you keep starving the classrooms, I guarantee you, your tutorial center will be an empire.

While this instructor did not clarify what he meant by "the basics," we think that he meant smaller class sizes, full-time rather than part-time instructors, adequate faculty development, and other institutional resources we discuss in Chapters 8 and 9—conditions under which instructors are better able to weave remedial components into regular classes, as we show in Section III. Thus the "empire" of remedial education in many colleges reflects a choice to reduce the resources allocated to basic instruction in regular courses and then to increase formal remediation for students who can't learn in such courses.

Literacy as a Skill

The worst teaching in remedial education, the kind that was likely to collapse into "drill and kill," is commonly based on a conception of literacy as a skill. These classes emphasize cognitive procedures such as decoding words, using punctuation appropriately, learning the meanings of unfamiliar words, and mastering specific forms of writing such as the three-paragraph essay, the business letter, or the memo. Here is one such class, taught by the teacher complaining that her students didn't know that *a* is not a verb:

> At the beginning of the class the instructor urges the sixteen students to attend an upcoming theater production. She hands back a grammar test, asking: "Do you know why you did bad?" Students nod and smile, taking this as a statement of fact rather than a reprimand. Then the instructor tells students to open their books. She writes on the board, "A sentence is a group of words . . . ," asks students to complete the definition, and gives a mnemonic technique for remembering the definition of a sentence. She talks about sentence fragments for the next ten minutes, writing a definition of a simple sentence on the board, then giving examples and a trick method for identifying sentence fragments.
>
> Then the instructor talks about compound sentences, gives tips for remembering conjunctions, and reads sample sentences from the book. A student asks a question (the first time this has happened in this class, after a half hour of teacher talk) about whether one can substitute different conjunctions in a given sentence. The instructor goes around the room, calling on students to read conjunction exercises out loud. She asks, "Why do commas go in particular places?" Students offer answers.
>
> The instructor shifts to prepositions. Again the same pattern emerges—first a definition, then some explanation, then the class completes fill-in-the-blank exercises orally. The instructor says that if one specific student gets all the answers right, the whole class will get bonus points. She gets them right.
>
> The instructor follows same pattern for complex sentences. At the end of the ninety-minute class, the instructor gives the next assignment, which includes grammar exercises.

Her course syllabus reads:

> The purpose is to demonstrate how language functions so that the student, understanding the "how" of the language, can simply apply the knowledge of function to any given syntax or structure. The course also stresses mastery of fundamental skills such as sentence sense.

The problem here, one much discussed by educators, is whether expertise in language use is the result of learning rules and applying them, or the consequence of active participation in meaningful activity involving language. One answer is that students need both, though participation in language use is essential while learning rules is not. But many remedial classes, especially those in English or language arts divisions, flow from the view that learning rules comes first.[17] Classes like this also support the view, widespread among students, that learning grammar will lead to effective language use.

When colleges develop sequences of remedial courses, they often betray the dominance of skills-based approaches. For example, here is a developmental instructor describing the "empire of remediation" at her college:

> The very first developmental class is 093-094; they're usually taught ten credits together, and one's usually a reading component and the other's usually a writing component. And so 093-094 is very much focused on grammar. And 095-096 is still very focused on grammar, but [requires] a lot more reading and [discussion]. And 097-098 is the last class people take before going to transfer. And it's very similar to what you saw 099 doing—reading and writing. People are moving toward actual paragraphs; they're trying to put paragraphs in combination to make a point, [and] they're learning to recognize when they've made a point and when they haven't. [There] are still a lot of grammar problems, but the focus isn't quite so much on [that]; it's more on ideas.

So students had to take twenty units before they got to a course where they're "moving toward actual paragraphs." That's a long time on grammar drill, and even in the last course "there are still a lot of grammar problems."

Some instructors questioned the study of grammar but nonetheless went along with it as a departmental requirement:

> This is very difficult material, you know. It's sort of idiotic to present basic grammar as a beginning English course. Basic grammar is very difficult.

The difficulty of teaching grammar rules was clear from moments like this, in a business English class. The instructor was handing back a fifty-question quiz titled

"Independent Clauses Without Conjunction, Series with Internal Commas." A student asked this question while they were reviewing the quiz:

> Student: "Why isn't there a comma after 'before 1990' but there is after 'before long'?"
>
> Instructor: "I noticed that, too. It's one of those rules. Let me look it up."
>
> The instructor looks in the book, finds the page. He reads silently, then says aloud: "It seems to me that it is because the pause is necessary for clarity. 'Before long people' would be confusing without the comma, whereas 'before 1900 people' would be okay."

However, the student did not appear convinced; unlike other grammar rules they had been learning, "clarity" is an ambiguous rule, interpretable only within a community of practice.

These kinds of remedial classes are entirely predictable, since class time is usually spent drilling on technical aspects of reading and writing.[18] Such classes suffer from a problem of content, since they focus only on technical features of reading and writing, rather than the content that can be learned through reading and writing and that might interest students. One dean of developmental studies described this view of learning without recognizing its problems:

> You have your categories of skills—actually, beginning in the third grade or the second grade. Children hear stories and enjoy the appreciation of words. Then the skills get more complex, you do greater comprehension skills, you do greater vocabulary skills, you introduce critical-thinking skills. By the time you get to the junior-high and high-school level you should be talking about college study skills that enable you to study a great deal of complex material and absorb it.

She conceptualizes various listening, speaking, reading, and writing activities as "skills" and arranges them in sequential order, with each skill separate from the material itself. As she continues:

> Then when they get to those very tough courses, anatomy and physiology, and they get to the more difficult research courses, and to the more difficult occupational technical courses that will lead them into a profession such as nursing, they have these skills already, so that all they have to do is deal with the content.

Similarly, the director of a basic skills programs described a computerized remediation program, adding that the center was not to be used for "tutoring in a specific discipline; it's for instruction in general, study skills, or reading and writing."

Symbolically, the separation of skills from content is reflected in the curricular separation of remedial courses from content courses, in the administrative separation of departments that teach remedial courses (often called developmental studies) from those that teach content- or discipline-based courses, and in the physical separation of learning labs from other classrooms.

The idea that remediation has to precede content learning creates a teaching problem. Students normally enter community colleges to master the academic subjects required for transfer or the occupational courses necessary for employment. Then they find themselves in remedial classes where the instructor has abandoned all content in order to focus on forms and abstractions, in which they are drilling on homonyms and synonyms, percents and fractions. As one remedial instructor described the disjunction between conventional courses and remedial courses:

> There's a canon in chemistry—there's a body of knowledge that for the last five centuries, in the Western part of the world anyway, has been transferred on to the next generation. Well, think about the teaching of reading. They tend not to really worry about content. There's no canon, body of [knowledge] . . . The method is what's important. It probably doesn't matter what you're reading, but it makes a lot of difference in chemistry.

Many instructors solve the problem of content by making grammar or arithmetic the content of remediation, without any application. Others use readings from newspapers, anthologies, student writings, or other examples from the "real world," but often find that they have to back away from discussions prompted by these readings because the purpose of the class is not to explore such material. Often instructors cut off discussions of content, as in this reading class:

> A reading instructor in the Midwest passes out copies of a local newspaper. Students choose their own articles and start to read. The instructor has already told them that they are to argue their own interpretations of what they read, but two students, in reporting their readings, find themselves starting to compare conflicting opinions on abortion. The instructor quickly cuts off the discussion, saying, "We each have a right to our own opinion," and then moves on to the next student. This happens to be an older man, reading an article about bad conditions in schools in poor neighborhoods, who says, "It's the job of the government to see that money is being spent fairly." Again the instructor cuts the student off and takes up another standard reading skill—context clues.

Just as a vocational instructor was likely to say that he couldn't teach reading or writing because he wasn't trained to do so, a reading instructor would say that she did not know enough about history, sociology, or business to carry the discussion forward in a responsible way, and therefore abandoned any content.

Sometimes the problem of content is resolved by creating a new course that used subject content to accomplish remediation, in what we have called support courses. One dean mentioned:

> If a student in a developmental writing course has to do fifteen writing assignments, then why can't those fifteen writing assignments be oriented toward the specialty that he or she is in? ... Then you get the tension from the other side, because the developmental writing instructor is saying, "Well, how am I gonna know if he or she is telling me the truth about welding or automotive?"

A course called Nursing Success Strategies was developed in response to the need among students for certain "skills," but faculty felt that generic courses without nursing content would not be useful. The instructor told us:

> We saw nursing students who wanted quick fixes, help for studying, taking tests, and retaining information and things ... so by the time everybody put their heads together we felt we needed a course.

Another program, this one in automotive repair, developed a relationship with the English, math, and reading departments.

> This morning the English instructor came here and she teaches English here and her written assignments are automotive-related. And the math instructor teaches right here and she's using applied-type mathematics that relates as much as she can to the automobile and other hands-on activities. Then we have a reading instructor who comes in and then their reading assignment for the week is the same assignment that I've given them in the automotive areas.

But these support courses are often constrained by conventional approaches to literacy and remediation. The English instructor described above was constrained by having to evaluate her students with standardized tests developed by the English department; the math teacher, also bound by her department's curriculum, expected no more than six of her twenty-four students to pass. So while the problem of content moved these occupational departments to develop related support courses, the skills-oriented pedagogy limited what the instructor could accomplish by constraining engagement with the content.

Literacy as Social Practice

Most instruction in the skills-based approach to remediation—as well as the multiple-choice tests that direct students into such courses—ignores the purposes of reading and writing, especially the ability to interpret what a text means and how it is used in social interactions among workers, citizens, family members, or participants in the "great conversation" among literate people. The problem of learning the meaning of a text, as compared with simply decoding it, was illustrated by a story told by a business English teacher, about a diligent student who resisted reading aloud in class, apparently because he could not read. When asked whether he could read in the sense of decoding the words, the instructor offered the following cautionary reply:

> Yes. But they don't understand the words. It's not there. It's a different kind of vocabulary. I would try to do so many little things to get them to understand what the class was about other than through reading. When you do that, it's like, "Yeah, yeah, yeah, I see what you mean." But if you don't do that, for some of our classes, it's like, "I don't know what you're talking about. I mean, I see the words, but they really have no meaning at all."

This instructor's solution was to devise ways of teaching content that did not depend on reading. But designing remediation that would be appropriate for students who can "see the words" but for whom "they really have no meaning at all" requires pedagogical approaches that involve more than the technical aspects of literacy.

In contrast to skills-based approaches, instruction that moves toward meaning making is usually based on a conception of literacy as a social practice—in which extracting the meaning from a text, or conveying meaning to others, supersedes the technical aspects of reading and writing.[19] One instructor noted that her students viewed literacy as a "school activity," not one useful in real life; her goal was to "see that they can participate in an intellectual and emotional life through print," a way of communicating both in the classroom and the world outside. In her basic reading class, the students had read a selection from *The Autobiography of Malcolm X*, where he is in prison and learns to read by looking words up in the dictionary. This text is read as a trade book by adult readers and by college-level students in history and English classes, but not often in remedial classes since it is considered too difficult and too long. However, the instructor was confident that these students, whom she described as "not independent enough to benefit from learning-lab work," could benefit from this book if it was taught in a way that demystified and made explicit anything they were unfamiliar with.

Given the low skill level of these students, the instructor did not initially focus on the text structure or other features of a whole text such as irony, characterization, or argument. Instead, she emphasized a more basic level, leading students to grasp the meanings of words unfamiliar to them. She did not tell them the meanings; instead, she put them through a labor-intensive activity, with the whole class learning about fifteen words in one session by examining the context in which they were used, the intention of the writer, parts of the word familiar to them, and the dictionary. (After all, the reading passage was about Malcolm X learning to read in somewhat the same way, though without the help of a teacher.) While this method was time-consuming, it seemed likely that students would be less inclined to forget words they learned this way, compared to simply being told the meanings. The instructor was also covering much more about the structure of words and their use in particular contexts than a didactic approach would.

For homework, students had been assigned to do "personal vocabulary words" on index cards. Each card showed the word they had chosen, its part of speech, other forms of the word, prefixes and suffixes, and its roots on one side of the card while the other side displayed its definition, the sentence in the book in which the word appeared, and the dictionary page. Here's what took place in class:

> Students pair up and read their vocabulary words out loud to each other. Working from their cards, they ask many questions of each other and the instructor as they try to understand the words. One student has trouble with the word *convey*. Instead of telling the student the definition, the instructor carries a book across the room in her outstretched hand. "Oh," says the student, "to carry it across." The instructor then reads the sentence again and asks the students if they have ever felt frustrated in trying to convey meaning in writing. "You know what you want to say, but the words don't come out," says a student. The instructor says, "This is the feeling Malcolm X was having. What solution did he find?" "He started writing down words from the dictionary," replies another student, acknowledging that this is what they are now doing themselves.

The slow but sure way that the students worked their way through the text, gathering meanings from their experience to fill each new word with significance, reminds us that to an adult learning a word, as compared to a child encountering a word for the first time, the meaning of that word is already complex and invisibly connected to many other meanings.[20] In contrast to the conventional remedial/developmental class's vocabulary drills, this instructor took advantage of the distinction between adults' learning and children's learning by leading students through an exercise in which the connection of language with their own experiences was clear.

Another instructor took three weeks at the beginning of each semester to determine the interests of each student, to use as the basis for further exercises:

> Another guy was particularly interested in Egyptian stuff, so when I taught phonics I pulled together a lot of alphabetic information, you know, where the alphabet came from, the different forms of writing, its movement, and then I had a lot of religious books, so I talked heavily about the Bible and the traditions, the alphabetic traditions.

In this class, the instructor explicitly taught the concept of "register," a technical term from linguistics referring to the vocabulary, phrases, and language habits characteristic of a social setting; for example, a doctor might use one register for speaking to patients, but another for other doctors or family. This instructor taught students to distinguish among sacred, formal, intimate, and vulgar registers, asking them to move the register of a poem from one to another and to identify words as belonging to particular registers. Students also developed "word histories" by tracing the evolution of a word's meaning. Her basic reading students completed the semester with a reading of *Oedipus Rex*—certainly college-level material, read by students who would not customarily be considered college-level. Needless to say, these exercises are much more complex than conventional vocabulary drill, and they all stress the communicative uses of language rather than its mechanics.

These differences also encompass forms of assessment. In contrast to conventional classes, in which students are evaluated by the formal correctness of their writing, this instructor evaluated her class by multiple measures, including how well students carried out some literacy activity such as reading a play together:

> We have a wide-ranging achievement test, which is an oral pronunciation test, and then the Stanford silent reading test. When it's writing, I use a pre- and posttest writing sample. But how do I really measure it [what students are learning]? I mean, those things are important; I'm not putting those down. But I really measure it by whether or not by the end of the semester they are reading together or writing together like a symphony, everybody striking their own notes and everybody in concert. I mean—when we read *Oedipus*, we have to be able to read it as one body. We have to realize we all have different parts but we're all producing this play together.

She spoke of a particular student who had a role in that play, stressing the fact that by the end of the semester she's willing to read the shepherd's part in *Oedipus Rex*—for her, the fact that this terribly overworked mother is willing to do a thorough study of a word history. Each person will buy in at a different point. You can't legislate which thing buying in means.

So students come in individually, and they "buy in" individually—but in the end language use requires a community, and the classroom becomes that community.

While all these exercises—the study of register, word histories, a reading of *Oedipus Rex*—might seem to be too difficult for remedial students, they are all linked by this teacher's commitment to a particular conception of language:

> I believe that ideas are inherently interesting to everybody, and that the great literature of the world is great literature because it's full of great ideas about human conditions. These people have a tremendous knowledge of the human condition. I pose the questions about schooling, about literacy, about relationships, about how to do things in the world, how to work, what does work mean. I think these are dynamite ideas and people learn skills in order to become closer to these ideas. So I mean, I don't motivate them. The materials motivate them.

And so, in this and other meaning-oriented remedial courses, the problem of content is resolved by incorporating two agendas simultaneously: one concerned with ideas, issues, and other forms of intrinsic meaning, and the other concerned with the structure of reading and writing. Students do learn to improve their writing, master conventional punctuation and expand their vocabularies, but there's some substance to these classes, not just rules of punctuation and vocabulary drills. As one instructor mentioned, "We don't do semicolon day . . . we hit those grammar issues as they come up, a little bit at a time," subordinating technical issues to the larger problem of constructing meaning through writing. And the substance contributes to motivation, in place of the listless attention that is so obvious in drill-oriented classes.

Teaching Remedial Math

Remediation usually requires teaching the technical aspects of a symbolic system in which ideas are communicated. In language use, these include the representation of word sounds by letters, the way words are arranged in a text, the conventions of various text structures. In mathematics, these include the meaning of numbers and computational signs, the formal properties of algebra, the ways of representing mathematical relationships in Cartesian coordinate systems. The math instructor quoted in the previous chapter made the link:

> We need to tighten up the precision of what we're saying.... An example is the minus sign. There are three different meanings for the same symbol. And my point is, it's much like in English. If you were learning English as a foreign language, and one day somebody says to you *to-too-two*, three words that sound exactly the same, meaning entirely different things, it must drive them nuts.

So one task of remedial math is to be explicit about the representation of mathematical ideas in symbols. However, a different dimension is how instructors treat the meaning embedded in mathematical notation—whether they treat mathematics as a set of technical operations to be carried out, or whether they are concerned with students understanding the meaning conveyed in mathematics.

Most remedial math instructors are, even more than faculty who teach basic reading and writing, likely to conceive of teaching as a series of drills in conventional procedures—arithmetic operations, the conversion of fractions and decimals, simple algebraic expressions—without much application or other content. Math becomes a series of formal operations without any particular use, and passing a remedial math class seems to be a particularly empty requirement because its relationship to subsequent classes, particularly occupational classes, seems so remote. These are the conditions under which occupational instructors complain about conventional academic practices: "That's where we lose our students—in basic skills, because they don't see the benefit of being there."

These math classes would be familiar to anyone who has been through elementary school. Typically, the instructor presents a formal operation and connects it to a skill mastered earlier (e.g., the relation of multiplication to addition, of decimals to fractions); then students practice on worksheets, or homework problems; finally they review their work in class, with instructors typically repeating instruction they have provided before. In community colleges, most remedial math is elementary-school math, and students have been exposed to such mathematics many times, with almost precisely the same teaching techniques. Unfortunately, there is little attempt to vary the form of instruction, to provide applications or other methods that might succeed where drill-oriented methods have failed before.

Here, for example is a math class that is part of a learning community linking basic writing, basic math, and a biology course for students hoping to become health professionals. In this class, math is treated as a set of operations that students learn to carry out correctly by repetition:

> The class is reviewing thirty-four problems for the midterm exam, covering fractions, multiplication with decimals, rounding off, percentages, areas and perimeters, squares, reading graphs, and long division. Many problems have emerged repeatedly; for example, the instructor

asks with some exasperation, "What's the quotient of 24 and 8? I went over this the first day of class." Some are straight arithmetic problems, while others are supposed to be contextualized by the science, like a problem of converting liters to milliliters ("What operation do you use?") or the problem of providing pills with a certain dosage ("How many 150 mg tablets would equal a dose of 450 mg?"). Students tend simply to guess what operation is appropriate, so with the dosage problem they are likely to reverse the operation (e.g., 150/450 instead of 450/150) or to subtract one figure from the other, generating truly implausible answers (450 – 150 = 300 tablets). There's little effort by the instructor to figure out the nature of the errors and correct them, or to replace guessing as a strategy. Lunch provides stiff competition for the content of this class, and many students drift into side conversations. The questions from students tend to involve what gets credit and what counts. A few procedural questions are answered by rules. For example, for a problem involved in transforming a fraction to a decimal, a student asks, "Why are you dividing by 100?" The instructor responds, "It's always 100—that's the rule for changing to percent." The instructor also teaches the following approach to problem-solving: When the question asks, "What percent of 84 is 105?" *is* becomes an equals sign, *what* becomes the unknown *n,* and *percent of* becomes a multiplication sign, leading to the following transformation from language to symbols:

What percent	of	84	is	105?
n	x	84	=	105

Students were being given the same rules that they had failed to learn in many years of elementary and secondary school, and the instructor—new, unsure of herself, and with few sources of help—had no idea what to do when students persisted in making the same errors. The extent of contextualization from biology was limited, and the class did not use any materials from biology labs that had given them problems. The approach to problem solving was formulaic, providing no guidance if a problem was worded in a different way.

But here's a very different approach to math, an elementary algebra class that is part of a learning community for older adults:

The instructor starts the class by asking if students have any questions. One student asks about a homework question, and the instructor starts a pattern he follows for almost an hour: He asks students to clarify the information available and bring in new information as appropriate, sets up the equations related to the information available, and writes the equation in both verbal and mathematical forms. He is in effect modeling the activities of a thoughtful mathematician first understanding a problem, then selecting a strategy for solution, then representing the problem in an equation, and finally solving the equation with a variety of different methods (like factoring, simplifying, and various short cuts). At one point he asks, "Are you ready for tricks?" He shows how to multiply both sides of an equation by the inverse of one term, and then asks, "What is the mathematical process?," encouraging and revising students as they try out their ideas. When a woman whose frequent giggles betray insecurity starts by saying, "I'm going to ask a stupid question," his manner communicates that there is no such thing as a stupid question. At another point he solves a problem in several ways, declares, "This is an extraneous solution," and discards it. On another problem, he shows two methods for solution; he points out that the usual, conventional method they might have learned requires more trial and error and that the alternative approach takes more steps but is more to the point. A student says she has his approach down pat but is confused by the alternative; the instructor clarifies the difference but says, "Hey, if you have a method down pat, stay with it. I'll show you the other method, but you stay with what works for you."

This instructor is less concerned with rules than with mathematics as a way of extracting information from a situation, and there is no authoritarian requirement of the "right" way to solve a problem; alternative solutions are fine as long as students understand their logic. The instructor is concerned with several levels of representation—the oral reading of a problem, a verbal understanding of what it is asking, its representation in both linguistic and mathematical symbols. The participation from students, rather than being confined to procedural questions about the test, are instead ways of exploring mathematical ideas. And the inattention, side conversations, and preoccupation with lunch so evident in the prior class have been replaced by a much higher level of engagement.

Another instructor in a basic skills learning community set up her classroom so that students actively use the language of math with each other:

> I'm emphasizing symbolic representations. . . . Many of our students have difficulties with vocabulary, and with symbolic representations and relationships, and that's pretty much what I'm trying to develop at this point, that math is a symbolic language, and it has its special vocabulary. . . . I want them to be active and I want them to be reading and writing and listening to each other, as well as talking.

In her classroom, students were divided into three groups of four students each, working out problems by reading, writing, listening, and talking rather than simply watching the instructor solve problems. Here's a description of a group:

> Group #3 seems to be working through the problems with minimal difficulty. The more agreed-upon answers they produce, the more excited they become. Their voices can be heard across the room (as can most other voices). They're reading, questioning, and restating their problem-solving methods. When one student is unable to solve a problem, another (or others) provides guidance. At least one member can be heard asking the others, "Do you understand? Do you see how I got that? How do we deal with this one?"

When math serves the additional purpose of representing physical relationships, the value of math as a symbolic language (rather than just as a set of operations) becomes even clearer. Here is a class described in the catalogue as Technical Physics, but which is really a basic algebra class for students in HVAC (heating, ventilating, and air-conditioning). They are a group of working-class males who typically have not mastered much math beyond arithmetic:

> On the board is a graph of P as a function of V. The instructor asks, "Someone want to read me these numbers?" and fills in a chart with the answers as a student reads off appropriate values. She then presents the formula for work (in the physical sense)
>
> $$w \ = \ nRT \ \ln(V^t/V^i)$$
>
> followed by some fill-in-the-blank exercises—"What's n? What's R?"—where the whole class follows along, understanding errors and correcting them. Students throw out relatively sophisticated questions of clarification involving the work done by the heat exchanged, and her answers stress thinking about heat transfer, not just about the algebra: "I want a way of thinking about this—not an answer about the algebra but about the underlying phenomenon. . . . Do not believe what the equation says, because different conventions can lead to different answers. Lead with your head, not the equation." Later she shifts to another topic—"Let's look at another pictorial representation of a cycle"—and directs the students: "Look up the Carnot cycle in the book. Are the arrows going the correct way?" She is getting them to think first about the process of heat transfer, then about its

representation in a diagram of the Carnot cycle, and then about its
algebraic representation. She asks, "What's the law of thermodynamics
we're working with here?" again asking students to move between a
principle governing heat and the equation describing the process.
Students have learned this way of thinking; one says, "I'm trying to
conceptualize how these three variables work together," and the
instructor responds, "You have to think about all three quantities, not
one or two"—a problem in multivariate nonlinear algebra that is well
beyond most algebra courses.

In this course, as in the previous example, the instructor is concerned not with
routine manipulation of algebraic expressions, but with the meaning of algebra,
its usefulness in representing phenomena of interest—heat transfer, information
in verbal forms. The translation of verbal problems into mathematical notation
is not a rote process of substituting symbols for words, but requires understanding of both heat transfer and algebraic conventions. Such conventions have to be
carefully examined, as "different conventions can lead to different answers."
Furthermore, the math in this class has some obvious content since this math
course is being taught specifically for an HVAC program. The problem of content-
free remediation has been resolved: This is a math class, to be sure, but it is concerned with something of interest to students, some sense that mathematics is a
useful activity in its own right rather than simply a prerequisite.

Remedial math classes in a meaning-centered tradition are harder to find than
remedial language classes following this approach. The discussions among math
instructors have not been as frequent as those among English and remedial/devel-
opmental instructors, particularly at the community college level; the interpretive
tradition, so much a part of debates over literature, doesn't have a clear analogue
in math.[21] And so some of the most lifeless teaching can be found in remedial
math classes, where students continue to repeat the same errors that have carried
them through elementary and secondary schooling.

III. REMEDIATION IN DISGUISE: THE CONVERSION OF ACADEMIC AND OCCUPATIONAL CLASSES

Despite the number of official remedial courses, remediation takes place in many
other guises, in classes not listed in course catalogues as remedial. These are often
classes with ad hoc remediation, as instructors discover the need to detour into
subjects that they might ordinarily expect college-level students to know. One
consistent feature of such disguised remediation is that instructors make explicit

the technical features of some kind of literacy, whether by demonstrating how to punctuate a sentence, defining a word, reviewing the solution of an algebraic equation, or teaching the use of an index. A student who did not understand these features would fall behind; by providing such explicit instruction, instructors enable students to keep up with the class—or, in some cases, allow the entire class to progress. And, as in "official" remediation, these teaching activities are not ends in themselves, but ways to remove barriers to learning course content.

Hidden or submerged remediation develops in many different ways, and it is impossible to detect without observing classes directly. It sometimes emerges, unfortunately, when the instructor discovers that virtually all students are under-prepared, and converts an entire class to basic skills. Thus we saw supposedly college-level courses in literature and composition—the basic courses commonly numbered English 1 or English 101—that had been converted to grammar drill, reading comprehension, and practice in writing simple essays. Similarly, a class in labor economics was converted into life skills and resume writing, a sociology class became an introduction to using the library, and a course called Office Information Systems was converted to grammar and spelling drills (business English) for potential secretaries and administrative assistants. These are cases where course labels and content have become disconnected from each other. In such examples, we usually saw the most unimaginative and didactic teaching: The instructor was typically unprepared to teach a remedial course, and so reverted to conceptions of literacy as a skill, which we observed in so many other remedial classes. These courses demonstrated the same separation of remediation from content, as the supposed subject of the class—usually the analysis of literature—vanished.

In other cases, instructors harness some kind of ancillary support to teach basic skills—either a tutorial center, an aide, or (for occupational classes) a support course such as technical math or business English. For example, one CIS instructor used a tutor this way:

> There are students who are poorly prepared when they get here. Sometimes it takes them more work to get through the course, a little extra study. I've been really, really, really fortunate to have a tutor just for CIS up in the library in our tutorial center. What she does is not teach them about subject matter; what she does is teach them how to study. She goes, "Oh, you know, half the time I'm not explaining what this and this is; I'm explaining they should be reading the chapter, answering the questions, looking at your outline." She says, "I'm teaching them how to study." I said, "That's great. Just keep doing that." So ill-prepared as far as just knowing how to study, I think a lot of my students are.

In this case, remediation is again separated from content. The tutor evidently stayed away from "subject matter" to concentrate on study skills, though presumably with the advantage of having students from a single class, with a limited set of assignments to master.

In other cases, however, remediation is woven into the fabric of the class, sometimes quite deftly, as instructors leave the official content of the class for a moment to emphasize a particular use of language, writing problem, math application, or notation system or diagram specific to an occupation. In a computer programming class, for example, an instructor found that he had to explain prime numbers. He then developed a simple flow chart of a computer program; his students, who in this class of fifty or sixty apparently felt free to call out with either questions or answers, got him to explain or even repeat a complete section as he went along. One student finally asked: "Why are these people asking all these Mickey Mouse questions?" The instructor answered, "Because it's helping them think." The student pressed on: "I don't mean to criticize, but I just think they're getting too serious." The instructor deftly passed this challenge to another student: "Bill, why do you think they're asking so many questions?" Bill settled the matter: "So they can go next door and run it." These are examples where it is not always apparent that remediation is taking place, eliminating the inevitable stigma associated with such activities. Moreover, the problem of content is resolved because such moments of basic instruction are directed to the course content and integrated into the sweep of the class.

Some instructors who practice this kind of embedded remediation have developed a clear explanation of what they are doing. For example, in a predominantly minority urban college in the Midwest, a microbiology instructor explained his perspective on "underprepared" students.

> Students at community colleges need a lot of guidance, teaching them how to think, what to do, sometimes even how to read. Sometimes they ask me a question. I just say, "Well, open your book to this page, let's go see." And it's there. The point is, they never really bothered to read it. Or even if they did, they misinterpreted it.

He did not say that his students needed a reading class or a basic skills course; nor did he negotiate down the content of his class. Instead, his approach was to provide appropriate, ad hoc remediation whenever it seemed necessary. He explained that he approached teaching science as teaching a new language:

> This is a science class. The vocabulary in the science is completely different from the vocabulary we use in a regular English or any other class. That's part of what our students are supposed to learn as they go, and that's another reason why we do have a

problem bringing them up to the level where we want them, because [not only do] they have to comprehend the basic language, English, but then you train them in what kind of seems like a foreign language to them.

He gave as an example the way he teaches what a "culture" is:

> Bacteria—we're talking about the culture of microorganisms—and yes, you can talk about the culture of people, you can talk about the word *culture,* which means how to do you derive these words. This is in the information pack I have given to them about the origin, derivations, how you pronounce the variety of scientific termi-nologies.

The foundation material that this instructor gave his microbiology students elaborated the concept of culture, making explicit the semantic connections that instructors of students with wider reading backgrounds would take for granted. His approach was parallel to that of the remedial English instructor who taught her students the word *convey* by "conveying" a book across a room. Both were brief asides that allowed students to define a word for themselves, distinguished the literal and metaphorical meanings, and brought students closer to a discussion of meaning. Similarly, the computer programming instructor described above paused in the middle of the class to ask his students why he was spending so much class time explaining ASCII. A student quickly responded: "Because you're trying to stress the importance of a universal language."

Another instructor, in an agricultural area, told how he taught students the lan-guage of his content area—beef and swine production. Students were learning how to understand the commodities markets; they would be working for large beef and pork production companies, selling and buying millions of dollars' worth of meat on the hoof or in refrigeration. Like the microbiology instructor, this instructor's focus was on the language:

> Terms? Let's use the right one. If you're going to drive a car, why do they call it a steer-ing wheel? Why do they call it an accelerator?

He described the development of students' ability to use the correct terminology as the years pass:

> We start out first-year, first-semester students, and we let them use some of the slang, with the understanding that we're going to correct you and say you should be using this term. Most kids are not scared of terminology if the words are small. But if it's this long, they question it, and if it's *this* long, let's not even use it, let's not even try to

pronounce it. And you can't believe how the competency can build just by taking
something like the livestock health class. A lot of big words, especially when it comes
to drugs. Let's just sound it out, go back to the old phonics, put it together. Pretty
soon [they say], "I never dreamed I could pronounce this word. Hell, I think I can
even spell it!"

And so, in small steps always connected to the content of the course, he led his students to greater precision and complexity in the use of language, with a result that
would make any English teacher proud.

With instructors who are appropriately student-centered, attuned to what their
students know and don't know, these small moments are constant, reflexive,
almost unconscious. As another example, a basic English class, part of a learning
community focused on biology for health professionals, had been discussing an
article entitled "The Seven Deadly Sins of Living" (about poor health habits) when
the instructor discovered that students didn't recognize the reference to "seven
deadly sins."[22] She then led them through a brief digression to St. Thomas
Aquinas, the origin of the term in medieval theology, and the continued use of
reference and metaphor. She mentioned about this interlude, "When I find
enormous gaps in knowledge, I sometimes can't help myself from leaping in."
These moments of instruction—often referred to as "teachable moments," taking
advantage of serendipitous events in the classroom—may not always be effective,
as this English instructor noted. The information in this instance was too arcane
to be readily retained, too disconnected from the rest of the class and the lives of
these students—welfare mothers struggling to get into the labor force. But the
constant exploitation of such moments provides students access to information
and analytic skills that would otherwise constitute barriers to their understanding,
without routing them away from the content of courses they have come to learn.

Like formal remediation, then, disguised or hidden remediation comes in
many forms, ranging from the worst cases—when an entire college-level course
has been hijacked for the purposes of basic instruction—to the most deft instruction with basic skills embedded in other content as the need arises. None of this is
planned by the college, and none of this can be recognized as remediation except
by observing the classroom. For this reason the official measures of remediation in
community colleges seriously underestimate what really takes place.

These forms of remediation will continue no matter what official policy is. If
the current hostility toward basic education at the college level succeeds in eliminating it or shifting the burden to another program, such as adult education, the
classes labeled "remedial" or "developmental" or "basic" could disappear from college catalogues. But despite what policy makers think they are doing, remediation
will persist in other guises: Instructors will continue to respond to their students

and their levels of preparation, and will continue to modify their courses accordingly. The only question is whether they do so with skill and foresight, aware of the pedagogies available to them, or whether they do so badly because they are unaware of how to teach the students they have.

IV. INNOVATIVE FORMS OF DEVELOPMENTAL EDUCATION: THE VALUE OF COLLECTIVE APPROACHES

Because remedial education includes both the best and the worst teaching, we saw many exemplars: the developmental English instructor who led her students through *Oedipus Rex*, exposing them to the power of great ideas; the basic math instructor who led her HVAC students through complex nonlinear equations, clarifying mathematics as symbolic representation of heating; the microbiology instructor who deftly integrated vocabulary and concepts like "culture" throughout his course. These classes have solved the problem of content by integrating basic skills with other kinds of content. They have moved toward more sophisticated conceptions of writing and mathematics (and other specialized literacies) as forms of communication rather than disembodied skills—and students in them are infinitely more engaged.[23] These are so different from standard remedial courses—with drills on grammar and punctuation, contrived writing exercises, endless repetition of decimals and fractions, and word problems completely removed from applications—that it is amazing to find them in the same institution.

These exemplars are forms of teaching that individual instructors can adopt for their own classes. But we think it's difficult to take an individualistic approach to remediation. Too many of the instructors we observed were squarely in a skills-oriented tradition; there was nothing in their background or training, and no institutional support, that could show them any other way to teach. And no matter how deftly individual instructors integrate remedial passages into their classes, ad hoc remediation can never be a comprehensive approach to the problems students bring to college, since it is so often reactive, fleeting, tangential to the subject at hand, unsystematic.

In fact, we were struck by our finding that most innovative practices seem to emerge from collective efforts, not from individual instructors. The most inspiring remedial instructors we observed were part of learning communities, where they had worked with other instructors to devise a *program* of courses for underprepared students.[24] And so the most promising approaches to remedial education are collective approaches, including a few developmental studies departments with coherent philosophies and institutionalized practices, and learning communities that resolve the problem of content.[25]

Institutionalizing Good Practice: The Developmental Studies Division, North County Community College

In most community colleges, developmental education is provided by departments that can charitably be described as loosely organized. While these departments typically establish exams guiding students into different levels, and provide two or three levels of "precollege" reading, writing, and math classes, there is little other structure. Most instructors are part-time, so there is little time for curriculum development, discussions with peers, or careful consideration of pedagogical alternatives. To be sure, there are remedial texts and computer programs and learning labs, and these help structure what harried instructors do on Monday morning when thirty to sixty reluctant students troop in. But for a subject as difficult as developmental education, there is neither the time nor the reason for careful deliberations about teaching. Many instructors acknowledged this problem. One, for example, was eager to find out from us what happened at other colleges: Do teachers rewrite the book? What are the little things a teacher can do to get content across to students other than requiring them to get it all from reading? And did that make the class less than college-level? What is the norm? How do other people deal with this? Such questions betrayed a lack of any forum for discussing remedial teaching.

However, we did come across one developmental studies division, in what we will call North County Community College, that established its own distinctive approach, with various mechanisms to institutionalize its philosophy and practice—illustrating that remedial education need not be so haphazard.[26] This department began to develop its own particular approach during the early 1980s, as enrollments began increasing rapidly. The balkanization within colleges means that departments can usually do what they want as long as enrollments are up and complaints are few. As the head of developmental studies described it,

> Our former president used to say "What are you people down there in DS doing now?" He said, "You were always trying something." And to him we were kind of a puzzle. But then when we were productive, he didn't bother us.

The division developed a coherent philosophy about developmental education, codified in two enormous volumes sometimes referred to as the "basic writing curriculum book." This describes a self-consciously hybrid approach to instruction. The head of the division complained that existing basal readers followed either a phonics strategy or a comprehension strategy, roughly equivalent to viewing literacy as a skill versus a social practice, and that debates about remediation have been similarly polarized: "We're back to the same old thing—top-down or bottom-up—and that's ridiculous." Instead, the philosophy of this department follows "transactional theory," in which language including writing is a "dialectic or interchange among writer, audience, and reality"—a variant, we should note, of literacy as a social practice rather than isolated skills. Writing is a "recursive activity" incorporating prewriting, rewriting, and revision, and includes "strategies for invention and discovery whereby instructors help students to generate content and purpose." The approach includes grammar, spelling, and other mechanics, but only in "the final stages of the writing process," since its use early in writing (as in "bonehead English") has been so counterproductive. The introduction to this curriculum book is an elegant approach to meaning-centered teaching, replete with examples from the latest research and practice; the rest contains examples, applications, and syllabuses in great profusion.

One purpose of the basic writing curriculum book is to codify the department's philosophy and practice, but another purpose is to introduce part-time instructors to the division's methods. As the division head described her intention:

> I wanted an adjunct faculty handle, so that my [part-time] faculty coming in would know exactly where the developmental studies courses stood, what the philosophy of the community college was. I wanted them to understand that these students were here to be taught, they were not to be discouraged or disparaged, and they were to be allowed to get on with better lives because of the impact we had on them here.

This curriculum book is therefore a training manual for the department. There are several other ways that the department ensures the quality of its teaching:

• There is a more rigorous and teaching-centered selection process for faculty than in most colleges. It asks applicants about their philosophies of teaching: "Do you know what's going on out there in the field. Have you read? Are you involved in and up-to-date?" In the field of remedial/developmental education, where there are several well-codified schools of thought (Goto, 1995) as well as a great deal of casual practice, such questions are highly revealing, and the division tries to hire individuals with compatible philosophies. The division also gives a classroom teaching test to see how applicants perform in front of students. These screens for teaching philosophy and ability take place before any other hiring criteria are considered. The head is quite aware that "each person [in the hiring procedure] seems to be looking for something different," many of them unrelated to teaching, and the initial screen for teaching is a way of ensuring that these extraneous considerations do not dominate the hiring process.

• The division observes its part-time instructors early in their teaching, and if a "traditionalist" (a skills-oriented teacher) has managed to slip through, the division tries to work with her:

> The one thing you do not do is to come and start beating people on the head [with the idea] that you have the answer and they don't. In other words, the people who went into the writing process tried not to beat up on the traditionalists, but continued to talk. Now, in the case of the part-time faculty, I observe them. If I see a traditionalist and that person is worked with, and things are explained to that person, and now we have this manual, and the person refuses to change, or refuses to do [or] at least try some things that would be of benefit to students, then the next thing you've got to do is to say, "Either you're gonna try it, or you have to go."

There's both carrot and stick in this vignette, of course , but the process works to create a uniform approach to teaching even among part-time faculty.

• The division meets regularly to develop curriculum materials. As one instructor explained, "Pretty much everybody's on the reading and writing committee, because that sets the curriculum; that's just what we do." This instructor also claimed that

> all our conversations are about what we can do to be better teachers. I feel that I've had more professional growth being in this department for a month than from all the conferences I've ever attended.

• The division encourages its instructors go back to university to learn more about teaching methods. Several instructors praised the preparation they had received in their university programs; in this region there are a few graduate programs (including those in adult education) geared to developmental education.

The rest of the college was quite conventional. We observed several classes taught by the English faculty that were grammar-based and dreary; a prealgebra (i.e., remedial) math course based entirely on lecture and drill; and a business writing class that proved to be a grammar-based remedial writing course with no applications to business whatsoever. Sharing across divisions is rare, as the head of the English department mentioned:

> A lot of the English instructors don't know what happens in a dev stud or ESL class. . . . There's just not enough interaction among the three areas [English, developmental studies, and ESL] for us to have any sense of what's being done at the different levels.

The college's effort to develop Writing Across the Curriculum had not gone far; as the head of English mentioned, "What we've done in that area is mainly talk."

The institution had applied for a FIPSE grant to reform "outmoded instructional strategies that aren't able to address adequately the needs of the nontraditional student body"—that is, ineffective lecture and drill methods. But the grant had not yet been awarded, never mind implemented, and the college had not taken any other steps to improve instruction.[27] The developmental studies department had created an island of exceptional practice, but its pedagogical developments, personnel practices, and support for instructors had not been adopted by the rest of the college.

Despite the real advances of this division, several problems persisted. In practice, remedial courses were often taught by individuals from English or part-timers who had not gone through the developmental studies process or explored its basic writing curriculum book. The division simply couldn't control everyone who taught in its "empire," much as it tried. And the division had not resolved the problem of content, since it was independent of academic and occupational subjects and had been unable to develop common approaches. This is an issue for which learning communities are virtually the only solution.

Learning Communities for Remedial Education

Some colleges have developed learning communities for some or all of their remedial/developmental education.[28] As in other learning communities, described in Chapter 7, these efforts join several courses that students take simultaneously. One is usually a content course, often one that students have previously struggled to complete; the other courses are remedial language or math courses. The combinations are endless and inventive. We observed learning communities pairing biology and English, history and English, computers and math, HVAC and math, and—winning the prize for most innovative title—one called "Reading, Writing, and Wrenches," initiated by an automotive instructor who worked with an English instructor to remedy the problems his students had with reading. Larger learning communities have combined biology (an introductory course for health professionals), English, and math, and we observed one in human services, English, and math—these latter two designed for welfare recipients trying to enter the workforce.

Learning communities resolve a number of problems simultaneously, including the problem of content. Because they include at least one content course, there is a body of material that students have chosen to learn, usually related to further vocational or academic goals, that provides the readings, examples, and applications for the basic courses. In pairings with academic courses, the specialized reading, vocabulary, and logic of particular disciplines—science courses with their new "language," or social sciences with their particular ways of constructing

arguments—provide the content for remedial coursework. Similarly, in vocationally oriented learning communities, complaints from occupational instructors
about losing students in basic skills—"My students say they don't want any damn
English"—are rare because English courses have been tailored to occupational
needs, shifted away from the interpretive practices and text structures of literature
courses and toward the instructional manuals, rate books, and other information
sources specific to occupations. Similarly, math classes can maintain a level of
sophistication while focusing on the applications pertinent to an occupation—at
least in the best cases, like the applied physics course described in Section II.

When the problem of content is resolved, the problem of motivation is also
overcome. In conventional remediation, students enter a college for academic or
vocational purposes only to find themselves doing sentence completion exercises,
arithmetic drills, and three-paragraph essays on contrived topics, and dropout
rates from these courses are alarmingly high (see Table 5.1). But within learning
communities students can more readily see the point of language or math courses,
since the content is connected to a subject they have elected and is different from
what they have encountered previously. These forms of remediation are fresh
approaches to the three R's (at least when they are designed collaboratively), not
just another round of the same material.[29] And like all learning communities,
these approaches provide students with supportive peers and instructors who
know them better—one of the first benefits that students mention. With all these
advantages, course completion rates and subsequent enrollment are higher for
students in learning communities than for those in conventional arrangements.[30]

There are some disadvantages, too. Learning communities for remedial purposes invariably have a "lead" course that drives much of the content in the language and math courses, and some instructors resent losing control of "their"
subject to the lead course. Sometimes an occupational focus for a learning community makes it difficult for English instructors to incorporate the esthetic and
moral dimensions of literature, and so the familiar battles about the relative balance of vocational, political, and intellectual goals ensue.

But the benefits of such learning communities are enormous. The obvious
question is why they seem so rare—why, for example, they have not superseded
the tutorial labs and dreary skills-oriented classes that we observed so often. The
principal answer is that they require institutional commitment, and sometimes
resources—commitment to scheduling classes in pairs or triples, commitment to
finding instructors willing to work together, commitment to enough staff development and planning time so that instructors can develop their curricula jointly.
The dependence of remedial education on part-time instructors, who often patch
together a living by teaching in several colleges, makes collaboration among teachers especially difficult. And so we often found colleges with one or two learning

communities for remedial purposes, but where the vast "empire" of remediation persists in conventional stand-alone courses and learning labs. In other colleges external funding has supported a learning community, but the program ended when the grant ran out. The commitment to learning communities as a normal approach to developmental education rather than an exceptional experiment is rare, a conclusion that is testimony to the power of enrollment-driven funding, conventional practice, and sheer inattention to the institutional requirements for improved teaching.

The examples of learning communities, and the well-developed approach in North County Community College, suggest that remedial/developmental education is especially likely to benefit from collective rather than individual approaches to instruction. Certainly individual faculty on their own can develop innovative remedial courses, moving away from the deadly drills and repetitive practice of skills-oriented courses. Competent instructors can lace their classes with small and informal remedial interludes, providing underprepared students with the technical mastery they need without labeling it remedial. But these efforts are too haphazard and serendipitous to take care of the massive amount of remedial/developmental education required by the open-door college. In contrast, those colleges sponsoring learning communities as vehicles for remediation, or supporting departments with coherent philosophies and policies, have made institutional commitments to improving the quality of such instruction.

Finally, we can see how detrimental the current proposals to eliminate remedial or developmental education from community colleges would be. In the first place, they couldn't succeed. Remedial education would continue in informal and ad hoc ways, by instructors committed to their students and willing to address the problems they come with. But most of these instructors would be unprepared to teach remedial education and would fall back on drill-oriented approaches. Even the most skilled instructor would be unable to do more than respond in unsystematic ways to the issues that popped up in specific classes; ad hoc remediation, no matter how skillful, can never be comprehensive. In the second place, shifting remediation to adult education or voluntary programs would exacerbate the problem of content. The separation of verbal and mathematical "skills" from issues of substance can be overcome only if remedial education is integrated with academic and occupational subjects, as it is in support courses and learning communities. We conclude that if community colleges are to remain open-door institutions, they need to maintain their commitments to remedial/developmental education.

NOTES

1. There has been a long debate about what to call it, with "remedial," "developmental," and "basic" education all having different histories and proponents. Goto (1995) reviews these debates carefully and concludes that the amalgam "remedial/developmental" is most appropriate—though in this book we sometimes simplify this to "remedial education" despite its pejorative connotation.

2. See Mansfield and Farris, 1991 for the amount of remediation in two- and four-year colleges. Estimates between 25 and 50 percent of coursework are contained in Grubb and Kalman, 1994, and Riggs, Davis, and Wilson, 1990, estimate that 78 percent of courses in Tennessee's community colleges are remedial.

3. We did not observe enough ESL classes to come to many conclusions about this kind of instruction. The problems experienced by ESL and remedial students are distinctly different, and most instructors think that the solutions should be different as well. However, ESL classes are often oversubscribed, and so many immigrants end up in remediation instead. This creates pedagogical problems for instructors with distinctly different groups of students, and it may be less effective for second-language learners as well.

4. Remedial education within community colleges is isolated not only from the rest of the institution but also from debates over basic skills instruction in four-year colleges, where there has been a much livelier theoretical and pedagogical debate. However, most of the issues about status and practice are precisely the same; see Hull, undated, for a review of issues in writing programs in four-year colleges.

5. This definition is taken from Goto, 1995, and has been modified to include a broader range of activities other than courses labeled remedial education and to allow instructor recognition of the need for remediation.

6. See, for example, Traub, 1994a and 1994b, and McGrath and Spear, 1991, on students who have not mastered the conventions of academic discourse, or Richardson, Okun, and Smith, 1983, on "bitting," or breaking complex texts into small parts. We note that teaching is particularly invisible in both Traub's work and McGrath and Spear's work, since none of these writings takes much care in describing what teaching in remedial classes is like.

7. However, these writing assessments are likely to depend on the specific prompt used, and their scoring can be unreliable. There is, to our knowledge, no review of the assessment practices used for directing students into remediation or any evaluation of their validity and reliability.

8. According to the American Council on Testing, 27 percent of students who go through an initial orientation and testing procedure using the ASSET test never enroll at all. See American Council on Testing, 1996, p. 6.

9. The MALDEF case is an interesting example of frustration over standardized tests. California adopted a "matriculation" requirement in which entering students would be assessed and then placed appropriately. In practice, colleges implemented matriculation poorly and unevenly, often requiring standardized tests for inappropriate purposes. The purpose of the MALDEF case was to force colleges to develop more sensible and sensitive procedures. But legal challenges are crude instruments of education policy, and the result—eliminating the power of colleges to require remediation—is as likely to err against the interests of students through underinclusion as the original procedures may have erred through overinclusion. Oral communication, Susan Brown, Legal Counsel for the Latin Issues Forum, San Francisco (formerly an attorney with MALDEF), January 1998.

10. Some colleges have created semester-long courses or seminars related to career explo-

ration; LaGuardia Community College has used its co-op program in a similar way (Grubb and Badway, 1998).

11. For colleges in regions of the country with many immigrant students, facility in the English language is a special problem. Existing tests cannot distinguish between facility in English and command of the linguistic and mathematical concepts being tested, so they are particularly inappropriate for language-minority students (Hofstetter, 1998; Hofstetter et al., 1998). However, the methods for developing more sensitive assessments are barely under way.

12. We found a very few examples of locally generated aptitude tests for occupational classes. One automotive instructor had developed his own test of manual dexterity to weed out students who he felt were unsuited to the auto trades. However, the college subsequently prohibited him from using it because of a potential discriminatory effect against women and minorities. The problem in this case is precisely that of conventional standardized tests: Because they have not been validated, the suspicion is high that standardized tests may be excluding individuals who could benefit.

13. ACT, which provides such a follow-up test, reports that only two community colleges in the country have used this. Personal communication, Robert Elliott, March 1997.

14. The "assignment problem" has been rarely discussed, except obliquely and incompletely in debates about whether community colleges "cool out" students or not. The assignment problem is an exceptionally difficult issue because the information necessary to determine what explains different outcomes is usually missing; in the absence of such information, partisan and political debates take place. For a brief discussion, see Grubb, 1998a.

15. In this book, we examine only the pedagogical dimensions of remedial/developmental education. But many students needing remedial education also experience other barriers, including constraining or abusive families, mental health problems such as bipolar and depressive conditions, alcohol and drug problems, and the like. As one instructor noted, "Developmental/remedial classes have problems other than simply lack of language skills; they have a whole host of what I would call personal or interpersonal skills that need development . . . problems that are what I would call structural problems—situational problems, personal problems that are probably interfering or are barriers to their education." Although comprehensive programs would identify and correct such barriers, most colleges don't have the facilities to do so. See also Quint, Musick, and Ladner, 1994, or Quint and Bos, forthcoming, on the barriers to mothers in the New Chance program.

16. We did not visit more than a few learning labs because our interest was in teaching and because they tend to be much alike from one college to another. Except as a method of quick review for older students who have previously mastered basic skills, these labs strike us as pedagogically primitive and inappropriate for community college students. They tend to use the simplest forms of drill-oriented instruction, either in workbooks or on computers; the computer programs are, almost uniformly, workbooks transferred to the computer screen. As one director noted, "In my mind a lab is a more skill-centered type of curriculum." See also Section II of Chapter 7, on the unimaginative use of computers.

17. In the vocabulary developed in Chapter 4, about two thirds of remedial classes took an authoritative approach to interpretation, where the conventions of standard English were the sole authority. Of these twenty-one classes, seventeen were explicit about language use—a characteristic of remedial classes. We characterized seven as cooperative because they incorporated some kind of small-group work; ten were more individual in their focus.

18. In the terms developed in Chapter 4, these are explicit, individualistic (or competitive), authoritative classes. The only difference between these and the dominant type of class—tacit,

competitive, and authoritative—is that remedial instructors are generally explicit rather than tacit about the technical features of literacy, since they are explicitly teaching grammar, word usage, and the like.

19. In the vocabulary of Chapter 4, these classes are explicit about literacy, distributed in the locus of authority, and cooperative. About one third of developmental classes took this form.

20. "The characteristic feature of the adults' verbal meanings is that the word preserves in itself all systems of connection inherent in it, beginning with the very elementary and visual and ending with the very complex and abstract. . . . An entire complex of relations is hidden behind each word"; see Luria, 1969, 137. On the work of Luria, a colleague of the Soviet psychologist L. S. Vygoysky, see Cole, 1997.

21. But see, for K–12 math, the standards of the National Council of Teachers of Mathematics (NCTM, 1989). Although the level of math in community colleges is similar to that in upper elementary grades through high school, community college instructors have not been active in NCTM and its efforts to devise new approaches to teaching and curriculum.

22. This choice of reading is an example of how an excellent instructor can tailor materials to fit her class. In this case, a learning community focused on biology, she managed to find a reading that was simultaneously about health, was at a more advanced level than most remedial texts (since it was from the *New York Times*), contained an embedded mathematical problem related to the math course, and presented some indirect and much-needed lessons to students about healthy living.

23. We judged these classes and instructors to be exemplary based on our observation, not on evidence about performance in subsequent classes, progress through the college, employment effects, or other indicators of outcomes. The evaluation of remedial education is still in a primitive stage; for some of the issues, see Grubb, 1998a.

24. Of the specific instructors we have profiled in this chapter, only the microbiology instructor was not part of a learning community—though they are using methods that instructors could use on their own. In part this may happen because particularly innovative instructors are more likely to create teaching-oriented communities for themselves, as we noted in Section IV of Chapter 1. But we also think that participation in a learning community stimulates the process of discussion, feedback, and reflection that allows instructors to improve their own practice, and so we suspect that learning communities have contributed to the development of innovative practice in remedial education.

25. Our conclusions about collective approaches are close to Shaw's (1997) observations. She describes the remedial programs in three community colleges, each with a distinct philosophy that influences individual instructors: an inflexible and rather punitive policy at what she calls Bootstrapper College, a consistent ideology supporting both formal and informal remediation at Nurturer College, and an inconsistent set of policies at Service Provider College.

26. We came across this exemplar by accident, when two instructors presented a paper at a College Composition and Communication conference. This college is not particularly well known, either in the remedial education community or in its own state, for its remedial efforts—which we take as an indication that there is no widespread discussion about what good practice is or which colleges exemplify it. This developmental studies division has many of the same practices as the exemplary teaching colleges we examine in Section V of Chapter 8, and illustrates that a division can support good teaching in isolation from the rest of the college.

27. This FIPSE grant is an example of a point we make in Chapter 9. The institution, like many others, was relying heavily on an external grant to reform its teaching, but whether an external grant can generate reforms that become institutionalized is doubtful.

28. Some colleges have also developed learning communities for ESL, pairing an ESL course with a content course, with the same logic as developmental learning communities. One model that has spread throughout California is the Puente ("bridge" in Spanish) program for Spanish-speaking students, incorporating some multicultural subjects as well as bilingual instruction; see, for example, Cazden, 1996.

29. See also the analysis of learning communities in Chapter 7, Section III, where it is clear that unsuccessful examples—where instructors have little time to collaborate—do not have any pedagogical advantages.

30. See the evidence cited in Chapter 7, Section III, especially MacGregor, 1991; Tokina, 1993; Tinto and Goodsell-Love, 1995; Tinto, Goodsell-Love, and Russo, 1994; and Tinto, Love, and Russo, undated.

6

STANDARDS AND CONTENT
The Special Dilemmas of Community Colleges

Our nation is awash in talk about standards. In K–12 education, many different standards have been proposed for students, for teachers, and for specific disciplines, backed up by statewide testing programs and even national standards and exams.[1] In postsecondary education, without traditions of external examinations, states have wrestled (mostly unsuccessfully) with how to set standards for their colleges and universities (Dill, Massy, Williams, and Cook, 1996). Employers and policy makers concerned about international competition have embraced "world-class standards" as their grail, and the federal government has begun experimenting with skills standards in occupational areas (Bailey and Merritt, 1995). Critics of education have weighed in with their own laments about declining standards: Those from the right have offered detailed recommendations (e.g., Hirsch, 1987; Adler, 1982), while other advocates have deplored the reduced expectations for low-income and minority students (Hopfenberg and Levin, 1993). No sin is worse than lowering educational standards, nor—it seems—is any more common.

While the temperature of discussion surrounding community colleges is somewhat lower, the specter of low standards has stalked these institutions virtually since their inception. As "junior colleges," they were created to be subordinate to four-year colleges, and their lack of admissions requirements has made them suspect, sometimes derided as "high schools with ashtrays." The phenomenon of "transfer shock"—where students transferring from two-year institutions to four-year colleges suffer a drop in their grades, and often drop out—has been a recurring challenge, and employers have complained about the quality of graduates from two-year colleges as well as high-school graduates (Van Horn, 1995). Even though public debate over standards and content has been less strident, the same issues are present.

But the problem of standards in community colleges is infinitely more complex than in most other institutions. These colleges are, by design, the lowest tier of higher education, a way back into the academic and economic mainstream for students who have not done well the first time around. By necessity, then, many courses are pitched at an introductory or remedial level: Most math classes are pre-algebra, and (as we saw in the previous chapter) many English classes are either formally or informally remedial. This by itself does not imply that community colleges are guilty of "low standards," since students arriving without sufficient preparation in a discipline need such introductory courses. Typically, within the same institutions, more advanced courses are also available, and we have given numerous examples of classes with high standards, in which instructors were taking their students with great facility through sophisticated material. Examples of these are the geology, child development, and microeconomics classes described in Chapter 2; the English class for welfare mothers profiled in Chapter 2 and Chapter 7; the most sophisticated of the occupational courses described in Chapter 3; and the many innovative programs described in Chapter 7. It is more appropriate to understand community colleges as places where *multiple* standards operate simultaneously, reflecting the vast variety of students and their purposes—the issue we address in Section I.

Rather than emphasizing the levels of courses, we examine standards by asking whether the content that the instructor intends to teach is reaching students. This is often a function not of the content defined for the class—the level of textbooks and reading, the formal curriculum—but of the ways instructors teach that material. During our visits, we saw not only inspiring classes, in which students were moving rapidly through sophisticated materials, but also classes that were dismal, brain-deadening, and often humiliating to students. One goal in this chapter (particularly Section II) is to explain these distressed and collapsed classes, classes that seemed to be emptied of content, where there was little chance of any learning going on. We interpret them not principally as the result of incompetence or laziness, nor of bad teachers who should be drummed out of the classroom, but rather as due to the institutional context of teaching. If colleges pay attention to the quality of instruction, then faculty can learn to change the many small practices that contribute to empty classes. But if colleges are indifferent to the quality of teaching, then inattention to teaching surfaces in low standards.

There are several different mechanisms to enhance standards, and we cover most of them in this chapter. Institutions may enhance standards by admitting only highly competent students, of course, but the practice of selection, while it does operate in subtle ways for certain courses (as we see in Section I), is not generally possible in open-access institutions. Alternatively, educational institutions can establish standards through the preparation of teachers, requiring that instructors have both content knowledge and pedagogical skills. But community colleges generally don't select or prepare instructors for mastery of teaching, as we show more carefully in Chapter 8, and instructors who may be well prepared in their subjects may still undermine standards through their teaching practices, as we describe in Section II when we illustrate how distressed and collapsed classes emerge.

Third, instructors can rely on conventional testing and assessment to hold their students to standards, but these create their own dilemmas, as we illustrate in Section III. While some community college instructors have been creative in developing alternative assessments, many continue to use conventional multiple-choice exams, with negative effects on many students. Finally, education standards sometimes come from external sources, including those of employers and of four-year colleges in transfer programs; but, as we argue in Section IV, these external standards are generally weak except in a few occupational areas.

The upshot is that the principal mechanisms of upholding standards in education don't work well in community colleges. So colleges face an almost impossible dilemma. The programs they provide, by turns academic and transfer-oriented, occupational, and remedial, are pulled among many different standards, particularly as they serve students with varying purposes and levels of preparation. But the forums for discussing the setting of standards are weak, since there are few colleges where there is any sustained attention to teaching or any mechanism of enforcing standards save a recommended outline here and there. In the absence of any institutional agreement, it becomes difficult to define any widely accepted standards. Therefore instructors must find their own way through the thickets of competing standards, and it isn't surprising to find great variation.

I. THE DILEMMAS OF STANDARDS IN OPEN-ACCESS INSTITUTIONS

A defining characteristic of community colleges is that they are open-access institutions. In some states, any high-school graduate can enter; in others, even high-school dropouts may enroll if they show an "ability to benefit." Many community college students have had mediocre academic records, and some—those who enroll for remedial purposes, and some immigrants from impoverished countries—have learned very little in their formal schooling.

But even open-access colleges have a surprising number of selection mechanisms, limiting the variety of students in certain classes. Indeed, much of the outstanding teaching we saw occurred in such "selective" classes, implying that a narrower range of students helps create the conditions for effective teaching.

Prerequisites

Among the most important selection mechanisms in many community colleges are the basic skills tests taken by entering students (reviewed in Section I of Chapter 5), which remove the least-prepared students from regular college-level courses. A few specialized programs have instituted their own admissions procedures. For example, some learning communities profiled in Chapter 7 have interview procedures that screen applicants for motivation; the PACE programs for older adults typically have application procedures that create more motivated and homogeneous student groups. Some occupational programs have their own screening devices. Health occupations programs typically require certain science prerequisites; because they are usually oversubscribed, there are admissions standards and waiting periods. Some technical programs have tests of mechanical aptitude; others have interview procedures that may serve as screens for ability and motivation. (For example, one auto instructor held orientation meetings where, he admitted, he would "scare away" about one third of potential students with stories of conditions on the job.) Some programs—early childhood education, for instance, or occupations involving customer relations—look for personality characteristics. Some occupational programs have implicit mechanisms of self-selection by gender, since they are dominated by men (automotive programs and the trades) or women (early childhood and health occupations). A few agricultural equipment programs that work closely with employers require students to be sponsored by local dealers before they can enroll, and some co-op programs require employer selection, so that screening is done partly by employers. Prerequisites are quite varied, then, and sometimes work in subtle ways.

Student Intentions and Interest

Enrolling in occupational courses normally means that a student has made a choice about a prospective vocation, ensuring higher motivation than in classes without selection by interest. Similarly, upper-division (or sophomore-level) academic courses are generally attended by students who major in these subjects, ensuring both certain levels of preparation and motivation. Unusual teaching environments attract a self-selected group; for example, learning communities on some campuses have generated special reputations, and appeal to students disposed toward their multidisciplinary, participatory style. Based on our observations and the comments of instructors, immigrant students in ESL courses are highly motivated. Certain specialized subjects attract small numbers of committed students, like the astonishing seminar we observed in a Muslim world studies program. Finally, evening classes tend to attract older students, usually employed during the day, who are seeking to improve their employment situation or move into new careers. Universally, instructors say that older students are more motivated and committed, and have more life experience that they can draw upon in class. The time of day therefore turns out to be a powerful selection mechanism.

In contrast, many first-level and transfer courses attract a wide range of students, including "experimenters" who are there to see what they might be interested in. Many instructors recognize that such experimenters are less likely to be committed to the subject as one English instructor commented:

> I think a lot of the people who don't make it through my course, it's not through lack of my motivating them, it's simply through a lack of them being ready to be students or having any idea why they're here.

As a result, instructors who teach different classes often face very different groups of students. One psychology instructor, for example, noted that her Psych 1 class included many experimenters and transfer students accumulating credits without any real interest in psychology. In contrast, her class in human relations included more older working students who were seeking to upgrade their employment and who saw immediate applications in their own work. Among her classes, then, "the levels of motivation vary tremendously."

Student Persistence

A final mechanism of selection—more precisely, of *self*-selection by students—is persistence. In virtually all community colleges, attrition is very high during the first few weeks of a course, as high as 50 percent. Experimenters who find the course not to their liking, students who find the requirements too hard, and those whose personal lives become disrupted are among the dropouts. They leave behind students with more time and resources, who are almost by definition more committed and better able to do the classwork. As one instructor noted,

> A large number of our students drop. So the identity of our classrooms does change, because the people drop who have such overwhelming problems that they couldn't stay with the class, and were not sure they were ever gonna be college students anyway.

The result of these selection mechanisms is that, even in open-access institutions, many individual programs and courses are selective. Some of them are selective in multiple ways. For example, the child development class profiled in Chapter 2, Section I, was triply selective since there was a formal course prerequisite, most students were there as part of occupational programs in early childhood education or human services, and this second-year course enrolled only students who had persisted through a year of preliminary coursework. In such a class, motivation is high, competencies in conventional reading and writing are adequate, and students have substantial experiences of their own relevant to the class. These selection mechanisms significantly contributed to the active student participation that made this class so remarkable.

But many courses are not so selective. In the lower-level English and math courses that often prove to be remedial, in the first-level courses in natural and social sciences that students must take for transfer, in the day programs with young and uncommitted students, instructors experience the full diversity of the community college. The most thoughtful instructors have expressed the resulting problem as one of being caught between two conflicting conceptions of "standards." As an English instructor described the struggle:

> I think at the community colleges we have a real difficulty, because one has to be always playing two sets of standards off simultaneously. There's got to be some absolute standards, some sense of what the student needs to produce in terms of writing competence in a given course . . . so that, indeed, when he or she does transfer, that student will be competitive with the same students who started their freshman year in a four-year institution. But then we also, of course, have the range of skills within our own classrooms. So I tend to try to keep high standards in terms of my willingness to give what are traditionally called high grades but to solve the problem of the fact that students can't attain those standards initially by both allowing and requiring things to be redone. And I'll try to teach in better ways and I'll try to repackage the way I present the instruction and I give students both the opportunity and the responsibility to redo things that are below the standards that I think I really have to maintain.

In effect, there are both absolute and relative standards. Absolute standards govern the *level* of what any student in a college-level math or English or economics course should know. Relative standards refer to *changes* in what students learn, recognizing that students with inadequate preparation cannot achieve the same absolute levels in the same time as well-prepared (or four-year-college) students. This reflects a widespread perception among instructors that even if the improvement in competency in a community college is high, absolute achievement levels may remain lower.[2]

The difference between absolute and relative standards creates confusion for students as well as faculty. The same English instructor continued to talk about her students:

Most of them have no real sense of the standards that exist or where they really fit within them. Or if they do, that's such a difficult issue to face that they somehow consider that there's something wrong with the standards or with the college or with the teacher or with themselves. Very few of them can separate the notion of intelligence and the notion of being educated.... They get all confused between what's learning and what's intelligence; they get all confused between potential and achievements.... They equate potential with achievement, so if they didn't get it right, right away, they're not going to get it.

The inability of students to distinguish accomplishments (or what we call relative standards) from absolute standards leads them to think that they don't have the ability to achieve, and this in turn leads them to devalue their own potential to learn—"both of which are very nonproductive to addressing learning, both of which are totally debilitating conditions." The absence of any clarification to students about different conceptions of standards therefore undermines the educational enterprise itself.

One problem for colleges and their students is that discussions about standards usually refer to absolute standards, particularly in comparing community colleges to four-year colleges. It has been nearly impossible to conduct public discussions about relative or "value-added" conceptions of standards. In addition, articulating any conception of value-added or relative standards smacks of *lowering* standards, of settling for "lower expectations" for disadvantaged and working-class and minority students. So the question inevitably remains: How can instructors reconcile absolute and relative conceptions of standards? How can they try to attain some level of absolute standards with students who are by definition poorly prepared?

Many faculty respond to the dilemma of varying standards through pedagogical innovation. Like the English instructor just quoted, they lean on their students to work harder and longer and to redo unacceptable work. They "try to teach in better ways" and "repackage the way I present the instruction," usually shifting to more student-centered and active forms of teaching. They include the better remedial instructors we profiled in Section II of Chapter 5, who taught literacy as a social practice rather than an isolated skill; the instructors we describe in Chapter 7, experimenting with more constructivist teaching methods; and those who have devised learning communities, including those for developmental students. Indeed, among faculty who are particularly concerned about low-achieving students, a conventional wisdom has developed: Ordinary whole-class lecture is the least effective method of instruction, and discussion, small-group work, and project-based methods are more likely to be effective. As one dean of instruction expressed it,

Many of the faculty are still teaching with the same paradigms that were successful when we had a different student population. The future rests in the faculty's ability to develop alternative teaching styles.

In other words, middle-class students may be able to learn through lecture, but nontraditional students need other methods.[3] Even though the specifics of "alternative teaching styles" are often left vague, most instructors imply some version of the meaning-making approach we described in Chapter 1.

A further question is how faculty can "try to teach in better ways" and "develop alternative teaching styles" in institutions (like this dean's) with so little institutional support for pedagogical innovation. Individual instructors who articulate this position have usually come to their own teaching methods through experience as well as trial and error. For example, the English instructor quoted above explained the development of her practices quite simply: "I've been teaching in the community colleges for twenty years." But for many others, any hopes of pedagogical innovation are undermined by the lack of institutional support. For example, the difficulty of teaching students with low literacy skills provoked this exasperated comment from an anthropology instructor:

> The text is the basis for my lecture. . . . When I digress from the text, I find that I can't lecture. If I don't require it, they don't read it. You can't have interactions if they haven't read the material.

In a selective college, she could have solved this problem by admitting only well-prepared students. Since this solution was unavailable, she might have expected help in figuring out how to teach the students she did have. Instead, she felt isolated: The people who evaluated her for tenure had been high-school teachers, and were uninterested in both her teaching and her subject.

> There's no one who really looks at the content of my teaching or who's currently interested in my research. . . . I could be saying things that are absolutely wrong and they would not know the difference.

There was, in other words, no community of practice in her institution that could respond to the challenges instructors face in teaching students who don't read.

Unfortunately, then, many instructors are unable to make the transition to "alternative teaching styles" when they confront a wide range of students. They lack the preparation before they start teaching, and there's little support within most colleges to help them change. Instead, as we will see in the next section, they tend to take one of two other approaches, one of which we call "blissful indifference" and the other a more familiar route of accommodation, of reducing content to accommodate the variety of students. But these pedagogical strategies lead, more often than we like to think, to classes where very little learning is taking place. In the process, pedagogical responses to the variety of students operate to undermine standards.

II. WHEN THINGS GO WRONG: DISTRESSED AND COLLAPSED CLASSES

Some classes seem to illustrate everything that can go wrong in teaching. The content vanishes, the discussion is lackluster if not outright hostile, and most students fail to participate. Such classes are alarmingly frequent—perhaps one fourth of those we observed fell into this category. These are unpleasant places to be, and they represent a collapse of standards as well. Our purpose in examining these classes is to note some patterns in the ways things fall apart and to understand what pedagogical standard is being disregarded.

Classes can manifest several different kinds of trouble. In the first kind, which we label "distressed" because of the evident tensions, a struggle seems to be taking place between instructor and students. Students arrive late, leave early, cluster in the back rows, and whisper or sleep or study materials from other classes. The architectural history class described in Chapter 2, where most of the students left during the slides, is a good example, where students simply voted with their feet. In other cases of open resistance, students are actively disputatious or rude; they might, for example, argue combatively rather than productively. Then, if the instructor cannot reshape the conflict into a constructive dialogue, a class with a legitimate disagreement is likely to deteriorate. A class would also count as distressed when the instructor gets angry at students, perhaps insulting them in some way, or asserts procedural authority to stop a discussion that has gone too far. An example is the anthropology class described in Chapter 2: A student muttered, "How the hell do we even know how to make mud bricks?" in an overt challenge to the assignment, stopping the class dead in its tracks. The instructor, failing to get any real discussion going, then reverted to threats of a quiz and to simple slogans describing complex conceptions.

In another example, a physics instructor lecturing on acceleration asked students to draw a graph representing a simple concept. One student refused aggressively, saying he didn't get the handout. The instructor suddenly got angry; the class was shaken up. Pulling herself together, the instructor commanded, "Read the rest of the chapter"—but that was the end of activity in the class. In another class in which the instructor had asked students to define *humanitarian*, the problem of how to compare the humanitarian activities of rich and poor people began to stir the class. Students suggested that the very rich were not really being humanitarian when they gave to the institutions of their own class. The instructor, with a different definition in mind, commanded, "Get out your papers and write everything you know about technology," effectively silencing everyone. In these classes, there appeared to be a struggle between the instructor and the students, and it wasn't clear who would win—though the instructor always has procedural authority.

In the second (and more common) type of class, students seem to be going along, apparently cooperating with the instructor—yet something is wrong. Sometimes students put up with low levels of content or with an ill-prepared instructor. In other cases, students sit amiably while a class is pitched at the wrong level—too fast, too difficult, or (in one case) delivered in rapid colloquial English to a class of ESL students. We call such classes "collapsed" because the content has leaked out of them and they have simply deflated. They don't show the tension typical of distressed classes, but there isn't any content, either. We interpreted these classes as places where a struggle had already been resolved, perhaps long before the semester began. Students have come to accept the authority of the instructor and the order of the classroom, no matter how little takes place. These classes have attained the equilibrium we mentioned in Chapter 1, in which teacher and student expectations are aligned, but it is a low-content equilibrium.[4] The battle for control of the class has been won, but the war has been lost.

Distressed and collapsed classes, with either active or passive resistance, have certain features in common. They are likely to be lectures, or lecture/discussion marked by fill-in-the-blank or IRE questions. The instructor generally holds a firm grip on the meaning of what is being taught; in the vocabulary we developed in Chapter 4, these are classes in which the instructor is authoritative, yielding no interpretive power to students. Often, given the academic background of students, these classes do not provide enough technical information about what is being learned, such as the significance of the x- and y-axes on a graph, or the difference between an index and a table of contents. The lack of any explicit teaching of technical details means that some students are left behind for lack of background knowledge, not by what they are learning. These classes are also marked by "passive" teaching methods: The instructor is not using a pedagogical strategy requiring the student to do the hard work of learning—interpreting, analyzing, explaining, assembling, or summarizing. Instead, the instructor carries the entire burden of delivering content to students orally, and the students sit passively, listening, usually taking only the most minimal notes.

Student resistance, whether active or passive, may come from several different sources.[5] Sometimes it comes from students being in such stultifying classes that they lack any motive to participate. Sometimes passivity comes from students who have been socialized to be passive, who have spent their high school years "trained" to be quiet participants, with little demanded of them; many instructors (like the one profiled in Chapter 2, Section I) who have not resocialized their students then face sullen, quiet students instead of the active contributors they want. And many students lack any real sense of how much work is expected of them in college, as the English instructor quoted above expressed when she said that "most of them have no real sense of the standards that exist." As a result, instructors confront resistance from students who literally have no idea that the demands on them are reasonable, and they face passivity from students who are used to sitting quietly through didactic classes. But without an ability to disentangle these different kinds of resistance, to recognize them for what they are and then correct them, some form of lowered expectations is often the only response.

Blissful Indifference

Frequently, distressed classes develop from a particular instructor's response to the problem of maintaining standards in an open-access institutions—an approach we call blissful indifference. A large number of these classes march students through a standard textbook, with instructors lecturing and making concessions neither to innovative pedagogies nor to their students' levels of preparation. Instructors who adopt these practices are likely to be quite starchy about their responsibilities; for example, the architectural history instructor described earlier and in the next section declared, "I'm going to give a slide recognition quiz. If they haven't seen it, they'll flunk." Or as an extremely didactic biotechnology teacher— one with a dry and monotonous style, who made little attempt to "check in" with students—explained his approach,

> At first there were a lot of complaints that I was going too fast. I told them to go back and look at their notes. . . . If they go back and read their notes, they'll work through it and understand. So they blame it on me, but it's their responsibility to learn. I can't make them learn. They have to come motivated to learn. And some of them don't understand what that means.

Indifference to what students are and are not learning—plowing ahead with lecture, no matter the level of comprehension—is a way of maintaining standards and guaranteeing coverage, though the consequence is likely to be a high rate of attrition and failure. This is a nonresponse to the problems of having varied students—it amounts to "faculty teaching with the same paradigms that were successful when we had a different student population."

The tactic of blissful indifference has emerged in the past in discussions about the "right to fail." In the early 1970s, when it became clear that community colleges experienced high dropout rates, a debate ensued about whether the responsibility for success lies with students or with the colleges themselves. One view was that students had a right to enter community colleges but that the responsibility for completion was theirs alone—their "right to fail" was the corollary of their right of entry. One instructor described the atmosphere that was "going on back in the fifties and sixties":

> If you learned anything, you acquired it on your own. No one was there to assist or help you. . . . So the guy gets in and he goes to school, and all through life people have been telling him school was there to help him. When he gets into the classroom he sits in the classroom and he tells the instructor that he has a problem. The instructor will tell him, you know, "Read the book," or "Go to the library and read this book"— never try to find out what his or her problem was and understand it. And this occurs several times to the individual, and the individual gets frustrated. They drop out.

Over time the discussion about the "right to fail" has moderated, replaced by a more sophisticated discussion about what to do about high rates of noncompletion. The development of remedial/developmental education, more student-centered approaches to teaching, and of student services such as counseling and tutoring all reflect the notion that the community college should take more responsibility for the success of students. But the tendency to place full responsibility for learning and completion on students is deeply rooted in all educational institutions.

Accommodation

Another way to cope with the variety of students in a classroom is a process we (and others) call accommodation.[6] Accommodation is always a process of lowering standards, though it happens in several ways. One form occurs when students resist learning, particularly in authoritarian and didactic classes, and teachers then lower their expectations in return for decent behavior and minimal compliance— a negotiated truce. For example, the reduction of cultural anthropology to simple slogans, described above, occurred partly because of student resistance to this instructor.

A slightly different form of accommodation occurs when instructors discover, or believe, that their students are not competent to meet high standards. One instructor admitted that she chose a difficult text for her Psych 1 course, to impress four-year college instructors for those very few students who did transfer, but she cut back on the amount covered because students were unable to make much progress in a difficult text. Another, teaching in a middle-class college, noted that he did not have "the best of the crop" of postsecondary students:

> I tend to water it down a little bit. . . . If I had a group of students who were all the equivalent of [university level], I would teach it a little differently. I would be much more severe in tests and so forth. I would be asking nothing but essay questions, and I would go into much greater detail in some areas. And I think I'd be a little bit more demanding than I am with this sort of mixed group.

In reality, this instructor would not change his pedagogy at all for better-prepared students; he would simply demand more from them on tests. In this form of accommodation, instructors faced with lower levels of academic preparation maintain the same teaching methods but reduce their demands.

Accommodation can also come from sympathy with students and their complex lives, as well as from thinking them incompetent. Instructors recognize that their students have lives that are considerably more difficult than those of "traditional" students. They almost always work, many have family responsibilities, and the poorest of them are beset with family abuse and community violence. Instructors don't want to make their students' lives any harder. One psychology instructor explained his lack of required writing in this way:

> It's optional, that they can do it if they want, because most of them are working a couple of jobs, raising kids and taking a full load . . . and they just, I mean, they hardly have enough time to study, much less to write for hours. . . . I have a very wide C range, so that allows most people to at least get C's and not have to worry about failing.

Similarly, the English instructor described in Section I of Chapter 2 characterized her students in these terms:

> Students' lives are so incredibly complicated and busied up compared to twenty-five years ago. . . . I just decided this semester not to make their lives any harder by being mean to them. . . . So I've just decided to try to make the class as palatable as possible without reducing the standards. As enjoyable as I can. And try to be, you know, as decent, so I'm not one more thorn.

Despite the aside about not reducing standards, this instructor limited the content of her classes substantially, and she was intensely conflicted about it: "I'm not sure this is even good. Someone said to me, 'Well, you're just codependent, you're just aiding them in their troubles.'" Another expressed his ambivalence in similar terms:

> I think, generally, we're [community college instructors] too loose in our standards. Because we want to . . . it comes from a good heart . . . we want to be forgiving, you know, we want to help students as much as we can, we've got this sort of bleeding heart for all the students. But I think maybe we've gone too far with that, and now it's time for a little tough love.

A symptom of accommodation is homework. Many instructors noted that students simply do not do homework—indeed, we observed all too many classes where only a few students handed in problem sets and essays—and they explain this by the pressured lives of their students. The English teacher just quoted also commented,

> I've even asked them why don't they do the reading. . . . The answers are very interesting to me. They're not convincing, but I think they're convincing to them. They say they don't have the time. There's so much work, they're taking other classes.

The amount of homework assigned in most classes is quite small. It's very common to find that reading lists for a fifteen-week semester total 100 to 125 pages, a week's reading assignment is a five- to eight-page article, and required essays are two to four pages long. The four-year-college standard—where one rule of thumb has been that students work three hours outside of class for every hour in class—is clearly not being met in community colleges, under the assumption that part-time students cannot do that much work.

When instructors meet the low preparation of students with low expectations, three pedagogical ploys contribute to diluting content: content is converted into facts and slogans, entertainment displaces content, and content is dominated by anecdote and opinion.

Converting content into facts and slogans. In many classes taught in a didactic and teacher-centered (or text-centered) way, the content is converted into brief slogans or expressions for the students to memorize. Sometimes this happens under duress. For example, the anthropology teacher described in Chapter 2, faced with a class that was by turns hostile and apathetic, finally ended up with a series of brief declarations that she threatened to include on a subsequent quiz:

> Instructor: "If you can't remember [these concepts], I'll have to ask you to study them again and I will retest you. . . . You should not forgot

RCD [radiocarbon dating], you should not forget systems theory, you should not forget cultural materialism, you should not forget that culture is integrated. So before we go on, can someone tell me what systems theory is?"

Student: "You have been dependent on each other."

Instructor: "Well, to be more specific, that each subsystem within a culture is interdependent, so the agricultural system will affect maybe the marital situation, the marital system will affect the religious system, and as there is change in one you will see a change in marital patterns and many trade patterns. Cultural materialism is about what?"

Student 2: "You are what you're wearing."

Instructor: "You are what you wear, or you are what's in your house, so when you look at the materialist nature of society we can tell a lot about that society. Radiocarbon dating: What is that used to date?"

Student 3: "Advanced materialism?" [This is a wild and irrelevant guess.]

Instructor: "Very few of you talked about radiocarbon dating being used to analyze the materials in that household."

These students were therefore learning anthropology as a series of slogans—cultural materialism, systems theory—whose meanings they memorized for a quiz, rather than as a discipline with broad questions about culture that can be used to illuminate a variety of societies (including our own). Similarly, a philosophy instructor summarized the writing of several philosophers by brief slogans—Kant by the categorical imperative, James by pragmatism, Sartre by existentialism. Philosophy became a series of individuals associated with phrases, not a way of systematically addressing complex issues. The English teacher in Chapter 2 had drilled students on the definition of ellipsis, as if that fact would help their writing. Similarly, one can see sociology reduced to a series of theorists, psychology reduced to a procession of personality theories, and history converted into names and dates and big events.

Community college instructors fall back on this approach for different reasons. When students are inattentive—because they are in lectures unrelated to anything of interest—instructors are sometimes driven in desperation to slogans as a way of ensuring that students learn *something*, no matter how trivial. In other cases, instructors may assume that students don't have the ability to discuss sophisticated concepts. More to the point, some instructors have never seen how initial exercises, small-group discussions, and skillful questioning can bring even unprepared students to discuss quite complex subjects. The requirements of coverage in introductory courses—Sociology 1, Psychology 1, and the like—also drive them to simplification and sloganeering. And the extensive use of multiple-choice tests, or tests that ask for short responses, exacerbates the tendency to reduce complex disciplines to simple facts and short slogans.

Entertainment. In some classes, various forms of entertainment displace much of the content. For example, one business instructor, a real *mensch,* enlivened his class with a long series of funny asides, affectionate jibes ("Now get it down, loves: Span of control is the number of people who report to a manager"), and concocted examples of hypothetical business situations. At one point when students couldn't agree, he said, "Let's get one of Greenberg's famous votes," and had students vote on the possible correct answers. This procedure generated a great deal of razzing between the two sides and certainly enlivened the class. But as a pedagogical device a vote is counterproductive, since it implies that issues of fact should be put to a vote. The instructor ended up giving the right answer anyway, making the vote irrelevant except as a form of entertainment. This class appeared to be fast-paced and lively, but the humor masked a text-driven class with contrived examples, where the instructor avoided many real business problems facing his students (like store closings in poor neighborhoods and unemployment among minorities). Another instructor described his basic approach in similar terms:

> I view teaching a whole lot as a theatrical event. I like to perform, to stand in front of a group of students and discuss a math problem and cajole them and joke with them and . . . eventually get them to tell me some right answers along the way.

At the end of the theater "some right answers" might emerge—a conventional combination of fact-oriented instruction with "agreeable diversions."

The use of humor is one of the standard bromides for good practice in teaching. But the difference between motivating students so that they will absorb the material of a lecture and simply reducing a class to entertainment involves fine distinctions about the ways humor is used and the extent to which it displaces rather than reinforces content.[7] Without more attention to pedagogy—without, for example, feedback from supportive observers about whether an instructor uses humor too much or inappropriately—instructors are left to their own proclivities, and the result can undermine standards as easily as enhance them.

Anecdote and opinion-mongering. Another pedagogical device that tends to empty a class of content is reliance on personal anecdote and opinion, from both instructors and students. Sometimes, of course, these anecdotes are connected to the content of the class; as we pointed out in Chapter 3, occupational instructors often tell stories about their own work experiences to convey lore about the real world of practice. But in many other cases these anecdotes are simply other forms of entertainment. For example, one instructor of cultural anthropology, in the midst of a class on research design, kept wandering into a reminiscence of his past in Romania, highly engaging to students but unrelated to the subject at hand. In another example, an instructor in a class called Cultural Aspects of Health Care spent virtually an entire class on a personal story about racism in the South. Again, it was highly engaging to students, many of whom (as well as the instructor) were black; but it had nothing to do with the content of the class, which was intended to read a textbook cover to cover.

Unfortunately, when instructors trade anecdotes and stories, students begin to do so as well, and their contributions then reinforce the lack of content; one example was the biology class described in Section IV of Chapter 2. In some cases, entire classes degenerate into little more than uninformed opinions about an irrelevant topic. For example, here's a segment from a Psych 1 course, taught by an instructor who arrived late, without notes or preparation, and who had to ask students where the class had left off. The ostensible topic for the day was intelligence.

Instructor: "Can you think of a movie actor who is intelligent relevant
  to their environment?"
Student 1: "Madonna."
  Students laugh and comment to each other.
Instructor: "She's a prime example. In my opinion, she is very intelli-
  gent. Did you see the book *Sex*? Last semester students in my class
  pooled their money to buy it and then raffled it off."
Student 2: "That's not her intelligence, she has agents and publicists."
  Another student discounts this statement, referring to the fact that
Madonna hires those people. The instructor comments, "Who isn't as
intelligent? Brandon Lee wasn't intelligent."
  Other students pick up on the digression, asking questions like
"Who is he?" "When did he die?" "Who was Bruce Lee?" "It is a mys-
tery how he died. Something like the Mafia."
Instructor: "Excuse me. I don't think he [Brandon Lee] was adjusted
  very well, he put himself in the hands of others. There were other
  accidents on the movie set."
  By this time students were talking among themselves, with no clear
lecture or discussion going on. The instructor commented that
Madonna was intelligent, but that Marilyn Monroe probably wasn't.
Then he moved a little closer to the topic.
Instructor: "What I'm trying to do with the definition of intelligence is

to expand it." He writes "measuring intelligence" and "IQ—intelligence quotient" on the board, and students copy them down; ostensibly he is shifting to issues concerning the measurement of intelligence.

Instructor: "I'm not going to define it [IQ] because it isn't important to me. If it is to you, you can look it up."

This class is an extreme case of opinion mongering and anti-intellectualism, but examples like it occur in many classrooms. Some instructors even bless the unargued opinions of students. For example, in a course called Language and Society, the instructor took a series of euphemisms from the textbook and asked students "whether they have a problem with these or not." Rather than examining the conditions under which euphemisms arise, he declared, "This is a matter of opinion, so there is no right and wrong like that." One student made a distinction between cussing and swearing, reserving the latter for violations of the Fourth Commandment. Without investigating why such a distinction might be meaningful, the instructor simply responded, "That's your personal definition and no one can argue with you. You can tell them that I said so." (The authority relations embedded in this sentence are especially odd.)[8] Consistently, therefore, a class that could have investigated the way language varies across social settings was converted into simple opinions, with students giggling as they got to say dirty words in public.

A related way of undermining content is for instructors to accept whatever interpretations students offer as equally valid. For example, the poetry instructor profiled in Chapter 2 allowed her student to interpret the phrase "parting green from green" as referring to green water and green land, while in the context of the poem the image almost certainly expressed the parting of green branches while walking on land. The teacher accepted a second awkward interpretation ("Good, that too, both correct") without having students contrast their differing views. We rarely saw instructors challenging students about their interpretations, asking students to clarify their views, or otherwise signaling that an opinion might be "wrong." Instructors trying to socialize students away from fact-centered approaches are often grateful for anything they can get from students, but by being so accepting they are implicitly teaching them that anything goes.

We also suspect that instructors emphasizing student support are more likely to permit anecdote and opinion. For example, the instructor in Cultural Aspects of Health Care was especially emphatic about the need for instructors to be caring and supportive of students. Personal stories (like her story of facing racism in the South) were a way of establishing a good relationship with students. Anecdotes and opinions were accepted from students because challenging them—probing how their stories are related to the course, or asking the basis for an opinion—

would put students on the spot, might threaten them if they could not respond, and would clarify the instructor's role as a teacher rather than friend. However, it isn't supportive of students to allow them to slide through without learning much. In contrast, an excellent English instructor expressed her conception of teaching as "a balance of rigorous standards, and encouraging and supporting students." But simultaneously challenging and supporting students requires highly skilled teaching, and without any pedagogical preparation, some instructors find it easier simply to accept whatever students have to say.

The process of accommodation is an endless and subtle one, as writers on K–12 education have insisted. Because of it, nearly everyone participates in the process of lowering standards: the institution by its jigsaw puzzle of contradictory selection mechanisms without addressing the difficulties of shifting standards; instructors by their sympathy for students and many forms of accommodation; students by their endless negotiation with instructors about grades, tests, and the length of reading lists. It's simple to deplore lowering standards, but it is a complex process to withstand.

The responses to the problem of standards in open-access colleges—pedagogical innovation, accommodation, or blissful indifference—are quite different, obviously. Pedagogical innovation attempts to increase relative standards (or "value added"), often with absolute standards in mind. Accommodation lowers absolute standards and may also abandon relative standards. Blissful indifference tries to maintain absolute standards but may succeed with so few students that the average result is little or no progress. The three "solutions" quite often reflect allegiances to different pedagogical approaches as well. Those in the meaning-making tradition, with its commitment both to certain forms of student-centered learning and to intrinsic motivation, are most likely to embrace pedagogical innovation. Practitioners of conventional skills and drills sometimes take the tactic of indifference and sometimes, worn down by students and their resistance, follow the route of accommodation. Those adhering to student support tend to follow the more obvious forms of accommodation, particularly in failing to challenge students. The choice among the three is value-laden, and it depends on conceptions of the obligations of teachers, students, and institutions. But these are also pedagogical choices, because instructors who do not have access to pedagogical alternatives, or who cannot figure out how to make reasonable demands on their students without driving them away, have no option but to end up with lower standards or high attrition.

The only hope for escaping this dilemma is for instructors to develop greater control of their teaching. They need to have some sense when fun and games or storytelling gets out of hand. They need to understand when they should challenge students, and how they can do so without losing the students' allegiance. But in community colleges—as in every other educational institution where instructors close their doors once class begins—there are virtually no mechanisms for helping instructors achieve this balance. There are very few examples of co-teaching and very little observation of classes by peers or administrators (as we will clarify in Chapter 8); there is no one to provide instructors with feedback on their practices. Pre-service training in pedagogy is virtually nonexistent, and—except in a very few colleges—in-service training and staff development is diffuse and unhelpful. There are no forums for faculty to discuss their approaches to teaching, the problems they experience, the alternative solutions available. The lack of institutional support for instruction, by leaving faculty to their own proclivities, therefore has the unintended effect of undermining standards and content.

III. THE DILEMMAS OF TESTING AND ASSESSMENT

Yet another way for instructors to ensure that standards are being met is to assess students periodically. Those that do not meet some predetermined standard simply fail the course, and by elimination those who pass have met the standard. Testing and assessment have multiple purposes, however, in addition to setting and certifying standards. They also provide diagnostic information to instructors and to students themselves about how well they are learning, and they provide motivation for students to learn, in order to pass the course. Finally, assessments—particularly where they are established outside a class—often contain pedagogical incentives, embodied in the common concern about "teaching to the test." A multiple-choice test emphasizing facts or discrete skills may lead instructors to teach these facts and skills, while essay exams and portfolio assessments will lead to very different pedagogies. The roles of exams in setting standards, diagnosing learning, motivating students, and encouraging certain pedagogies are not necessarily consistent, as we shall see.

Community college instructors give many tests and quizzes—at least every other week, if not weekly. (The common exceptions are occupational instructors; their use of workshop-based projects as assessments is examined later in this section.) The vast majority are multiple-choice tests, even true/false tests; many are done on Scantron forms for easy grading—not an insignificant consideration if an instructor has five classes of twenty-five students each. Instructors often provide warnings about their content—"This is important, it might be on an exam"—and course syllabuses typically describe what will be covered on tests. In many classes, tests are the ultimate expression of skills-oriented approaches. They reflect the reduction of complex competencies into facts and simple skills, and they reinforce the authority of the teacher and the teacher-centered classroom. There aren't many surprises here: Instructors teaching their subjects as facts and skills develop multiple-choice tests that measure these facts and skills.

However, the diagnostic or educational value to students of these tests is limited. It's quite typical, as we noted in Chapter 2, for instructors to begin a class by reviewing a past test, providing the right answers, and sometimes giving some elaboration of the answers. But these are typically low-energy periods: A test review is an entirely teacher-directed activity, and students often appear distressed by their low grades rather than challenged. The pedagogical approach of learning from mistakes—of diagnosing what kinds of errors are common, how they might arise, and how students can avoid them in the future—is one we almost never observed.

The value of tests in setting standards is quite limited for the simple reason that the majority of tests are created by instructors for their own classes and therefore embody the standards of the individual instructor, not those of an institution or external body. The only exceptions are the few colleges with department-wide tests as mechanisms of imposing common standards. Some textbook-driven classes using tests provided in the textbook also meet an external standard of sorts. Otherwise, the standards embodied in tests are idiosyncratic and shifting. The admission of the architectural history instructor quoted above—"I tend to water it down a little bit"—describes his tests as well as class content. As one math instructor described the problem:

> In mathematics we teach—a number of us teach the same classes and we more or less agree on the same text, but then I think we each do it our own very special way—tremendously different attitudes about it. I wish that the department would consider going to uniform exams because I'm afraid at times that some people are failing—not delivering. Some of the teachers may not be delivering everything they could be delivering. But as far as I can tell, there's no receptivity for that—so we're basically independent agents.

The motivational power of tests is similarly quite checkered. There's no question that students do respond to tests, since "studenting" behavior—"Will it be on the test?"—is common. But sometimes tests are used for punitive purposes; here's a crisp example of this pattern, with a boot camp analogy thrown in:

> I noticed that about a half dozen of the students would leave when they'd start showing slides. . . . That's pretty dumb, but, you know, they're right out of high school—"Well, I can do this. We don't need to stay and look at these things." And I'm going to give a slide recognition quiz. If they haven't seen it, they'll flunk.

The interviewer then asked if they knew that such a quiz was coming up.

> Not yet, they don't. My feeling is, and this is sort of a harsh feeling, that when I went
> to high school, I almost flunked out. And then I went into the Navy, a V-12 program,
> went to the University of Texas, and flunked out. And I had to go to boot camp, I got
> on a ship, went off to the Pacific in late '44, and I came back—I was grown-up. . . .
> So, in flunking out, I learned something. . . . So if I flunk somebody here, I don't feel
> sorry for [him]. It's an education. Say, okay, society says you're failing. Shape up or go
> do something else.

There's little chance, we think, that forcing students to attend slide slows with surprise quizzes will cause them to retain much about the power and glory of architecture. Another instructor, who also used tests in punitive ways, described the effects tests have throughout the semester:

> The first thing [in the semester] a lot of students are curious and open-minded and
> a lot of them are happy to get in because some of the classes are full and everything is
> fresh and new. Some could care less like from day one, but I think the majority of
> people when they come in, before they start to have assignments and test dates, feel
> curious. I guess it's when you get down to the work, the assignments and the first
> test, that students start to feel a different way.

So the initial blush of curiosity and open-mindedness is squeezed out of students by tests—hardly a testimonial to their motivating power.

Alternative Assessments

A large number of instructors recognize how counterproductive multiple-choice, fact-oriented quizzes are—particularly for the students in community colleges. As an early childhood educator expressed the problem:

> In terms of testing, it's hard for some of the students to write down their thoughts or
> their interpretations . . . and testing is really an issue for some of our students. They
> just freak out, you know. We have a lot of re-entry women who haven't been in
> school for a long time.

To avoid these negative effects, a number of instructors have devised alternative forms of assessment. One common approach is to provide options for extra credit, since extra credit allows students to choose how they will be graded, provides incentives for additional work, and increases the grades students can earn. For example, one English instructor described herself as the "extra-credit queen" in her college and gave students many options for extra credit, including attendance at lectures, plays, and even art galleries as long as they wrote a two-page paper about it—partly to get students outside of school and thinking about the uses of language in different settings. Another pattern is to allow students to redo work; for example, one developmental instructor devised a grade of R (for "repeatable"):

> If it's just not passing quality, if it doesn't do what it's supposed to do, and if they didn't master anything we talked about, they get an R, which turns into an F; but it's an invitation for them to rewrite if they want to.

A more complex tactic is to get students to choose grading options from a menu of alternatives. One English instructor allowed students to choose among alternatives—a major paper worth 2 points, an elective paper worth 1 point, various computer exercises for 0.5 point, timely work for an extra 0.1 point, exemplary work for an extra 0.3—as long as the point score totaled 4.0. The purpose was to make assessment consistent with the pedagogy of the class, which maintained a balance of teacher- and student-centered methods ("It's important to keep a balance going; if it's all student-centered, then that's a failing"). This assessment system represented such a balance: The options were established by instructors, and the final decisions were made by students.

Another instructor, in physics, had also devised options for students who failed tests, where the option took the form of collaborative work:

> I have a way of grading them which has a lot of options. If you flunk an exam, there's an option. You can now do, let's say, two extra assignments outside. You have to find yourself a couple more team members and work together. . . . That's very motivating, I found out. You know, it really is amazing: They put in a heck of a lot more work than the exam was worth and they learn the topic much better than any other way because . . . they meet in the library, they meet in the coffee shop. . . . The other thing that's motivating about it is that you cannot face your team without doing something because after a while you've just simply dropped out of there.

Another collective option was developed in a learning community for older students (the PACE program described in Chapter 7). Students took a test individually, then retook it in small groups collaboratively; their final grade was the higher of the individual score or the average of the group score and the individual score. This allowed a low-performing individual's score to be pulled up by a group score.

More important, the process of taking the test collaboratively meant that students were working collectively and teaching each other while being assessed.

Yet another alternative assessment was devised to cope with the variation among students. In this case, a learning community included both younger and older students; "the sixteen-year-olds are clearly not as sophisticated as the older students" and were less likely to have completed writing requirements. Students could enroll for either English 101 or English 102, a second-level course, and their papers were graded with two different sets of expectations. At the same time, students enrolled for English 101 could see the different expectations for more advanced students:

> They [the younger students] struggled with getting beyond telling me what the story is about, and at the end of the quarter, they have a better understanding. Now Whitman in "Song of Myself" is really talking about existentialism and its conflict with his idealism of self, you see, so they move along that continuum. All the while, we're pushing harder and harder to help them move from this very simplistic level of, "Well, this story is about . . ." so that by the end of the quarter they are really beginning to understand more what college expectations are.

While the dual grading system responded to the dilemma of absolute versus relative standards, it also had its own educative value.

Finally, a team-taught learning community illustrated how an assessment can be devised by a class itself. The English instructor led a class in test-taking strategies, including how to identify the main points in short essays. In small groups, students then selected topics from the other subject of the learning community—social studies—while the second instructor of the team transcribed comments on a laptop computer. During a break, he formulated practice test questions, and students took this "test" after the break. This was, in effect, a student-generated and collective assessment, one that emerged from discussion among students.

These alternative assessments are much more than mechanisms of setting standards and assigning grades. They try to take the fear out of grading among students who react badly to conventional tests. They convert assessment into an inherently educative activity, and—in classes that aim to be more student-centered—are partially constructed by students themselves. They provide motivation for extra work—perhaps a sneaky kind of motivation ("They put in a heck of a lot more work than the exam is worth"), but one that works more effectively. In the end, they are part and parcel of pedagogies that differ in all their details from the standard lecture with tests that simply scare the hell out of students.

Occupational Projects as Forms of Assessment

For occupational instructors, assessments normally include projects carried out in workshops, instead of or in addition to paper-and-pencil tests. Often instructors combine both forms of assessment. For example, one instructor noted: "I teach electronics, which is 90 percent cognition and 10 percent manipulation." He therefore uses essay exams to test the cognitive dimensions of his class and lab-based assessments (demonstrations of wiring arrays) to test manipulative skills. Some do not rely on conventional tests at all. As another electronics instructor noted:

> I have a contracting business. I don't want anyone that works for me to go home and study tonight for what he's going to do tomorrow, okay—I want him to go out on the job with some knowledge that he has acquired, accumulated over a period of time, and not cramming. So I don't judge mine from tests or anything. My total judge as to what the student has acquired is out there in the laboratory.

This statement also clarifies that project-based tests are performance-based, and performance is a function of both accumulated knowledge and manipulative abilities (or other noncognitive "intelligences"). Students cannot fake performance or cram for such a test, nor are there idiosyncratic "interpretations" that instructors might be conned into accepting; either circuits and motors and many other projects work or they don't. The projects in occupational workshops combine learning, practice, and assessment, and it isn't necessary to have separate periods of time allocated to artificial tests.

Occupational instructors also frequently note that project-based assessments are more appropriate for the students in occupational programs and for the demands of employers. An HVAC instructor noted that, because of their preparation, his students wouldn't do well in conventional tests:

> Some people are really good at hands-on, aren't so good at tests. So if I give you the test, then if you fail the test you're still going to pass the course if you can physically do the work—and that's what you need to do when you get out on the job.

The electronics instructor cited above, the one who judged students entirely on the basis of lab work, echoed these comments:

> Where you find individuals that lack dexterity or the hands-on, then they place a lot of emphasis on the technical information. Whereas employers are not concerned with your knowledge of technical information; they're concerned with your ability to perform the work.

So work-related and project-based assessments have two further advantages over conventional pen-and-paper tests: They are more supportive of the "tactile" students in occupational courses, and they are "authentic" in the sense of being job-related.

While occupational faculty are virtually unanimous about the value of projects as assessments, this approach is more problematic than instructors acknowledge. In the first place, the emphasis on manipulative skills rather than cognitive understanding among some instructors—an emphasis on the "vocational" over the "academic"—may serve students well in entry-level jobs but deny them the abilities for long-run advancement. (This is part of the debate over broad versus narrow conceptions of occupational education, a subject to which we return in Section IV of Chapter 7.) Second, the realism of the occupational workshop is sometimes suspect since—as we examined in Chapter 3—occupational students are working on outmoded equipment, do not work at the pace required in production, or learn more general skills than the product-specific skills used in workplaces. These problems manifest themselves in assessments as much as in teaching, and some claims on behalf of project-based assessment should be tempered.

But there are no forums for discussion about occupational assessments. Aside from programs that are subject to external occupational standards (examined in the following section), there are no standard-setting agencies or organizations where assessments are debated. Like many other aspects of occupational education, project-based assessment has many inherent advantages over the most common forms of academic assessment, but it has emerged "naturally," without much debate or discussion or opportunities for improvement.

IV. EXTERNAL STANDARDS AND THEIR EFFECTIVENESS

The final mechanism for ensuring high standards in education is to impose external standards—typically, tests set by external agencies that students must pass, or content requirements set externally. Aside from Florida's "rising junior" exam for all students entering their junior year—including community college students who transfer—there are no universal exams in postsecondary education. However, there are still many external standards applicable to community colleges.

In academic subjects, "rigor" is usually defined as meeting the requirements for transfer, and most colleges have designed their academic curriculum by consulting the four-year institutions to which students are likely to transfer. As a dean of a technical institute described the process:

> We became a comprehensive community college about five years [ago] even though
> we didn't have any transfer courses. . . . We've invited our transfer institutions, Iowa
> State, University of Iowa, UNI, South Dakota, University of Nebraska, Wayne State,
> and then the privates in this area, to develop our curriculum for us. They come in
> and spend two real intense days. They not only have developed our curriculum, we
> are assured transfer with that curriculum. They take it back and rewrite their own,
> because they know this was the best, this compilation of what everybody is doing.

The assumption here, clearly, is that "what everybody is doing" is best, and that what is best for four-year colleges is also best for community colleges.

However, the standards developed for transfer courses are based on the syllabus and content of a course, not on issues of pedagogy or how that content is delivered. Therefore the real content—the curriculum actually taught, rather than the formal curriculum—may be quite different from that envisioned in articulation agreements. This happens, for example, when a syllabus contains more than an instructor actually covers, or when an instructor chooses a harder textbook to impress four-year colleges but fails to cover much of it, or when instructors engage in the forms of accommodation we described in Section II.

A clear illustration of how content can vary despite transfer requirements is the comparison among courses with the same title in a single institution.[9] In one community college, for example, a common syllabus had been adopted for Psychology 1. But one instructor taught the class "by the book," presenting the chapters in the textbook-centered approach we described in Chapter 2; a second instructor made almost no mention of the text and converted the course into an applied course for students going into the helping professions, relying on student experiences and anecdotes; and the third teacher, described in Section II above, converted the course into a random discussion of topics such as the relative intelligence of Madonna and Marilyn Monroe. In another institution, one English instructor led her students through a high-level discussion of readings, concentrating on such meta-analytic issues as the requirements for appropriate inference; another teaching the same course had to work hard to drag facts about a piece of literature from her students, and spent a great deal of time reinforcing grammatical rules. In a biology class for nonmajors, one that counted as lower-division science for students transferring to the nearby flagship campus of the state university, a "field trip" involved a forty-five-minute walk to a neighboring wetlands to collect one insect; students then had to draw the insect and label the head, abdomen, and thorax. And, as we saw in Chapter 5, many college-level English and math courses are transformed into remedial/developmental courses when instructors find high proportions of students without the skills necessary for "college-level" work—but these courses still meet transfer requirements.

Sometimes the exigencies of trying to get students through a program take precedence over any standards set by transfer requirements. In one learning community, the four instructors wanted to give credit for a transfer-level math course but could not figure out how to integrate math with the other subjects. They settled for giving credit for computer science (which counts in that state as math) and required them to use word processors—so students were getting math transfer credit for word processing. Another learning community, geared for working adults, devised a schedule that would allow students to fit the program in on nights and weekends, including four hours per week of prescribed videos. In practice several students admitted that they did not complete this component because there was no check on them, and they therefore received full credit toward transfer for a substantially shorter program.

Transfer requirements are weak forms of external standards, then. Anyone can write a syllabus that meets the requirements of articulation agreements, but content and standards depend on what instructors do in class. In effect, transfer agreements constitute *voluntary* standards, useful for conscientious instructors but without much effect among others. This observation leads to an obvious explanation for "transfer shock": Some students transferring to four-year colleges go through a period of low grades because the standards of their community college courses have not been as high as those in four-year colleges.

If external standards for academic courses are weak, they are virtually absent for remedial/developmental courses. In theory, community colleges establish remedial courses for those students unprepared for college-level work. But "college-level" work is ill-defined; while a few states (like New Jersey) have set statewide norms for remedial programs, most institutions set their own. And even where developmental studies departments have created coherent programs, as the example of North County Community College in Chapter 5 illustrates, these are still internally defined standards.

Some occupational courses are subject to external standards. Licensing exams apply, for example, to nursing and most other health occupations, to airplane mechanics licensed by the Federal Aviation Administration, and building inspectors and construction managers who must pass state and local tests about building codes.[10] In other occupations, standards are voluntary—as in welding, where the American Welding Society has promoted voluntary standards, or in automobile repair, where NATEF has done the same.[11] Even in a state where licensing is not required, an instructor related that his students are likely to take the test "to prove that he or she does know what they're doing," so that the NATEF standard is still employed as an indicator of quality.[12]

Advisory committees for occupational programs also serve to set standards.[13] Such committees have pressured some programs into incorporating more communications skills, more reading and writing and other forms of "academic" content; as one occupational dean mentioned,

> The thing that amazed me, which I was very pleased by, and I think was a little more than the faculty thought it would be, was the high level that the advisory committees wanted them to have in reading and in writing and in math.

Another occupational instructor, in dental assisting, noted that her advisory committee met only once a semester but that "there are people on the committee that I can get to very quickly if I have a question"—so that advisory committees can serve as sources of continuous consultation. Like voluntary standards, advisory committees cannot be as uniform in their influence as external licensing exams, but they do serve as external sources of authority for those instructors serious about keeping up with good practice.

A final kind of occupational standard is potentially quite powerful but, unfortunately, relatively rare in community colleges. Where colleges have internships and co-op programs, the need to prepare students for work placements constitutes another kind of external pressure. One nursing instructor mentioned her goals:

> A goal is to have them pass the exam and have a good internship. I mean, I feel very successful when they come back with good evaluations of their internships. It makes me feel that they've gotten the essence of what it is to work in health care, and that they've done a good job.

In her description, the exam and the internship are roughly equivalent kinds of standards, the first covering the "body of knowledge" necessary in nursing and the second covering the "life skills" and behavior required on the job.

While internships and cooperative education are relatively rare in community colleges except in nursing programs, where they exist they have powerful effects on standards.[14] Probably the best examples exist in two-year colleges in Cincinnati (Villeneuve and Grubb, 1996). Standards are maintained in several ways. Students must have completed all remedial work before starting a co-op placement, must have earned a certain grade-point average, and must have completed a certain number of prerequisite occupational courses. Students are also selected by employers, and employers work with occupational instructors to make sure that students learn certain competencies before they start the work-based component. Implicitly, employers and technical colleges have developed a high-quality equilibrium. Colleges are aware that their students must be well prepared if employers are to participate; as one co-op coordinator noted,

If [employers] got clunkers every time, if they got somebody who couldn't do the job or learn the job—they would, of course, generally be able to deal with that on a once-a-year basis [but they wouldn't put up with it often]. If a coordinator doesn't screen an applicant sufficiently for the job—I mean, if you put a student out on a job, for example, in drafting or in CAD, and the student hates offices and wants to be in a factory or outside—that is not [going to work well]. So there's a certain amount of common sense to make sure that the situation works right.

For their part, employers understand that low-quality placements do not attract the best students:

I inform [employers] if they have a low campus image and nobody wants to interview with their company—because students bring this back, too, you know. There's nothing that can kill a program quicker than students coming back and complaining about their co-op job. There's a lot of buzz on campus about different businesses and where the good jobs are.

All participants understand that the high-quality equilibrium can persist only if each side keeps up its end of the implicit bargain. The result is that co-op programs in Cincinnati enjoy high standards in both the college-based components and the work-based ones.

In general, then, external standards are most powerful in occupational programs, though even here they are often voluntary.[15] The external standards imposed by transfer requirements are weak and easily evaded, and external standards are completely missing for remedial/developmental education. The result is that community colleges must rely on internal or professional standards in order to maintain the quality of their programs—that is, on the norms of individual instructors. But this returns the issue of standards and content to the realm of teaching: If instructors lack the pedagogical facility to maintain their own standards and to meet the demands of teaching disparate students, then it is all too easy for standards to fall.

V. THE INSTITUTIONAL DIMENSIONS OF STANDARDS

At least four structural features make standards especially difficult for community colleges. The most obvious is their allegiance to open access, which brings to them both students who are not academically well prepared and instructors with a substantial allegiance to these nontraditional students. The issue of what high standards mean given such a diversity of students—the issue of absolute versus relative standards—is difficult enough given the uncertainty about what "college-level" work should be and the infinite variety of student backgrounds. It is nearly impossible when there are no public forums to discuss these issues, when instructors have to work them out on their own.

A second structural feature is the lack of preparation for teaching. Community colleges tend to hire faculty based on their advanced degrees in disciplinary areas or, for occupational faculty, their experience in industry, assuming that subject-matter expertise is sufficient for teaching. One English instructor said this about the mediocre teaching of writing:

> I think most people are trained to teach in their discipline and are not trained to teach writing at all. Most of us go to graduate school and they teach us about the history of whatever, and then they kind of leave the teaching aspect of our profession to work out for itself.

These practices reinforce the dominant conceptions of standards as *content* standards, based in the disciplines. But the problems with standards we have described in this chapter are not usually due to ignorance of content. They are due instead to a lack of facility with different approaches to teaching, an ignorance of the methods that might allow faculty to work with a broad range of students without either eliminating content or leaving many students behind, or an unconscious use of methods they think will grab students—humor, anecdote, personal stories—without understanding the damage they do to content.

But there are still other institutional pressures that work against standards. One involves enrollment and funding. For colleges that live or die by enrollments and the revenue they generate, high drop rates—rates at which students leave courses partway through the semester—carry fiscal consequences for the institution. Some institutions calculate drop rates for all courses and let instructors know when their rates are unacceptably high, and instructors themselves monitor their own classes. An instructor in construction management noted,

> The other thing [causing student dropout, aside from financial pressure] is, frankly, how much work I give them.... This [course] here, I'm backing off. I had thirty-six registered. I'm down to probably about twenty or twenty-two. So when you see that great a disparity then I have to take a look at myself and say, whoa, you know, what's going on here.... If they just took the one course, it might be okay, but a lot of them are taking two or three of my courses, so I really have to take a look, a real strong look at how much work I give them. That, I suspect, is one reason why they're dropping out of that course, see.

From their side, students monitor classes and often know who the tough teachers are, and many instructors believe that students take courses partly on the basis of instructor demands. As one instructor complained about the process of lowering standards,

> I know that a lot of students on campus choose classes by the kinds of exams the instructor creates. If they're multiple-choice and there are no term papers, that class is usually very full. A lot of instructors don't choose to give critical-thinking tests because that also requires a lot of grading. So we've gotten into a very bad pattern here.

These pressures for enrollment are ever-present: Instructors can't teach their favorite courses, hire new faculty, or get capital funds if their enrollments are low and drop rates are high. If high-quality teaching doesn't enhance enrollments, then reducing standards is the only way to do so.

Finally, and at a more abstract level, the dominant purposes of open-access institutions are not particularly consistent with high standards.[16] The expansion of community colleges has been driven by two broadly vocational purposes: individual mobility, or the desire of individuals to use education to advance their own positions, and social equity, the use of education to provide equality of opportunity to lower-income individuals, minorities, immigrants, the handicapped, and other groups. For these purposes, high standards serve a purpose only if they help individuals advance in the labor market. If they don't—if educational credentials matter but content doesn't—then individuals have an incentive to extend their schooling and acquire credentials but not to work unduly hard to do so.[17] Under these circumstances, advocates for educationally disadvantaged students (including minority and disabled students) pressure for "their" groups to be admitted to postsecondary education, while high standards are often resisted because they look like gatekeeping mechanisms to keep such students out. And so the dominant purposes in community colleges create pressures—from students themselves, sometimes from instructors, frequently from counselors and tutors and other advocates for students, often from administrators conscious of funding sources and the institution's role in the community, sometimes from advocates of minority students and from the legal system—that tend to grind down commitment to standards.

From an institutional perspective, the question is whether community colleges can confront these issues of standards and content directly and can then can take steps to enforce higher standards, through internal or external mechanisms. We suspect that the most successful approach would be a combination of external standards, set outside colleges, and internal standards, embedded in the attitudes and approaches to teaching of faculty themselves.[18] External standards can give faculty additional authority that they may not have on their own, and they can force reluctant instructors to improve their standards. Internal standards are necessary to influence the day-to-day content of classrooms, and adopting external standards without giving the faculty the ability to respond is worthless or even counterproductive if it results in many poorly taught students flunking externally set exams.

Creating external standards is a complex task requiring cooperation among instructors and among colleges, cooperation with employers (in the case of occupational standards), and probably some coordination through state (or possibly federal) policy. If poorly done, external standards can lead to inequity, the encouragement of inappropriate pedagogy, and an emphasis on irrelevant or outmoded material. Creating internal standards—the enforcement of standards through teacher training and preparation, through appropriate classroom practice (including testing and assessment), and through selection mechanisms, where necessary—returns colleges to the same issues of improving instruction that we have stressed throughout this volume. Neither is simple, therefore. But in the absence of such *institutional* steps, the maintenance of standards will remain the responsibility of individual instructors—and standards will continue to vary enormously.

NOTES

1. See, for example, the special issue of *Phi Delta Kappan*, June 1995 (Vol. 76, No. 11), on various aspects of the standards movement.

2. The little research that has been done on this subject confirms these perceptions. In comparing a sample of students from two- and four-year colleges, Pascarella, Bohr, Nora, and Terenzini (1995) found no differences in achievement test scores at the end of freshman year once achievement differences upon entering and other individual characteristics were considered. However, achievement for community college students remained lower at the end of the year than that of four-year-college students. The unpublished posttest figures for two- and four-year-college students, respectively, were 59.28 and 60.21 for reading, 56.17 and 56.98 for math, and 59.34 and 60.10 for critical thinking. Personal communication, Ernest Pascarella, June 1997.

3. We note that there is little empirical evidence about this proposition, though Knapp et al. (1995) provide some evidence that low-income elementary students learn more in classes with meaning-centered approaches. The historical and theoretical argument has been made in Grubb, 1995a.

4. Thus we can see high-content equilibria, in the best classes, and low-content equilibria. As in other situations with multiple equilibria, a high-content equilibrium requires several conditions to be achieved on the part of both instructors and students and therefore may be unsta-

ble—if students don't want to work that hard, if they are not prepared for active participation, or if faculty respond to initial resistance from students by reverting to lecture and drill.

5. There has been an infatuation in this country, as in Great Britain, with the work of Willis (1973) and the resistance that he describes in working-class boys in a compulsory secondary school; for a community college analogue in this country, see Weis, 1985. However, we do not think that this kind of resistance—which is intentional and politically motivated, and rooted in Great Britain in class antagonisms that are much less overt in this country—explains the behavior of community college students. No students and no teachers that we have encountered have expressed their behavior in consciously political terms the way Willis's lads did. The resistance we describe is educational rather than political, the result of being in classes with little content.

6. See, for example, the literature on K–12 teaching, especially Sizer, 1984; Powell, Farrar, and Cohen, 1985; and Sirotnick, 1983.

7. John Dewey was especially critical of the overuse of play as an "agreeable diversion"; as he said in *Democracy and Education* (1916, 194–95): "Sometimes, perhaps, plays, games, and constructive occupations are resorted to only for these reasons, with emphasis on relief from the tedium and strain of 'regular' school work. There is no reason, however, for using them merely as agreeable diversions."

8. This class took place in a Midwest community college dominated by the text-centered instruction we described in Chapter 2. In these classes, there are often two sources of authority: the text, which goes unquestioned; and personal opinion, which also goes unquestioned. There seems to be little possibility for well-argued interpretations, including those based on contravening texts or evidence; the whole point of meaning-making is simply not part of the agenda.

9. The demonstration that courses with similar titles can have vastly different content is a staple of the literature on secondary schools. See, for example, Powell, Farrar, and Cohen, 1985, on the "horizontal curriculum"; McDonnell, Burstein, Ormseth, Catterall, and Moody, 1990.

10. In some cases, like early childhood education, licensing requirements are stated in terms of course requirements and therefore have little effect on standards within courses.

11. For a listing of different occupational skill standards, see Wills and Lurie, 1993. However, neither this compendium nor the other recent writing on skill standards has examined the frequency and effects of occupational licensing and voluntary standards; this discussion has taken place in an empirical vacuum.

12. The use of voluntary standards by community colleges depends on perceptions of their value in the labor market and their adoption by employers. Automotive instructors and occupational deans were divided on the value of NATEF standards, for example, with some claiming that the standards were useless in the local labor market while others declared that no self-respecting program would forego NATEF accreditation.

13. There may be conflict within colleges about this kind of standard-setting. An economics instructor told us that, as he perceived it, the standards for occupational course content are actually set by the local business communities: "The local business community literally tells them what curriculum they want. I was just appalled to hear that." Here is an instance of multiple standards, where occupational instructors are pulled by the demands of employers while academic instructors with other conceptions of education are horrified.

14. Work placements are phenomena where virtually all colleges offer something, but to very few students. For example, Stern et al. (1995) found that almost nine hundred community colleges offer some form of work experience, but they serve very few students in most institutions; see also Bragg, Hamm, and Trinkle, 1995.

15. It is possible (if unlikely) that the development of skill standards will stimulate further

external standards; see Bailey and Merritt, 1995. In countries with greater commitment to externally set standards—like Great Britain, with its National Vocational Qualifications (NVQs)—the nature of occupational assessments is a matter of great debate. However, such issues do not arise in vocational systems driven by enrollments, such as that of the United States.

16. This section borrows from David Labaree's (1997) analysis of K–12 education. The dominant rationale for public schooling in the nineteenth century—to socialize the populace for a democratic nation—required high standards for all students so that they could participate in a democracy on relatively equal footing. Similarly, the purpose of social efficiency—of preparing a labor force with the abilities required by employers in production—also requires high standards, since plumbers and philosophers alike need to be highly competent. But political socialization and social efficiency have been much less important in community colleges than individual mobility and social equity, which are purposes that tend to undermine standards.

17. In the K–12 context, the same phenomenon operates; as Bishop (1989) has argued, there are economic returns to the quantity of education but not to quality, because quality is hard for employers to observe and reward. The result is that the incentives for students are to prolong their education while working as little as possible.

18. Note that Dill, Massy, Williams, and Cook (1996) argue for strengthening internal standards only.

7

INNOVATIVE PRACTICES
The Pedagogical and Institutional Challenges

In an institution as varied as the community college, there's bound to be a great deal of innovation. The college's image as a teaching institution suggests that, freed from the constraints of research and academic tradition, it can more readily experiment with different approaches. And virtually every college—certainly every college we visited—has some experimentation, from individual instructors moving toward more student-centered methods, to efforts to incorporate computers, to one or two learning communities.

The origins of these innovations differ substantially. There's no general pressure on community colleges to reform—no national wave of dissatisfaction (as there is for K–12 education), no discussion of national tests and curriculum frameworks. The most recent federal legislation dumped an additional $6 billion a year into higher education through tax credits, which are funding mechanisms that completely ignore the quality of education—despite continued rhetoric about the preparation of the American workforce. Unlike K–12 education, where numerous states have mounted sustained efforts to improve their schools, there are few powerful state reform efforts for community colleges.[1]

As a result, the impetus for reform is more local. Some of the innovations we discuss in this chapter are currently "in the air." Nationwide, there's been much greater interest in the past ten years in constructivist and student-centered teaching, though there's no central movement to change teaching. The use of computers has been a topic of discussion for nearly thirty-five years, and colleges have certainly increased the numbers of computers; there's been, as we shall see, much less attention to how faculty use them. Linked courses and learning communities that group students (and instructors) for several classes are often initiated by a few faculty. Even though the Washington State Center for Improving the Quality of Undergraduate Education has promoted their use throughout the Pacific

Northwest, and a few colleges use them widely, they are still not widespread. And the integration of academic and vocational education, which has been around for a long time in applied academics courses, has received new impetus from federal vocational funds since 1990—though most colleges seem unaware of legislative requirements. As a result, innovations are uneven. Instructors experimenting with small groups or computer networks teach next to colleagues who continue to lecture, experimental learning communities draw small numbers of enthusiastic students while the rest of a college continues teaching as usual, and a few colleges (profiled in Chapter 8) support instruction through all their institutional resources while others pay little attention.

In this chapter we examine several emerging practices: the shift toward more constructivist and meaning-centered teaching; the use of "technology," meaning computer-based instruction and distance learning; learning communities; and the integration of academic and vocational education. Other innovations bandied around—Writing Across the Curriculum, for example, or the use of classroom assessment techniques—were too rare in the colleges we observed to examine separately. All the innovations we examine have the power to change teaching substantially, though they are not yet widespread. The question we pose throughout is whether emerging practices, everywhere apparent in community colleges, will expand to become common practice, or whether they will remain limited and incomplete.

I. MOVING AWAY FROM LECTURE

Many community college instructors are uncomfortable with conventional lecture. They recognize that lecture is not the best way to convey information— "They all throw the notes out as soon as they get their grade, and they don't remember"—and many have started to adopt the language of constructivist practice, as we saw in Chapter 1. Discussion is the dominant way they balance lecture, whether in academic or occupational classrooms. As we have pointed out, especially in Chapter 2, discussion can take many forms, from fact-oriented questions that permit no student initiative, to halting conversations that take place when students are uncomfortable with seminar formats, to fluid conversations with genuine student contributions. Simply providing openings in a conventional lecture is not enough; the kinds of questions instructors pose and the ways they prepare students for discussion are crucial to a student-centered classroom.

Another consistent problem with discussion formats, as every teacher knows, is that participation varies dramatically among students. Sometimes this seems to be purely individual, but a pattern emerges in many classes: The students who tend to participate are often those who are better educated, including individuals with baccalaureate degrees who attend community colleges for occupational preparation ("reverse transfers"); those who are older and have more experience (particularly occupational experience) to relate; and those who are native-born, since foreign-born students have often been educated in classrooms that are rigidly teacher-centered. (These patterns are particularly evident in remedial or ESL classes with students from many different countries; see Goto and Masuda, 1994.) The variation in students therefore presents challenges to instructors who want to shift toward more participatory classes. Some faculty devise mechanisms for calling on students, some encourage participation through small-group discussions, and some (particularly in language classes) use reading materials from a variety of cultures, providing natural openings for foreign-born students. But it's quite common for discussions to be dominated by a few individuals. While this may be true even under the best of circumstances, the varied backgrounds of community college students contribute their own special difficulties.

Common as lecture/discussion is, there's very little debate about discussion. Instructors clarify that they are trying to use discussion to move away from lecture and to involve students, but they rarely mention how to create a lively discussion. The flow of discussion is often attributed to whether students have done the reading, but rarely is it treated as the instructor's responsibility, or the result of the way instructors pose questions or prepare students for interaction. We saw few workshops devoted to the art of question and answer included in staff development activities. However, the process of shifting from didactic and teacher-centered approaches to more participatory classes cannot happen quickly, merely as a result of an instructor attending a workshop and deciding to change his or her teaching style. As Tharp and Gallimore (1988, Ch. 10) have stressed in describing a master teacher working with an elementary-school teacher over five months, teaching involves deeply rooted impulses based on conceptions of learning, and change usually requires instructors to modify their basic ways of thinking about teaching as well as their persona in the classroom. Another perspective—from mentor teachers or peers—and extensive practice are necessary, and this kind of support is rare in community colleges. In its absence, trial and error or "learning by doing" becomes the dominant way instructors develop: "I simply learned [to teach] by doing—and that's not always the best way," as a business instructor described in Chapter 1 noted.

Another common practice as instructors move away from lecture is the use of small-group work, also referred to as "cooperative learning." Many classes include small groups, particularly in academic subjects such as English where instructors have students form groups to discuss a reading. Occupational classes use small groups to work on specific tasks or projects, often because there's not enough equipment for all students to work on their own. Instructors discuss the value of small groups in several different ways. Sometimes the purpose appears to be motivational; as a director of developmental studies mentioned,

> When you have a buddy or you have a group with whom you're working on something, the learning can be greatly expanded. Because these are your peers. And if your peers—some of your peers—are successful, then there's that competitive thing. You can say, "Well, look, if he does it, I can do it." So it's definitely a boon to the lower students—the student who's missing a lot of skills.

And while most instructors are unconcerned about the composition of groups, a few recognize that the groups themselves have educational value as students learn from others who are different. One physics instructor prevented women from banding together because then "they don't move," and with a group of Peruvian students, "I have to break them up so they will get a bit more English."

In general, the use of small groups seems to work well in several different dimensions. A larger number of students participate in discussions; the discussions among students are often more lively and engaged than are whole-class discussions. When faculty present large and difficult questions, small groups provide a way for students to think through them, whereas such questions thrown out to a class are usually met by blank silence as students struggle to make sense of them. In occupational classes, small groups enable instructors to demonstrate more detailed procedures, and to address specific problems, in ways that are difficult with an entire class.

But, as with everything else in teaching, the use of small groups can break down, often because instructors use them in inappropriate ways. For example, in an ESL course incorporated into a health program, the instructor divided students into small groups to discuss the text (*The Language of Health Care*), but when they reconvened as a class she asked for volunteers (rather than group representatives) to address her questions. This negated the purpose of convening in small groups, and the widespread participation that had taken place in small groups ground to a halt. In another case, students in a learning community discussed a text in a fluid way with a great deal of student initiative and interaction. Then, when placed into small groups to discuss the theme of the "other," their confusion about the task and about the meaning of the "other" meant that small groups made little progress on the task and then degenerated into personal opinions. The problem in this case wasn't that students were uncomfortable with discussions among themselves, but that the instructor hadn't clarified the task.

A common problem in using groups is the variation in how they function. In a particular remedial writing class, one group spent most of their time socializing; a second group was dominated by two students; a third group took the assignment quite seriously and participation was widespread; a fourth group was dominated by several women who talked about their personal experiences; and two remaining groups were quiet, with relatively little participation. Like the patterns of student discussion with a class, active participation in groups doesn't simply happen by itself; instructors need to prepare students for the most productive behavior within them.

Sometimes instructors use small groups in ways that simply replicate the teacher-student relationships of lecture. One composition instructor who taught in a textbook-driven fashion, with a great deal of intimidation from the tests her department required, was explicit about her intentions: to "get a strong student to add his or her voice to work in a small groups and explain why it's important to accomplish these tasks, do the grammar exercises." In a business class, the instructor formed students into small groups with the admonition "Let's have a good discussion, let's make sure everyone understands these concepts." However, the charge to each group was to find answers to fact-oriented questions from the text, in which accounting principles had been reduced to simple facts to memorize. Typically, the group leader read the question and provided his or her answer, which other students usually accepted with little discussion.

In another example, the instructors in a nursing course arranged students in small groups "teaching each other the material." But within each group, one student simply read terms from the text (e.g., "blunted affect") and then read the textbook definition while others wrote them down—an example of textbook-driven teaching conveyed to small groups. Then the instructor asked each group to come to some consensus about a series of questions—for example, the appropriate living situation for a schizophrenic—that, one might think, would generate considerable debate. But discussion within groups was lackadaisical and inconclusive. Here's one of the discussions:

> Student 1: "Twenty years old, I can't see him living with his brother."
> Student 2: "But you don't want to take him out and put him in a house living on his own."
> Student 3: "Well, we'll see." [Followed by silence within the group.]

The instructor then gave the "right" answer, without asking for any debate or contribution from the small groups. The third student's comment meant, "We'll see what the instructor says"; there was no point in thinking hard about the issue because the instructor was going to give the "right" answer in any case. One instructor commented, "It's called cooperative learning":

> It activates the learning process rather than the teacher being so prepared and deliv-
> ering the notes; it puts more of the activity and involvement on the student.

She noted that she and her co-teacher were "trying to do as little formal lecturing as possible, and really activate the learning," but they (like the business
instructor) had managed to convert small groups into textbook- and fact-centered
instruction.

Some of these examples reveal relatively simple errors in using small groups,
easily corrected by providing clearer instructions or by having groups respond to
the class as a whole. But the other examples reveal how hybrid teaching can go
wrong. Instructors who are wedded to conveying fact and content, or who teach in
textbook-driven approaches, may pick up small-group methods as new forms of
active teaching, but they convert them to their own, unchanged pedagogy.

Several other practices associated with more active or student-centered teaching illustrate the same problem. In the nursing class mentioned above, the class
engaged in a role-playing game called Family Feud, in which students played family members with different mental illnesses. The class was certainly lively, as different students played their different roles. However, the instructors stressed getting
a short list of "correct" descriptors for each illness. This prevented the exploration
through role playing of ambiguities and varying interpretations of behavior,
which are central in virtually all types of mental illness. In another example
involving role playing, a business instructor had his students play the roles of business leaders with different styles. But he scripted the roles precisely:

> I'll look at the groups and pick people that can fulfill the roles I want. One will be an
> autocratic style, one a social laissez-faire leader. Another one might be democratic.
> They'll have different problems to solve.

In scripting the "roles I want," he converted what could be a student-directed exercise into a teacher-dominated one, in which students had little to say about the
effects of different leadership styles on decision making.

The "writing process" is a well-developed approach to writing that concentrates on writing as communication, subordinating spelling, grammar, and other
mechanics of writing to its content and persuasiveness. However, this approach to
writing can be thwarted through interruption. For example, an English instructor
began his class with brainstorming, an initial step allowing students to develop
ideas without concern for mechanics. However, he then began talking during the
period of brainstorming, described their papers in insulting ways ("dishwater
dull"), shifted to grammar rules that he had the class repeat in unison, and handed
back papers with nasty asides ("Prove to me that TV has not made you passive").

Quite apart from his demeaning treatment of students, his interruption of brainstorming and concern with grammar undid whatever the writing process might have to offer.

A final category of constructivist teaching that can easily go wrong is problem- or project-based teaching. When carefully constructed, problems can present students with realistic applications of academic or textbook material, in settings that force them (rather than the instructor) to develop the methods of solution. Problem-based teaching is particularly common in occupational areas, where instructors use real problems—cars that don't run, circuits that don't work, or cakes that collapse—to develop solutions. In subjects such as business or health occupations, which don't have physical projects, instructors often pose scenarios (a particular business complication, a patient with certain complaints) and ask students to develop alternative approaches. But the selection of problems, and the guidance of students as they solve them, is crucial to the success of this method. Often, particularly in math classes, the "problems" are conventional word problems. One example was the remedial math class for welfare mothers described in Section II of Chapter 5, where the instructor presented a formulaic approach to solving problems. Not only were the problems trivial, but this approach also truncated the process by which students develop their own understanding of how to tackle problems.

The contrary issue arises when instructors develop problems that are too complex for students to solve. In one electronics class, for example, the instructor assigned students to build a circuit. However, the components had multiple bugs in them, and the oscilloscope for testing the circuits had been deliberately miscalibrated, so there were too many overlapping problems for the students to resolve. Furthermore, the instructor made many sarcastic and belittling comments during the students' flailing efforts. He complicated the problem before they understood simpler issues, and when they failed he took them step by step through the appropriate solution, in the end substituting a demonstration for student-led solutions. A class intended to move students from electrical diagrams and algebraic calculations (theory) to actual circuits (practice) wound up simply demoralizing them.

Overall, the efforts to teach in more student-centered or constructivist ways should be celebrated, for they relieve the evident tedium of lecture, motivate students, provide some truly impressive discussions, and bring in applications and "relevance" with many benefits. But these efforts can go wrong, and they often do so when instructors adopt them without changing their approach to teaching—when they remain focused on facts and knowledge transfer, when they continue to use humiliation as motivation, when they continue to dominate classroom discussion. The *practices* instructors use are often less important than their *understanding* of teaching—just as, in constructivist approaches, understanding is more important than specific practices such as long division or mastering a spreadsheet program. And this kind of understanding is not something that can be picked up from casual conversations or random workshops; it requires more sustained efforts.

II. TECHNOLOGY IN THE CLASSROOM: THE DISAPPOINTMENTS OF INNOVATION

In community colleges, as in the rest of education, technology has become the latest, hottest development. Promoters have promised that it can revolutionize teaching, reach new audiences, and reduce costs. They claim that technology and the Internet can transform every classroom into a "global classroom." The president of the American Association of Community colleges has declared that the benefits of technology seem "endless and intoxicating"; others have called the transformations of information technology "inevitable and irreversible."[2]

But the delirious promoters of technology rarely stop to ask basic questions about teaching and learning with new technologies—about how teachers actually use them, or what pedagogical problems they help resolve. These are empirical questions, ones that must be answered by seeing how instructors use technology in the classroom—the pedagogy of technology. In this section we examine how the community college faculty we observed use computers as aids to instruction, and how distance learning takes place.

Computer Technology as an Aid to Instruction

Our most obvious finding is that the use of computers is quite rare. In the 257 classrooms we observed, we can describe every instance of computer use—all eleven of them.[3] Unless our sample of classrooms is badly skewed, the use of computers is still highly limited, and the applications are divided between a few innovative uses and many more humdrum applications, including drills.

A more important conclusion is that computers are used by instructors in ways that reinforce their own well-developed pedagogies. The clearest example was a biology instructor, well known in her college for multimedia applications. Her teaching style was relentlessly didactic: She presented diagrams of the body and explained each part without any overall sense of the organism and its functioning—the kind of fact-intensive and part-to-whole teaching typical of many science instructors. Her multimedia system turned out to include ten thousand images of different animals. She used the computer to sequence various images and then projected a series of photographs, commenting about their similarities and differences. Of course, the multimedia system was a real convenience, since it included an enormous bank of images and allowed her to arrange them in any way. But the computer was only a store of information that she used in fact-intensive lecturing—an information dump.

A dean of instruction in another college—highly regarded in its state for supposedly innovative teaching—described computer use in precisely the same way:

> Our aim is to change how instruction is delivered. For example, in the social sciences we are converting a regular classroom into a multimedia classroom ... so the instructor can go in there and have their lecture outlines and everything done, and anything they need, like the historians who like to have a lot of visual aids. So that when they go in, it's already there; they don't have to bring anything.

So a multimedia system is purely a convenience; it lightens the burden of carrying around a lot of visual aids. In addition to this (presumably expensive) multimedia lab, the dean related a story about a faculty member who developed a computer program for music "which gives you a formal definition," describes various phases of the Renaissance, and presents snatches of music as well as literature of the period. The dean was proud of the fact that it cost $700,000 to develop. This is a nice way to bring together music, literature, and images, though it still uses the computer only as a store of information for didactic classrooms. We also wonder whether it would do more for students to spend $700,000 on a single lesson or to spend it wisely on staff development, particularly given the limited resources for improving instruction in most colleges (see Chapter 8). In these examples, colleges are investing in computers *rather than instructors*, presuming that fancy slide shows and multimedia presentations are more educative than instructors with a better command of teaching practice.

Other instructors use computers as the basis for drill. Remedial English teachers often use computers for drills on vocabulary, grammar, and other exercises in the skills-and-drills tradition. Oddly enough, only two of the thirty-six developmental instructors in our sample used a computer-based program. One used a program called College Reading Skills, financed by federal funds for vocational students, so "I haven't had a hand in choosing that software." She had wanted another well-known program called Plato, which the college couldn't afford. But both Plato and College Reading Skills are drills converted to the computer screen—as are the vast majority of remedial reading programs (Grubb and Kalman, 1994; Weisberg, 1988). Another remedial instructor noted that computers enhance student participation, because they have to be involved during a computer-based class. However, she described the computer as a kind of toy, more "fun" for students—a return to entertainment value. The computer may have been a convenience for these two, but it was pedagogically indistinguishable from conventional workbooks.

On the other hand, several English teachers used computers in more interesting ways. One taught a computer-based writing class where students posted preliminary versions of their essays to an electronic site. Other students could comment before the essays were rewritten, a procedure in which students could take on the role of critic as well as writer. Using computers also allowed the instructor to create records of students' writing throughout the semester so that he could monitor their progress. The same instructor also used computers for the more mundane aspects of writing—spelling and routine grammar. He was trying to figure out how to get his critical-thinking class onto computers:

> The way that I teach the class now, if I have a class of thirty students, there are going to be somewhere between six and ten who are going to be active. . . . But I think if I can get them in the classroom with the computers, there are ways to get responses from everybody. . . . We can be having a discussion, and I can say, "Okay, everybody, take five minutes and compose a free response or answer this question [on the computer]," and so then everybody has had to be engaged in giving me a response.

This instructor noted "some negative aspects to having the technology between the teacher and the student," principally because community college students are generally not familiar with computers. Once students overcame the initial barrier, the computer was useful in promoting both small-group work and highly individualized instruction:

> Once that's overcome, then all the other possibilities are much more facilitated by the teacher being able to contact individual students, by being able to arrange small-group experiences, by being able to give a range of different assignments so that students at one and the same time can be working on a whole array of different activities, depending on where they are.

His colleague also had students write on computers, and noted that computers helped his students gain fluency: "On the computers you can get these long intricate stories because they can type them really fast." He used computers to allow students to share their writing: a student would start a story, pass it by computer to another student, who would add a section, and so on through the class—a form of collaborative writing. He also noted that editing and rewriting are easier on computers, and he had developed a series of macros that gave students brief paragraphs of correction—for example, about run-on sentences—"because English teachers wind up saying the same thing over and over." Students kept journals (which he checked via computer) to develop their fluency, because "you learn how to write by writing":

> If they write every day, even if they're not aware of it, their sentences are getting more complex, their vocabularies are improving, and they're just writing better, just for the active writing, because they spent so little time writing in their lives before.

These two English instructors were constantly thinking about how computers could be used to further the kind of active instruction that they favored. But, aside from some discussions with other teachers on the Internet, they were working on their own.

The use of computers in math classes follows a similar pattern. Many developmental math instructors use computers for drills on arithmetic, conversions among fractions and decimals, and simple word problems. At a more sophisticated level, one math instructor wanted his students to be "literate with calculators." He used computers for graphing equations, some simulation exercises, spreadsheets, and simple logic games. Only one math instructor in our sample made extensive use of computers. He used computers for graphing equations, and he had a videodisk player for straightforward information about physics applications. He also used a curriculum called MBL (Microprocessor-Based Lab), a formalized way of using computers in "workshop physics." This particular instructor had developed a community of like-minded instructors, both inside and outside of his college, including a network called TYC21 (for "two-year college") funded by NSF for physics teachers. In his case the use of computers was again an extension of his basic pedagogical approach.

The other uses of computers we observed were more idiosyncratic. A business instructor used a computer-based simulation (Entrepreneur, published by Houghton Mifflin), lasting an entire semester, in which students worked in groups to solve various business problems. One learning community used a laptop computer to create practice exams from student discussion, an innovative approach to assessment that we described in Chapter 6. One learning community used a videodisk player controlled by a computer to show films; the computer-driven system made it easy to move back and forth within a film, but provided little other than this convenience. And one learning community for older adults "required" students to enroll in a telecourse for four hours per week, which took the form of videotapes they could take home. However, the telecourse was never referred to in the conventional class, and a few of the instructors even disparaged the telecourse. It turned out to be a convenient way to give students sufficient hours of credit, but otherwise lacked any educative value we could detect.

Evidently, as their advocates have often said, computers are highly flexible, but their use in education depends critically on the pedagogical approaches of instructors. A more interesting conclusion is that computers *reinforce* the pedagogies instructors bring with them. An instructor who stresses didactic delivery of facts, like the biology teacher we described, can find many computer programs and the riches of the Internet to expand the facts she can present, but computers will be used only to reinforce fact transmission. A remedial instructor who believes in drills can find many software programs to provide drills, but if anything these programs are inferior to existing workbooks because of their rigid structure and very short reading passages. On the other hand, meaning- and student-centered instructors can turn to computers as well, though they will find few existing programs to meet their needs. The creative uses of computers depend first on faculty with appropriate pedagogical methods, and then an understanding of how computers might be used. Instead, the current approach is to give faculty access to computers, software, and training that focuses on the technical rather than the pedagogical aspects.[4]

Without paying attention to the pedagogy underlying computers, certain uses of computers to solve routine problems inadvertently truncate the process of learning. Several English instructors noted that grammar checkers could be used mechanically, but then students would not be able to reproduce standard English away from a computer:

> If this is the essence of what they know—push the button and bring up the grammar checker—and they still don't know how to do it if they don't have the computer, then that's where the loss is. Because the person is not learning.

Similarly, while graphing calculators have reduced the tedium of graphing equations, a math instructor noted that students have to be able to graph by themselves if they are to understand what graphing really is. And one instructor teaching the history of theater feared that computers were being used simply as a form of "razzle-dazzle" entertainment:

> This whole MTV thing, I mean, this whole approach to multimedia also scares me a little bit, because it's all put into a context of short spurts. People say, "Well, you know, you've got to jazz up your class." Well, my point is that if I can do what I do with a pencil and piece of paper and a couple of overheads and a couple of slide projectors, then why do I need this other stuff? . . . Are we trying to razzle-dazzle them because they have razzle-dazzle minds, or do we try to get them to be patient, to try different things, to think in a different way?

Other faculty were critical of how technology has been introduced into their colleges. One of the creative English instructors described above complained about "technology day" on his campus:

One of the computer people came in with one of the machines and showed us how to do all this stuff on the machine. But it only works in courses which have right answers, and English doesn't have right answers. You put an assignment out there and they all do it differently and they all can be right.

Another individual, a computer enthusiast himself, had been asked by his administration what computers and applications they should request. But these administrators wanted to buy computers before knowing how they might be used:

We're being driven sort of by the wrong things, almost. These people [administrators] were being technology-driven and not applications-driven, and so that would be sort of a classic example of the cart leading the horse.

It's possible that more widespread use of technology is just around the corner, though we don't think so. The most recent hot development—the Internet, promising access to information galore—provides an illustration. Several instructors mentioned that they desired to get students on the Internet but had generally failed. They couldn't get the right kinds of powerful computers, and not enough students had their own computers: "The Internet didn't go too well, it's too clumsy, it's too awkward, it's too complicated." Furthermore, the Internet is simply a vast information source. For individuals who are not adept at using information—who have trouble picking out the main point of an article or synthesizing several short articles—providing even vaster amounts of information is not the solution. There isn't much attention in most classes to existing information sources—college and community libraries, encyclopedias—partly because students don't do much homework or "research" for papers, anyway; it isn't clear why they need the complex resources of the Web when simpler resources are unused. The Internet might be sexy, but without changes in how instructors use information sources, it will be more a marvel, another form of entertainment, than a new form of education.

Like the promoters of technology, we too think that computers have tremendous potential in community college classrooms, and the few creative applications we saw are convincing. But the main uses of computers, as repositories of facts and mechanisms of drill, are neither novel nor especially educative, and some applications (grammar and spell-checkers, some calculator use, some graphing programs) are counterproductive. The issue of how to use computers has been rarely raised within community colleges, and many institutions have spent vast sums on them without thinking much about their use—and without putting comparable resources into staff development. As the director for the Center for Teaching and

Learning at Westville Community College (profiled in Section IV of Chapter 8) stated the problem, "We have been pretty successful in getting funds for hardware, software, and connectivity; it's much harder to find resources for faculty development and support." Therefore the most powerful developments have come from individuals working on their own, using computers to extend their personal approaches to teaching. Until colleges understand the pedagogy of computers, we fear that the imaginative uses will continue to be idiosyncratic and limited.

The Pedagogy of Distance Learning

Like computer-aided instruction, distance learning has been promoted as a solution to several problems including vast distances, which impede face-to-face instruction, and limited populations, which preclude a wide variety of offerings.[5] More expansively, proponents of distance learning have enthused about the "global classroom," where students can gain access to any subject or lecturer at low cost. Recently a fiscal rationale has joined these educational reasons for distance learning: Distance methods may be cheaper per student because an instructor can teach many classrooms simultaneously, or lectures can be taped for use at other times.[6]

Distance technology can vary enormously. In the early days, distance learning took the form of correspondence courses, where institutions sent individuals print materials by mail, students sent back essays and tests, and instructors sometimes talked with students by telephone. One-way television or video has provided an advance over correspondence courses, though this method can provide little more than lecture. Most advocates now promote distance learning with fully interactive classrooms permitting the free interchanges of lecture/discussions. In the most sophisticated examples, the instructor is in one classroom with a class of students. He or she has at least two television monitors for each remote classroom and can orient the cameras to focus on either individual students or the entire class. These monitors are visible in each remote class as well, so that all students can see what is happening in every other class. Students have voice-activated microphones in front of them, so their comments can be heard clearly by the instructor as well as by students in every remote site. Instructors can therefore create small groups that can report back to the class as a whole, as well as whole-class discussions. Virtually any kind of teacher-student and student-student interaction is possible. The question, however, is whether the potential for discussion is realized, or whether instructors slip back into lecture because of the inevitable technical barriers.

Our observations of community college classrooms included five examples of distance learning, four of them in a state that has linked all secondary and post-secondary institutions.[7] Though our sample of distance learning is small, it is sufficient to point out certain pedagogical problems, especially if the technology is limited by cost considerations.

In some cases, instructors were simply lecturing. In other cases, instructors tried to have discussion punctuate the lecture. In one such class, these discussions turned out to be conversations between the instructor and one site at a time, while the other sites were quiet. The instructor reported that the distance technology was not difficult to use, but it seemed an impediment in several small ways. There was a great deal of confusion about what page in the text the instructor was on, and the fuzziness of remote audio communication compounded the confusion. An electronic pause followed each question and answer, making interchanges slow and awkward. The teacher played to the camera, not to students. This was an unimaginative teacher in the textbook-driven mode, somewhat hampered by technology.

Yet another class illustrated several problems inherent in distance learning. The class began with an interpretive question from a remote site; the instructor did not push the student to develop his interpretation further but instead gave a simple evaluation. We suspect that the ability of instructors to press students, rare enough in conventional classes, is more difficult in a distance classroom, where the simultaneous challenge and encouragement to the student take place over television monitors rather than in person. Then the instructor moved into lecture. Students in remote classes were not paying attention, perhaps because a page from the text rather than the image of the instructor was inadvertently transmitted to remote sites. The instructor failed to notice both the incorrect transmission and the inattention. The discussion that did occur came from students in the instructor's classroom, not at the remote sites; during a break a student at a remote site complained that the instructor was hard to hear. The instructor noted that the problem of nonparticipating students at remote sites was common, partly due to the technology and the need to "hit the mike":

> It [nonparticipation] bothers me, and it's typical. The [state distance learning network] does add the extra problem of . . . you have to hit the mike. And I have a number of students who, I can point them out to you in every single classroom, who have not yet hit that mike unless I specifically point to them and call them by name and say, "Would you hit the mike and talk to me?" They don't break that barrier.

The instructor recognized the problems of classroom control as well, stating that "on the fiber-optic system there's very little classroom control." He stated that "it takes a special sort of student to work well on this system"—those who are mature and self-disciplined.[8] While he used small-group discussions in his regular classrooms, he did not in distance classes.

When the technology is less sophisticated, students are forced into passive roles. In a class in American Indian history at Choctaw Community College, the nature of the lecture/discussion did not change markedly from the instructor's regular history class to his distance class in ethnic studies. But the technology provided one-way audio and video only, and students in the remote sites couldn't participate at all; they were purely passive spectators.

There are, then, many limitations of distance technology, and instructors seem to underestimate the demands of the medium. While instructors have the entire repertoire of personal performance, video, audio, and overheads at their command, the management of this repertoire is similar to the role of a film director. The instructor must play the roles of teacher, actor, and director—not an artistry that faculty are prepared for. As usual, the preparation of instructors for distance teaching is quite limited. In the state that has linked all its colleges, the only help to instructors was a program called Firepoint, which generates computerized slides so that "once the presentation is underway he [the instructor] does not have to deal with the technology." This provides help with the mechanics of slides, but not with the techniques of discussion via distance methods. A technician in charge of setting up distance learning viewed it as a way to extend the span of the teacher-as-entertainer: "Instructors are basically hams, and this gives them a bigger audience to act to." The state's network included several people who help instructors, but more with technical and logistical problems—for example, getting written materials back and forth—than with pedagogical issues. Like the use of computers, distance learning is treated as a technology rather than a forum for teaching, and the lack of staff development undermines its potential.

If distance learning is used in situations where students would otherwise have no access, then it is obviously better than nothing at all, especially for independent and motivated students. But the use of distance techniques for financial reasons—to reach more students at lower cost, to enhance the "productivity" of instructors—is quite different. The substitution of distance methods for conventional instruction works to the disadvantage of students who need more instructor attention and more active participation, and these are precisely the kinds of students who come to community colleges in droves. Above all, when fiscal imperatives dominate educational motives, then cheaper technologies are likely to be used in place of the most interactive and expensive ones. Cheaper equipment includes systems without voice-activated microphones, so students have to "hit the mike"; systems with one-way video, so instructors cannot see students in remote sites; systems with lower-quality monitors and audio components, so communication takes place through a haze of blurry images and fuzzy sound; and systems that break down more often, so remote students get only bits and pieces of what instructors present. In the extreme case, instructors will simply be video-taped for students to watch at their leisure, ensuring the total domination of didactic methods. Under these conditions, distance learning will simply become a caricature of what it could be, driven by the logic of efficiency.

Realizing the potential of new technologies is no different from developing the instructional power of old technologies or of faculty themselves. Appropriate preparation of instructors is necessary; otherwise many revert to familiar practices and didactic teaching. Therefore effective use of computers and distance learning requires investment in *both* instructors *and* technology. But technology is often being used to *substitute* for investment in instructors. The result is often a learning lab with students carrying out drills at banks of computers, or lecture over one-way video. Independent students and those needing only a brush-up may do well, but community college instructors agree that their students require more encouragement than any machine can give.[9] And if distance learning methods are used to cut costs, the result is to substitute low-cost equipment for fully interactive distance classrooms and to skimp on instructor training, leading inevitably to "talking heads."[10] Finally, if innovations are to be more than random and idiosyncratic, community colleges must develop systematic institutional support, including the financing of both capital costs and staff development. Otherwise, the uses of new technology will continue to be as disappointing as they now are.

III. LEARNING COMMUNITIES: THE BENEFITS TO STUDENTS AND FACULTY

One common form of fragmentation in all of education is the practice of teaching courses that are independent of one another, a practice reflecting the fragmenting tendency of "skills and drills." Even though courses may be arrayed in logical sequences, coordinating them remains difficult. Student practices—taking courses randomly as "experimenters," or failing to complete programs—further undermine whatever coherence there may be in a series of courses. As one instructor in a learning community mentioned,

> At a school like [this college] there's no real collegial identity. It's almost like a supermarket where you come and push your cart around, and you take this and you take that and you move around, you know, in a circle. I mean, even the structure physically of the school sort of reinforces that.[11]

One solution to such fragmentation has been the creation of learning communities (LCs) or linked courses, where a group of students takes two or more courses at the same time, and instructors coordinate their teaching—sometimes even by team teaching.[12] Such learning communities enable faculty in one course to present the prerequisites for another course—for example, the math or language requirements of a business or biology course—and to develop the applications of one subject in another. Other kinds of learning communities permit a particular topic—immigration, for example, or the senses, or identity and multiculturalism—to be explored from several disciplinary perspectives. Because they are multidisciplinary, learning communities also provide students with the intellectual resources and perspectives of several disciplines. And they create a community of peers. As the instructor who complained about his college being a "supermarket" noted:

> There is no, of course, dormitory life or on-campus life because of the fact that no one is resident at the school. And that means that many students are hungry or want some sort of experience that marks them as being part of a group. And they find that in [this learning community], which is often called a college within the college ... our students find in the learning community the closest thing to a real college, and having a continuity with classmates.

This comment is interesting for contrasting a community college with a "real college" that incorporates "continuity with classmates," and it highlights a substantial benefit of LCs.

Learning communities can be used in at least three distinctive ways. One is a problem-focused approach, in which a particular educational problem is resolved through learning communities. For example, one college found a high rate of failure in a basic biology course necessary for health occupations, partly because its math and language requirements were relatively high. The college then created a learning community of biology, English, and math instructors. The use of learning communities for remedial/developmental education and ESL, described in Chapter 6, can also be interpreted as problem-focused examples. Second, learning communities can create multidisciplinary approaches to general education by developing a theme for several instructors from different academic disciplines. This has been the emphasis of the Washington State Center at Evergreen State College, and is particularly prevalent in the Pacific Northwest. Third, learning communities are often developed to meet the needs of particular groups of students, particularly nontraditional students. The PACE (Program for Adult College Education) programs are learning communities for older employed students, with schedules and subjects designed to meet their needs. In California the Puente project has developed learning communities for Latino students in approximately thirty colleges (Cazden, 1996; *Puente*, undated). They typically emphasize language and cultural issues, and include counselors working along with faculty to provide help with financial and personal problems that may arise. At Laney College in Oakland, Project Bridge serves underprepared students (largely black) in an LC format (Griffith, Jacobs, Wilson, and Dashiel, 1988; Wilson, 1994). LaGuardia Community College has decided that all of its programs for welfare recipients should take place within learning communities, to create supportive networks and to address remedial needs with links to occupational courses.

The advantages of learning communities are enormous, and some of the most innovative and engaging teaching takes place in them. In the case of the biology/English/math LC mentioned above, the biology instructor made constant reference to the reading and math prerequisites from the other two courses. The English instructor had developed readings about health-related issues that served the multiple purposes of increasing the sophistication of reading, motivating writing exercises, and introducing students to a variety of health-related careers, personal issues (like smoking and alcohol abuse), and public issues. She also stressed the kind of scientific reasoning that the biology instructor wanted students to master: "Take it back to what you're doing in science: What's the first thing a scientist does?" She pressed students to develop hypotheses, test them with evidence, and make inferences from the evidence at hand. In an LC for individuals wanting to enter social welfare programs, including a remedial English course, a sociology course, and Introduction to Human Services, the English instructor had devised readings about the lives of black and Latina women, generating discussions related both to the themes of the LC—the life course and the strains of modern life—and to the students' own lives.

In many cases, particularly in problem-focused LCs, one course remains essentially the same, and other courses modify their content. For example, the purpose of the biology/English/math LC was to enable students to pass the biology course; the math and English courses modified their content more than the lead course did. Similarly, in a computer/ESL pairing intended to allow recent immigrants to move into computer occupations, the ESL course incorporated readings and vocabulary focused on computer use, but the lead computer course did not change at all. In such cases, several classes become support courses to the lead course. The success of the learning community depends on the extent to which the instructors in these support courses modify their content and on the use the central instructor makes of the support courses. Not surprisingly, there's some loss to the support courses. An English instructor noted, "You can't do everything," and fiction and longer texts had been eliminated in orienting her course around health topics. But there are substantial compensations, including the reinforcement among courses and the development of group motivation.

One strength of LCs comes from the roles faculty can play, particularly in team teaching. One is that faculty from several different disciplines are in the room, providing different perspectives, so students "get a real range of response from the different discipline areas." Another is that instructors can argue with one another, providing varying interpretations and modeling for students the active debate and discussion that they want to encourage:

> I'll pose questions from out in left field. . . . Sometimes I have real questions about the work myself that I can't get, you know, deal with when we have our tutor meetings, or that none of the students are bringing up.

Sometimes instructors engage in role playing to convey these differences, though some find it artificial and prefer questioning as more reflective of real intellectual discourse.

In some LCs an instructor will pose questions that both clarify the content of the course and model a certain intellectual stance. For example, in a biology/English pair, the English instructor asked questions during the biology component—"How can you infer that from the data?"—that pretended a certain ignorance but were artfully composed to draw out the difficult issues of evidence and inference within a scientific context. Students participated with similar questions of their own—not with questions of fact and procedure—and they reported that "it's easier to make the links between the subjects, to see how they fit." Similarly, in another LC that included social science and English, each instructor questioned the other; they were modeling a certain kind of questioning as well as providing contrasting points of view. One reported that they were trying to "break down the apathy that students often feel in traditional English classes where they're asked to be passive participants," and the presence of both instructors helped socialize students to more active roles.

One common benefit of LCs is that they create communities among students. Students report that they come to know their fellow students better and are able to work with them more both in and out of class—in contrast to conventional practice in community colleges, where students typically find a new group in virtually every class they take. These communities are especially important in PACE programs, originally developed at Wayne State and supported by the AFT to empower workers through education. The same ethos remains at one of the PACE programs we observed; the older students "aren't interested in the wild and wonderful things we did in the old days of the experimental colleges," one instructor reported, but they support one another through the LC format.

A less recognized benefit of LCs is that they enable *faculty* to create communities—in contrast to the predominant isolation of instructors (see Chapter 1 and Section I of Chapter 8). The English teacher in the English/social science pair mentioned above had participated in order to develop new teaching methods, because she felt her teaching had gone stale. An electronics instructor joined an LC because of the isolated conditions of his teaching ("I feel very isolated, because my labs are here, I teach my classes here"). He reported that within the LC "there's been a lot of informal sharing of teaching technique" even though "that wasn't a goal, that wasn't on our agenda." Here are the reactions of another instructor:

> It's very, very enriching to see other teachers work, teachers who are already quite adept, quite experienced, veteran teachers with enormous reserves of technique.... So there's an enormous kind of fertilization, different sorts of ideas, and also you get a chance to run things up the flagpole, and so there's that kind of enrichment that would never be possible in the normal traditional venue where you are going into the classroom every day by yourself. And you might get some feedback from students [or] from the division chair and other peers, but it's not the same. This is continual. This is every week.

When faculty work together, then, LCs look like continuous forms of staff development—the kind we propose in Chapter 8. Of course, it's much harder for part-time instructors to engage in this kind of interaction. Sometimes highly committed part-timers participate, but often they lack the time. Then, as one noted of his LC, "it's not been a teaching exchange."

There is now evidence that LCs do indeed help students. One college documented that its remedial students in LCs did better than those in conventional courses (Gudan, Clack, Tang, and Dixon, 1991), and MacGregor (1991) similarly reported that developmental students in a learning community did as well as "regular" students despite lower placement test scores. Tokino (1993) found students in learning communities to have significantly higher levels of academic achievement than students in regular courses, and Tinto and his colleagues (1994, 1995) found higher rates of persistence compared to students in regular courses, perhaps because of their better integration into the college. And nearly everyone has cited higher motivation among students in LCs (MacGregor, 1991; Tinto, Goodsell-Love, and Russo, 1994). Despite some methodological problems, the direction of research reinforces the support from faculty and students themselves.

Of course, as with every other teaching innovation, the simple structure of LCs—grouping courses together—is not enough to realize their benefits. In several cases the weaker faculty in learning communities were grudgingly "drafted" rather than self-selected. In other cases, there is no connection between the classes. For example, in one LC the Introduction to Computers course was paired with an introductory business class, but neither instructor made any reference to the other class; these were parallel courses, not integrated courses. In another college, four faculty—in electronics, social science, English, and architectural history—

developed a theme-based LC, but the references among classes were sparse or missing. In situations like this, *students* bear the entire burden for integrating material from different courses.

In still other cases, the instructors are too different in their approaches to teaching for the LC to become a coherent community. This is a particular problem for learning communities that are consciously constructivist and student-centered. As one instructor in such an LC mentioned, "This is a problem when new teachers come into the program. They're so used to lecturing, and they worry that students won't cover the material." For example, a biology/English LC on the theme of the senses included a didactic biology instructor and a more meaning-centered English instructor. The biology periods were fact-oriented and textbook-driven, the English sessions were much more interpretive and based on active discussions rather than lecture, and neither component made much reference to the other. The LC looked more like a form of parallel play than an intellectual community. An ESL instructor with a well-developed "ESL method"—a form of hybrid instruction—paired with a didactic computer instructor noted, "It's hard working with another instructor locked into a lecture format—horrible because lectures don't reach 'new students.'"

In the biology/English/math triple we have mentioned, an inexperienced and insecure math teacher concentrated on conventional procedures and drills, modifying her courses only a little (e.g., by adding metric conversions) to fit the other two courses. Similarly, in the social services/English/sociology LC, the sociology professor was didactic, rigid, and demeaning to students, and made no reference to the other courses. His approach to teaching converted students who were active and engaged in the other two classes into passive note takers who were often confused when his textbook presentations conflicted with their own experiences and ambitions. If faculty can't or don't plan together, if they make no references to other classes in the LC, or if their pedagogical approaches are wildly different, then it's difficult for an intellectual community to emerge from the pieces.

Similarly, the PACE programs we saw varied substantially despite their common origins. One (described briefly above) was responsive to the demands of its students for well-structured if somewhat conventional teaching. This program had developed mechanisms of selecting teachers, training new participants, and developing common approaches through regular meetings, much like the developmental studies program described near the end of Chapter 5. By contrast, in another PACE program, the instructors reported that the students "don't like the idea of collaborativeness in a lot of ways." Both the time and the intellectual demands on students were low, and the program had done little to prepare new instructors for discussion-based teaching. In yet another case, a College for Working Adults based on the PACE model and located in the Midwest, the most conventional textbook-centered teaching prevailed. This program adopted the PACE structure but none of its philosophy. Like the LCs that practice parallel play, teachers taught their subjects conventionally.

Of course, colleges have some ways to ensure that LCs succeed. One is the selection of faculty. Instructors in an LC will often recruit others who they think will work well, and faculty participating in LCs are often those searching for collegial opportunities. Faculty who don't like collaborative teaching leave LCs. The sociology instructor mentioned above had announced his departure, to the relief of other members. In addition, some colleges provide special forms of staff development for new faculty in LCs—one operates a summer institute, and the Washington State Center operates summer workshops for both two- and four-year colleges. And the very process of joining a learning community provides its own form of staff development, as instructors work with one another to shape the curriculum. One instructor noted that a colleague was

> very dyed-in-the-wool, very old-fashioned, very behind the times, and trying to bring him along so that he's up with those of us who are a little bit more with it has been fun. Part of [an LC], I guess, is in-service training.

However, this innovation requires certain kinds of institutional support—unlike the efforts to move toward more student-centered teaching or to incorporate computers, which can be adopted by instructors working alone. Learning communities don't just happen, as several administrators stressed. They have to be created by identifying instructional problems that an LC might resolve or themes that students might enjoy, by finding subjects with natural rather than forced relationships, by identifying faculty who are willing to collaborate, and by recruiting students in large numbers since many won't show up. In colleges where LCs are rare, the very idea of an LC must be publicized because of its unfamiliarity.[13] As a flyer for one learning community, in a college we'll call Paradise, advertised to students:

> You will join 24 other students who will take all of the same classes during the fall semester. You'll get to know other students in your major, your faculty, automotive technology, and reading, writing, and math at the same time. It's the Paradise advantage: a team approach to learning and career development.

Other institutional imperatives threaten LCs. One is the issue of funding, which is partly about turf and partly about cost. Department chairs can be barriers: They often want to build up courses in their departments, and may be reluctant to release faculty to interdisciplinary efforts. One dean mentioned that a budget crisis had spurred department chairs to cancel all the LCs: "When they had the option, why should they support the cluster? They would rather close down the clusters and support their own sections and their own faculty." To prevent this, a few institutions have created special funds for LCs. In still other cases LCs have been funded by outside grants, sidestepping internal battles at the cost of being vulnerable to external funding.

In addition, LCs often cost more[14]—for staff development or for smaller classes if students don't enroll—and the requirement of joint scheduling means that an LC cannot be larger than the enrollment in the lowest-enrolled course.[15] In colleges that are enrollment-driven (as we will examine in Chapter 9), LCs are often unpopular with administrators and subject to envious criticism from other instructors because of small class sizes. Here the divide between administrators and faculty is particularly sharp. In one college an LC focused on automotive trades was being phased out; a vice president felt that the enrollments didn't justify the special efforts, while instructors were livid that the institution was "abandoning" these students. When administrators emphasize enrollments and instructors stress teaching quality, there's little common ground.

In addition to the constraints of enrollment and funding, the mantra of flexibility also threatens LCs. Community colleges have stressed the importance of flexible schedules to meet the needs of students with the multiple demands of employment, family, and schooling. Creating cohorts of students taking several classes together limits this flexibility, and one administrative objection is that students won't constrain themselves in this way. But this common reaction supports flexibility and course fragmentation over the benefits of student communities, implicitly reinforcing learning as a largely individual responsibility rather than as a social enterprise in which students learn from each other.

As a result, LCs are often isolated innovations within their colleges. Except when they have been institutionalized through special funding, or where they are widely used for general education, it is common to find only one or two LCs in a college, often funded from outside grants. The instructors are often interested in teaching innovations for personal reasons and "kind of find one another," as good teachers seem to do. But these are fragile innovations, as the history of PACE programs illustrate. When the external funding runs out or an instructor wants to do something different, the programs often collapse—without having had any influence on practices in the rest of the college.

Learning communities have enormous promise. They can be used to address specific instructional problems as well as to create communities of students and faculty. But they face individual and institutional barriers. Faculty have to be willing to teach in more collaborative and integrated ways, and colleges have to be willing to support practices that look quite different from familiar course offerings. Without both individual and institutional support, learning communities tend to collapse back to "business as usual."

IV. INTEGRATING ACADEMIC AND OCCUPATIONAL EDUCATION: BROADENING VOCATIONAL PREPARATION

Like learning communities, efforts to integrate academic and vocational education help remedy the fragmentation of the curriculum and shift the burden of coordinating subjects from students to instructors. This kind of integration also responds to some problems specific to occupational education. Ever since the inception of vocational education early in this century, periodic appraisals have criticized it for becoming too narrow and applied, too distant from its academic underpinnings. The suggestion to integrate vocational instruction with academic content has been often made, and just as often unheeded (Grubb, 1995b).

More recently, employers and others have claimed that the workforce now requires higher-level competencies than it did under older forms of production following Taylorist principles. The development of more flexible production with fewer layers of supervision means that workers need communication skills, problem solving abilities, initiative and judgment, and other higher-order competencies (SCANS, 1991; Stasz et al., 1993; Osterman, 1994)—competencies that traditional occupational education may not provide. Some instructors also recognize these trends. As one mentioned,

> The automotive technology fields is getting to be much more of a cerebral, thinking-type field. In the olden days, it used to be something you could just learn by doing it. Nowadays it's something you have to learn by reading the books.

Sometimes they find it difficult to convince their students. An instructor in a program combining plumbing, heating, ventilation, and industrial electricity mentioned that his hardest task is persuading students

> that there's more to it than the hands-on. It's the planning, the thinking, the organizing, the layout, the design. Otherwise they're not going to get the good jobs out on the street, and they're gonna be a gofer and they're gonna be a helper if they can't do the head work.

One solution, then, is to incorporate more academic content into occupational programs. An automotive instructor related that his industry advisory committee pushed the program into integration because not just interpretation of technical material was needed, but communication skills and interpersonal relationships between the public, employer, and fellow employees were most necessary.

Harsh reality has played a role in some colleges, as occupational instructors have found completion rates falling among students unable to read at appropriate levels:

> You know, that's the students we were losing—the ones [who] didn't have those study skills ... maybe they hadn't been to school for a while or maybe when they were in school they didn't have those skills, so ... they were interested in the technical material but didn't have the other skills to keep up. "Gee, automotive—isn't that just workin' on cars?" Well, no—there's a lot of theory and a lot of textbook information that goes with it.

In other cases the initiative has come from the state level; as a dean of occupational education mentioned:

> The governor has indicated, through the Higher Education Coordinating Board, that all programs, especially those that are vocationally and technically oriented, will address the basic skills issues that are needed by the Texas quality workforce, as well as part of Texas being part of the global economy. ... So, yes, while we're here to provide the technical skills, we also have to work on basic skills as well.

And federal policy has played a role, with the 1990 amendments to the Carl Perkins Act requiring that all federal funds for vocational education be spent on programs that "integrate academic and vocational education ... so that students achieve both academic and occupational competencies."

The need for curriculum integration arises in part because of a pervasive problem in occupational instruction. Even if instructors recognize the need for academic skills—and many complain about the low levels of basic skill among their "tactile" students, as we saw in Chapter 3—the solution isn't always obvious. Occasionally occupational instructors are self-conscious about infusing more academic content into occupational classes. The child development instructor portrayed in Chapter 1 integrated child psychology into her courses and used writing assignments in explicit ways. Two auto instructors in the same institution purposely incorporated "learning skills"—problem solving, critical thinking, the benefits of cooperative learning—into their handouts and problem sets.

But infusion as a strategy of integration relies on the abilities and proclivities of individual instructors. Those who do not see the need for integration or those who feel unqualified to venture onto academic ground are unlikely to teach reading, math, or other skills considered "academic," as we pointed out in Chapter 4. As one occupational dean noted, in calling for collaboration between occupational and developmental faculty:

> There are technical faculty who feel they're not qualified to do a lot in the area of writing development. . . . Their question is, "I'm a welding instructor—do I have to have a second specialty in English?"

Teachers might incorporate writing into a class, or problems that require math, but they would not usually review the mechanics of reading, writing, or math.

More structured approaches to integration can take several forms.[16] One involves learning communities, like the LCs in the problem solving mode described in the previous section. Often, LCs used for remedial purposes or ESL are tied to occupational subjects. The other common form of curriculum integration—similar in intent, though more modest in scope—includes applied academic courses, where an academic subject is modified to develop the applications necessary for particular occupational subjects. Such courses may cover a broad range of occupations—for example, applied math or technical math may be developed for several occupations—or a narrower range, such as business English, technical math for nurses, agricultural economics, or business economics. Applied courses cover the topics necessary for an occupational area rather than leaving out important topics, and the applications and materials are drawn from occupational issues rather than from literature or everyday life (as in consumer math). Such specialized courses get around the objection of occupational instructors to the "irrelevance" of conventional courses. An auto instructor described the advantage of collaborating with a basic skills instructor to develop an applied course:

> As we get more and more technical in automotive—I mean, we're just gettin' overwhelmed with all of this technical information, the manuals. . . . We tried some things like, you know, having students take just study skills classes to improve their reading, but they just couldn't see any relevancy, you know. The people who taught those classes didn't teach 'em for automotive, they just taught 'em as generic classes. . . . The lady [who] worked with me in the integrative study skills was really interested in having some meaning to her classes, [so] that they could actually put it to use. She came into each class, so some of the things she talked to 'em about [were] modeled then, so they had examples of how to use [them].

In addition, occupational instructors may be better able to motivate their students to learn academic material than academic faculty can:

If a student goes to the counseling office and the first thing the student is told
[about] is assessment and testing and developmental courses, many students are
turned off by that. And what many of the technical faculty have said is, "Refer those
students to us. Let us talk to them about what their goals are in the technical field,
and then we can show the relationship between the technical courses and the reading, the writing, the mathematics, and the assessment, so that [students] are not
turned off by the terms."

Applied academics courses are, not surprisingly, enormously varied, since they
are usually locally developed—"*applied* means forty different things," noted one
applied math instructor. One sophisticated version was the applied physics class—
essentially a class in applied algebra and calculus—for students in an HVAC (heating, ventilating, and air-conditioning) program described in Chapter 5. The class
reviewed a nonlinear formula that a conventional algebra class would treat simply
as an algebraic expression. However, this instructor stressed the importance of
understanding how algebra represents physical phenomena, and of moving
between the algebra and the heating issues they were discussing:

I want a way of thinking about this—not an answer about the algebra but about the
underlying phenomena. . . . Do not believe what the equation says, because different
conventions can lead to different answers. Lead with your head, not the equation.

Throughout, the instructor elaborated the interpretation of equations, whereas a
conventional math class would simply present them. She stressed the "literacy" of
algebra—the fact that math is a representation of a phenomenon (here, heat
transfer) rather than something to be manipulated for its own sake.

Similarly, in a course on applied science and technology—part of a learning
community called Reading, Writing, and Wrenches—the instructor presented formulas for compression ratios in car engines. After working with the formulas in
conventional ways, he then asked, "If you want a certain compression ratio, what
are the options?"—moving from the mathematical representation of compression
and force to the problem as an auto mechanic might experience it. After some
alternatives were presented he asked, "Of those choices, which is the most likely?"
making the point that alternatives that are mathematically equivalent may not be
practically equivalent. The instructor continued reviewing various formulas and
problems until a student asked, "Do they just run the numbers until it looks right?
You know, in the factory?" and the instructor responded with an elaborate explanation of how engineers test engines and establish miniature production lines to
develop formulas. The instructor moved constantly between mathematical representation, applications on the shop floor, and the "real world" of production facil-

ities. This was math "in context," presented in the applications that students can see in both workshops and on the job.

But this approach is hardly universal, and conventional pedagogy abounds in other applied courses. For example, a business writing class spent several periods reviewing grammar. The students were editing sentences from a learning guide (essentially a programmed text) with no business examples at all, with the instructor essentially irrelevant except to respond to a few factual questions. As the instructor described her conception of the course:

> I try to get across to the students how important communication is, and how people out in business really stress good communication skills. And what is written is there in black and white. And you don't want to have anything that's going to be distributed outside the company or within the company that would be embarrassing to you.... Grammar is very important, because the construction of the sentences and the placement of your clauses and, like, misplaced modifiers and ... their punctuation—those are the things that people are depending upon you, as maybe a secretary.

Unfortunately, this limited conception of communication skills is quite different from the national debate about higher-order abilities for flexible workplaces, and ignores the range of competencies a good secretary requires. Similarly, a math instructor taught a class called Math for Technology, designed for students in electronics, auto, and drafting/CAD programs, using curriculum materials developed by the Council on Occupational Research and Development.[17] He presented in a standard lecture format, covering graphing and formulas for linear equations, with a few IRE questions but without any applications to the occupational areas. The math instructor in the biology/math/English learning community described in Section II of this chapter provides yet another example; while she modified her content slightly for the biology course by including metric conversions, both the content and the pedagogy were otherwise quite standard. Applied academics courses provide vehicles for integrating academic and occupational education, but—like learning communities—the form is less important than the way instructors use it.

A final (and relatively rare) form of curriculum integration involves multidisciplinary courses. These hybrids take subjects conventionally considered academic and develop their perspectives with occupational applications. For example, they may examine the literature of workplaces and occupations, or the history of technology and society, or the public and political issues surrounding employment, occupations, and technical change. The syllabuses for such courses are often quite exciting, since they integrate several disciplinary perspectives and applications.

They usually invite students to contribute their own work experiences and suggest other active teaching strategies.[18]

However, the one example we observed of such a course—one called Working in America, using an anthology of fictional readings about work (Sessions and Wortman, 1992)—turned into a conventional lecture. The instructor first lectured about conceptions of work in different cultures, asking a few questions to see if students were following. She then read from Nathaniel Hawthorne's "Young Goodman Brown" and asked a few questions, generating simple phrases rather than extended discussion. She presented slides of different artworks related to work (like Grant Wood's "American Gothic"), giving her own interpretation rather than soliciting student views. Her approach converted a great deal of material into facts and slogans, accompanied by some moralizing ("fear, clarity, power, oneness, belonging to a community—these are the things that motivate us to do what we do in life") and a great deal of her interpretation, but little student contribution or investigation of *their* work in America.

The idea of integrating academic and occupational education is powerful, as we have stressed elsewhere. It can provide the academic foundations that occupational students need, enhance the range of competencies they master (including the higher-order skills so much in demand now), and prepare them for a greater variety of occupational possibilities beyond entry-level work. Such integration can bridge the divide between the "academic" and the "vocational," a divide that many instructors and educational reformers from John Dewey on have disliked. But, as with the other innovations we have examined in this chapter, realizing its potential lies in the details of execution. When instructors fail to modify their content, or when they have impoverished conceptions of higher-order skills, these integrated approaches look no different from conventional offerings. When their approach to teaching is didactic and student-centered, the possibilities of allowing students to incorporate their own work experiences and to reflect upon their occupational ambitions are lost. As with other innovations, the basic approach to teaching of different instructors determines much of the success or failure of curriculum integration.

Finally, the support of community colleges for the integration of academic and vocational education has been distinctly mixed. The advisory committees that could lead to integration often meet infrequently (Grubb, 1996b, Ch. 6). Within colleges, the support for learning communities is quite varied, as we saw in the previous section. In many colleges, occupational instructors told tales of academic instructors reluctant to participate in applied or integrated courses. One auto instructor complained about departmental constraints on applied courses—"The English department is always a big thorn"—and several occupational departments developed their own applied courses because of the lack of cooperation from math and English teachers. As we will document in greater detail in Chapter 8, many institutions fail to support innovative teaching. The instructor of Working in America complained,

> I don't feel a lot of support from the college, and I think it comes from the fact that they're so budget-minded—administrators are always looking at the bottom line, and even if they have come from the classroom themselves, that's long past.

And many occupational instructors are not convinced of the need for integration. They continue to emphasize occupation-specific skills (just as many academic instructors stress disciplinary content), and they resent having to share their time with subjects that they think students should master elsewhere.

On the other hand, changing a practice as deeply rooted as the separation of academic and occupational education necessarily takes time, and the pedagogical innovations central to the most successful examples of integration are also difficult to instill. Partly because of alarms about the "workforce of the twenty-first century," the advantages of integration are becoming better-known in many colleges, and interest is building.[19] Like the other innovations in this chapter, the direction of change is clear. The question is whether colleges can provide the institutional support to extend this interest and to ensure that curriculum integration becomes more than a relabeling of conventional practice.

V. THE FUTURE OF INNOVATION: SUSTAINING THE "TEACHING COLLEGE"

The history of American education has been marked by cycles of change, of "reforming again and again and again," as Larry Cuban (1990) described the patterns in K–12 education. Something of the same pattern can be detected in community colleges, where experienced faculty remember a period of innovation during the 1960s and early 1970s, which gave way to "privatization" and the sanctity of the individual classroom. Now there seems to be a revival of innovation. The use of computers is high on almost every list of changes, and the others we have examined in this chapter—the shift toward more constructivist or student-centered teaching, the use of learning communities and other collaborative efforts, programs that integrate academic and occupational content—are well known, if not always widespread. Is it possible that colleges are in the midst of a revolution in approaches to teaching?

We'd like to think so, because there is evidence—greater student engagement as instructors move away from lecture, harder data on the effects of learning communities, statements from employers about the importance of higher-order abilities—that such innovations do benefit student learning. But before we trumpet the future of teaching, some caution is appropriate. Some developments have been more slogan than content, and some practices have been adopted without much thought being given to their underlying philosophy. The cheering for "technology" in the classroom is one example. Its partisans have not distinguished between practices that simply replicate old-fashioned drills or enhance the conventional information dump—now relabeled "multimedia"—and those used in the writing process, in math, or in business simulations that make full use of the computer's power in constructivist ways. Similarly, the ineffective use of discussion, the adoption of small-group methods for fact finding, or learning communities or applied math courses that merely relabel older practices are innovations only in name. A deeper understanding of pedagogical assumptions is necessary to convert slogan into innovation.

It's difficult to produce the shift in basic approaches to teaching necessary for these innovations, as Cuban (1993) clarifies for K–12 education. The long odysseys of individual community college instructors, as they have felt their way through trial and error away from conventional didactic methods, attest to the difficulty of changing basic conceptions of what knowledge is important and what roles students should play. But without such a shift, any particular practice—this year a computer, next year distance learning, five years down the pike yet another idea—will be adopted in partial and incomplete ways, changing the outward appearances of classrooms but not the basic forms of teaching and learning.

This returns us to a point we have made repeatedly. While individual instructors can and do change their teaching, the process by which they typically do so—trial and error, with a little help from their friends—isn't particularly efficient, effective, or uniform. Many instructors don't make this odyssey, and the worst isolate themselves from their peers, so there can't be much influence (as we saw in Chapter 1). Instructors themselves complain about how lengthy the process is and how uncertain "learning by doing" can be. The desire that many instructors express for a more collective approach to teaching, in which faculty observe and learn from each other, reflects deep dissatisfaction with the current state of teacher preparation and development. And so even the innovations that instructors can adopt on their own—like small-group practices, projects in place of lectures, or computer-based methods—would be enhanced by institutional mechanisms of support, by the workshops and teacher centers and mini-grants we describe in the next chapter. For other innovations, such as learning communities and integrated instruction, the need for institutional support is more obvious. In its absence, they appear in colleges by ones and twos and cannot possibly change the basic nature of teaching and learning for many students.

Institutional support means more than money. It includes promotion by administrators and their intervention to coordinate many parts of a college, from deans to instructors to keepers of the master schedule. But these are cases where resources make a difference. In some colleges, resources are simply unavailable for luxuries like team teaching and staff development. Even where they are available, single-minded attention to enrollments, budgets, and efficiency—or "budget-minded administrators always looking at the bottom line"—undermines any commitment to teaching practices that do not increase enrollments, even though they may be more effective. Most subtly of all, those practices that might be adopted for pedagogical reasons—distance learning to meet the needs of remote or snow-bound students, computers to bring new kinds of instruction, learning communities to enhance connections among subjects—are invariably undermined when they are promoted for fiscal reasons. Thus distance learning and computer instruction as mechanisms for reducing the costs of instructors invariably lead back to "talking heads" in place of interactive methods. Learning communities that teach large numbers of students with low-cost part-time instructors undermine the planning among instructors and the interactions among students that are essential to this form of teaching. More money may not necessarily lead to innovation, as we stress in Chapter 9, but the search for "efficient" (or low-cost) instruction inevitably leads back to skills and drills. And so the innovations reviewed in this chapter will not endure, we think, unless colleges support them with the institutional resources they have at their command. Only when these resources are appropriately used can they create true teaching colleges where innovation abounds, as we clarify in the next chapters.

NOTES

1. There are some partial exceptions: Oregon has promoted the improvement of community colleges through institutional mechanisms, and Florida has done so through marketlike mechanisms including competition and performance-based funding (Grubb et al., 1999). However, most of the recent state reforms have concentrated on training and welfare-related efforts and neglected the educational side.

2. See the special issue of the *Community College Journal*, 66 (2), Oct.–Nov. 1995, pp. 4, 14.

3. We did not select classrooms in order to see or avoid new technologies, so from this perspective our sample is random. For an appraisal of how little effect computers have had in community colleges, especially compared to the rhetoric, see Doucette, 1994. We suspect that the use of computers for drills in developmental English and math classes is considerably greater than we detected, though we know of no census of community college practices that would determine whether this is true or not. In K–12 education, Cuban (1986) and Tyack and Cuban (1995, Ch. 5) have pointed out how little technology has ever changed schools.

4. For a recent report that highlights this point, see the Panel on Educational Technology, 1997—for example, the second recommendation: "Emphasize content and pedagogy, not technology" (p. 7).

5. For a review of distance learning in community colleges, with a series of profiles of individual colleges, see Lever-Duffy, Lemky, and Johnson (1996). While their introduction mentions the instructional challenges of distance learning (see pp. viii–ix), it doesn't look at how distance learning is carried out.

6. On ways of cutting costs in community colleges, see Beckman (1996), Section 3 on "Networks, Technology Training, and Distance Education." The discussion of substituting capital for labor harks back to Bowen's (1968) observation that productivity increases are lower (and cost increases therefore greater) in the public sector than the private sector because of the difficulty of substituting capital for labor.

7. This state may not be a good test of the potential for distance learning because it is dominated by textbook-driven instruction (described in Chapter 2). It isn't surprising to find most distance learning in this state to be didactic, because most teaching in these community colleges is didactic.

8. There's a general recognition that distance courses require more independent and autonomous learners; see also Linn, 1996.

9. The existing metanalyses of computer-aided instruction conclude that outcomes are slightly more positive in computer-based teaching, though the differences are not statistically significant (Kulik, Kulik, and Cohen, 1980). Brawer and Cohen (1989, 152–53) review several community college studies about computer use with distinctly mixed effects on achievement. However, these analyses do not clarify what kind of teaching has taken place in either the computer-aided class or the regular ones. The finding that computer-aided instruction is not more effective than conventional teaching may simply mean that skills and drills has dominated both.

10. See again Linn, 1996, for the conclusion that the cheapest forms of distance learning are poorly suited to helping students become autonomous.

11. This description of the community college as supermarket precisely replicates the metaphor of the shopping-mall high school developed by Powell, Farrar, and Cohen (1985).

12. Learning communities encompass linked or paired courses, course clusters, and coordinated studies; see Matthews, 1994; Tinto, Russo, and Kadel, 1994; and Smith, 1991, for various descriptions.

13. In colleges in the Pacific Northwest, the common use of LCs for general education requirements means that they are well known; in another case, LCs are so common that almost 10 percent of students are enrolled in one, so again the experience with LCs is common. However, in other institutions, one might find one or two LCs with perhaps sixty to one hundred students in an institution with a total enrollment of five thousand to ten thousand students—so LCs are almost invisible blips within the college. The problem of scale is part of creating a college culture in which LCs are well accepted.

14. Occasionally the obverse is true. One PACE program seemed to cost less per student because the program had fewer contact hours than regular courses and used inexpensive part-time faculty. While the administration liked it because of its "enrollment/FTE ratio," both the part-time faculty (causing high turnover) and fewer contact hours undermined the quality of the program.

15. This is a tricky institutional barrier. Suppose an LC includes a social science class that would normally have an enrollment of forty to fifty, an English class with an enrollment of twenty-five to thirty, and a remedial/developmental class with an enrollment of twenty, where

these limits are often set by college or district requirements related to safety and workload. Either the LC includes twenty students—so that the English and social science classes are underenrolled—or non-LC students are enrolled in the English and social science classes, undermining the point of the LC.

16. We have previously written extensively on the integration of academic and vocational education, in secondary schools (e.g., Grubb, 1995b) as well as community colleges; see Grubb and Kraskouskas, 1992; Grubb, 1996b, Ch. 5; Grubb et al., 1997; and Badway and Grubb, 1997.

17. The Council on Occupational Research and Development in Waco has developed a series of applied academics courses—in applied math, applied communications, applied physics (called Principles of Technology), and applied biology and chemistry—that instructors can use "off the shelf." These courses are probably the dominant forms of integrating academic and vocational education in high schools, but we found most community college instructors disdainful of these courses; because the content is relatively elementary, the applications are contrived and overly general. They strongly prefer to develop their own applied materials.

18. Several of these syllabuses are reprinted in Badway and Grubb, 1997, Vol. II.

19. We draw in part on extensive experience presenting workshops on curriculum integration for numerous colleges and consortia.

8

THE INSTITUTIONAL INFLUENCES ON TEACHING
The Potential Power of "Teaching Colleges"

As we have seen, the variation in teaching practices within community colleges is enormous. Often, the differences seem highly individualistic: Good teachers often emerge after individuals begin questioning their methods and change their approaches through trial and error (as we saw in Chapter 1). Conversely, unskillful instructors are as likely to be in colleges with strong reputations as in weak colleges, and they can be found in all fields of study. The apparently random distribution of good and bad teaching seems to confirm the biases of those who think of teaching as an innate ability—"good teachers are born, not made."

But this interpretation is, we think, incorrect. If educational institutions do little to foster good teaching—or if they make ineffective efforts—then indeed the quality of teaching is idiosyncratic and random, as individuals develop teaching abilities on their own. However, in a few colleges we found teaching to be of higher quality overall, and faculty unanimously reported that the college did everything within its power to improve instruction. Under these conditions the quality of teaching is more likely to be systematic rather than idiosyncratic.

In this chapter we examine the variety of institutional policies that influence teaching. There is a large number: personnel practices (in Section II), instructor training and retraining (Section III), the influence of administrators and the culture they establish (Section IV). The basic structure of a teaching position (examined in Section I) is an influence that isn't immediately obvious, though it is one of the most critical. Other mechanisms of influencing teaching have never been tried in the United States; the inspection system used in further-education colleges in Great Britain is one we examine briefly. Finally, funding patterns and state and federal policy exert their own influences, though we postpone them until Chapter 9. A "teaching college," therefore, is an institution that directs each of these influences to improving teaching, rather than serving other purposes unrelated to instruction.

In our interpretation of institutional effects, we rely on our interviews with instructors and administrators, of course. But a caution is necessary: Instructors sometimes cannot imagine what their institution might do because the question has never been asked, and because they conceive of their roles entirely within classrooms. Often, for example, instructors interpreted questions about "institutional support" as queries about supplies and materials for individual classes. Here's an auto instructor whom we asked what his administration could do:

> Stay out of my way, which they do, and I really have enough money to buy—yeah, you could always use more money, because I could use better equipment and tools and whatever. But for the most part, I'm just talking about—I mean I'm pretty well satisfied. We've got some '94 and '95 transmissions here—what more can you ask for? I mean, you can't do much more than that.

"What more can you ask for?" There were many more things he needed than some '94 and '95 transmissions. This instructor had complained about students with inadequate reading levels and low levels of motivation. He acknowledged only a passing acquaintance with faculty outside the auto group, including the English faculty whose help he could have used. He hadn't even begun to think about innovative practices that auto instructors elsewhere find useful—the integration of more academic content into occupational programs, the voluntary credentialing established by a trade association (NATEF), the links to employers created by high-quality co-op programs—and that require administrative support. When teachers live their lives wholly within their classrooms, they can't always articulate how their colleges could influence teaching practices or think about how things might be different.

Much of this chapter is distressingly negative. Many community colleges are not, contrary to rhetoric, teaching institutions, because they do not use their institutional policies and resources to improve the quality of instruction. We think the real story is to be found in Section V, which profiles three community colleges that do focus their energies on teaching. These exemplars clarify that community colleges can be the teaching institutions they aspire to be.

I. THE BASIC STRUCTURE OF INSTRUCTORS' ROLES: FRAGMENTATION AND ISOLATION

The most basic fact of instructor's lives is that, if they are conscientious, they are overloaded. The typical teaching load is five classes, which usually meet three hours per week, and somewhat more for occupational instructors. Institutions make their money on enrollments. Therefore, many instructors face between 25 and 35 students per class, or perhaps 150 students at a time; grading the frequent quizzes and papers therefore adds considerably to the fifteen to twenty hours per week of contact time. Full-time faculty are also responsible for institutional maintenance; in a period when the numbers of part-time faculty have been increasing, the price of being a full-time instructor is having to supervise part-time instructors and carry out administrative chores.[1] Here's how one faculty member, a dedicated and innovative business instructor, described his job:

> I'm required to teach five classes a semester, and there are some semesters when I've had five different preparations.... Number two, you're required to have at least five hours of office hours per week for students. You're required to sit on collegiate-wide committees. As a faculty member in business, there's an expectation that I have to be involved with and linked with the business community, and doing things to make our program in the college more visible and certainly more credible. At the same point in time, I'm expected to continually upgrade my skills.... If there were a strong commitment [to teaching], I think that the shift would be on knowing that a person who is hired as a faculty member is that—is a teacher, and that it's a full-time job, and that you cannot break it into different segments of being this, this, and this.

The pressures he describes are those of fragmentation, of being pulled among several responsibilities, with the result that instructors cannot concentrate on teaching.

For occupational instructors, the demands are increased by the need to drum up financial support for materials, equipment, and work-based placements. As an instructor in a medical office program described the problem:

> The things that are going on in the institution that affect my teaching is the lack of support that I feel from people really understanding how demanding the clinical placement is.... That can add up to many hours. They [the administration] don't consider that at all. They just expect me to get it done, and fortunately I've been able to do that, but it's very tiring, very tiring.... What I've gotten back is, "Well, I'm just sorry, ma'am, but we don't have any money to hire anybody to help you. You just have to do the best you can."

The position of an instructor is conceptualized and paid as a set number of contact hours, with time allowed for preparation and grading. But the other duties that instructors have to perform—institutional maintenance and development, raising money, developing internships, contacting employers for placement, keeping up-to-date for occupational instructors —are invisible and uncounted.

Part-time instructors are in an even worse position because they are not paid for anything other than teaching. Their participation in the life of colleges—including teaching-related discussions and workshops—is very limited. As one full-time instructor described the participation of part-timers,

> I'm not saying that the part-timers lack dedication or all that, but there is less reason for them to commit extra time and energy to the college when, as they see it, they aren't getting the benefits they deserve, they aren't getting paid for any of their prep time, or their time doing paperwork or any of their office hours.

And part-time instructors feel the pressures acutely.

> Yeah, well, there [are] lots of committees and, you know, like critical thinking and things like that. But, you know . . . I'm a part-time instructor as well, and so I'm also teaching in other places, and so I don't have the time to spend doing a lot of the in-services and things that I wish we had. . . . There are always things that are going on that are very helpful, I think. But personally, as an instructor, because I'm part-time and because I have to teach in lots of different places to supplement my income, usually I don't have the time to do it. Which is sort of the problem, I guess.

Some community colleges are beginning to look the way some business firms do: There's a relatively small core of full-time faculty who are responsible not only for teaching but also for "managing" part-time faculty—for devising course outlines, sometimes for hiring and monitoring the part-timers. So neither full-time nor part-time faculty can devote much energy to rethinking their teaching. "Teaching" becomes defined as covering a specific course and outline, and the main problem is meeting logistical demands—ensuring that teachers cover specific subjects in particular rooms at certain times of day. In this kind of institution, attention to pedagogy gets lost.

A second defining aspect of instructors' lives, as we first saw in Chapter 1, is isolation. While many individuals feel that isolation is an innate part of teaching, it has many institutional roots. The sovereignty of individual instructors is a legacy of four-year colleges, where academic freedom has often been interpreted (or misinterpreted) as guaranteeing the right of instructors to teach as they will. Community colleges that are trying to follow the four-year college mode resist any infringements on academic freedom. The independence of teachers is also a feature of high schools, from which many older community college instructors came.

The differentiation between full-time instructors, teaching full-time traditional-age students during the day, and part-time instructors, teaching part-time
and older students at night, contributes to the sense of fragmentation as well. As
one instructor complained,

> I have no idea who's teaching Marriage and Family 101 on Wednesday nights. . . . I
> know her name [only] because I've seen her name on stuff. People get hired, oh, for
> an Exceptional Person class. I've met him once; I don't know him. I developed the
> course, I wrote the course guide; I know this course. And I offered him any assis-
> tance he needed. He said, "Thank you," and walked away from me. I have never seen
> him since. I have no idea what he's doing with that class, and I know it sounds turfy,
> but I want to know what students in the program that I'm responsible for are leav-
> ing here with.

In this complaint, the full-time instructors who are responsible for devising
coherent programs of study do not have the opportunity to monitor those programs. The college has become a set of independent courses, where instructors are
interchangeable cogs in a large teaching machine, rather than an institution where
coherence matters.

The recent history of the community college may also have created isolation as
a "solution" to diverse views about teaching. One longtime English instructor
described the process his institution went through in the 1960s and 1970s:

> During the first ten or twelve years of being here [in the 1960s], there was a lot of
> active attention given to sharing teaching experiences. It was relatively easy to visit
> other people's classes. . . . As a result of that, some factionalism began to develop
> because certain teaching modes were perceived as the desirable ones and certain sub-
> ject matters were perceived as the desirable ones and people for whom those were
> not their natural modes or their subject matter interest began to resist and some fac-
> tions, political factions, began to develop. There was a kind of—what did we call it in
> those days?—do your own thing. . . . All of that resulted in, I think, about the middle
> seventies in a real ascendancy of privacy. The classroom is my place. After that it
> became very difficult to talk about teaching other than with just good friends, as a
> professional activity.

Another echoed the fact that community colleges had developed isolated cultures
by the 1970s, and resisted any efforts to create collegiality:

> My experience when I came to [this college] in 1977, it was kind of an old-guard
> teaching faculty that was very much into leaving each other alone, and I came in, you

know, Mr. Hotshot—okay, I want to do this, and talk with people, and collaborate. People would give me really cold responses, like, "Well, you know, don't push too hard, you know, we all do our thing, and we trust that we're doing a good job."

Many of the instructors in innovative programs, like learning communities, described themselves as holdovers from the 1960s. But *if* that were a golden age, it gave way to a much more individualistic approach to teaching.

Above all, the isolation of instructors is created by the lack of any activities that might draw them together *around teaching*. Opportunities for learning communities and collaborative teaching are rare. Staff development activities are formulaic, contrived, and often not focused on teaching, as we will show. In most institutions, there are no mechanisms to evaluate other instructors—for example, by observing other classes—and therefore no reasons to discuss the quality of teaching or to reflect on one's own practice. Except where colleges have created teaching centers, there are no forums for faculty to discuss their teaching. And, as we have already seen in Chapter 1, the department is not a reliable source of collegiality, since it is often too small and too varied. Instructors are often "wrapped up in our individual work . . . I'm not sure what collegiality would be based on."

The isolation of teaching is a problem for several reasons. Without any central forum for discussion, the status of teaching is almost invisible, or inaudible. Discussions about instruction may take place among a few interested faculty that "kind of find each other," but otherwise there's no place to have such a discussion. As we saw in Chapter 1, instructors often learn about teaching from colleagues, but colleges and departments that thwart collegiality make it less likely that instructors can learn in this way. Finally, the lack of collegiality means that innovative practices often don't influence other instructors. In most colleges with learning communities, for example, we found one or two learning communities funded from outside grants. But they were not replicated by other instructors, and their essential lessons—about the need to provide students with more coherent programs, to integrate across disciplines, to provide more active project-based work—were unrecognized in the rest of the institution.[2] In North County Community College, the developmental studies division had developed an innovative pedagogy (profiled in Section IV of Chapter 5), but the other two divisions of the college concerned with language and literacy—English and ESL—were immune to its good practices. The director of developmental studies commented, "There is just not enough interaction among the three areas [English, developmental studies, ESL] for us to have any sense of what's being done at the different levels." It's startling to visit an exemplary program and find that other faculty in the same building have no idea about its existence—but that is consistent with the fragmentation and isolation typical of most colleges.

Such fragmentation, while quite common, is hardly inevitable. The colleges we profile in Section V have come up with central visions and planning processes that bind faculty together in common purposes instead of dividing them. In K–12 education, a long history of reform efforts has led to a similar conclusion about the conditions necessary to enhance instruction: "Teachers learn by doing, reading, and reflecting (just as students do); by collaborating with other teachers; by looking closely as students and their work; and by sharing what they see."[3] Without such internal coherence, without a sense of collegiality across the entire campus, teaching is difficult to improve, because it remains an individual effort.

II. PERSONNEL PRACTICES: THE CONFUSION OF MULTIPLE GOALS

One way to promote good teaching is to select and promote only the most skilled instructors. In this section we examine three personnel practices that could affect teaching: the hiring process, the promotion and tenuring process, and salary systems and other incentives. In Section III we review the education and training of community college instructors, the policies that colleges can use to develop good teaching rather than select for it. The question is not whether these practices can by themselves guarantee good teaching; they obviously cannot, given the multiplicity of factors that affect instruction. Rather, our question is whether community colleges consistently use their personnel practices to promote good teaching rather than other goals.

Hiring Practices

A college that is single-minded about teaching would, we presume, use the quality of instruction as the first among several criteria in hiring. But there are many other goals in hiring, and—except in a few rare cases—the quality of teaching seems to sink to the bottom of the list.

Hiring procedures for full-time faculty have become incredibly complex and bureaucratized—partly under the pressure of affirmative action, which emphasizes squeaky-clean procedures. Here's a *partial* description of a typical process by a dean of instruction:

> Departmental units will identify their needs and will then walk through the process to establish whether or not the institution will decide that that is a priority. If it is a priority, then those positions will go down to the district office and they will be advertised. Once they're advertised, the faculty members are selected by the academic senate, the administrators are selected by the administration, and classified

[staff] are selected by the classified [staff]; they come together and will work with the job description. Prior to it going out, by the way, they will also be given some training in the area of what to look for in hiring, what to look for in a candidate, what the affirmative action rules and regulations are [*sighs*]. The position is advertised; once it is advertised for four to six weeks, then the committee will engage in a screening process. Prior to engaging in the screening process, the committee will identify selected questions that they want [to ask], they will agree on the answers that that question ought to generate, and, you know, the other kinds of things—who's gonna go first, who's gonna go second.

She went on to describe the interview process itself (which in this institution involved reviewing the candidate's disciplinary qualifications and asking about imaginary classroom scenarios), the process of selection, the recommendation to the president, the final approval by the academic senate, college-level administration, and district-level administration. The process is so detailed and so unwieldy, and involves so many people from such diverse interest groups, that it's hard to imagine that any one consideration (like the quality of teaching) could ever survive. Many people whose interest in teaching is limited (like classified staff) have a say in the matter, as do others—particularly administrators—whose commitment to teaching is checked by other goals. One head of developmental studies described such a process this way:

Each person seems to be looking for something different. You know, the instructors are looking for a real comrade—knowledgeable, flexible. They are also looking for somebody who can work well with them because they team up a lot, you know, they've got a lot of committees. Then, when I [as an administrator] look at the person, I look at somebody [whom] I perceive from the other end. Can this person work with not only certain individuals, but can the person work well within the group? The whole group. . . . And I guess the president is looking [to see if] the person [is one] to join the union [*laughs*], who adheres to the mission of the community college, is not egocentric and can only work with DS [developmental studies] but can work with a variety of different people.

Even in this brief description, a number of qualities aside from teaching ability are important: flexibility, ability to work easily with others, disinclination to join a union (or, from the vantage of a union representative, the inclination to join), adhering to the mission of the community college. Consistently, the following criteria prove important:

• Content mastery is usually ensured by requiring a master's degree or, in occupational areas, years of experience in the field. However, content mastery does nothing to ensure command of pedagogical methods. Indeed, the focus of even master's programs on research, and the increasing preference for Ph.D.'s, has placed an increasing number of would-be researchers in community college positions.

• Affirmative action is, as one instructor put it, "a real sore subject." Recruitment committees are under great pressure from administrators and committee members to hire minority faculty and women in nontraditional areas.[4] Several instructors told stories of recruitment committees sent back to the start when their finalists did not include any minorities or women. Others mentioned cases where a president had specified targets for hiring certain numbers of minority faculty. The operation of affirmative action has made many white and Asian-American faculty members quite bitter. One gifted English teacher said that affirmative action on his campus "has subsumed every other consideration" in hiring. Still another said, "We won't take a chance on someone who might be a brilliant instructor" because affirmative action made the process too cumbersome.

This is not the place to rehearse the difficult and emotional issues involved in affirmative action. Our point about affirmative action is not that it is wrong—indeed, we support it wholeheartedly—but rather that it has been given such priority, and has such complicated hiring procedures, that it has buried the issue of teaching quality.

• Familiarity with community colleges and allegiance to its sacred norms is an important hiring criterion in many colleges. People who don't know the lingo about "access" and the "people's college" and "teaching institutions" simply aren't hired. Indeed, one college with problems hiring minority faculty has developed a training program to recruit black and Latino individuals from M.A. programs. The "training" concentrates on teaching them about the community college so they can compete in job interviews.

• Policy toward part-time faculty sometimes gives them priority for full-time positions, to develop a system of promotion for part-timers.[5] But this policy is counterproductive as a selection mechanism for teaching because part-time faculty members are usually hired in very casual ways—sometimes without interviews or procedures of any kind, when a college finds that it has to staff a section by the following Monday—and with only cursory reviews of their subsequent teaching.

There are many other idiosyncratic criteria that recruitment committees use. That's precisely our point: Recruitment committees look for so many different and potentially incompatible qualities that facility with teaching falls near the bottom of the list. As one instructor summarized the entire process,

> I think the criteria are phony. There's a lot of politics involved, a lot of affirmative action, the selection process itself—the numerical selection process, I think, guaran-

tees mediocrity. . . . That's not to say that we haven't hired some good young teachers, but I think it was despite the process rather than because of the process. Everybody is so frightened, you know, what we won't do is take a chance on a person who might be a brilliant instructor because that person falls outside of the parameters of the instruments used to evaluate.[6]

In addition, *most hiring committees do not gather any valid information about teaching.* It has become common to require a "teaching demonstration," but in every case we learned about, it is so short and artificial as to be laughable.[7] Many colleges schedule a five- to fifteen-minute demonstration to the hiring committee; several instructors noted that they had no advance warning of the short lesson required. It's hard to imagine how even the most gifted instructor could strut her stuff in ten or fifteen minutes. The most active forms of instruction, like small-group discussions and projects, take longer than that to set up. The most skilled forms of lecture/demonstration generally begin with some didactic material that is atypical of the class as a whole. Finally—as we stressed in Chapter 2—meaning- and student-centered instructors have to socialize students to the particular expectations and goals of their classes, a process that takes several weeks at least. Short demonstrations to educated adults (not students) cannot be good indications of the skill and control that constitutes good teaching.

In the absence of any real information from "teaching demonstrations," other feedback comes from the interview process, including responses to artificial teaching scenarios mentioned above. We doubt that committees can pick out "good teachers" on the basis of interviews. The best instructors we observed come in so many styles, with such different personalities and modes of self-presentation, that a short interview is unlikely to be reliable. Furthermore, as we clarified in Chapter 1, what instructors say about their teaching differs from what they do. Many didactic instructors claim to use discussion and small-group techniques when in fact they don't.[8] So the information that committees get about teaching is much less reliable than the information they collect about race, ethnicity, gender, formal qualifications, and prior experience.

Based on what instructors have told us, then, teaching ability is one of the least important factors in hiring. But it needn't be that way. For example, in the developmental studies department we profiled in Section IV of Chapter 5, the department imposes an *initial* screen for an individual's teaching philosophy:

They [the recruitment committee] ask 'em some pretty gruff questions. . . . So they would like to know, very often, "Well, what type of philosophy do you adhere to in writing? Whose theories and writings do you most adhere to?" So, you see, that one question has many implications: "Do you know what's going on out there in the field? Do you understand a reading philosophy or a writing philosophy? Have you read? Are you involved [in] and up-to-date [with] what's going on?" So people will come in, and [if] they don't really know that much, are at a loss.

The importance of having an initial screen for teaching is that the other criteria for hiring—affirmative action, allegiance to the community colleges and all the rest— can still have their influence, but only within a pool of individuals committed to high-quality teaching. A hiring procedure with an ordered sequence of criteria could put teaching first, rather than—as seems typical—having it come last.

Promotion and Teaching Evaluations

A second selection process takes place as faculty are evaluated for promotion and tenure, and one might expect to find teaching evaluations prominent in promotion decisions. Almost universally, however, instructors responded that the process for evaluating and promoting faculty is "not meaningful" or "just a rubber stamp." In several cases a college had been unable to agree on an evaluation system, so there simply wasn't one: Individuals were promoted after a certain period of time—usually four years—and were paid according to experience and formal education. Most colleges do have procedures to evaluate instructors, including a review of student evaluations and an assessment of contributions through committees and other non-class activities. But the evaluations are often not very meaningful. The head of English at North County Community College mentioned, "I personally don't think that's a very strong incentive [to improve teaching]," and the head of developmental studies described it derisively:

All they have to do is fill out a sheet, answering questions such as "Did I adhere to the rules and regulations of the school?" [*Laughs.*] You know, "Do I talk with my students? Do I try to help them individually? Do I try to boost their morale?" You know, various sorts of questions, and there are not many. "Do I work well with my supervisor?"—that kind of thing.

Usually such evaluations lack power because almost no one is denied tenure, as one instructor pointed out:

We have a faculty member here in our department that we hired, and we hoped that he would come along and really be productive, and he's not. I think we either really need to sit on him and make him accountable and help him to be better, or we need to get rid of him. And we won't, and he'll be here until he dies, probably. . . . I think you'd have to be grossly incapable to be let go.

Another noted, "You really have to screw up to be denied tenure around here." The tenure review may provide some feedback to new instructors about their strengths and weaknesses, but it doesn't kick out many bad teachers. And since very few colleges provide any meaningful in-service education, a probationary instructor would typically have nowhere to turn for help.

Sometimes evaluations include an observation of teaching by administrators and (rarely) by peers. When administrators review teaching, the observations depend on the skill of the administrator. But, as we will see in Section IV, most faculty regard administrators as impossibly distant from teaching; they are mired in other considerations (like enrollment) and often have not been in the classroom for a long time. Some deans of instruction come from the ranks of counseling, or through "leadership" programs to train administrators, and so they have never been instructors. And some administrators charged with reviewing teaching have philosophies of instruction that are quite uninspiring. One dean of instruction with a strong reputation admitted that he rated faculty members based on "hearsay"—what faculty members said about other faculty in private—as well as his own observations. Here's how he described one instructor he had recently observed:

> I was really impressed with what he was teaching, how he was teaching, how he had broken it down, how he kept repeating basic ideas, how he came back again and again and again so that a student understood the concept. I don't see how anybody could have gone through that lecture without knowing what [the instructor] was talking about.

But sheer repetition is not effective teaching, and his comments betrayed no appreciation for alternative approaches. In many colleges, administrator review can't be a powerful method for improving teaching, as their judgments are too unreliable, too uninformed by any understanding of what good teaching might be.

If evaluation of teaching is meaningless for most probationary teachers, it is rarer still for tenured faculty. This is serious because of burnout. A teaching institution would continue to monitor the quality of instruction and would provide some support—a change in subjects taught or teaching format, or further staff development, or a well-timed sabbatical—if the quality of an instructor's teaching began to suffer as a result of burnout or battle fatigue. But this almost never happens; the tenure process assumes that once an individual has been deemed fit for teaching, he or she will stay that way.

The marked tendency for faculty evaluation to be a "rubber stamp" is not universal, and some colleges have instituted classroom observations that are oriented toward improvement. In one college, the administration and union finally developed an evaluation process after ten years; one instructor commented, "It really has some potential, and it is teaching-centered." The dean of instruction was widely praised by faculty for her understanding of teaching; the assistant dean who carried out the evaluations described what she looked for in these terms, which we interpret as a statement about hybrid teaching:

> I like to see active classrooms. I like to see instructors that are experts in their field of knowledge and know how to incorporate students into their teaching so that students are, at least during a portion of the class, actively participating.... Do they start on time? Do they know what they're talking about? Do they conform to the course outline? But I'm looking to see what kind of student interaction they've got going. Is the classroom comfortable? Are the students willing to speak up? Is there a method for a faculty member assessing the learning, what's going on in the class, and altering it as it goes?

In another college, the dean of instruction observed probationary teachers with other faculty members. The dean, well regarded in the community college world for her promotion of learning communities, ran staff development seminars devoted entirely to teaching approaches, which probationary teachers were required to take. In this institution, faculty members agreed, teaching evaluations were both meaningful and tied to mechanisms of improvement.

While most classroom observations are carried out by administrators, in a few institutions faculty observe one another.[9] Setting up this process has not always been smooth—there is not, in this country, any tradition of teachers at any level observing one another—but it has the seeds of creating more collegiality within an institution. As a dean of business described the process,

> We're relatively new to peer evaluation, and peers are loath to discredit their colleagues.... If everybody's looking at it as just "Let's do the paperwork and get this thing over with," it's not gonna have very much effect. We had this very discussion in our own division a few weeks ago, and there was a debate. One of the persons says, "It has no value, it's a sham, we don't get anything out of it," and the other side of the room says, "Wait a minute! You know, I don't agree with that. I learn, as a peer, when I observe. I'm learning an awful lot." ... Then somebody else says, "Well, it made me think through what I'm doing. You know? Maybe stop and consider, am I doing all the things I need to be doing?" So it sort of brings you up short [and] makes you think about it a little bit.

Developing the culture required for peer observation—a "basic attitude"—is a tricky process. It can be undermined if faculty come to see its judgments as illegitimate, or if a union rejects peer observation on principle, or if too many faculty treat it as "paperwork," or if administrators abuse the process in various ways.[10] But this college and others have made peer observations work, and in the process restored teaching to a more meaningful component of evaluation.

The lack of any serious evaluation of teaching in most community colleges means that the hiring decision is the crucial step. Once hired, an individual is likely to be given tenure; once tenured, there is no further concern with the quality of teaching. But the hiring process, as we have already seen, generally incorporates very little concern for instruction. So personnel practices are almost completely ineffective in promoting good teaching, and the burden therefore falls almost entirely on the education and training of instructors.

Pay Scales and Merit Pay

Community college instructors are paid based on experience and formal credentials. Merit pay, or pay scales that consider the quality of teaching, are quite rare. The message implicit in this convention is, of course, that teaching does not count; as one writing instructor complained,

> How does the pay raise come? If good teaching [equals] doing well on the pay scale, then it's rewarded, and then good teaching is the center of everybody's attention. If publishing and making presentations and being presidents of organizations gets rewarded financially, then that's where your . . . your heart's where your money is.

Or, as an innovative auto instructor expressed it, "Money is a pretty good incentive to do a lot of things—a lot of people don't do 'em just for the heck of it."

The only form of merit pay we encountered was in Colorado, which has required all its colleges to develop pay-for-performance systems. There has been very little money available to allocate through this mechanism, and therefore many faculty have questioned whether it is worth the time involved—though apparently the principle of merit pay has not been questioned there. In addition, South Carolina has recently adopted a voluntary staff development effort, which can lead to a certificate for eighteen hours of time spent, and colleges may include this certificate in their annual performance reviews (Bower, 1996). This is a step toward providing activities related to teaching, but it is not really a merit pay system because—like basing salary on formal schooling—it rewards course taking, not performance. Finally, much to our surprise, two of the thirty-two institutions we observed have begun to provide some pay increase for publication—precisely the wrong policy for an institution that aims to be a teaching college.

It's difficult to recommend performance-based pay because its success in other educational institutions has been quite limited. In K–12 education, for example, schools often find that the conflict over defining and measuring merit is not worth the cost to collegiality. Merit pay systems have worked well only in districts where pay is above average, working conditions are good, and teachers and unions have successfully collaborated over time—conditions that are missing in many community colleges.[11] Merit pay might therefore create divisions, whereas one goal of a teaching institution should be to create community. The benefits of observing teaching in classrooms, creating collegiality through peer observation, and taking the quality of teaching seriously in regular reviews can all be realized, we suspect, without moving to merit pay. However, if "your heart's where your money is," the lack of merit pay is yet another signal that teaching doesn't much matter in community colleges.

III. THE EDUCATION AND TRAINING OF INSTRUCTORS

Since personnel policies are so ineffective in promoting good teaching, the burden falls on the education of instructors. Indeed, as we saw in Chapter 6 on standards, most postsecondary institutions in the United States rely on instructors' mastery of content and individual commitment to ensure high standards, because there are few external regulations. Community colleges can affect instruction through pre-service education or the formal requirements for being hired, in-service education and staff development, and (rarely) faculty centers.

Pre-Service Education

Almost universally, community colleges require their academic instructors to have master's degrees in order to ensure subject mastery (though the hiring of part-time instructors is usually less stringent). Occupational teachers generally have substantial experience in their occupational area. While these practices are often determined by local colleges, some states reinforce them through certification procedures.[12]

However, very few community colleges impose any requirements for preparation in teaching itself. A number of instructors noted how odd this is, given the conception of the college as a teaching institution. As one instructor said,

> The irony is that we're not taught to be teachers at the college level. . . . We teach high-school teachers how to teach. . . . We teach administrators; you can go get your Ph.D. in administration. But we don't teach college teachers how to teach. They just throw you right in it. . . . Nobody is sitting there talking about the pedagogy of teaching college students, you know, the whole philosophy. I find that very strange.

Another noted that "most of us go to graduate school, and they teach us about the history of whatever, and they kind of leave the teaching aspect of our profession to work out for itself." Only a few instructors went to graduate programs that emphasized community college teaching.[13] Preparation specific to teaching is generally rare, then, even though dedication to teaching is supposedly a defining characteristic of community colleges.

Among the institutions we visited, the only exceptions were colleges in Minnesota, where occupational faculty only must complete a six-course sequence within their first three years, and colleges in Iowa, where new instructors must take a workshop for new teachers—an interim measure, a "Band-Aid type of thing"—and then complete coursework within five years in methods of teaching, student evaluation, curriculum development, foundations of the community college, and human relations.[14] Overall, instructors in Iowa are quite positive about the requirement.[15] A dean of health occupations described the preparation:

> Part of their education has been taking courses where they could begin to identify that having additional teaching skills would be helpful; because you are a nurse and know how to *practice* those skills, you don't necessarily know how to *teach* these skills. . . . So [the state's requirement] helps with the basic entry-level understanding of being a teacher and what it's all about.

To be sure, there has been considerable controversy in this country about teacher preparation. Many teacher training programs are considered quite weak, and they are often blamed for the problems of education. But, at least in K–12 education, there is considerable evidence that untrained teachers are disastrous for students.[16] Equally important, community college instructors seem to regard pre-service education about teaching as appropriate to their work. Given the long process of trial and error that has led many innovative instructors to their teaching approaches, pre-service instructor education could speed up the development of teaching appropriate to community colleges.

Mentoring New Instructors

Preparation in pedagogy might also be effective in the initial period of teaching. In K–12 education, these first few years are widely acknowledged to be crucial, and many districts have developed systems for mentoring new instructors, providing staff development and other support specifically geared toward new teachers. The results are not only improved teaching, but also higher retention rates as fewer teachers burn out because of stress.[17]

But special attention to new instructors is rare in community colleges. A number of instructors referred to the "sink-or-swim" method common in community colleges: "They just throw you right in it." One instructor recalled his first semester this way:

> When they debriefed me after the first class I taught in [this region], they said, "How's it going?" And I said, "Not too damn good, because these people are coming in there and I'm teaching business communications, I assume they can write a sentence and a paragraph; they cannot." And rather than them being aghast, as I was, they all went, "Get in line. Every single instructor we've ever had—adjunct, full-time, or otherwise, centers, on campus—has the same problem. This is a universal problem, so quit whining."

The lack of sympathy seems harsh, but the absence of institutional support is common. While all faculty have access to staff development, such activities are rarely directed specifically at beginning instructors, and they fail to provide the personal and class-specific attention that might benefit new faculty.

As with other institutional policies, there are notable exceptions. The college we call the Community College of Westville requires that probationary teachers go through a minimum of ninety hours of staff development in the Teaching/Learning Center. Another institution has a process of designating "lead instructors," who are released half time from their regular teaching to help new instructors. Yet another designates a committee for every new teacher. Its purpose is in part to determine tenure, but the committee also provides advice and support to the faculty member it reviews. The developmental studies program at North County Community College has a mentoring process where the division head, or another experienced teacher, works with new part-time instructors. And many learning communities have an informal process in which instructors discuss joint and related classes, which is simultaneously a way of providing guidance to new members of the learning community.

The exemplars of mentoring for new instructors are comparatively rare, however. Given the frequency with which instructors learn from others around them (as we documented in Chapter 1), a mentoring process would provide such exemplars early on. It might also shorten the process of trial and error that otherwise takes so long to produce innovative teachers and works so unevenly.

In-Service Education and Staff Development

When we asked administrators what their institution does to support good teaching, their second response—after repeating the mantra that community colleges are "teaching institutions" without research responsibilities—was to note their staff development activities. Most institutions have sabbaticals, funds for attending conferences, workshops, and seminars given by outside speakers. But while some institutions have used staff development to focus on pedagogy, most colleges have used in-service education in unfocused and thoughtless ways.

Some institutions include sabbaticals, though they tend to be rare—perhaps one or two faculty per year, who typically return to a university to continue their own subject-specific education. More frequently, colleges provide funds for faculty to attend conferences or summer institutes, largely to keep up-to-date or extend their knowledge in their subject areas. One might wonder whether travel funds accomplish much; as one writing instructor noted acidly, "A lot of people like to travel," and conferences are often located in suspiciously beautiful places. A more important objection is that these forms of staff development (as well as sabbaticals) emphasize mastery of subject matter rather than teaching methods, and they benefit individual instructors rather than groups or departments. Conference-going could benefit larger groups if, for example, faculty members attending were required to give workshops to fellow faculty members about what they had learned. But this never happens; as one instructor noted, "We really don't get too much of that—the schedules are so busy, and I mean, we have a hard time getting a business department meeting scheduled." In effect, most staff development emphasizes teaching as an individual activity, dependent only on subject mastery.

The most common form of staff development is the seminar with outside speakers. In some institutions, such seminars are used to examine forms of teaching, and some instructors learn important tips from such programs. But they are systematically marred by several common failings. One is that the subjects vary wildly, and many have nothing to do with teaching. When an institution provides a smorgasbord of topics, they may include CPR, or how to take a vacation, or investment alternatives, or the introductory meeting at the beginning of each term when administrators say grand and motivating things. One instructor mentioned that his department organized its own staff development because the college efforts were so useless:

> We've gotten approval from our dean to hold our own meeting, rather than going off to some of the flex-day ones, because they're not real relevant to what we're trying to do. One of them is a hike up onto the ridge here. It's a great outing, but I walk up there every other day, and if that's the best of what they have to offer for some of the flex days, I'm not really interested in that.

And a smorgasbord approach cannot possibly provide a faculty with a common understanding of teaching, since everyone attends different seminars. Staff development becomes another kind of perk serving individual ends, rather than an activity that might systematically improve instruction.

Another great failing of staff development days is that they are typically one-shot activities with outsiders, and do nothing to generate a culture within an institution supporting teaching. A number of instructors mentioned that they disliked getting "fancy educators to come and talk to us about things," as if there were no expertise internal to the faculty. Many others noted that outside speakers might provide instant inspiration but no lasting effect. As one instructor described the effect of a well-known speaker:

> It's called staff development; it's supposed to make you a better teacher. . . . John ——— came one year and was very inspiring. It's almost orgasmic to be in a room with John and hear him speak, but you recognize that an hour after he leaves and you've come down, it's kind of like a Sylvester Stallone movie; it's very exciting while it's going on, but an hour after it's over, reality comes back and you have to go get in your car and go home. . . . John didn't stay here; John didn't provide daily inspiration; he didn't send daily memos; he didn't say, "Attaboy," you know, and nobody said that, and so obviously that kind of thing falls apart. . . . When the inspired leadership is gone, you fall back into routines.

The upshot is that staff development is not taken seriously by many faculty. As one outstanding English instructor commented about the "contrived" in-service program, "A lot of people treat it as a pro forma activity; they're required to put in so many hours, and they make it clear that they're putting in the hours."

A third problem is that staff development often treats teaching as a simple skill, one that can be imparted by a short-term activity—an afternoon workshop on cooperative learning, for example, or project-based learning, or the use of computers in writing. But while some approaches to teaching can be presented in a short period of time, their successful use generally depends on instructors changing their ideas of who they are, how they ought to relate to their students, and what the purposes are of conventional subject matter. These transformations in conceptions of self and teaching cannot be accomplished within an afternoon. In effect, conventional workshops are didactic, skill-oriented presentations of complex practices, while learning new ways of teaching requires more constructivist approaches in which instructors reinterpret the entire teaching enterprise. The relearning process not only requires a longer period of time, but also benefits from a community of like-minded individuals working on the same issues—stable networks of peers, rather than others randomly attending an afternoon workshop.[18]

In contrast to conventional workshops, some of the best colleges have staff development activities that depend on the internal resources of the institution—on learning from fellow faculty members. As an early childhood instructor at Choctaw Community College mentioned,

> One of the things we do well here is that we honor our expertise. We don't just look to people who are more than a hundred miles away. I can learn from Steve, I can learn from Marilyn—I have! . . . People have taught me a lot about cooperative learning, learning to learn, brain-based learning, Writing Across the Curriculum, and that's fit in really well with my early childhood background. So this has been a wonderful place to continue to [learn how to teach].

Similarly, the developmental studies department at North County Community College has its own "staff development," without relying on outsiders, through the mentoring of new instructors and the constant interaction among instructors. One new instructor commented: "I feel that I've had more professional growth being in this department for a month that from all the conferences I've ever attended."

In their criticisms of conventional staff development, faculty seem to be asking for activities that are internal and continuous, rather than external and episodic. They want ongoing workshops that create groups of faculty members who observe and discuss teaching regularly, relying on their own resources and using outside experts only occasionally.[19] Almost without exception, instructors who bemoaned the lack of collegiality indicated that they would welcome discussions of teaching and opportunities to visit each others' classes. A business instructor who described teaching as a "very individualistic endeavor" wanted to have a college-wide forum to discuss teaching, and to be able to observe his colleagues:

> I'd like to have the opportunity to observe and be part of a process of continually improving, by either in-service or observing my colleagues, or something that would provide me the opportunity to improve in my craft.

Another mentioned,

> I think that if resources would be available so that people have some time, take time, to collaborate with one another, the results would be beneficial to students. . . . I think that if you bring four instructors together to set up a program, that they might talk with one another.

A number of institutions have developed precisely such forms of in-service development. Metropolis Community Colleges, profiled in Section V of this chapter, offers several semester-long seminars every term, relying principally on discussion and reading among instructors. Each focuses on a different aspect of teaching—collaborative learning, for example, or the use of projects, or learning communities. One technical college has an ongoing seminar, intended to raise awareness of literacy among occupational faculty. Best of all, several institutions (including Choctaw and Westville, profiled in Section V) have developed faculty centers. These are typically offices that run seminars on different aspects of teaching (including special seminars for new instructors), provide individual help for faculty who request it, and maintain libraries of materials on teaching methods. Instructors can come to faculty centers with problems, and the centers can respond flexibly—either individually or collectively, if the problem is a common one. They are also continuous, allowing faculty to try new techniques and get feedback on their efforts. And they are symbolically important, representing an institutional commitment to teaching and faculty development, in place of the random offerings of most workshops.

To be sure, even faculty centers may be limited in their effects. As one instructor noted of her college's Center for Teaching and Learning: "The better teachers are the ones who get involved." This is consistent with our observation that the best teachers reach out to construct networks of like-minded instructors (see Chapter 1). But the point is not that a faculty center can guarantee the participation and improvement of the worst instructors; of course it can't. Our point is that faculty centers, and other staff development that is internal, continuous, and collaborative, can provide the resources necessary to improve teaching and change the culture of community colleges.

Other Forms of Teaching Improvement

Community colleges have at different times supported other more specific efforts to improve teaching. Their effects are generally quite limited, however, again because they tend to reach self-selected individuals. One of the oldest efforts to change teaching has been Writing Across the Curriculum (WAC), in which writing instructors encourage their peers to incorporate more writing—even (or perhaps especially) in subjects such as math and occupational areas.[20] A handful of the instructors we interviewed mentioned WAC programs as helpful. Despite their longevity, their reach has been limited. Most programs rely on volunteers as instructors, and the added burden causes substantial turnover. The participants are volunteers as well, and again it's likely that only the more engaged instructors participate. We suspect that occupational teachers are underrepresented because of their time pressures, because many do not accept the need for more writing, and because the writing promoted by most English teachers is inappropriate for occupational purposes (Grubb and Kraskouskas, 1992).

Similarly, a large number of community colleges have supported classroom assessment (or classroom research), which provides instructors with diagnostic devices—like concept maps, student goal rankings, learning logs, and one-minute papers—to make students more self-conscious about their learning and to help faculty see what their students are learning (Cross and Angelo, 1993; Cross and Steadman, 1996; Angelo, 1991). As in the case of WAC, a few instructors mentioned participating in classroom assessment programs, and a few reported continuing to use classroom assessment techniques. But classroom assessment tends to follow the pattern of most staff development. Only a few teachers attend such workshops, and they are likely to be highly self-selected; workshops tend to be one-shot efforts, without continuing support; and they are typically used by individual instructors in their own classes, rather than creating a common culture focused on teaching. In one college, classroom assessment was the basis of an ongoing seminar—as Cross and Steadman (1996) recommend—and therefore allowed instructors to create a community of discussion and support. However, this extended use appears to be rare, like other collective forms of staff development.

Finally, one institution required all faculty to be trained in the Vogler process, which creates a standard approach to syllabuses. This forces all faculty to consider their teaching, course goals, and behavioral objectives, and all course outlines followed the same format. But, valuable as this may be, it cannot influence pedagogy and the daily interaction of the classroom.[21]

These three examples focus on limited aspects of teaching—on writing, assessment, and course outlines, respectively. To be sure, they may provide some motivation for instructors to change their methods more broadly. For example, WAC in some institutions has turned into Writing for Understanding, in which writing encourages students to reflect on other activities and to think more critically. Similarly, classroom assessment includes some techniques encouraging instructors to rethink their basic approach to teaching. But, except in the hands of the most skilled leaders, they remain limited approaches to the vaster landscape of teaching, unable to change the culture of instruction.

IV. ADMINISTRATORS AND THE CULTURE OF COMMUNITY COLLEGES

The influences of administrators on teaching are profound. They establish the tone and culture of their institutions—the attitude toward instruction, whether good teaching is important or not, the sense of internal cohesiveness or, conversely, of fragmentation and independence. The best institutions—the true teaching colleges we profile in Section V—have administrators who are committed to teaching and who have managed to orient every single policy in their colleges toward the improvement of teaching. Sadly, such individuals are rare. Over and over, instructors report that administrators are ignorant and often indifferent about teaching, and their howls of anger are startling.

One way to understand the centrality of administrators is to see how they affect a college's culture. In several colleges, the faculty reported that a change in administration made all the difference. The exemplary institution we call Choctaw Community College attracted a new president in the late 1980s, someone supportive of innovation and collegiality. Older faculty uniformly recalled the "dark" and "dismal" years of his authoritarian predecessor, when managerialism destroyed all collegiality and innovation. As one exceptional faculty member described the difference,

> That was probably the very grim period of administrators making decisions, and [decisions] came down to us, as opposed to more of a cooperative, participatory. . . . I mean, it's not that we [now] have total autonomy and we make all decisions and the administrators don't; that's not at all true. But there is more input, more teamwork, more respect for each other's perspective and the integrity of the work that we do, and we all work hard, and we all try to appreciate that yes, we may have different roles, but we're here as a team for the purpose of instruction.

Another technical college had been ruled by an authoritarian president from the trades. When we visited, it was in the process of transition under a new president and dean of instruction more supportive of faculty participation and teaching. The new dean admitted that "we've got a problem with trust . . . people were not involved—I mean, they were just told what to do and they did their job." While instructors were unsure whether the new administration could turn the college around, they were hopeful that the new president would bring a new atmosphere.

Most community colleges have not had such pronounced changes in administration. The roles that administrators play emerge from the comments of instructors in many institutions, in all areas of the country. In one institution, for example, virtually every instructor spoke of the administration in the same terms: "We could get by without any administrators." "The less administrators interfere, the better." "I'd rather be left alone." At another college, an instructor in a learning community reported:

> We'd be better if they just called in sick every day. . . . It's really disquieting for me to say that, because I think we should all be working for the same thing, but for the

most part they're operating in some other fantasy world . . . for the most part, I don't think they have much effect on my teaching.

Almost universally, faculty report that administrators are uninvolved in teaching issues: They don't visit classrooms, they don't know what's going on in classrooms, and—apparently—they don't care. A culinary arts instructor noted the problems with making instructors accountable:

> The problem with the administrators administering that [accountability system]— you'd have to have it before a board or something like that, because the administrators mainly just talk to themselves. What that does, that reinforces misconceptions about who teachers are and what they do. So that makes their [administrators'] view of them [instructors] very skewed and oftentimes not correct. They are—how should I say this—I don't want to use the word *petty,* but they do exercise sometimes a rather willful wielding of power.

An instructor in another college laid the blame on the very different priorities of administrators:

> The administration has nothing to do with effective or innovative teaching. They're so busy counting beans and filling out forms and doing things like that, so busy in the mechanics that the creative and the innovative is way, way in the back seat, you know.

Another noted,

> I don't feel a lot of support from the college, and I think it comes from the fact that they're so budget-minded, always looking at the bottom line . . . they focus on image; they talk about promoting the college through the public relations office and getting articles in the newspaper, rather than building up the students, the professional development of the staff and faculty.

The problem of administrators who are ignorant about teaching is doubly difficult for occupational instructors, since most administrators come from the academic side. As one auto instructor noted, commenting in addition on the physical isolation of occupation programs, "The faculty, as well as the administration, do not know what I do back there." Yet another observed, "No one gives a shit what I do as long as enrollments are up." The special problems of finding money for equipment, lining up internships, keeping up to date, and establishing linkages with the business community—all serious demands on time—are unknown to academic instructors and unappreciated by most administrators (as we saw in Chapter 3).

The profound ignorance of most administrators about teaching was revealed quite directly by the recommendations of several deans. In a few colleges, we asked deans of instruction to recommend exceptional teachers so that we could see what their conception of "good teaching" looked like. In one institution where the dean of administration was a former counselor, he recommended two exemplary instructors in learning communities. But he also recommended an embittered auto instructor who had all but abandoned his students, and a CAD instructor without any experience who taught the subject as a set of computer commands. Another dean—one with a strong reputation for supporting good teaching—recommended that we see the mediocre anthropology instructor profiled in Section I of Chapter 2. Neither of these colleges had any procedure for observing classes; where administrators do not observe teaching, there is no way that they can know the quality of instruction on their campus.[22]

Even worse, in many institutions instructors perceive administrators to be actively hostile to innovation and disdainful of faculty. As an instructor at Choctaw Community College said about the "dark days" of the former president,

> His favorite word, which we've heard for the last fifteen years, is, "Well, you'll have to take it out of your hide." And that has bred a lot of resentment and a lot of people have backed off from innovation because of that. He'll say, "Gee, I'm glad you're doing that; that shows you're interested." But he doesn't seem to understand what it is you *are* doing.

An instructor at North County Community College contrasted her department's administration with that of other departments:

> A lot of times, your administrators, the first thing they're gonna say to you is no. And then you have to start defending and trying to convince them and sometimes you can't, sometimes you can't. These people [the division's administration] have a totally open mind, which is very unusual, I think, for top administrators.

Even where administrators support innovation, their support tends to be verbal encouragement of those who are experimenting on their own, rather than time and money resources for more instructors to innovate. In one institution with a strong reputation for transfer, the dean of instruction was praised by all instructors for her support of teaching. But she had not managed to institute any meaningful staff development, instructor evaluation, or college-wide change, and any instructional change was up to individual instructors. One innovative math teacher put it like this:

> There's a few people on the faculty that are really interested [in teaching] . . . we kind of find each other. They [the administration] to some extent recognize people who are doing innovative things and provide support, some support. Mostly it's usually verbal; it's not usually time and it's not usually money. I think they do their best to showcase and comment on and encourage innovation. I wish there was more. In the math department we still have 60 percent of the department that just lectures. They don't do feedback, they don't do groups, you know. They just lecture and students get through it.

The dean's interest in teaching was not enough, since it had not led to any institutional efforts to improve the quality of instruction.

The effect of administrators being ignorant of teaching, or even hostile to innovation, is that instructors tend to withdraw from the institution into their own classrooms. As one particularly innovative English instructor remarked,

> The rest of the management of my college [aside from the president]—well, let me put it this way: I stopped playing Mother May I? when I was in first grade. Basically they do not, in my opinion, offer enough respect and enough space for people to be innovative and creative and whatever. So I have total autonomy in my own classrooms. We all do essentially. But I am pretty nonparticipatory in the more structured college activities right now because they're [the administration] not interactive with me. They're sort of pejorative.

Another talked about the dispiriting effect of having administrators who are indifferent to teaching:

> It might be hard, you might bring some of that attitude [of administrators] into the classroom and it might affect the students. You know, I'm . . . I'm just going to do my job and get out of here. You know, if you learn it, you learn it; if you don't, you don't, because who gives a care anyway. They [administrators] don't care about me and— not all instances, but some instances where when you sit in the faculty lounge and hear teachers talk, it's like, my God, what's going on in the classroom if you feel this way about the college?

Another consequence of administrator indifference is that many powerful forms of teaching cannot be sustained by faculty because they require collective action that only administrators can provide. Individual instructors can be excellent on their own, of course, and sometimes groups can band together in small collectives—in learning communities or in specific departments. But learning communities prove unstable and ephemeral without institutional support, and individualistic approaches lead to as many dreadful teachers as terrific ones, while leaving a vast number of middling instructors without much help. The establishment of personnel practices focused on teaching, staff development that emphasizes the improvement of instruction, and mentoring all need administrator support and institutional resources.

The news about administrators is not all bad, of course. The exemplary institutions we profile in the following section have administrators who not only value good teaching, but have set up institutional mechanisms to develop it. However, the hostility toward administrators is so profound that we need some explanations of the divide. One is the problem of managerialism that has plagued almost every level of the American educational system. As Cuban (1988) has stressed for K–12 education, administrators can see themselves primarily as educators concerned with the quality of teaching and learning; as managers focused on enrollment targets, budget requirements, space needs, and other noneducational goals; or as politicians promoting the institution within the community. Each of these roles is necessary to the maintenance of strong educational institutions. The three roles need not be embodied in one person; it is possible to split them and allocate them to different administrators. As one instructor described his president,

> The president is a wonderful person, but she is not an educational person. She thinks she is, but she's not. She's a manager. She's good at the financial, she's good at the political, but she's very weak in instruction, but she, I think, understands that, so therefore allows people who are stronger to have more influence.

But where managerialism takes over completely, it has the effect of demolishing educational leadership. The English instructor we quoted above, the one who refused to play Mother May I? described the consequences quite precisely:

> I've had it out with my current dean. I went and asked him something and he pulls out the contract and I said, "I don't need you to read the contract for me. I know how to read. I'm looking for moral and educational leadership here and I'm not getting it. . . . I am *not* looking for a manager. . . . I am looking for someone—an educational administrator who leads us toward educational goals and administers the stuff that gets done in order to bring them to fruition. I do not wish to be managed. I manage myself." [*laughs*] . . . At our college it's always management, management. Collective bargaining has partly played into that, but I don't need to be managed.

When administrators do participate more actively in teaching, faculty respond positively. One economics instructor who disparaged administrators as "careerists" who should "stay out of the way" nonetheless recounted his president's efforts:

> Our president came to a workshop [on effective teaching] and was interested enough to put herself up in front of a group of teachers and teach a fifteen-minute segment and have us evaluate her. I think that was the best thing she ever did . . . that kind of thing does a hell of a lot for faculty morale.

But save for a few examples, instructors live in a different world from administrators who are "busy counting beans and filling out forms." The division between administrators who manage and faculty who teach is, evidently, detrimental to the cause of teaching and learning.

Managerialism may be reinforced by common practices throughout American education, and by collective bargaining that reinforces a sharp division between management and labor, but it is also promoted by the training that some community college administrators receive. Many have come through community college "leadership" programs that pay scant attention to teaching.[23] As one English instructor described his administrators,

> Aside from [one administrator], I would say that there's probably no administrator on campus who is really even conscious of what's happening in that way [in teaching]. Community college leaders . . . by the kind of people they recruit to be in the [administrator training] program, and in some ways because of the curriculum that the folks that are pickin' 'em [create], they're encouraging this creation of community college administrators, community college presidents who aren't necessarily teachers—in fact, probably aren't teachers. And we have a lot of sort of generic administrators, generic managers, who run community colleges. And they haven't come up out of the classroom. Our current president has never been a teacher, and so he . . . you know, it's pretty hard to talk to the person about our needs.

But administrator training programs cannot be blamed for the distance of all administrators from teaching, because many deans and presidents have come up through the ranks of teaching. To take a more sympathetic and structural view of administrators, they too are trapped in institutional roles that *require* them to be concerned first and foremost with enrollments, budgets, ensuring sufficient instructors and classrooms and light bulbs, so that innovative pedagogy is the last thing on their minds.[24] Here's an assistant dean of instruction describing the priorities in setting up a new program:

It works like this: you have to generate this much FTES [full-time equivalent stu-
dents], which is a fixed revenue, and you have to meet a certain productivity goal, a
certain number of students per teacher on the average. Both those goals are set by the
district, and then you get the money which equals those goals. So when we are
shrinking enrollment and generating less FTES, we basically have less money available. So it's hard to support programs like multimedia, which is a developing program, a new program.

Purely instructional concerns—whether a multimedia program would benefit
students, for example—are in practice swamped by revenue and productivity targets that are established outside the college and driven by overall enrollment and
funding concerns. Meeting these targets is this administrator's first priority, since
failing to meet them means the institution won't be adequately funded. While she
has been working hard to establish a new evaluation system, including classroom
observations, she has so many competing goals that promoting the quality of
instruction does not come first. A few faculty expressed sympathy for administrators. An English instructor in the college where the faculty uniformly wanted the
administration to "leave them alone" acknowledged,

> We do not have department chairs here . . . so with only three assistant deans taking
> care of so much, they're just overworked—we're about as flat [a hierarchy] as
> you can get . . . so as far as what's happening in the administration right now, they're
> just taking care of what they have to take care of or what needs to be taken care
> of first, and I have to say that they are not doing anything aggressively as far as
> fostering innovation and, you know, effectiveness of teaching. They're just tak-
> ing care of things as they come along, almost like crisis management. Hopefully
> that will change in the future, but it's kind of been like that for the last couple of
> years [sighs].

But such sympathy for the plight of administrators is rare since, overworked
though they may be, they still set the conditions that discourage innovation and
attention to teaching.

Part of the problem comes from administrator turnover; instability in leadership is detrimental to effective instructional policies. When asked if her institution
was innovative or experimental, one vice president for academic affairs responded,

> I don't think we are. We've had seven presidents in ten years. And the school district
> put some of those people in here as part of a rotation . . . so they had no idea what a
> technical college was about. And some of them were put in here as a dumping
> ground. . . . The sum total of all that changeover in administration all the time, and

not very good administration, is that [this college] has just kind of plodded along, doing what we do, and not innovating very much.

Here are the comments of another:

You know, [this college] changes presidents and deans like most people change clothes [*laughs*]. From my perspective it is an administrative training academy, and we pay people to come here for two years, get trained, and then they go on to another job. So the administration really doesn't have—you know, they come in with a lot of big ideas but, you know, one president comes in and wants to take away the diesel building and build a music hall instead. Well, it's too late. She couldn't do it because the plan had gone to the state ten years earlier. Then somebody else comes in and decides they want to take all of our equipment money and give it to the library for a new computerized card catalogue.

This comment is not just about turnover; it also reveals that when new administrators come, they bring their own priorities, fail to consult the faculty, and institute changes that may make no sense—before moving on to greener pastures.

In institutions where administrators neglect educational issues, mutual blaming takes place. In one college whose faculty clearly regards the administration as useless, here is the reaction of the dean of instruction:

The door is open to faculty and they're encouraged to engage in staff development. But what I believe is that too many faculty members do not take advantage of the opportunities that are available and not enough are thinking about their development as it relates to new teaching strategies and styles. I think that there is a weakness in the way we evaluate and monitor staff development as it relates to faculty members improving their teaching—we have very little leverage. If a faculty member decides that he or she does not want to improve their teaching, there is very little that can be done by an institution. . . . I would venture to say less than 20 percent of the faculty are engaged in what I would consider learning new teaching techniques and styles . . . and I don't believe it's incentives. I think there are a lot of incentives. I don't believe it's because faculty don't care. I believe that a lot of faculty members have given up.

There are several noteworthy elements of this passage, particularly the fact that the dean acknowledges a "weakness" in the way the college monitors faculty but never proposes doing anything about it. The dean feels that there are sufficient staff development activities, though staff development takes the form of "flex days" that faculty consider worthless. But the saddest aspect is that a standoff has developed:

The faculty sees the administration as worthless, and the dean sees the faculty as responsible for mediocre teaching because they have "given up."[25] In some cases, outright hostility is the result. One head of a vocational center said,

> Someone once asked me, "Jim, could you run a high school?" I say, "Damn right. Give me the building, give me the kids. I get to machine-gun the staff." Because we really need to start over, building the philosophy.

In such cases, mutual blaming allows individuals to go on acting as they have been, comforted that mediocre teaching is not their fault. These are conditions in which any improvement is difficult to begin.

The division between administrators with managerial and political priorities and instructors concerned entirely with teaching therefore has many roots. But it consistently works to undermine the attention to instruction in the "teaching college." It leads to administrators who are distant from classroom concerns, ignorant of what their instructors are doing, hostile to innovation because it disrupts well-established routines, and inclined to blame the faculty. It leads to administrators and instructors responding to very different imperatives. It cannot reconcile, for example, the need to improve instruction through meaningful staff development with the very real need to balance the books. In the end, this division promotes the isolation of instructors and good teaching as an individual effort, because too few administrators realize how much they influence the culture of the "teaching college."

V. EXEMPLARS OF "TEACHING COLLEGES"

Overall, we observed twenty-two community colleges in enough depth to get a reasonably detailed picture of how they affect teaching. In fifteen of these institutions, sad to say, we could find little evidence of an institutional commitment to teaching. Staff development was weak or unfocused, hiring and promotion policies were unconcerned with the quality of instruction, administrators supported little innovation, and the faculty and administration were at a standoff. These were often institutions where a few innovations persisted—several included some learning communities, another developed a widely cited learning community for poorly prepared students—but these innovations were limited. Their practices had not spread outside a small group of committed and dedicated faculty, and the administration tolerated rather than promoted innovation.

Four of the community colleges we examined were distinctly mixed in their institutional support for teaching. One provided support for a number of learning communities, though overall the division between administrators, concerned with funding, and faculty, concerned with effectiveness, was marked. Another case was a technical college changing from a former president, an authoritarian individual who had been poisonous to the culture of teaching and learning, to a new president who was more collaborative and supportive of faculty. One was an institution where the dean of instruction was widely viewed as knowledgeable about teaching, though only recently had the college instituted some changes. These included instructor evaluation with classroom observation, a teaching-centered orientation program for new instructors, and a staff development program that includes more teaching-related workshops. Both institutions might be on their way to being "teaching colleges," though at the time of our observations it was too early to tell.

In contrast, in three colleges, the faculty almost uniformly reported that their administrators are committed to teaching, and there was no mistaking the institutional culture of innovation and experimentation.[26] These institutions use virtually all the policies at their disposal to enhance instruction.

Choctaw Community College

Choctaw Community College has emerged from a "dark" and "dismal" regime of an authoritarian president in the early 1980s—"kind of a black period for Choctaw, very hard-line management, faculty were extremely upset." Its current president received high marks from faculty for creating an atmosphere of extensive faculty participation and support for good teaching. The process was not easy or swift—"It took him ten years, and I think it was probably five years before lots of people really came on board," commented one innovative instructor—but virtually every faculty member and dean described the results in the same terms. In addition to new procedures for decision making, this college has adopted several practices related to teaching:

• An Opportunity Center provides support to faculty for their teaching in several ways, including seminars and workshops. (See Lauridsen, 1994, for other information on teaching centers for faculty.) A small grant program provides funding for innovative practices, and many instructors have used these to change both their pedagogy and the structure of courses.

• The staff development program is based on providing a variety of teaching-related experiences for faculty members. The manual for staff development is explicit about the fact that content mastery is not sufficient for good teaching and that instructors should be proficient with a variety of pedagogical approaches.

• The evaluation of faculty involves classroom observation by both peers and administrators, guided by a Faculty Appraisal Planning Worksheet. This directs observers to note many standard aspects of teaching (whether the instructor is well prepared, whether he summarizes major points), but also to rate faculty on emphasizing conceptual understanding, encouraging class discussion, clarifying student thinking by having them apply concepts and identifying reasons for their questions, and encouraging different points of view.

• The institution is committed to linked courses and learning communities, and there are numerous offerings bringing together academic areas and integrating academic and occupational subjects.

• Administrators were planning an induction process for new faculty, and a writing center to help faculty teach writing.

The result of these practices is an institution with a great deal of innovative teaching and collegiality. The comment in Section III—"We honor our expertise; we don't just look to people who are more than ten miles away"—came from this institution. We found none of the split between academic and occupational faculty that permeates most community colleges. Instead, occupational instructors accepted the importance of academic subjects and collaboration from the academic side. One instructor, a non-nurse teaching in a nursing program, told a story of two nurses from a neighboring community college questioning her legitimacy in a nursing program, causing her to reflect on collaboration at Choctaw:

> That was the first time I really sat back and looked at myself and thought, Is it not interesting that I'm not in a climate where the nurses *know*? They are not the experts in *how* to go about studying, or *how* to take tests, or *preparing* for those tests, and they're willing enough and confident enough that some of us *do* know, and they'll pull on that expertise. And the thing with math: We're willing enough to say to Tom, "You can do this." So it was really different to see them [the two nurses from a different college] feel that this was their sanctuary—one should not tread on this ground.

If the proof of change is in the teaching, this college has clearly turned its attention to the quality of instruction, with all of the institutional resources at its disposal.

Community College of Westville

At the Community College of Westville, unlike Choctaw, there is less praise for a single individual such as the president, but like Choctaw the institution includes an amazing variety of mechanisms to enhance teaching.

• A Teaching and Learning Center provides many services to faculty, "to facilitate the learning community concept, or developing a learning college," as its director described it. Its activities include customized assistance about teaching to individual faculty members; workshops on specific subjects that groups of faculty request (like incorporating computers into instruction); working with students with inadequate reading levels, alternative "learning styles," and multicultural issues (in a city with large black and Latino populations); and "team-building" seminars held off campus on subjects like risk taking, time management, and coping with change. The center manages mini-grants that faculty can get for curriculum development. The center also surveys students, employers, and recent graduates, so that any external information about content and pedagogy can be quickly translated into workshops and other forms of staff development.

Various administrators and faculty, as well as the head of the Teaching and Learning Center, stressed its value in providing a wide and flexible array of support for faculty. As the vice president of instruction described it,

> The Teaching/Learning Center is, it's kind of nonjudgmental help. I mean, you don't have to go to your dean or me and say [*whispering*], "I don't know how to do this." You go to [the head of the center] and say, "I want to do this, and I need a team." And so she'll tell you about some of the English faculty who've been really good working on teams and like to do that, or some of the math, and they'll pull together a team and they'll do it.

• The college has its own system of faculty credentialing, a delegation of the state's credentialing power. As the vice president for instruction explained, "Because we do our own, we think that it's more relevant, and we can tie it into what they're teaching." New faculty are on probationary status for three to four years, during which time they participate in special workshops for new faculty and an additional thirty hours per year of professional development. For tenured faculty, a five-year recertification process encourages them to continue developing their teaching abilities.

• The college has several cross-curriculum efforts, including a "skills across the curriculum" program that emphasizes five particular competencies: reading, writing, speaking and listening, valuing diversity, and computing. A handbook on the integration of critical skills provides illustrations of how to incorporate the five skills into different types of classrooms. Most of the sample assignments include both reading and writing as well as group work where students interpret what they are doing to the class and evaluate each other. The examples also provide illustrations of integrated teaching across disciplines. Throughout the handbook there is no distinction between academic or transfer classes and occupational classes—all have an equivalent pedagogical footing. In addition, a Writing Center has been established with FIPSE funding, to help instructors with the teaching of writing.

• A number of departments have developed "content guides" for their courses, partly to standardize course content and partly to help part-time instructors who, in other institutions, are dumped into the classroom without any help. These content guides are revised every five years; they also incorporate the five critical competencies. In at least some cases these content guides incorporate pedagogy as well. For example, the sociology department incorporated "feminist" or more learner-centered pedagogy, a "big shift for a couple of the other sociology faculty."[27]

•The college has adopted a form of merit pay developed by the faculty. Merit is measured on a five-point scale, determined largely by student evaluations, administrator observations, and evidence of service to the college and community. Because there has been very little expansion in funding, the amount of merit pay is trivial—perhaps a few hundred dollars. Nonetheless, the faculty recently voted to keep the pay-for-performance system when given a chance to scrap it, since it has provided faculty more contact with deans and given deans a better understanding of what happens in classrooms. This experience suggests that merit pay need not be divisive, and can provide the basis for more contact between faculty and administration.

• The college has developed a series of linked courses designed for Latino students, funded with a FIPSE grant, that pairs developmental courses with core courses.

In addition to these specific practices, the college has developed a culture, with procedures to match, that the vice president for instruction described as "getting the data." When we asked what the institution did to improve instruction, she replied:

> I think it's getting the data. I think the faculty know a lot of the data. . . . If I'm not graduating any ethnic minorities, I know it. If you start publishing data across the college that says that, then I sit and I start thinking, hmmm, maybe we could be doing something differently. So I think that the kind of data we put out makes people bring things they know in the back of their heads to the front of their heads, and start deciding to do something about it.

"Getting the data" reflects an institution-wide sensitivity to outcomes, using various conventional measures (persistence and graduation rates, employment rates after graduation) plus scores on tests administered by the Educational Testing Service, the "ETS academic profile." Part of the institution's culture is that problems identified by these measures are not left alone, "things they know in the back of their heads." Instead a specific program of improvement is developed by faculty and implemented (often with the help of mini-grants). This college is not, therefore, driven only by enrollment and revenue goals, like so many other community colleges; it has taken clear steps to become concerned with how much their students know and what they do after leaving the institution.

Finally, like Choctaw, Westville seems to have developed a more collegial structure, in which faculty participate at many stages of institutional development. The mini-grants for innovative teaching came about as the result of just such a process. As the vice president for instruction described the college's reaction to a standardized test:

> Our students were at the zero percentile on that test: we had the lowest incoming students of any school that took the test. It was funny, because the administration went, "Oh, my God, this isn't Cleveland, this isn't L.A., this is Westville!" And our faculty said, "We've been telling you this! We've been telling you what a difficult population we have." And so we said, "Okay. What can we do to help you so that you can help the students?" And that was what they said—they wanted the mini-grants. So that's why we give mini-grants.

One could argue that this vignette illustrates a division between faculty and administration over difficult teaching conditions, but in the end a problem-centered solution won out in which the faculty had a real voice.

Metropolis Community College

Metropolis Community College is located in one of the largest cities of the country. Its students include a kaleidoscope of every race and ethnicity that has ever come to this country. Many of them are victims of the city's poor school system, and many of them are recent immigrants. The college is housed in a large building in a poor and bombed-out area, a grim illustration of how Americans have let their central cities deteriorate. But this is one of our favorite community colleges, because inside it is vibrant, innovative, and constantly changing—everything that a teaching institution under difficult conditions should be.

The founding president of the college instituted a culture of innovation and experimentation that, faculty agree, has stayed with the institution. The dean for instruction has been in many ways the guiding light in the college's emphasis on teaching and learning—she is highly visible for her promotion of learning communities and of active forms of teaching. But while she is central, the underlying ideas have been institutionalized in many ways. Again and again, faculty mentioned to us: "You better believe it: This is a teaching institution."

• The college has promoted learning communities in many ways, primarily in a "problem solving" mode. In addition, the college has come to understand that developmental education and ESL are best delivered through learning communities. When it sets up programs for welfare recipients, it also insists that they be done through learning communities. In order to "protect" this teaching arrangement, a separate budget has been established for learning communities.

• The dean for instruction runs seminars for faculty members on different aspects of teaching and leaning—for example, small-group work, teaching culturally diverse students, project-based teaching, racism and sexism, developing case studies, new-student and faculty perceptions. Unlike conventional one-shot staff development activities, these last an entire semester. Rather than having outsiders come in with glad tidings and then disappear, the seminars are vehicles for faculty to create a learning community of their own. The dean conducts these workshops as she would a student-centered class, with the faculty participants running different sessions and preparing exercises based on experiences in their own classrooms.

• New faculty are matched with mentors, and both mentors and administrators observe their teaching and provide various kinds of support. New faculty are protected from other responsibilities —to prevent the kind of fragmentation mentioned in Section I above. Evaluations of faculty involve peer observation (at least three times per semester), and every instructor noted that these observations are taken seriously in promotion and tenure. Consistently, the purpose is support of new faculty; as the dean of instruction mentioned,

> The thrust of the process is really to work with the faculty member, to make them the best possible person you can, rather than a process that's seen as punitive. And it gets the actual faculty into the process.

• Like Choctaw Community College and the Community College of Westville, Metropolis has separate resources to support faculty initiatives. There have been many innovations funded over the years, including a course for early math support; a problem solving seminar; a reading/math cluster developed by two faculty; assignments in psychology to use in co-op placements; and a practice of including counselors in classrooms to see what works and what doesn't. The idea behind these innovations is that some will work well and become institutionalized, while others will not—a reflection of the culture of innovation.

• Some departments meet regularly—three to four times per year—to discuss common teaching problems, syllabuses, readings, and the like. In some cases departments have developed collective understandings of what classes should emphasize. For example, the instructor of an extraordinary English class for welfare recipients (profiled in Chapter 2, Section IV) noted that an emphasis on textual references was part of the department's standard practice. An ESL instructor mentioned the "ESL method" common in her department, a combination of conventional drills and reading and speaking about real-life materials.[28] In developmental studies, the entire department moved from what one instructor called a "skills" approach to a "content" approach, emphasizing study strategies, metacognitive skills, and theme-based learning, all based on K–12 research on reading and constructivism.

The Metropolis faculty seems more aware of what other faculty do than instructors in most community colleges. They speak knowledgeably (if warily) about the strengths and weaknesses of each other's teaching. Classrooms are more open and teaching is more public than in most community colleges, because of learning communities, the faculty development seminars, and peer observation. Discussions about instruction are part of the common currency of the institution. One fledgling (and not yet confident) human services teacher summed up the attitude:

> Metropolis is a *great* place to be a teacher. If you're serious about effective teaching, there's support to struggle with the issues. Good teaching is rewarded. You don't have to be perfect, but you have to be honest and open, to try hard. This is a rare find.

The only problem is that the importance of teaching makes instructors extremely busy; as an innovative and conscientious English teacher remarked, "They work you to death."

Drawing on the Ideal of the "Teaching College"

Other institutions we observed have taken smaller steps to promote teaching and learning. Several colleges have adopted a large number of learning communities, particularly colleges in the Pacific Northwest under the influence of the Washington State Center at Evergreen State College. One or two other colleges have adopted centers for teaching, to provide an umbrella for various workshops, mentoring practices, and mini-grants for innovation. One technical college developed a Critical Literacy Seminar for occupational instructors to explore issues in teaching (like learning styles, small-group work, and writing), though none of the topics was specific to occupational instruction. A few colleges have adopted mentoring practices for new faculty, and one or two have instituted peer observation and teaching-based evaluations of faculty. Several colleges have presidents or other administrators who are trying to reemphasize teaching and learning, according to faculty. But what distinguishes the practices in Choctaw, Westville, and Metropolis, and the developmental studies division of North County (profiled in Section IV of Chapter 5), is that improvement of teaching and learning drives virtually every policy.

Community colleges do have an advantage over other educational institutions: They can, if they choose, rely on the ideology of being a "teaching institution." One college with a rather mediocre record of teaching has recently tried various ways to improve instruction. After long battles it has adopted an instructor evaluation program that includes classroom observation; a teaching-centered orientation program for new instructions has been instituted; the staff development program, while still contrived in many ways, incorporates more teaching-centered workshops, including some on classroom assessment. In describing these recent (and still small) efforts, an innovative English instructor noted the importance of community college ideals:

> I think we have a tradition that is honored, I suppose as much in the breach as not, but we do have a tradition as seeing ourselves as the teaching college. This is the place ... that has always been a teacher-centered institution and, unfortunately, many of the faculty members, I think, have not seen that that means teaching-centered. So a lot of what goes on here is serving the personal interests and concerns of faculty members rather than serving their role as teachers, as classroom teachers. But I think that, at least, the tradition is there and it can be called upon when the occasion warrants.

More to the point, the tradition can be called upon if the institution wills it—if the administration and faculty decide to make teaching a priority. Then there are many institutional mechanisms to give content to this priority, and to convert the promise of the "teaching college" from rhetoric into reality.

NOTES

1. The proportion of all instructional faculty and staff who are part-time increased from 52.1 percent in 1987 to 60.2 percent in 1992—the highest of any type of postsecondary institution. See Kirshstein et al., 1997, Table 2.1.

2. The exceptions are the colleges that have made an institution-wide commitment to learning communities, particularly those located in the Pacific Northwest because of the influence of the Washington Center on Improving the Quality of Undergraduate Education, located at Evergreen State College in Olympia, and a few other colleges, such as LaGuardia (Matthews, 1994), that have made learning communities a priority.

3. See Darling-Hammond and McLaughlin, 1995, 598. The issue of collegiality has been extensively examined in K–12 education, and it proves to be crucial to the ability to innovate—because innovations require support from other instructors and tend to wither away if instructors must develop them independently. Some schools have moved toward a model in which teachers form a collective with responsibility not only for improved teaching, but also for many administrative and managerial tasks, breaking down the conventional separation of "teaching" and "administration." See also Little, 1987 and 1996, and Lieberman, 1995.

4. This seems to be true even in regions of the country such as the rural and upper Midwest, where there are exceedingly few black and Latino students.

5. In one college, this policy is tempered with a desire to find "new blood" by hiring some proportion of instructors from outside the ranks of part-time instructors. This caused a great outcry

among part-timers—a good example where a political conflict over hiring has nothing to do with teaching.

6. The "numerical selection process" refers to a scale developed in the college, where points were awarded for particular answers to specific questions. This particularly rigid format arose from the need to standardize interviews for affirmative action.

7. But see Shulman's (1995) proposals for the pedagogical colloquium.

8. See also Harkin and Davis, 1996a and 1996b. They came to the same finding with instructors in further-education colleges in Great Britain.

9. In a few colleges, union rules have precluded observation by peers; this reflects the long-standing antipathy of conventional unions toward having workers judge one another lest they be co-opted into the tasks of management. In these colleges, one hears about "management" rather than administration; for example, one instructional dean declared that "evaluations here are done strictly by management" because of union rules.

10. Because there are so few examples of peer observations, we do not have more precise information about the conditions which contribute to their success or failure. Somewhat better information is available from Great Britain, where there is a long tradition of observing classes by Her Majesty's Inspectorate. Currently there are various inspection systems, and their success depends on many small details of the process; see Grubb, 1998b.

11. See Murnane, 1984. We note that research universities usually have evaluation and promotion systems (and therefore salary) based on merit, where research and publication are the dominant components of merit. This system works well only when there is a discipline-based consensus about what good research is. It has been much more difficult to come to any similar consensus about good teaching.

12. McDonnell and Zellman (1993, Table 3.3) report that only fourteen states have any certification requirements for occupational instructors. The Iowa Board of Education Examiners (1991) found that eleven of the forty-one states that responded to a questionnaire licensed community college instructors, requiring an M.A. or equivalent experience for occupational instructors. No states other than Iowa and Minnesota appear to require preparation specifically in teaching.

13. See also DeBard, 1995, who reported that 3 percent of instructors come from programs specifically focused on community college teaching. However, it is possible that this fraction is increasing, because 15 percent of new hires come from such programs.

14. In addition, occupational instructors in California used to complete a twelve-unit program designed to prepare faculty coming in from industry for teaching—a requirement that has since been abolished in order to move closer to a "collegiate" conception of instructors. Universally, occupational instructors who had been through that program approved of it; they felt their teaching was superior to that of academic instructors with no preparation in teaching at all.

15. The Iowa Board of Education Examiners (1991) determined through a survey that the majority (about 74 percent) of faculty approved of the state's licensing requirements. The only instructors who did not were those with Ph.D.'s.

16. See for example Darling-Hammond, 1994 and 1996; Ashton and Crocker, 1986; Guyton and Farokhi, 1987.

17. Some community college districts report turnover among part-time instructors as high as 50 percent in the first two years.

18. The point about changing dispositions about teaching has been well articulated in the K–12 literature on staff development; see, for example, Floden, Goertz, and O'Day, 1995. They emphasize the creation of teacher networks as more constructivist approaches to reform,

because they allow teachers to change their conceptions and dispositions within a community of like-minded peers.

19. See also the project on peer review of teaching developed by the American Association of Higher Education (Hutchings, 1994), and the associated workbook (Hutchings, 1995). Unfortunately this project includes no community colleges.

20. On WAC, see Stanley and Ambron, 1991. Another effort to improve the teaching of writing is the National Writing Project, which uses teachers to teach their peers about the writing process, but NWP is now in only a few community colleges.

21. This process can easily lead to competency-based approaches to teaching, and then to skills and drills—particularly in occupational classes. See Achtenhagen and Grubb, 1999.

22. For the same reason, it's foolish to carry out research or award certificates for good teaching based on recommendations of administrators, because they simply don't know enough to make reliable judgments. For examples of studies based on administrator recommendations of supposedly exemplary teachers, see Baker, Roueche, and Gillett-Karam, 1990, and Easton, Forrest, Goldman, and Ludwig, 1985.

23. This is common, but it need not be the case. In K–12 education, with the development of teacher-led schools and governance patterns in which administrators and teachers share administrative roles, there has been greater interest in creating programs that prepare administrators with a greater concern for teaching. A fledgling literature has developed on administrators who are more concerned with teaching and learning and who work with teachers in more collegial ways; see, for example, Porter, 1995, and Lytle, 1996. However, we know of no efforts to develop postsecondary programs along these lines.

24. The resources for administration in community colleges are also relatively low: Administrative spending per full-time equivalent student in 1994–95 was $1,336 in community colleges, compared to $2,436 in public four-year colleges, $2,516 in public universities, and $4,896 in private universities. NCES, 1997, Tables 341–44.

25. Similarly, Brewer (1995) found that administrators in the Wisconsin technical college system cite "faculty resistance to change" as a barrier, while faculty feel that administrators don't understand the time demands on them.

26. Almost uniformly but not quite, since poor instructors can isolate themselves from the rest of the institution (as we saw in Chapter 1). Thus one mediocre instructor at Metropolis Community College felt that the institution was unsupportive of teaching—contrary to all his peers. In this case a didactic and authoritarian instructor found his conception of teaching at odds with practices in an innovative institution; rather than understanding his own limitations, he blamed the institution.

27. For an example of a self-consciously feminist approach to pedagogy, see Noddings, 1992. What some individuals call a "feminist" pedagogy relies on the supposedly "female" qualities of caring and sensitivity to others, similar to the "student support" model of teaching described in Chapter 1.

28. The "ESL method" she articulated is a good example of carefully considered hybrid instruction. However, in other ESL classes around the country, instructors are not aware of any "ESL method," so this method has been locally developed.

9

FUNDING AND POLICY
The Neglect of Teaching

The issue of funding might come first rather than last. Consistently, instructors and administrators in community colleges complain about the lack of funding—for salaries, for supplies and equipment, for ancillary services like staff development and student support, for innovative practices like team teaching and learning communities. Their proposals to improve teaching are invariably followed by complaints about resources, with the implication that only money prevents community colleges from becoming "teaching institutions." Instructors and administrators alike mention funding right off the bat when discussing their top priorities:

> Enrollment issues is what it boils down to, as I see it—money issues. We've been asked to do more with less. At this college, I think as a whole we've done pretty good at that. But it's getting down to the bare bones, and getting to be more difficult to do.

> I think the lack of financial resources is something that has impacted everybody, and it's not just the instructors—I know the administration has been impacted as well. . . . It just means that people have to do more with less, and it filters down, of course, to us. . . . Money is driving the problems right now. It's the money problem, and enrollment.

Resource issues are overwhelming because of a hierarchy of need implicit in the way most educators think: Fiscal survival is necessary before any institutional improvement, including teaching, can be addressed. As one auto instructor explained the difficulty of focusing on student outcomes:

> Until we get a system that rewards placement, never mind about all these other things [like completion], then I don't think you're going to see big-time changes. . . .

321

You can't blame the college administration; you can't even blame the district administrators because their job is to get the institution to survive. That's number one, that's first of all the need to survive and then after we get survival down, then we need to worry about the specific things—are the kids becoming mechanics, and everything else. And they never get that far. It's just fighting for survival.

Everyone complains about resources, of course, but there is substantial basis for these complaints. In 1994–95, public two-year colleges spent an average of $6,346 per full-time equivalent student, compared to $12,925 per student in public four-year colleges, $18,950 in public universities, and $35,745 in private universities. Funding in community colleges is more comparable to K–12 funding—which averaged $5,988 per pupil that year—than it is to spending in other institutions of higher education.

Furthermore, the *increase* in spending per pupil has been much lower in community colleges than in the rest of higher education. Expenditure per student, adjusted for inflation, grew 8 percent between 1976–77 and 1986–87; since then it has wobbled around from year to year, increasing overall by only $140, or 2 percent. Over the same eighteen-year period spending per pupil in four-year colleges grew relatively steadily, by 21 percent in public four-year colleges, 29 percent in public universities, and 57 percent in private universities.[1] Over the past decade, then, real funding per pupil in community colleges has been essentially stagnant—though this has been a period in which more students have come to community colleges needing remedial/developmental education, guidance and counseling, and (we would argue) active and innovative teaching. Thus the *disparity* between stable funding and increased needs has become greater and greater: "The student that we're getting is less prepared, so the trend is that we're running out of resources very rapidly." The basic political decisions about these institutions have provided access to higher education for larger numbers of students, but with considerably fewer resources compared to four-year colleges.

But the issue of funding is more complex than merely an accounting of dollars—particularly when we are concerned about the quality of teaching. In K–12 education, for example, funding per pupil has expanded substantially, from $1,903 in 1960–61 to $4,116 in 1980–81 and $5,582 by 1990–91 (in 1992–93 dollars; see Hanushek, 1996). Similarly, efforts to equalize funding between rich and poor school districts, extending back to the turn of the century, have been promoted for their presumed effects in narrowing the educational gap between rich and poor students. But schools don't seem noticeably more effective than they were ten or thirty years ago, and greater equity in funding has not narrowed educational differences in any obvious way. Around these debates a research literature has developed that purports to show that "money makes no difference"—that differences among schools or among students in funding per student, in teacher-pupil ratios, in teacher experience, in space and science labs and library books don't affect outcomes such as test scores. Even after considerable wrangling over the technical details, the most positive statement is that funding might make some difference, under some conditions—but this pallid conclusion is hardly a clarion call for more funding.[2]

However, the research showing that "money doesn't make a difference" is fatally flawed, in our view, by failing to consider the process by which funding is translated into student outcomes. The "production process"—what goes on within the school including pedagogy, the central issue of this book—is left as a black box, opaque and unexamined. Once we ask how resources might be translated into student "outputs," then the conclusion that money makes no difference starts to become comprehensible. If pupil-teacher ratios are reduced but teachers continue to lecture, then there can be no improvement in what students learn; even if teachers use the smaller number of pupils to provide more one-on-one instruction, the difference is slight.[3] If some experienced teachers are burned out and continue to use the same dog-eared notes from year to year, while others improve their teaching through trial and error (as we saw in Chapter 1), then *on the average* teacher experience cannot affect learning—even if it makes a great deal of difference in *some* cases. If teachers with higher credentials or more in-service education spend their time mastering disciplinary specialties or attending worthless staff development (see Chapter 8), then credentials and staff development cannot improve learning. If computers are used in unimaginative ways (see Chapter 7), if libraries have books but instructors assign little reading (see Chapter 6), if administrators drive up costs but concern themselves with enrollments rather than teaching (see Chapter 8), then resources cannot affect educational outcomes. Only if resources are used in ways that directly benefit teaching in some way is there any hope that money can make a difference.

This means that researchers examining the effectiveness of funding, administrators considering how to use additional resources, and policy makers contemplating increases in funding need to understand how they might influence the experiences of students. Otherwise—as we argue in Section V below—it is easy to think of ways to spend more money in community colleges without changing the outcomes.[4] As a state community college director stated, clarifying what he would do with three wishes,

> I would *never* say money because money does not get you anywhere if you don't have a dream in place of how it is going to accomplish something.

In this chapter, we examine the "new school finance" of community colleges— the ways in which resources have influenced teaching practices—in contrast to the "old" educational finance, where the effect of money was taken for granted. In Section I we clarify the ways that constrained funding affects teaching practices, drawing together many strands of analysis from throughout the book. In Section II we focus on the use of part-time instructors, which is one of the dominant ways colleges economize. In Section III we examine the common reliance on external funding for innovation. Then we examine the ineffectiveness of state and federal policies in supporting teaching. The final section examines how resources might profitably be used in the event that they increase.

I. THE EFFECTS OF FUNDING ON TEACHING

The *level* of funding is one concern of instructors and administrators, because it results in fewer instructional resources per student in community colleges. In 1994–95 such funding averaged $3,111 in two-year colleges, compared to $5,402 in public four-year colleges, $6,710 in public universities, and a whopping $13,701 in private universities. Right off the bat, many conditions affecting teaching in community colleges are caused by the relatively low level of funding. Instructors typically teach five courses per semester in most institutions, rather than three or four, as in most state colleges, or two courses, as in research universities; the resources available for staff development are relatively low; and most colleges have a hard time finding funds for teacher centers, mini-grants, learning communities, and the other innovations we examined in Chapter 8. Innovations requiring funds are far below the priorities of providing the basic facilities and instructors necessary to keep the doors open.

In addition, the *method* of funding is important, because it determines the incentives that institutions face. Most states fund their community colleges on the basis of enrollments, usually measured by full-time equivalent students (FTEs); even those states that use some form of negotiated funding use enrollments to determine changes in funding.[5] Only eight states use differential funding, in which certain expensive subjects (health occupations or technical specialties such as electronics) receive additional resources. Capital funding is determined by a combination of formula and project funding; in turn, departments generally have to apply to their colleges for capital funding. Finally, some states earmark resources for specific purposes. For example, California has separate funding for staff development ("flex days") and for reducing the numbers of part-time faculty; other states fund computers, basic skills programs, libraries, and other special programs (Honeyman, Williamson, and Wattenbarger, 1991, Tables 11 and 12). These practices vary enormously from state to state, making generalization difficult.

The effects of enrollment-driven funding are pervasive. One effect is that programs with higher costs—especially occupational programs with high expenses for materials and equipment, as we clarified in Chapter 3—are more difficult to sup-

Pressures on Instructors

Because enrollments count so heavily, instructors come under subtle pressure to keep their enrollments up—even at the expense of standards. Most colleges calculate enrollments per class—what an administrator quoted in the previous chapter called "productivity goals"—and so instructors and departments are under constant scrutiny to keep their "productivity" up. When students shop around for easier instructors, the combination of institutional incentives and student searches generates pressure on instructors with higher standards. In addition, some colleges calculate "drop rates," or rates at which students drop courses after initial enrollment. Instructors with high drop rates may decide that they have been demanding too much, as one instructor noted:

> When you see that great a disparity [between initial and final enrollment], then I have to take a look at myself and say, whoa, you know, what's going on here? . . . I really have to take a real strong look at how much work I give them.

The result, over time, is to cause instructors to rethink their demands, the numbers of quizzes they give or papers they assign—a subtle but constant pressure against maintaining whatever standards they start with.

Effects on Teaching Support and Innovation

Under enrollment-based funding, any activity that does *not* generate additional enrollments is likely to be cut when resources are tight. Such vulnerable activities includes many that support teaching and learning, including staff development, release time to update courses or plan new programs, the time necessary for mentoring new instructors or peer observation, teacher centers, and the additional resources necessary for joint teaching and learning communities. Relentlessly, pedagogical innovations have to overcome the presumptions of funding mechanisms geared to enrollments.

In a different kind of educational institution, one might think first about the instructional and material resources necessary to run effective programs, and then develop funding mechanisms to support such programs. One automotive instructor contrasted a manufacturer's training center—ten students per instructor, a large variety of cars to work on, and instructor time for updating courses—with the program he could run in a community college:

> As long as the community college is set up—it's based on ADA, you know, you need twenty students in a class, they're looking at retention. . . . I mean, there's no release time for anybody to do anything except teach. If you said, "I would like to get a semester off to develop a new course," they would say ha, ha, ha; they'd just laugh at you, it

would just be a big joke. So as long as the basics are in there, the funding mechanisms, the way that the district is financed, the way the teachers are paid . . . the momentum is just to kind of keep going in terms of the way you're [already] doing.

Staff development is similarly vulnerable to reductions in funding because it does not generate any revenues. As one instructor said,

When funding becomes tighter, when there are more strictures, when there are more demands on fewer dollars, faculty development is gone—first thing out the door. You can justify anything that has return dollars in the other column. [But] faculty development is like planting seeds, and you do not necessarily have a measurable, observable harvest.

Some institutions—colleges such as Choctaw, Metropolis, and Westville, described in Chapter 8—find the funds for teaching-centered activities. Some of their teaching-oriented policies—the priorities of administrators, hiring and promotion policies, the emphasis on continuous staff development—cost almost nothing, though others require additional resources, including teacher centers, mentoring of new instructors, mini-grants for instructional innovations, and support for learning communities. These institutions don't have more resources than the average community college in their states, nor do they have disproportionate amounts of external funding. Instead, they establish institutional priorities enhancing teaching, rather than allowing external funding formulas to dictate their allocation of resources. Once internal funding decisions are uncoupled from external funding formulas, and the quality of teaching is the top priority instead of expanded enrollments, then colleges can find the resources to support improved teaching.

Of course, funding need not be based simply on enrollments. When we turn to recommendations in Section IV, we find alternatives to the current enrollment-based funding—for example, formulas that reward initial enrollments, several points of progress through programs, and final completion or success measured in various ways—that would eliminate the biases inherent in enrollment-based funding. If the quality of teaching becomes a priority, for local colleges and state policy alike, then some basic funding changes are both necessary and feasible.

II. THE RELIANCE ON EXTERNAL FUNDING FOR INNOVATION

When funding is limited, it is difficult to pay for innovation with "hard" funds— the core funding provided to community colleges though tax revenues and tuition. Therefore many teaching innovations are funded by "soft" money, by special grants from outside the institutions. When instructors and administrators speak about innovation, they invariably mention the need for new sources of funds—for grants of some kind.

Three kinds of external grants are particularly important in community colleges. The first are grants from employers. These include gifts of equipment and materials to help occupational programs keep up to date, as we saw in Chapter 3, and internships and co-op positions, to provide work-based education for occupational students. The second are federal grants for occupational education. These are supposed to support efforts on behalf of various special-needs students and various kinds of program improvement; many efforts to integrate academic and occupational education reviewed in Chapter 7 have been funded with federal revenues. Third, the Fund for the Improvement of Postsecondary Education (FIPSE) supports a variety of teaching innovations in community colleges, ranging from learning communities to writing centers. While the scale of these reforms is usually limited to a specific course or center, FIPSE funds are sometimes used for institution-wide reforms. For example, North County Community College (profiled in Section V of Chapter 5) applied for a FIPSE grant for institution-wide improvement in teaching, covering Writing Across the Curriculum, an Applied Skills Center to include more reading and writing in occupational areas, and an initiative to knit together the efforts of the English, developmental studies, and ESL divisions. There are other sources of external funding, including special funds from states and other federal programs (for example, math and science initiatives from the National Science Foundation), but these three appear to be the major sources of funding for innovation.

It's important to appreciate external grants: the innovations we have described throughout this volume depend heavily on them. But each funding source has its costs. In the case of contributions from employers, occupational instructors have to work hard, essentially on their own, to generate such contributions, and their efforts are unrecognized and uncompensated by community colleges. Some occupational instructors are active in searching for funds and in maintaining contacts, but others are not. Therefore ties with employers are idiosyncratic—excellent in a few departments, mediocre to nonexistent in others (see also Grubb, 1996b, Ch. 3). In establishing links with employers, colleges and instructors must work against the particular culture of American firms, which have been more reluctant to support training than their competitors in other countries (especially Germany and Japan). But correcting a deeply rooted antitraining culture requires a widespread and *institutional* effort, not the individual efforts of particularly active occupational instructors. Only where such ties with employers are regularized can students and instructors count on the participation of employers—as in the co-op programs in Cincinnati and in LaGuardia Community College (Villeneuve and Grubb, 1996; Grubb and Badway, 1998) or the efforts of John Deere dealers throughout the Midwest. Until community colleges as institutions undertake such efforts—or the federal government does so on their behalf, through legislation such as the School-to-Work Opportunities Act of 1994—we cannot expect employers to provide much sustained support for innovation.[7]

Federal efforts, through funds for vocational education and through FIPSE, are similarly checkered in their effects. On the one hand, many individual initiatives of great promise have been supported by these funds. On the other hand, these efforts tend not to be systematic. A few colleges and a few states have used federal vocational funds for improvements, such as tech prep programs and efforts to integrate academic and occupational education. But these initiatives have generated much more change at the high-school level than in community colleges.[8] For the most part, colleges continue to use such funds for relatively routine purchases of equipment, upgrading of occupational courses, and remedial education. This is testimony that funding for keeping occupational courses up-to-date is in short supply, but it is hardly indicative of pedagogical innovation. And as valuable as FIPSE funds have been, they have not resulted in widespread changes even within the institutions they have funded. In the institutions we observed, innovative FIPSE projects were located adjacent to the most pedestrian teaching, without any spillover from one to the other. There is even less communication among community colleges. While FIPSE has published a series of booklets entitled *Lessons Learned from FIPSE Projects* (e.g., Marcus, Cobb, and Shoenberg, 1993 and 1996), there haven't been many efforts at replication from federal or state initiatives.[9] There's no widespread learning from these efforts.

A serious problem with external grants is that their results tend not to be institutionalized or adopted as routine practice, using the "hard" funding of colleges. At the outset they *cannot* be institutionalized because by definition such funding may disappear at the next funding cycle; therefore external grants tend to be spent in ways that have only temporary effects. Purchasing materials (including computers) is a good example: Such materials do not create fiscal and moral obligations to continue funding from "hard" revenues. If new personnel are hired, they are always temporary or part-time, so they can be let go when special funding ceases; because they are temporary, they are low-status and peripheral to the college. In addition, outside grants are often obtained by individuals within the college, like unusually innovative instructors. Both administrators and other faculty view these as the property of the applicant—"Joan's FIPSE grant" or "Bill's funding from employers." Joan and Bill probably see it that way, too—after all, they have put in the extra hours to get funding—but it means that projects with external funding are viewed as individual efforts, not experiments that might spawn institution-wide reform.

The pressure to get external resources for innovations is understandable in a period when public funding appears to be steadily dwindling. But external funding has never been a good way to reform institutions—particularly if we want good teaching to be viewed as an institutional commitment rather than as an individual and idiosyncratic effort. Establishing community colleges as teaching institutions will require funding for teaching that is more stable, more universally "owned" by administrators and instructors, and more central to the core purposes of colleges than external funding can ever be.

III. THE SHIFT TO PART-TIME INSTRUCTORS

An obvious result of fiscal pressures on community colleges is the use of part-time instructors. The problem of part-timers is an excellent example of how funding subtly affects many aspects of an educational institution, including the basic roles of all instructors.

The use of part-time instructors is a good idea that has gone wrong because of fiscal motives. Originally, such teachers were hired in order to bring certain kinds of expertise into the community college—occupational instructors in certain specialties, for example, or individuals with experience in industry or government, or other individuals who want to "give back" to the community of learners but don't want to be full-time teachers. Virtually everyone agrees that part-time faculty enrich the community college. As one instructor described the advantages:

> I think the key there is that they are by far the best resources for introducing new technology, new concepts, and practice into the educational process—because they bring with it not the academics of it, but the practical exposure and experiences that are currently out there in industry. Two hours ago I was working on the cutting edge of new technology, stuff that's not even sold to the public yet.... I could be introducing that technology right here so that the students could be cutting into a new direction.

But more recently fiscal pressures have caused colleges to teach even their core subjects through part-time instructors. The simple economics are relentless. In one community college where we were able to get precise figures, a new full-time instructor earns $44,850 per year (including benefits) for teaching ten classes, for a cost of $4,485 per class. Part-time instructors are paid $35.88 per contact hour without benefits, or $1,829.88 for a three-hour course over a seventeen-week semester, or only 40 percent as much.[10] Since instructional costs average 49 percent of community college budgets, no efficiency-minded administrator can afford to take a principled position against using part-timers. In addition, part-timers can be hired and fired at will. Where programs must expand or contract—as with occupational programs over the business cycle, for example, or remedial or ESL classes with unpredictable demographic changes—the use of part-time faculty helps colleges be flexible and responsive. Part-timers also lack offices, phones, secretarial support, and other ancillary services that might enhance their participation in the college but that also impose real costs. The fiscal logic of part-time employment has taken over virtually all colleges. Currently, a slight majority of instructors (52 percent) are part-time, though—since their teaching load is smaller—they teach only 37 percent of courses.[11]

The most immediate effect of using so many part-time teachers is to undermine their own careers. These part-timers do not fit the original mold of individuals with full-time careers who are teaching on the side. Instead, many of them must patch together several part-time teaching positions to earn a living, becoming "freeway flyers" commuting among institutions:

> We all have to work somewhere else. It means having to move around during the day and keep track of different institutional things, and it's tiring and it's frustrating because you don't get benefits here. We don't have job security. I choose to put in a lot of overtime, [but] some people are working more than I . . . some people are driving around a lot, and that takes up a lot of time.

Such multiple commitments constrain their time and limit the energy they have for teaching.

Another effect is that part-time instructors are paid for their teaching, but not for office hours, staff development, preparation time, and coordination with other faculty. Part-timers come in, teach their classes, and leave, like workers on piece rates. They could be paid for these "extra" duties, but of course this makes no sense if they are hired in order to economize. The result is that they participate very little in college activities. As one part-time instructor expressed her dilemma:

> Yeah, well, there [are] lots of committees and, you know, like critical thinking and things like that. But, you know . . . I'm a part-time instructor, and so I'm also teaching in other places, and so I don't have the time to spend doing a lot of the in-services and things that I wish we had. . . . I mean, there are always things that are going on that are very helpful, I think. But, personally, as an instructor, because I'm part-time and because I have to teach in lots of different places to supplement my income, usually I don't have the time to do it. Which is sort of the problem, I guess.

In addition to their lack of participation in staff development, part-timers are also absent from most committees within community colleges, so their interests are unrepresented. And oddly enough—since part-time instructors are often hired specifically for their experience in business and industry—part-time instructors are generally less well connected to the local labor market than are full-time instructors (Brewer and Gray, 1997), partly because of time constraints.

Part-time faculty are also underrepresented in teaching that requires greater collaboration with other faculty—particularly learning communities and related efforts at integrating academic and occupational education, which we examined in Chapter 7. We stress that there are part-time faculty in learning communities, and some of the most dedicated faculty we saw were part-time instructors who could afford to devote more time to teaching. But it is much more difficult for them to find the time for planning with their full-time colleagues. One full-time member of a learning community described her problems in coordinating with a part-time instructor:

> It would be good if we do as much linkage as possible, because that is the goal—it's like a coordinated studies [course], you know? . . . But no, with the computer teacher, I did not and could not, for several reasons: Number one, the computer teacher is a part-timer, and this computer teacher, in particular, who has got the class for two quarters, has about four other part-time jobs, and so he gave me his home number and I called him once and he refused to answer my call. . . . So I just didn't want to call him anymore. You know, I don't feel good calling people in their homes. You know, they have a life. They should have a life.

In another case, full-time biology and developmental teachers were matched with a part-time math instructor who was new to teaching. Their inability to find enough common planning time meant that the math component was inconsistent with the other two subjects: The math teacher was more didactic, more conventional in her ordering of mathematical topics, and less connected to the other two courses. Administrators also find starting new programs with part-timers more difficult; as one commented about a new environmental technology program,

> Our problem with that has been we're running with part-timers who are marginally committed, or you have peculiar personalities, and it's hard to run the program in a coherent fashion.

Part-time status doesn't prevent participation in such innovative teaching arrangements, then, but it impedes the coordination that is at the heart of the most successful efforts.

A less obvious effect of having so many part-time instructors is that it undermines collegiality. In many departments, a large number of part-time instructors slip in and out of their classrooms without much interaction with the rest of the institution. They are hired casually, and rarely are they reviewed by other faculty. They don't have offices and office hours, or telephones at the college, so they are not easy to contact. They are not around for committee meetings and other informal contacts. In sum, they are not part of the community of the college; they are even more isolated from other instructors than their full-time peers. And this kind of isolation influences not only their feelings toward the institution, but also the perspectives of full-time instructors.

This statement of the full-time instructor on p. 284, complaining about a part-timer teaching her course, can be read as an expression of turfism and resentment, but we interpret it more as a complaint about the destruction of collegial culture and mutual responsibility. Part-time faculty make such mutual responsibility impossible. The vice president of one faculty union described the problem this way:

> No one looks at the student evaluations to see what the student input is, no one evaluates these off-campus people, and I understand it's a logistical nightmare, but our reputation as a college is being built or destroyed by those folks, probably to a greater extent.

Finally, the use of so many part-time faculty members structures the positions not only of part-time faculty, but also of full-time faculty. Full-time faculty bear the entire responsibility for institutional maintenance and improvement: They sit on the hiring committees, the curriculum committees, the faculty senates, the planning committees. In many departments, full-time faculty develop the core courses that part-time faculty teach; they establish the instructional framework, and then hire the part-timers who carry it out. The basic structure of faculty roles—the sense of being fragmented by too many responsibilities, the feeling of being broken into "different segments of being this, this, and this" (page 282)—is forced upon full-time faculty members by the use of so many part-timers. One instructor commented that her institution had finally decided to hire more full-time instructors because "there's just too much work for all the full-timers to do." Someone needs to carry out the essential tasks of institutional maintenance, but some community colleges have stripped down the full-time faculty to the point where these tasks cannot be adequately performed.

The final question is whether the quality of teaching among part-time faculty is different from than that of full-time faculty. Certainly the structural and institutional conditions for part-time teachers are dreadful. But for all these differences, we found no evidence that part-time instructors are, in any sense, worse teachers than full-timers.[12] Several of the most dynamic instructors we observed were part-timers, as were some of the most successful participants in developmental education, learning communities, and other innovative teaching. The different approaches to teaching that we identified in Chapter 1 can be found among both full-time and part-time instructors. None of the truly terrible instructors—those who managed to be abusive to students and to eliminate any content from their classes—were part-timers; they tended instead to be experienced full-time teachers who had gotten burned out. Based on our evidence, then, part-time instructors can be found in almost all ranges of teaching quality and approach.

Why is the teaching among part-time instructors comparable to that of full-time instructors when the conditions they face are so much worse? The answer, we think, is that the institutional conditions supporting good teaching are missing in most colleges, for part-time and full-time instructors alike. Neither personnel policies nor pre-service and in-service education provides much support for good teaching, even for full-time instructors. Collegiality is lacking for full-time instructors as well as part-timers; the culture established by the many administrators who are ignorant about teaching applies equally to all. Under these conditions, good teaching is dependent on the vagaries of individuals and their own development. Since good teaching is essentially random, it is as prevalent among part-time instructors as among full-time instructors.

Furthermore, colleges that take teaching seriously make special provisions for part-time instructors. For example, the developmental studies division at North County created its manual of practice partly to provide direction for part-time faculty; the division provides additional guidance, observation, and support for them. Choctaw and Westville both have teacher centers providing an array of services to part-time faculty as well as full-timers. Westville, like the developmental studies department at North County, has developed "content guides" to help part-time instructors get started. At Metropolis, part-time instructors tend to be well represented in faculty development and in learning communities. The institutions that have made teaching an institutional priority have remembered the volume of teaching done by part-timers—after all, "our reputation as a college is being built or destroyed by those folks"—and have done whatever they can to support part-time instructors. In a different way, their practices minimize the differences in teaching between full-time and part-time instructors.

But this conclusion points to a real danger. *If* community colleges all took teaching seriously, the way a few of them do—if they devoted all their institutional policies to the improvement of instruction—then any instructors who remained isolated from these institutional efforts (including part-timers and recalcitrant full-timers) would be more conventional, less innovative instructors. Community colleges that take seriously their roles as teaching institutions need *both* to change their policies toward teaching and learning *and* to ensure that part-time instructors can participate fully. Otherwise, a gap in the quality of teaching would surely develop.

The use of so many part-time instructors is similar to the practice of many businesses, which have relatively few permanent employees supervising a large staff of temporary employees. Employers claim that competition has driven them to these practices, just as administrators feel that fiscal constraints have forced them to use part-timers. Applying this particular model to instructional institutions suggests that teachers are interchangeable parts in a large "firm" producing courses, or that English 10 and Business 101 can be taught by anyone with the appropriate credentials. The model assumes that educational programs can be subdivided in this way, that continuity among classes and collaboration among faculty are unimportant. These are old assumptions, underlying the standardization of both secondary and postsecondary courses.

The alternative is represented by departments that devise coherent programs, with linked courses and interdisciplinary teaching, in which instructors form collaboratives in order to improve their teaching. Sustaining this approach—an educational *community* in the truest sense—is much more difficult when part-time instructors are widely used for fiscal reasons. We conclude, then, that valuing the quality of instruction requires fewer part-time faculty—and, therefore, additional funding for community colleges, put to specific use.

IV. STATE AND FEDERAL POLICY: WHAT ROLES TO PLAY?

A federal system poses the question of what roles different levels of government should play. Formal schooling in this country developed first as a distinctly local endeavor, and "local control" has been a mantra for those resisting both state and federal control. In postsecondary education, the early domination of private colleges, and the culture of institutional autonomy and academic freedom that developed, have been powerful arguments against government control, even when state and federal governments provide extensive funding. Community colleges lie at the intersection of both arguments: As community-serving institutions, they can claim the need for local control, and as institutions of higher education, they aspire to the autonomy and freedom of research universities.

In practice, both state and federal influences over community colleges have remained relatively weak—particularly on issues related to teaching. Formally, education is the responsibility of states. States provide the largest amount of funding for community colleges—about 43 percent of overall revenues in 1994–95, compared to 31 percent from local sources, 21 percent from tuition and fees, and 5 percent from federal sources—and they dictate the mix of purposes and institutional types.[13] But aside from funding, most states tend to neglect community colleges. They confine their regulatory efforts to course and program approval, in an effort to prevent duplication; even these efforts are likely to be little more than rubber stamps for what local institutions want to do.[14] There is almost no control of curriculum (much less than for the K–12 system, for example), significantly less regulation of instructors through teacher licensing and credentialing, and few analogues to the kinds of exit exams and competency exams that proliferated in K–12 education during the 1980s. Even in the basic area of statistics, most states gather information only on enrollment. Only five collect information about any measures of academic achievement; only fourteen have any information about job skills, largely by surveying employers; and only twenty follow completers to ascertain their employment status (McDonnell and Zellman, 1993, Table 3.6). By and large, states lack even basic information to know whether local colleges are succeeding in any way.

In addition, there has been relatively little effort to define and promote exemplary practice, including good teaching practice. In K–12 education, many states have worked hard to devise school reforms of great variety and complexity. But at the postsecondary level, this kind of reform is missing. The institutional measures described in Chapter 8 that could promote improved teaching—requirements for instructor preparation like Iowa's; a network of teacher centers; high-quality and continuous staff development efforts, including mentoring for new teachers—are either rare or nonexistent. Enrollment-based funding creates incentives to eliminate such "frills" and to reduce the number of full-time instructors. Most state policies tend to *undermine* efforts to improve the quality of teaching.

The effects of federal policy on teaching are similarly limited. To be sure, the federal government has provided funding for the improvement of postsecondary occupational programs through the Carl Perkins Act; the 1990 amendments to the act stressed efforts to integrate academic and occupational education, as well as tech prep programs to link community colleges with high schools. But in these efforts, as in most federal programs, community colleges have been stepchildren. The Perkins Act and its predecessors have focused on secondary rather than postsecondary programs, and its provisions have always applied awkwardly to postsecondary institutions. Federal funding is tiny, amounting to roughly 5 percent of total funding in two-year institutions and perhaps 2 to 4 percent of all revenues for postsecondary occupational education (Grubb and Stern, 1989). As we noted in Section II, these funds typically have been used for relatively routine expenditures—equipment and remediation—that arguably should be supported from state and local revenues, and that are only marginally related to the improvement of teaching. In addition, the well-regarded Fund for the Improvement of Post-secondary Education (FIPSE) and other programs such as those offered by the National Science Foundation do support some curriculum development in post-secondary education, but such funding is unplanned and uncoordinated. A few institutions here and there benefit from improved courses, but the amounts to two-year institutions are tiny, the innovations are neither evaluated nor well pub-licized, and the effects on community colleges as a whole are small.

Federal grants and loans provide resources for students to enroll, but they are ineffective mechanisms of improving the quality of educational institutions.[15] Most recently, the Clinton administration pushed through Congress a package of tax credits worth an additional $6 billion per year, but this substantial increase in federal resources will not support improvement in any way, and relatively little of it is likely to come to community colleges. Like state policy, federal policy provides relatively little support to enhance the quality of teaching and learning, despite the large sums spent on postsecondary education.

As many commentators have noted, federal and state policy are driven more by concern with *access* to postsecondary education than by *completion* or *effective-ness*. A greater concern with completion and other measures of success would require both federal and state policy to place greater emphasis on aspects of teach-ing that might promote greater rates of completion. It's not hard to think of state and federal policies that could enhance the quality of teaching:

• States could impose certification requirements for community college instructors, as Iowa now does. These programs could include the theory and prac-tice of alternative pedagogies; the special problems of teaching underprepared students; the particular teaching problems arising in specific disciplines, whether academic or occupational; the collaborative teaching practices of learning com-munities and integrated academic and vocational programs; and the background and current role of community colleges. Ideally such preparation would extend into the first few years of instruction, to give new teachers a forum to resolve the early problems they experience.

• Similarly, states could require the certification of administrators, particularly since there is widespread dissatisfaction with their inattention to instructional issues. Greater knowledge about the varieties of teaching and greater familiarity with the institutional mechanisms of enhancing teaching could then be embedded in programs to prepare *educational* leaders for community colleges, rather than managers and administrators.

• States—and the federal government, through matching funds—could pro-vide funding for teacher centers (like those at Choctaw and Westville) and for mentoring programs for new teachers. Because states control the funding that supports staff development, they could replace one-shot workshops given by outsiders with more continuous and collegial forms of staff development.

• States could provide funding for local programs of mini-grants, to help teachers develop new courses and improve the quality of their teaching. One advantage is that states could collect information about promising practices from colleges, carry out more rigorous evaluation of their effectiveness, and provide assistance in disseminating promising practices.

• States could institute systems of inspection for community colleges. As practiced in colleges of further education in Great Britain, inspectors from outside a college, joined by individuals from within the institution, observe classes within specific colleges and investigate the institutional support for instruction. Inspection has become a way of opening up classrooms, of making the quality of teaching the subject of public discussion, and of providing feedback to individual instructors in collegial and supportive ways. Inspection also emphasizes the institutional responsibility for classroom practices, rather than treating the quality of teaching as individual and idiosyncratic. To be sure, inspection is a complex process, and it can easily become punitive and blaming (as in elementary-secondary education in England), but the details of inspection can create procedures that are supportive rather than degrading (Grubb, 1998b). As a mechanism of creating a larger community around teaching, inspection with some combination of inside and outside personnel provides one of the best ways of improving the quality of teaching.

• States now fund an enormous amount of remedial education, not only though community colleges but also through adult education, job training programs, and miscellaneous other settings. But the quality of teaching in such programs is almost never discussed. With the exception of some innovative community colleges and some idiosyncratic adult education efforts, teaching usually relies on the worst forms of skills and drills (Grubb and Kalman, 1994). Most programs are completely ineffective in moving their students to levels of competence that permit entry into middle-skilled jobs or further education. States—with the assistance of the federal government, which has initiated many of these programs—could implement mechanisms to improve the quality of teaching in the wide range of remedial programs, at both community colleges and elsewhere.

• The federal government could continue its support for specific innovations, such as the integration of academic and occupational education, tech prep, the integration of work-based learning into both occupational and academic programs, and improvements in math and science education. However, these initiatives should be written to apply to the special conditions in community colleges, rather than being afterthoughts of programs aimed at other levels of education.

Both state and federal governments should do more to synthesize the results of such innovations and to promote them in other states and localities.

• The federal government could help the states improve the quality of education by avoiding middle-class tax expenditures and instead supporting instruction-related practices such as teacher centers, mentoring and induction programs, mini-grants, inspection systems, and the improvement of remedial education. In partnerships with states, the federal government could also serve as an information broker, evaluating the most promising practices more carefully and helping to promote them among the states. This would also help create a national discussion about community college teaching where one does not exist.

• Both state and federal governments could examine their funding mechanisms carefully, to identify the incentives to undercut good teaching practices. States should therefore consider alternative forms of performance-based funding, and mechanisms that eliminate the bias against certain programs (like occupational education). The increasing reliance on part-time instructors hampers other efforts to improve teaching, and the fiscal incentives to use ever-greater numbers of part-time instructors need to be reversed. Until these incentives are reformed, community colleges will confront pressures against improved teaching that they cannot overcome by themselves.

Finally, we stress the relatedness of these reforms. State efforts to reduce part-time instructors will not improve teaching unless there are also other mechanisms of improvement—better preparation in teaching methods, teacher centers, induction and mentoring systems—for both part-time and full-time instructors. Greater federal or state funding for staff development, or for inspection mechanisms linked to improving teaching, will not work as long as administrators remain indifferent to teaching. Greater federal funding for innovations will not make much difference if state administrators are preoccupied only with the flows of money, or if local colleges do not understand the pedagogical purposes underlying innovations. Above all, creating larger communities concerned with the quality of teaching and learning—in place of the isolated groups that now exist in learning communities, in a few departments with coherent philosophies and practices, and in the few community colleges that are truly teaching institutions—will require pervasive and systematic reforms.

V. THE POTENTIAL EFFECTS OF FUNDING ON TEACHING

We have implicitly argued that additional funding may be necessary but not sufficient to improve the quality of teaching. Some institutional policies to enhance teaching are relatively costless—for example, hiring and promotion policies that take teaching seriously, and administrators who are supportive of teaching rather than ignorant or indifferent. Other policies are more expensive, but their effectiveness depends on how they are used. For example, staff development funds can be used for one-shot workshops with outside speakers, or they can be used to create communities of faculty that are more likely to sustain innovations. Mini-grants can be used to fund teachers' sabbaticals and trips to conferences, with no institutional benefits, or they can be used to support innovative teaching that can then spread throughout the institution.

Similarly, the state and federal policies discussed in the preceding section require additional funds, but this money needs to be spent in particular ways. A great deal of money is poorly spent, and at the same time many valuable improvements are poorly funded. Resources may be necessary for improvement, but they are rarely sufficient.

Another way to see this point is to perform a mental experiment, based on two scenarios. The first asks what would be likely to happen if community colleges received increases in real funding per pupil. We suspect that additional resources would be sprinkled over a number of different purposes.[16] Instructors would get some salary increases; a few more full-time instructors would be hired to replace some part-timers. A college might agree to teach a few more sections of low-enrollment courses—for example, sophomore courses necessary for transfer, some specialized occupational courses—and might provide some additional funds for occupational equipment, computers, and other capital outlays. Some funding would be made available for staff development, but its form would depend on the staff development already in place. Metropolis and Choctaw Community Colleges would probably funnel such monies through their teacher centers, but most colleges would slightly expand their smorgasbord of one-shot workshops, conference travel, and sabbaticals. Centers for remediation, tutoring, and minority students might get a little more money, as would student services such as guidance and counseling. Each institution probably has a promissory note that would fall due—attention to the library or a mentoring center, an initiative to increase minority faculty, or reconstruction of a dilapidated building. No doubt some money would be squirreled away for a pet project of the president—perhaps a satellite campus, an economic development program, or a high-profile computer initiative. Each of these changes is worthy in its own way, but their direct effects on teaching would be minimal.

The second scenario assumes that public funding will continue to be squeezed, following the argument of the instructor who commented that "we're running out of resources very rapidly." Pressures will grow for community colleges to take more students without increasing their funding proportionately, thereby reducing funding per student. Expanded enrollments will probably include more students with inadequate high-school preparation, more immigrant students, more welfare recipients being pressured to get off public assistance, perhaps more students redirected from expensive four-year colleges.

In this case, we suspect that fiscal pressures would be spread around. Class sizes would rise somewhat, leading to more lecturing, fewer writing assignments, more Scantron-graded multiple-choice exams, and fewer complex projects. The use of part-time instructors with weak institutional allegiances would also increase. Low-enrollment classes would be eliminated, and pressures would continue to build against programs with costs in excess of "benefits" (state and local aid plus tuition), such as health occupations and technical programs. Instructional materials would dwindle, as would funding for capital outlays including up-to-date occupational equipment. Remedial education would increasingly take the form of computer- or workbook-based learning labs, with little instructor time, rather than the more intensive efforts of learning communities or the carefully developed practices at North County Community College. Student support services—tutoring, guidance and counseling, and special minority programs—would be squeezed, as would support for faculty development and workshops. Colleges might experiment more intensely with distance learning, as a cheap way to generate greater enrollments, and with video-based "teaching" methods. None of these would *necessarily* affect the quality of teaching. Part-time instructors are not on the whole any worse than their full-time counterparts; most staff development is not particularly effective anyway; many instructors lecture as it is, and another five students wouldn't make that much difference. But each of these changes makes teaching more burdensome, makes improvement more difficult, and forces administrators to act more like budgeteers scrambling for money rather than educational leaders promoting a vision of the "teaching college."

From these two scenarios, we conclude again that money doesn't *necessarily* make a difference to student outcomes. Increases in funding can be spent without substantially improving the quality of teaching, and decreases in funding may take forms that don't substantially affect teaching. But improvement does generally require additional resources, carefully spent, and reduced funding makes the task of improving teaching ever more difficult.

The effects of decreased funding we have just outlined would probably hurt most the students who are now most attracted to the community college—the nontraditional students, the ones who have not done especially well in high school, the students returning to college after years of unsatisfactory employment, new immigrants in need of language instruction. These are students who by their own admission prefer the smaller scale of community colleges, the smaller classes, the learning communities where they are available, the sense that faculty and staff are looking after them. Increases in class sizes and other changes that make a community college a more impersonal place will affect them especially.

Efficiency has long been one of the imperatives of public education (Callahan, 1967), and community colleges are particularly susceptible to budget cuts because of their promise of low-cost access to postsecondary education. But efficiency in the form of cost cutting tends to turn educational institutions into screening mechanisms. Those students who are already competent and autonomous learners can make progress on their own. The ones who need better teaching and substantial support are more likely to drop out, and when they do, it *appears* that they leave because they fail to learn enough, or maintain their grades, or accumulate enough credits, and so students themselves are blamed for their failures. But the real fault lies in the way we have structured most educational institutions, as places where only certain kinds of students can learn well. Community colleges, with their greater commitment to nontraditional students and their promises to be "teaching colleges," have the best chances to escape this conventional approach to education. To do so requires appropriate levels of resources. But it also requires that resources be carefully spent to improve teaching and related services in the interests of nontraditional students. Money itself is never enough.

NOTES

1. Expenditure figures come from NCES (1997), Tables 336, 341–44.

2. For reviews of the literature on the relation between outputs (test scores) and various school resources, see Hanushek, 1986 and 1989. The rejoinder from Hedges, Laine, and Greenwald (1994) disputes the technical details of the analysis that Hanushek performed, but it does not challenge Hanushek's conclusion on substantive grounds. See also Hanushek's (1994) response, and Hanushek et al., 1994, for the conclusion that money might make some difference.

3. If class size is reduced from thirty to twenty, and instructors use half their time for whole-class instruction and half for one-on-one teaching, then this results in an increase in "personal attention" of 50 percent—but in a typical course of fifteen weeks, three hours per week, this amounts to an increase in "personal attention" from .75 hours to 1.125 hours—a trivial 22.5 additional minutes of teacher time per student.

4. In K–12 education, this point has been made in a very different literature, on "school effectiveness." This research has contrasted schools that, considering the family backgrounds of their students, are doing better than expected with those doing worse than expected. The conclusions point to differences that, by and large, do not require additional funding: for example, effective schools are reorganized around learning standards subject to greater accountability, and led by principals with clear visions. What seems to make a difference, therefore, are not resources per se, but resources used to improve the culture of an educational institution and to focus on instruction.

5. On funding formulas for community colleges, see McDonnell and Zellman, 1993, Ch. 3 and Table 3.5. Only eight states use FTE, but another fourteen use enrollment in cost-plus funding; still others incorporate it into negotiated funding.

6. This statement reflects a particular model of educational institutions that we should make explicit. If a college attracts a variety of students, as community colleges do, then the marginal cost of completion will be lowest for the best-prepared students and those with middle-class backgrounds. The marginal cost per completion will increase as completion rates increase, since the institution will be trying to get students with greater academic, financial, and motivational needs to complete, requiring more resources in the form of remedial/developmental education, financial aid, counseling and guidance, and other support services. If the resources of educational institutions are kept low, they act as a kind of filter, allowing only the best-prepared students to complete—and it shouldn't be surprising that those who complete are the students with the best academic preparation and middle-class backgrounds.

7. The School-to-Work Opportunities Act of 1994 is potentially a vehicle for promoting employer cooperation with high schools and community colleges, since it encourages work-based learning integrated with school-based learning. However, we despair that this act will ever accomplish much: funding has been paltry, national leadership and vision have been absent, most state plans have been marred by interest group squabbling, the program emphasizes high-school rather than community college efforts, and the initial implementation has been disappointing (Hershey et al., 1998). This legislation will end in 1999, and is unlikely to be reauthorized.

8. The efforts to develop tech prep programs have so far resulted in more changes at the high-school level, though it is possible that colleges will start making more changes; see Grubb, Badway, Bell, and Kraskouskas, 1996. Similarly, the changes made in response to requirements about integrating academic and occupational education have been more substantial at the high school level; see Grubb and Stasz, 1993, and Boesel, 1995. In part this has happened because federal legislation has always been written with secondary schools in mind. For an extended argument that Congress should consider separate legislation for community colleges, see Grubb and Stern, 1989; NCRVE, 1995; and Boesel and McFarland, 1994, especially p. 3.

9. The publication of findings is not the best way to replicate best practice in most educational institutions, and more active and personal methods are necessary—like the creation of networks.

10. These figures change slightly among colleges; in another system where we observed, the ratio was 43 percent. We suspect, based on other salary schedules, that this ratio varies from about 35 percent to 50 percent, though such figures have never been systematically collected.

11. The results are calculated from the *Digest of Educational Statistics, 1995,* Tables 220–21.

12. We were able to locate only a small number of part-time instructors to observe because of the logistics of contacting them, and it is possible that those part-timers we did observe were the most dedicated. In addition, our judgments about the quality of instruction are qualitative ones, and it's possible that more precise ways of rating teaching would reveal differences. However, our finding of no powerful difference between full-time and part-time instructors is consistent with other evidence like that in Willett, 1980, based on student evaluations.

13. There is substantial variation among states in the level of local versus state resources. See NCES, 1997, Table 328.

14. On state policy for community colleges, see McDonnell and Zellman, 1993, Ch. 3. Even the program approval process is relatively toothless because state enforcement is lax and state officials lack the information to know what is happening at the local level (Grubb and McDonnell, 1991).

15. While there have been proposals to modify student aid to encourage student completion (Fischer, 1987), these efforts have never gone very far since such restrictions might undermine funding for the low-income students that student aid is intended to help (Manski, 1989).

16. The notion of sprinkling money over a number of different purposes reflects a view of the community college as full of small interest groups, each demanding more resources for its own purpose without an overarching vision.

10

ALTERNATIVE FUTURES
Creating the "Teaching College"

When instructors contemplate the future, the prospects frighten them. Most foresee increasing numbers of students, with ever-greater educational and social needs, while budgets continue to stagnate. As one instructor elaborated the problem:

> We have so many critical problems we don't know where to start. We make an assumption that we're going to be getting more students. We're also making the assumption that the student that we're getting is less prepared. So the trend, over the last few years, is that we're running out of resources very rapidly.

These trends are often expressed as fiscal concerns, and then as relentless time pressure. As a nursing instructor mentioned, "It just means that people have to do more with less, and it filters down, of course, to us [instructors], too."

In an institution in which enrollments and their correlative funding drive all decisions, it's not surprising to see concerns expressed in fiscal terms, but there's much more to instructors' fears than anxiety about their own jobs or salaries. The collision between increasing numbers of students with lower levels of preparation and constrained budgets can lead only to one dreadful outcome or another. Colleges can abandon their commitment to open access by formally or informally instituting admissions requirements. They can abandon existing supports for underprepared students, such as tutorial and advising centers and remedial/developmental education based on intensive teaching and learning communities. They can cheapen instruction by hiring yet more part-timers, replace skilled remedial instructors with banks of inert computers filled with drill-based programs, shift to technology-based instruction like distance education with talking heads, squeeze the budget for equipment and materials, or further increase teaching loads. But they can't follow these practices and continue to trumpet themselves as "teaching colleges."

Furthermore, fiscal constraints do not permit experimentation with new approaches to teaching that so many instructors and administrators call for. An English instructor expressed her fears for the future:

> One of the major problems in the community colleges is how to repackage instruction to meet the needs of students and at the same time maintain and allow them to attain high standards.... I'm very concerned that as the community college becomes more and more the college of choice for the first two years of education, that either the standards will just be lowered for everyone or that the whole bottom portion of our student body—those students that do not have achievement but in my opinion *do* have potential—will simply be dropped back out of the system again, the way they perhaps were many years ago, before the big open-door policy in the seventies, because they are a difficult group to teach.... Then what happens to the students that have not been given the egalitarian education that they deserved, who have only potential to see them through and very little achievement up to now and, therefore, who for many community college instructors are difficult to teach? ... It's more and more likely that our students, for whom we are the one place that could give them that one last difference, will get dropped out the bottom.

The greatest fear among instructors, then, is that the second-chance mission of the community college cannot be maintained if increased demands confront dwindling resources.

Another concern, at least among some older faculty, is that the animating spirit has leaked out of the community college—the commitment to a broad array of students and to innovative teaching that motivated many faculty during the 1960s and early 1970s. Many instructors in learning communities and other novel teaching arrangements described themselves as children of the sixties, and complained that more recent faculty didn't have the same commitment and fervor, that for them teaching was only a job, or that they were wanna-be researchers disappointed at ending up in community colleges. One reminisced that his college was "founded by people who were idealist—the idea was that this was a democracy and that equity was the key concern"; another declared that "the strength of the college has been its faculty, who are very unusual, who were born out of the sixties." An innovative developmental studies director complained:

> Our culture's really changing here. Through retirement there's definitely been a changing of the guard. A majority of the people in this division right now are people who came of age in the sixties. And without people even knowing it—it's

something that people, I think, aren't conscious of, they bring that value system or that worldview.

A few instructors noted a reinforcing shift in mission, in that the only real expansion of funds is coming from workforce development programs for employers, and such efforts can only distract colleges from their commitments to underprepared students and to teaching.[1]

It's hard to know what to make of these complaints, since it's easy to romanticize the activist 1960s. Older faculty are just as likely to be critiqued by their younger peers for ignoring the racial and cultural complexity of students now, for "teaching with the same paradigms that were successful when we had a different student population," as to be revered for their commitments to equity.[2] But the legitimate kernel of these concerns is that community colleges *should* be institutions with a driving mission. When business as usual becomes the order of the day, they will become just like other colleges, just another brick in the wall of higher education, with nothing distinctive to offer.

Instructors become especially bitter when they see that they can't influence the conditions of their own teaching—when they see that they will have increasingly underprepared students without any help in teaching them. As an electronics instructor complained,

> It doesn't seem that the administration is concerned about what goes on in the classroom. The only thing they're concerned with is that we are here to meet all the requirements that the state demands—course outlines in a specific manner in their office, that's all they're concerned with. They're not concerned with what the content of that outline is, whether it's feasible or not to teach it, you know, deliver it or not . . . whether the students are going to benefit from that, no one cares. And that's a sad state and that's why I want to get out of it. . . . I wanted to try and make a change. Now I want to get out.

These complaints are disheartening on an individual basis, because they signal instructors who are unhappy with the conditions of their work and who must surely be less effective. But there are larger reasons to be alarmed, since individuals in a state of fear and despair can't take risks or innovate. They can't afford to try new approaches to teaching, because that might generate poor evaluations from students used to different approaches, or low enrollments that cause "productivity" formulas to penalize their department. The institution can't try innovative arrangements—pairing academic and occupational instructors, or moving away from traditional drill-oriented remediation, or learning communities, or unconventional forms of staff development—because they can't guarantee the outcomes. Failures look like gigantic wastes of resources in institutions that don't have any to spare. The internal debates in these institutions often look like the politics of resentment: Any group that tries something new is suspected of wanting resources that others won't have, of "privileging" one group of students or one mission over another, and any innovation is resisted by others.[3] Stasis sets in: Underfinanced and overwhelmed institutions are not fertile grounds for reform and innovation.

Many of these alarms about the future seem justified. Community colleges are under serious financial pressure and are battered by conflicting demands from many different constituencies. The conflict between open-access and collegiate standards is the most obvious, and there are several others that we clarify in Section I. But reconciling these conflicts—rather than giving up on them, for example by letting underprepared students "drop out of the bottom"—requires more careful attention to the quality and effectiveness of teaching. And so we have come to an answer to the question, raised first in the Introduction, of whether good teaching matters. It does matter, particularly in educational institutions with conflicting purposes and goals, those without the ability to select their students—like community colleges.

By now, we have also developed a more complex understanding of what "good teaching" means, illustrated by the variety of practices we have observed in academic, occupational, and remedial classes alike, in superb classes as well as "collapsed" or "distressed" classes. In Section II we review the different elements that go into teaching and conclude with an observation we have been making all along: that good teaching is almost always a collective activity in some way, even if it takes place behind closed doors with a single instructor. And if good teaching is collective, then it requires a collective and therefore institutional response.

In the final section, we return to a dilemma first identified in Chapter 1: the conflict between the individual and the institutional, between conceptions of teaching in which instructors are "thrown right in" the classroom to learn by trial and error and those that insist on institutional responsibilities for the quality of teaching. We recap the recommendations that have emerged, particularly from Chapters 8 and 9, about the responsibilities of instructors themselves, of administrators and individual colleges, and of state and federal policy. These directions provide ways for all colleges to become true teaching institutions.

I. THE CONTRADICTORY ROLES OF COMMUNITY COLLEGES AND THE ROLES OF TEACHING

What do we want of our educational institutions? What do we ask of the schools and colleges we have created for specialized purposes, to teach the young—and increasingly the middle-aged and elderly, the "lifelong learner"? And therefore what do we ask of teaching itself, of the quality of instruction, of the preparation of instructors? The fact that we make multiple and conflicting demands on these institutions, and particularly on community colleges, is obvious; but who then has the responsibility for reconciling these conflicting demands?

The most conspicuous conflict imposed on community colleges is that they are designed to be open-access institutions—the "people's college," "democracy's open door," or "second-chance" institutions—and yet still be part of higher education and the "collegiate" sector.[4] This conflict takes many forms, since it is such a defining element of community colleges. Debates about standards that make no concession to open access constitute one strand, leading to instructors as well as students who are confused about relative versus absolute standards (in Chapter 6). The critics of community colleges rail about "low standards" or "academic disarticulation" without confronting how much improvement is reasonable when students come poorly prepared for collegiate work. Criticism of remedial/developmental education, and of some applied and occupational courses as not being "college-level," is part of the same debate. Belittling remedial and applied courses for being "low-level" deflects attention from the fact that such classes can be either well taught and sophisticated or poorly taught with narrow skills-oriented approaches, as we saw in Chapter 5. This confusion in turn undermines the possibility of viewing such courses as opportunities for the same creative and demanding teaching that we look for in literary criticism, calculus, or microeconomics. Other manifestations of this conflict can be seen in the low status of remedial education and some forms of occupational education, the huge proportion of part-time instructors assigned to these courses, and the reluctance of some colleges to provide programs for job training clients and welfare recipients. And the "solutions" are all over the place. Some want community colleges to emphasize their transfer function and "collegiate" role, eliminating remediation and a great deal of occupational preparation.[5] Others—including those in four-year institutions who want to slough off their remedial programs to community colleges—want to convert them into entirely remedial institutions.

Part of the debate about what community colleges *should be* is a debate about what they *are*. Are they in fact "people's colleges," providing expanded opportunity to nontraditional students, or are they simply mechanisms for "cooling out" these individuals by diverting them away from four-year colleges and into lower-status institutions or lower-status paths like occupational education? Those who believe in community colleges' "cooling-out" function have often referred to Burton Clark's (1960a) observation—based on one community college in the late 1950s, evidence that is now badly out of date as well as absurdly limited—that counselors are to blame. This critique fails to get the terms of comparison right, since community college students are more likely to be individuals who otherwise would not have gone to higher education at all, rather than those who would have otherwise attended four-year colleges and graduated (Grubb, 1996b, Ch. 2). But this line of argument does reflect a different and more valid critique: The rates of completion for community college students are often abysmally low, and therefore any goals they set for themselves—whether completion of a baccalaureate degree, or of a certificate or associate's degree to provide access to improved employment—cannot be realized.[6] These open-access institutions for nontraditional students have replicated a traditional pattern whereby students who are poorly prepared, including many low-income and minority students, fail to make much educational progress.

A second great conflict within community colleges reflects their status as *comprehensive* institutions, with multiple purposes—academic, vocational, and remedial, as well as serving "experimenters" casting about for a future and avocational students expanding their interests. Americans have always preferred comprehensive educational institutions over specialized versions—comprehensive high schools rather than separate academic and vocational schools, and comprehensive four-year colleges in place of the specialized institutions (such as religious colleges, mechanics' institutes, and normal schools) that dominated higher education in the nineteenth century. In two-year institutions, specialized technical colleges have gradually given way to comprehensive institutions with both transfer and occupational programs. But despite the overt commitment to comprehensive purposes, most colleges are still dominated by "academic" norms. These include discipline-based conceptions of status, mastery of content rather than pedagogy, funding patterns suited to simple classrooms rather than the complex equipment and materials of occupational classes, and governance by individuals drawn from the high-status academic side with little understanding of either occupational or remedial teaching. So even as states have created networks of comprehensive community colleges, they have done little to shift the culture or funding of these institutions, and they have left vast reaches of colleges nearly invisible—including the entire occupational side as well as the "empire of remediation."

A third conflict involves our social ideals for education, which usually envision a coherent and integrated activity where a specialized program of ever-increasing sophistication (a "major") coexists with general education for broader purposes, encompassing both breadth and depth. But we have relentlessly built educational practices that encourage fragmentation rather than coherence. Development of the disciplines and subspecialties means that the relationships among subjects—interdisciplinary concerns—are neglected, and students often are unable to understand the implications for one subject of learning in another. The narrowness of job-specific occupational education may limit advancement, while the separation of academic from occupational subjects impoverishes both. The practice of creating prerequisites separates remediation from subject courses, exacerbating the problem of content we examined in Chapter 5. The teaching practice we have described as "skills and drills," based on part-to-whole instruction, emphasizes the mastery of discrete subskills, though the usefulness (the "relevance") of these skills is always in doubt. The increasingly common practice of students drifting around institutions, attending both two- and four-year colleges to pick up enough credits for graduation, undermines any one college's efforts to create coherent majors or programs of general education.[7] (States have encouraged this process by developing common course numbering systems and descriptions, bowing to the increased mobility of the populace.) The high rates of dropouts in community colleges make a mockery of institutional efforts to create coherent academic majors and occupational specialties. And the conditions of students' lives, "busied up" with the demands of work and family, fragment their time and attention in ways that instructors cannot influence. Most of these disintegrative and centrifugal forces are outside the control of community colleges: They describe the world we have constructed in the United States, one of shifting careers, shifting family allegiances, shifting identities. And so higher education itself looks a lot like work and family life: Students hold multiple, low-intensity, temporary "jobs" and bounce among them, unable to earn enough (or learn enough) in any one to make ends meet.

A final conflict is one we have only rarely noted in this book, though we suspect it merits greater attention. Community colleges are relentlessly local institutions. They attract their students from the community, they typically send their graduates to work locally, and they choose members of advisory groups from local employers and community leaders. The most active colleges become central to their communities, "the only game in town," providing a vast array of conventional programs, job training, adult education, welfare-to-work programs, and programs for employers. But increasingly they must prepare students for a global economy in which workplace demands for higher-order abilities are imposed by competition from far outside the local community. In rural areas with high outmigration, they must prepare their students to work in distant areas, in communities considerably less homogeneous than theirs. And in communities with concentrations of low-income students with restricted experiences, or immigrants new to this country, colleges serve as an introduction to worlds that students have never encountered. A few instructors noted the stress of preparing students for a broader world. Some faculty in the Midwest acknowledged the difficulty of preparing students raised in a relentlessly white, agrarian population for the variety of multicultural urban life. Others lamented the lack of realism among their students—"they don't know what they're getting into." But the conflict between the local and the global, embedded in the very structure of the *community* college in a world where communities cannot possibly be independent, is almost never a subject of conversation.

Resolutions to these conflicting pressures exist, though they tend to sacrifice one or another goal of community colleges. Some advocates, for example, argue that colleges should give up remedial education, in effect renouncing access and equity goals (McGrath and Spear, 1991; Zwerling, 1976). Others, by emphasizing equity and student support to the exclusion of other concerns, seem to be abandoning any commitment to content and standards (Griffith and Connor, 1994). Some contend that colleges should stress their academic and collegiate purposes, downgrading their vocational and remedial activities (Eaton, 1994). Others argue for dismantling the comprehensive college from the other direction, by specializing in occupational programs and workforce development. Some continue to trumpet the power of colleges as community-serving institutions without recognizing the dilemmas posed by national and international developments; others have declared the importance of globalization and high-performance workplaces for education, not recognizing the bind this creates for instructors trying to respond to local employers. These advocates are not so much trying to reconcile conflicting demands as they are promoting one side or another, often without being explicit about the conflict. And these conflicts are local as well; as a dean in charge of English, ESL, and remedial programs described the problem,

> They're [administrators are] getting mixed signals about what the people in the community want. Some of the folks they talk to who are in leadership positions say what's needed is academic transfer programs. Others say vocational programs are needed, and I'm not sure what direction to follow.

Many of these contradictions wind up in the classroom, even though they originate in social demands, in political decisions about funding, in cultural norms undergoing steady change, in international competition—events that are far from the classroom itself. But it is always the *instructor* who is responsible for reconciling such demands. Consider an instructor in English 101, the content of which is determined partly by articulation agreements with a four-year college and partly by state guidelines, who confronts a seriously underprepared student or one whose family life prevents her from devoting attention to a full-time courseload; an occupational instructor who is unable to get help in finding equipment and negotiating work placements; a part-time remedial instructor who falls back on workbooks and grammar drills because her institution doesn't have a coherent program like North County's Developmental Studies Division; an occupational instructor who is pulled between the demands of local employers and the calls for "higher-order thinking"; or instructors whose conceptions of literacy and language teaching clash. In all of these cases, lack of institutional support means that contradictions that should be resolved at an institutional level instead get resolved in an ad hoc manner, in individual and idiosyncratic ways.

This kind of reconciliation is unfair and absurd. It's also ineffective, since it leads to many classes where teaching is mediocre at best. Reconciling the conflicting demands on community colleges requires, in some cases, social and political decisions that must be made outside colleges themselves, particularly state (and federal) policy decisions about funding, practices, and regulation (examined in Chapter 9 and reviewed in Section III of this chapter). In other cases, no elegant accommodation may be possible. Institutions serving adults will always have to contend with the complexity of their lives, since adult students can never return to the luxuriant time and comparative simplicity of youth, the stage for which schools and elite colleges were originally designed.

However, teaching reforms and institutional practices that improve the quality of teaching can help reconcile the conflicting demands on community colleges. One way to resolve the debate between open access and high standards, for example, is to develop a better understanding of what educational institutions can do for underprepared students. This in turn requires understanding the differences between sophisticated remedial programs and classes whose low standards evolved because instructors traded away the content or watered it down through their weak command of teaching practices (as we illustrated in Chapter 6). Effective developmental programs are the *only* way to achieve high standards in open-access institutions, and such programs probably entail replacing ineffective skills-oriented practices with more social and collective conceptions, such as the consistent practices of North County Community College and the learning communities profiled in Section IV of Chapter 5.

Similarly, we think it likely that the nature of instruction is partly to blame for low completion rates and some dimensions of "cooling out." Classes with unrelieved lecture where only a third of the students pay attention, the "distressed" and "collapsed" classes we described in Chapter 6, and classes in which students are belittled are all examples where students have little reason to stay engaged. In other cases, students must follow integrative lectures or attend sophisticated seminars, but without the background information or any introduction to the more active forms of participation required by these forms of teaching. The disequilibrium that arises when instructors want active participation from students who have been prepared in more passive and authoritarian classrooms generates still other forms of disengagement, unless instructors consciously socialize their students to new classroom roles. And for those students who arrive underprepared, the vast amount of dismal remediation following skills-centered approaches is unlikely to engage their attention, and high rates of failure to complete remedial programs (see Table 5.1) result. These are students who are getting little support, from instructors or the institution, to help them through; they are nontraditional students in relatively traditional teaching and learning arrangements. As an electronics instructor described the problem,

> The community colleges were basically free, and they were to be the vehicle through which you progressed through in your education endeavors. However, there is a pyramid structure, and only one individual can occupy the peak of the pyramid, and what I discovered was that the community colleges were primarily there, as far as I'm concerned, to discourage those individuals that were pursuing a higher educational endeavor. And I'll explain to you how: If you learned anything, you acquired it on your own. No one was there to assist or help you. If anything, it was to make you more submissive to the role that or the status that you had attained in society alone. . . . So all through life people have been telling him [a new student] school was there to help him. When he gets into the classroom he sits in the classroom and he tells the instructor that he has a problem. The instructor will tell him, you know, read the book or go to the library and read this book—never try to find out what his or her problem was and understand it. And this occurs several times to the individual, the individual gets frustrated. They drop out.

These are cases where good teaching—teaching that is attentive to students and their preparation, that tries "to find out what the problem was and understand it," that self-consciously leads students to more active participation in their learning—is necessary to enhance the connection of students to the institution. Even if some decisions to drop out depend on financial and familial factors beyond the control of the college, improvement in teaching would at least do everything a college can do to help students realize their goals.[8]

The other conflicts in the roles of community college can similarly be remedied only by attention to the quality of teaching. The efforts to link remedial education with content courses, in learning communities and support courses, are ways of softening the divisions between transfer and remedial purposes. Efforts to integrate academic and vocational education reduce the distance between academic and occupational purposes, and learning communities can bridge other divisions within the comprehensive community college. Teaching reforms that unite instructors—for example, faculty centers that serve as resources for all faculty, treating remedial and occupational teaching with the same seriousness as English and math—are other ways of unifying colleges. In reconciling the *local* and *global* roles of colleges, only skillful teaching can lead students to see the variety of options they face, building on their experiences while leading them toward others. And all of these teaching-related improvements provide students with an education that is more coherent, less fractured by disciplinary boundaries and the disjointed concerns of individual instructors.

We conclude, then, that the common assumption that teaching matters is true *in this way*: When educational institutions are single-minded and relatively homogeneous—as are, for example, elite liberal arts colleges such as Amherst and Swarthmore, or single-purpose vocational programs such as cosmetology schools or electronics institutes, or graduate schools within major research universities— then students are highly selected or self-selected, conflicting purposes are absent, and the nature of appropriate teaching is relatively clear.[9] But where educational institutions are complex and multifaceted—and open-access, nonselective community colleges are certainly the most varied in their students and purposes of any in this country—then the teaching appropriate for any particular student is not at all self-evident. Even deciding what competencies are appropriate requires debate, as we showed in Chapter 4 regarding literacy practices, and as is also true for occupational education with its many competencies and for remedial education with its distinctly different approaches. The forms of teaching that seem so familiar—the synthetic lecture and the interpretive seminar in academic subjects—rely on assumptions that do not hold in community colleges; the workshop in occupational teaching and the teaching of remedial subjects require expertise that instructors untrained for teaching cannot have. Dumping these *institutional* problems onto unprepared instructors guarantees that they will be individually resolved, sometimes well and sometimes badly. And so confronting the teaching challenges of the community college requires that these conflicts be opened to public examination and debate, and then to institutional rather than individual resolution.

II. THE MANY FORMS OF "GOOD TEACHING": INSTRUCTION AS COLLECTIVE ACTIVITY

One of our tasks has been to make teaching in community colleges public and visible, and thereby open to analysis. Direct observations of classrooms were essential to this process, first to describe what goes on, and then to come to some judgments about what constitutes good teaching.[10] By now, we can see that good teaching comes in many forms. Since the improvement of instruction is so important in responding to the multiple and conflicting demands on community colleges, it's worth summarizing our conclusions about what such improvement might mean.

First and most obviously, the forms of teaching are not always what they seem. Lectures can become discussions; discussions can be lectures in disguise. What are supposed seminars can turn into teacher-directed classrooms, with students participating only under duress. Hands-on learning in occupational classes can be as didactic and passive (from the student's perspective) as the deadliest lecture. Group work and teamwork may replicate the fact-oriented and didactic practices of conventional classrooms rather than creating opportunities for students to discuss their own interpretations with one another. Learning communities and efforts to integrate disciplines can be changes in name only if instructors don't have the time to plan collaboratively. Computer-based methods and distance learning are useful only for drill unless instructors understand the pedagogy of these new technologies. Almost any teaching innovation can be undermined if instructors fail to understand and internalize the purposes of such practices. And so the overt forms of teaching—including the widespread antipathy of many instructors toward lecture and their avowed preference for discussion, or the allegiance of occupational instructors to hands-on methods—matter less than the details of practice and the skill of instructors in handling these different forms.[11] But these details are largely invisible. *We* saw them because we were looking for them, and because our method included discussion with both instructors and with each other, forcing us to be explicit about what we were observing. Experienced instructors sometimes come to understand them through trial and error and discussion with peers, but otherwise the details remain unknown even to practicing teachers.

A second conclusion about good teaching—and again, classroom observation proved crucial to this discovery—is that the skill of instructors in their classrooms requires control over many details of practice. The nature of questions and answers, the kinds of student questions an instructor encourages or cuts off, the applications developed, the references to other subjects and events and the extent to which students are prepared for them, the interactions in workshops or science labs, the tendency for instructors to carry out assignments rather than requiring students to learn how to do them—all these elements and more, many of them specific to particular subjects, influence content and the engagement of students. Many instructor have not mastered these details of practice or thought much about them despite their proclaimed allegiance to student-centered classrooms. Many of the "collapsed" and "distressed" classes we described in Chapter 6 ran aground on details of practice, including an overreliance on humor, the use of inappropriate examples, an easy acceptance of student contributions in the name of "student support"—all misuses of practices that have their rightful place in teaching. And the amount of belittling we saw, some of it unwitting and inadvertent, is again testimony to the lack of control many instructors have over the elements of teaching. But most instructors get no advice or support in rethinking their practices, since the details that undermine their classes are invisible to them, to their colleagues, to the administrators who presumably evaluate them—to everyone except the students who suffer under them.

In one dimension, the emerging orthodoxy against lecture and in favor of more student-centered or hybrid methods like lecture/discussion seems right. The inattention of students during straight lecture, with less than a third following along, taking notes, and responding to occasional IRE questions, is one tip-off to the weakness of conventional lecture. In contrast, the excellent "lectures" we saw, with virtually all students participating through questions and answers—the microeconomics and CIS classes described in Chapter 2, Section II, or the microbiology class in Chapter 4, Section I—weren't really lectures at all, since instructors managed to elicit student participation at many points. Even a textbook-driven class, normally the most quiet and passive of all types, could become more lively when an instructor gave students the responsibility for moving the class through the text. But the most powerful evidence, to us, is that the truly memorable classes we observed came not from these competent lecture/discussions (like the physical geography class profiled at the start of Chapter 2), good as they could be. The shining moments of teaching and learning in community colleges were memorable because of what *students* were doing, in classrooms where they were coming to astonishing understandings of their own under the steady guidance of the instructor "teaching from the sidelines." We think, for example, of the following classes we have already described:

• a remedial English class of African-American and Latina welfare moms exploring the textual details of a short story, relating its protagonist to their own odysseys under the guidance of their diminutive Chinese-American instructor;

• a seminar of students in the English component of a biology/English learning community, coming from a deadly fact-oriented lecture in biology but moving swiftly into complex moral and aesthetic reactions to a work of nonfiction;

• an applied math class of burly working-class guys in an HVAC program, mastering the details of multivariate nonlinear algebra, moving constantly between heating phenomena and their algebraic representation, under the constant prodding of their female physics instructor;

• a Growth and Development class in which students swiftly made a series of connections among their own backgrounds, the theoretical precepts of child psychology, and the practices and political dimensions of early childhood programs where they might find employment;

• a barn full of men in a dairy-herd management program, ankle-deep in cow dung, making the transition from the family farming practices of their childhood to the modern, science- and computer-based practices of the late twentieth century;

• a class of students in a remedial reading program, part of a learning community created for underprepared (and mostly African-American) students, wading into the complexities of register, voice, and *Oedipus Rex*;

• an economics class in which students fluidly interpreted a steady stream of diagrams, integrating both economic theory and applications in business structure, and elaborating the lecture through their own contributions;

• several learning communities and integrated approaches in which students were making the connections among subjects that instructors in independent classes simply assume, where the question "Why do I have to know this?" never arose.

These all prove to be student-centered and constructivist classes, where instructors have moved away from teacher-centered practices (or from authoritative to distributed conceptions of learning). The instructors' actions are worthy of study because they have created the conditions in which these shining moments can occur. But as we said at the outset, these classes are memorable for what *students* are doing, and in this sense the very best teaching we saw took place where students have been freed to come to their own understandings of reading, or math, or their future occupation, or the role of science or markets in society.

The students in these examples exemplify the range of those who attend community colleges. Some were conventional-age, middle-class students in a suburban college that transfers a high proportion of its enrollees to the nearby flagship university; others were older working-class men, the sons and daughters of working farmers, welfare mothers, or remedial students. Their instructors have found ways not only to teach the many groups that come to community colleges, but to develop truly memorable classes with them. Here too the emerging orthodoxy against lecture seems correct to us, particularly the version that holds that lecture and drill are ineffective with nontraditional students. As one dean of instruction mentioned, instead of "teaching with the same paradigms that were successful when we had a different student population"—which he described as "conventional lecture/demonstration"—"the future of good teaching at this college rests in the faculty's ability to develop alternative teaching styles, to address the various learning styles of students that are here." An English instructor with thirty years of experience echoed these sentiments:

> I would have to make some really basic changes in my sense about what I'm here for and what I'm here to do if I were looking for another ten years of this. We're really at a transition here, and the old or established ways are just not appropriate—just not going to be able to lecture to students or to assume that students come with the values and motivations or the reasons for being here that were true ten years ago.

We wish there were more "proof" of this observation.[12] The deadliness of the many drill-oriented remedial classes, rehearsing the same pointless grammatical facts and arithmetic procedures that these students have failed to master in their prior schooling, is testimony to the ineffectiveness of conventional approaches. Other evidence comes from students themselves, particularly those in learning communities who cite community among their peers as a major advantage *for learning* of such arrangements. And we remain convinced, as we mentioned in the previous section, that the high dropout rates in community colleges depend in part on the prevalence of traditional teaching for nontraditional students. Even if students themselves cannot articulate this link, mediocre teaching contributes to their lack of progress that leads, in and among the other barriers they face, to their leaving.[13]

Finally, we note the importance to good teaching of an equilibrium between students and instructors, of a common understanding of what education is and what should go on in the classroom. One kind of equilibrium emerges in text-book-centered classes and some occupational classes modeled after authoritarian workplaces, where students have been socialized to accept the authority of the instructor and the text, where they sit placidly and follow instructions no matter how trivial. No doubt these classes are effective in some sense, for they achieve coverage, and diligent students can master the explicit content of these courses. No doubt the United States would do better in international comparisons if all K–12 classes looked like this, and we shouldn't dismiss their value for some tasks and some stretches of time in almost every course. But students in these classes are too passive, and the material is too formulaic to prepare students for their own approaches to the world, whether the world of employment, of citizenship, or family and community life. And so the equilibrium that seems most effective is one where both instructors and students are prepared for the livelier exchanges, the student initiatives and challenges, the student-oriented elaboration and frequent departures from the class "script," and the full range of literacy practices that we see in student-centered and constructivist teaching.

When such an equilibrium does not exist, then classes often break down. Where instructors lament that their students are "so used to reading and accepting everything somebody says"—but have not socialized them to be more critical, or provided the preparation (the "scaffolding") for them to participate more actively—then we see classes where discussion is labored, where instructors struggle to pull answers out of students, where instructors do most of the intellectual work and in the end revert to lecture. When the contrary problem exists—teachers holding on to the authority to interpret all content despite students seeking active participation—then we find the "distressed" classes we described in Chapter 6, where overt challenges to the instructor's authority bring the class to a halt. There are many different ways for a disequilbrium between teachers and students to develop, then, but such breakdowns always reveal instructors who have failed to understand their students or failed to resocialize them—and they always undermine the possibilities for learning.

We conclude that "good teaching" is inescapably collective. It is collective at least in the sense that instructors must have the cooperation of their students, and must therefore have the facility to establish both motivation—the conventional part of bromides about good teaching—and consistent expectations of what will happen in the classroom and workshop.

But "good teaching" is also collective in a different sense. The control over the elements of teaching, the judgments of whether humor and applications and demonstration have been used appropriately or not, can be made visible and therefore available for modification only with external observation and feedback by others. Sometimes, for experienced teachers who have changed their methods through trial and error, this feedback comes from students themselves—"working with your students and finding out what works and what doesn't"—or from what they think is successful in the crucible of the classroom, "just a pragmatic way of trying to get things across." Sometimes this feedback comes from mentors, as we saw in Chapter 1, or from committed colleagues "who kind of find each other." Surprisingly often, the memorable teaching we observed came about in learning communities or from instructors who had created communities of like-minded individuals, where instructors observed others and were observed in turn. (Conversely, the worst instructors had managed to isolate themselves from their peers and their college, in effect hiding their bad practices from any scrutiny or possibility of correction.) And the praise for participating in communal approaches like learning communities mentioned in Chapter 7—"It's very, very enriching to see other teachers work"—exemplifies the interest of many more faculty in joining such collectives. So the best teaching involves some kind of cooperative activity, with students, with colleagues, and—for those forms that require widespread cooperation, like linked classes, learning communities, and the institutional practices we review in the final section—with administrators as well.

III. THE INDIVIDUAL AND THE INSTITUTIONAL REVISITED: THE RESPONSIBILITIES FOR "TEACHING COLLEGES"

Throughout this book, we have emphasized the enormous variety of teaching practices in community colleges. We found some patterns in this variety, to be sure. Those who had shifted toward more student- and meaning-centered approaches believed in a different form of learning, where students "need to work at constructing some of that knowledge," and many described a personal odyssey of moving away from lecture and teacher-dominated formats through trial and error, sometimes with the help of mentors or peers But we couldn't begin to say why some instructors had made this odyssey and why others had not, or which of them had actually changed their practices as a result. We could not tell how many were like the English instructor described in Section I of Chapter 2, who feared that "I'm simply not the right teacher, or I'm not doing it correctly" but lacked the resources within her college to make any changes. And so teaching—particularly the many forms of good teaching we summarized in the previous section—seems individual and idiosyncratic. "Teaching is a very individualistic endeavor," as one instructor expressed this convention.

But we have also concluded that good teaching is necessary to reconcile the conflicting demands placed on community colleges, and that it is inescapably collective. We have identified a variety of practices (particularly in Chapter 8) that colleges can pursue *as institutions* to improve the quality of teaching. Such institutional practices would also require colleges to conduct public debate and discussion about teaching, since it is impossible to reshape personnel policies (for example) without clarifying what aspects of teaching should be emphasized by hiring and promotion committees; it's impossible to institute a teaching center without clarifying what a particular faculty needs from it (*not* what an administration thinks the faculty need). The most important practices would also provide institutional support to develop competence in teaching as well as organizational practices such as the joint design of courses and learning communities, making teaching a more collective effort. Among the most important reforms are the following:

• Faculty roles would be structured so they are not pulled among so many responsibilities. This would also require reducing the number of part-time instructors, or at the very least structuring their work differently.

• Personnel policies would put teaching first rather than last among the criteria for hiring and promotion. This would include procedures for observing teaching, particularly in the interests of providing support and mentoring to new instructors, and of involving them actively in communities of practice and discussion around teaching.

• Colleges would require some preparation specifically for the conditions of teaching in community colleges, both before faculty start to teach and as they mature. As it now stands, faculty do not come ready to teach the students who enroll in community colleges, any more than the students themselves come prepared to attend college. To eliminate the surreal conditions produced when unprepared instructors confront unprepared students, colleges (and states) would develop programs, lasting from a summer to a year, to ready instructors for teaching.

• For continuing education, staff development would shift from one-shot, Friday-afternoon affairs—"fancy educators coming and talking to us about things"—to more sustained and collective efforts, creating debates about teaching *within* colleges. Peer observation of each other's teaching, faculty research about teaching, and exchanges with other colleges (perhaps as part of state-sponsored programs and national subject initiatives) would be parts of this process. The development of centers for faculty development and teaching, to improve the quality of instruction in multiple ways, would represent a focal point for such institutional commitments. Then other methods of improvement—Writing Across the Curriculum, for example, or classroom assessment techniques—could be used as the basis for collaborative efforts to improve teaching, rather than remaining individual and closeted.

• Administrators would become more engaged in classroom issues, either directly—through observing classes and participating with faculty in discussions of teaching—or at least indirectly, by considering all their decisions in the light of influences on teaching. In turn, a change in attitudes would require different forms of administrator preparation, perhaps more resources in administration, and certainly greater stability in collegiate leadership. As *educational* leaders rather than (or in addition to) "bean counters," administrators would be responsible, with the faculty, for creating a culture that supports teaching—that recognizes its complexity in *every* subject, that respects its collective nature, and that communicates these beliefs to faculty and students consistently. The power and authority in most colleges would become less hierarchical and authoritarian, to facilitate institutional decisions about teaching and to eliminate the deep hostility between administrators and faculty that now prevails.

These remedies shift teaching from an individual to an institutional responsibility. As we have seen in those few colleges that use these mechanisms consistently, such practices reinforce one another. A college with a supportive administration, where teaching matters, is more likely to concern itself with part-timers' teaching; an institution where teaching plays a serious role in hiring and evaluation is more likely to have continuous seminars and staff development focused on teaching improvement. In such institutions, there is less room for mediocre teachers to secrete themselves away. Students become collectively socialized to more active forms of learning, so the burden of reorienting students is widely shared rather than falling on the shoulders of a few. The presence of *many* policies related to the quality of teaching defines these as true teaching colleges, whereas isolated and ineffective practices—a Friday afternoon workshop here and there, a brief "teaching" demonstration by job candidates, a rhetorical commitment to teaching by a president who never goes near a classroom— do not.

Above the level of individual institutions, the states that create community colleges could improve the quality of teaching in other ways. One involves funding. Community colleges are, on the average, underfunded for the enormous teaching challenges they face; their funding levels compared to state four-year colleges are shameful. But rather than simply increasing resources across the board, increased funding would be more effective in improving the quality of colleges if it were tied to specific improvements: converting part-time teachers to full-time instructors, and reserving part-time positions for specialists from business and industry, for whom they were originally envisioned; reducing teaching loads while increasing responsibilities for teaching improvement and collaboration with other instructors (including roles as mentors to new instructors); increasing funding earmarked for materials, equipment, and coordinating internships for occupational programs. Instructional or faculty centers, devoted to improving the quality of teaching in many ways, merit separate state (and perhaps federal) funding, and establishing a network of such centers is something that states could readily undertake.

Other state policies to support instruction include the credentialing of faculty. Virtually all the instructors we interviewed supported preparation for community college teaching. The high level of support for the Iowa credentialing program, with its five-course requirement, and the approval of occupational instructors in California who used to complete a two-level sequence provide other evidence that well-designed programs would be widely accepted. States should therefore move to create pre-service and in-service requirements for community college instructors. This might also require state four-year colleges and universities to develop programs for teaching in community colleges; the proposal for a teaching-oriented doctorate is one way to achieve this (Glazer, 1983). Similar recommendations apply to administrator training, because if administrators are to be *educational* leaders, they must know as much about approaches to teaching and the ways institutions can affect pedagogy as they do about budgets and politics.

A third arena of state policy is the identification and dissemination of good practice. Individual instructors and colleges can by themselves look for ways to improve their teaching, but states are typically in a better position to survey the full range of practices, identify the most promising ones, carry out evaluations to test their effectiveness, and then disseminate the results to local institutions through workshops and other mechanisms. Currently, such state efforts are quite rare, though Minnesota funds a statewide Center for Teaching and Learning that provides some of this assistance. Such a role would require state agencies to think of themselves less as funding and compliance bureaus and more as educational agencies, concerned with the quality of instruction as well as the means to provide that instruction. While this kind of function would require a substantial change in many states, K–12 state agencies have been increasingly engaged in instructional reforms during the past fifteen years, and community colleges could certainly follow.

A final arena for state support involves data collection and analysis—not, we stress, in the interests of accountability (as is now all the rage), but in the service of improvement. Community colleges now have offices of institutional research, but with some notable exceptions they devote their energies to compliance reports, routine enrollment statistics, and public relations for the president. Instead, they could be analyzing different approaches to teaching—for example, different remedial programs' rates of completion and effects on student progress (like the results in Table 5.1), the value of applied and support courses for occupational students, the identification of "bottleneck" courses that prevent students from continuing their programs and the effectiveness of alternatives, the advantages of learning communities, the definition and measurement of standards. The states' role in fostering such local research would include additional funding for that purpose, as well as guidance in the data collection and instructional evaluation that would be most helpful to community colleges.

The federal government could also participate in such activities, as we stressed in Chapter 9. The federal government's role in community colleges has been minimal, confined to a little support through student grants and loans, a little bit of money for reform in occupational education, and occasional grants for instructional improvement through FIPSE, NSF, and other agencies. The 1996 tax credits—the Hope Tax Credit and Lifelong Learning Credit—expanded federal postsecondary funding by about $6 billion per year, and the amount of the Hope Credits was tied to community college tuitions, but little of these resources will flow to community colleges because of the structure of the credits. As we stressed in Chapter 9, money by itself is insufficient to improve quality. A more coherent approach would provide resources that improve instruction, for example by funding a series of faculty centers in conjunction with states. If "lifelong learning" in this country were ever to morph from vacuous rhetoric into reality, the federal government could play a leadership role through community colleges, which currently serve the widest range of students and the broadest variety of purposes. Rather than unrestricted support, federal funding for faculty and student centers—both focused on the special needs of learners throughout their lifetimes—would help local colleges and instructors respond to the particular needs of older and nontraditional students.[14] And, even more than states, the federal government has an important role to play in research and evaluation, and in identifying and disseminating good practice, since the federal reach encompasses the entire country.

Finally, if even a few of these methods of improving instruction were instituted, what would be the responsibilities of instructors themselves? After all, the failures of teaching are not always due to the institutional and policy lapses; they are sometimes individual failures, too. The instructors who isolated themselves from their colleagues, who berated and belittled their students, or who refused to think about pedagogical issues despite their lifelong roles as teachers bear some of the blame for mediocre teaching. We don't think that there are many personal characteristics required for teaching, since wonderful teachers come in a wide variety of personas, but there are a few. "You have to be honest and open, to try hard," as one instructor mentioned; a willingness to experiment is important, and many cited the need for basic sympathy and concern for students, widespread but not yet universal among community college instructors. And, because the improvement of teaching is inevitably a collective effort, individuals must be willing to work with colleagues, with sympathetic administrators, and with expert others.

And so we return to instructors and their practices, the bedrock of all educational institutions. There are already so many characteristics of community colleges that have gained their allegiance. They are, overwhelmingly, committed to the students and to the ideals of the "people's college." They recognize that these are the best forums for teaching in its truest sense, in helping students with varied motivations and preparation achieve their goals, rather than merely selecting students who can learn in any environment. As a veteran instructor noted about the community college,

> I can say that I can't imagine having a better job. I can't imagine as far as being a teacher, in terms of my career decision to become a teacher, I can't imagine that having been any better anywhere else.

When they express frustration, it's not with the ideal of the community college but with its failure to live up to its ideals:

> There's this irony: It's a teaching institution, but there's almost nothing for the teacher. The teacher's told to get in the classroom, teach his classes, and there are so-called staff development or professional development committees, and you can plug into one of their little workshops—it might last a few hours and that's the end of it. But there's no big investment in teaching your teachers how to teach, or teaching them how to research, teaching them how to assess the results of what they're doing, keeping them in communities so they talk to each other.

This instructor has expressed the heart of our recommendations: "teaching your teachers how to teach, teaching them how to research, teaching them how to assess the results of what they're doing, keeping them in communities so they talk to each other." Such changes would restore faculty and teaching to the primary roles they should play in any educational institution. And, in place of the dismal forecasts that envision instructors "doing more with less" and allowing needy students to "get dropped out of the bottom," the future of such institutions would be bright and shining, blessed with a new vision of what teaching institutions can be.

NOTES

1. Workforce development efforts usually neglect teaching, and because they serve employees, often of large firms, they do not usually serve underprepared, low-income, and minority students (Grubb et al., 1997). In addition, workforce development programs are too narrowly vocational for many faculty. More recently, in spring 1998, instructors have been concerned that welfare-to-work programs with their emphasis on "work first" and quick fixes to complex problems will distract community colleges from their commitment to teaching.

2. See also Barkley, 1993, a dissertation exploring the generation gap between older and younger faculty in community colleges.

3. In the worst of these cases, instructors who get outside funding for teaching innovation—FIPSE grants, for example—are resented for having smaller or fewer classes to teach even though they have gotten the funding on their own.

4. In Labaree's (1997) terms, this is a conflict between the purposes of social equity and individual mobility, on one hand, and social efficiency, on the other. Social efficiency dictates that only those who can be educated at reasonable cost be enrolled. Demands for more stringent admissions—for eliminating those students who are not "college material"—and for eliminating high-cost programs such as remedial/developmental education invariably express the concerns of social efficiency.

5. See, for example, Eaton, 1994, and many of the critics who fault the vocational direction of the community college, including Brint and Karabel, 1989, and Pincus, 1980. See also McGrath and Spear, 1991.

6. For evidence on noncompletion rates using two national longitudinal data sets—NLS72 and High School and Beyond—see Grubb, 1989; for more recent data based on the Beginning Postsecondary Survey data, see Barkner, Cuccaro-Alamin, and McCormick (1996).

7. On the problems of fragmenting general education in this way, see Smith, 1993.

8. The model of dropping out that dominates higher education is that of Tinto (1987), who hypothesizes that the degree of academic integration and social integration determine an individual's likelihood of dropping out. While academic integration is often operationalized in test scores for statistical analysis, engagement and disengagement with classes would also fit Tinto's description of academic integration. Because community colleges are commuter institutions without extensive extracurricular activities, the extent of social integration is low for most students—making academic integration a more important concern, at least within the restricted scope of Tinto's model.

9. We are *not* saying that teaching doesn't matter, only that the nature of good teaching is clear and instructors need not respond to so many conflicting pressures.

10. We hope that others will follow our practice of observing classrooms. In particular, we think that studies of both two- and four-year colleges that involve interviewing administrators

(or that use their recommendations to grant teaching awards) or interviewing faculty or students without observing their classes ought to stop immediately, because each of these sources of information is at best biased and at worst empty. What happens in classrooms has only a loose connection to what administrators, instructors, or even students themselves think is happening.

11. Once again, observation is necessary to uncover these practices, and the surveys of instructors about their preferred modes of teaching—as in Barnes, 1994—are likely to be only rough guides to practice.

12. See note 12 in Chapter 1, especially the work on low-income students by Knapp and his colleagues. Developing better evidence about the effectiveness of different approaches to teaching for nontraditional students would be an excellent project for the institutional researchers at community colleges.

13. The role of teaching quality in decisions to persist or drop out has not been investigated. In interviews with community college students (Grubb, 1996b, Ch. 2), they were likely to mention a lack of purpose, financial problems, and familial responsibilities rather than the quality of teaching. However, students rarely reflect on what good teaching might mean to them, particularly when they have been trained to regard schooling as drills and fact acquisition. We suspect that the lack of progress caused by mediocre teaching contributes to dropping out, even though most students end up blaming themselves or a lack of purpose rather than instructors or the college. The higher rate of completion in a learning community is the best evidence that teaching matters to persistence.

14. For a preliminary outline of such a plan, see Grubb, 1998c.

REFERENCES

Achtenhagen, F., & Grubb, W. N. (1999). Vocational and occupational education: Pedagogical complexity, institutional diversity. In V. Richardson (ed.), *Handbook of Research on Teaching* (4th ed.). Washington, DC: American Educational Research Association.

Adler, M. (1982). *The Paideia proposal: An educational manifesto.* New York: Macmillan.

American Council on Testing. (1996). *Six reports from ACT for ASSET and Compass Users.* Washington, DC: American Council on Testing.

Andrew, E.N. (1996). *As teachers tell it: Implementing All Aspects of the Industry* . Berkeley, CA : National Center for Research in Vocational Education, University of California at Berkeley,

Angelo, T. (1991). *Classroom research: Early lessons from success.* New Directions for Teaching and Learning, no. 46. San Francisco: Jossey-Bass Publishers.

Applebee, A., Langer, J., Mullis, I., Latham, A., & Gentile, C. (1994). *NAEP 1992 writing report card.* National Center for Educational Statistics, report no. 123-W01. Washington, DC: U.S. Government Printing Office.

Ashton, P., and Cocker, L. (1987). Systematic study of planned variation. *Journal of Teacher Education* 38(3):2–8.

Astin, A., Korn, W., & Dey, E. (1991). *The American college teacher: National norms for the 1989–90 HERI faculty survey.* Los Angeles: Higher Education Research Institute, University of California.

Badway, N., & Grubb, W. N. (1997). *A sourcebook for reshaping the community college: Curriculum integration and the multiple domains of career preparation* (Vols. 1–2). Berkeley, CA: National Center for Research in Vocational Education.

Bailey, T., & Merritt, D. (1995). *Making sense of industry-based skill standards.* Berkeley, CA: National Center for Research in Vocational Education.

Baker, G., Roueche, J., & Gillett-Karam, R. (1990). *Teaching as leading: Profiles of excellence in the open-door college.* Washington, DC: Community College Press.

Balmuth, M. (1985). *Essential characteristics of effective adult literacy programs: A review and analysis of the research.* The Adult Beginning Reader Project. Albany, NY: New York State Department of Education.

Barkley, E. (1993). *The new generation gap in the American faculty.* Ph.D. dissertation. Berkeley: School of Education, University of California.

Barnes, C. (1994). Questioning in college classrooms. In K. Feldman and M. Paulsen (eds.), *Teaching and learning in the college classroom* (pp. 398–409). Needham Heights, MA: Ginn Press.

Barr, B. R., & Tagg, J. (1995, November/December). From teaching to learning: A new paradigm for undergraduate education. *Change*, 13–25.

Beardsley, L. (1990). *Good day, bad day: The child's experience of child care.* New York: Teachers College, Columbia University.

Beckman, B. (Ed.). (1996). *How to do more with less: Community college innovations to increase efficiency and reduce costs.* Mission Viejo: League for Innovation in the Community College.

Berkner, L., Cuccaro-Alamin, S., and McCormick, A. (1996, March). *Descriptive summary of 1989–90 beginning postsecondary students: Five years later.* NCES 96-1255. Washington, DC: National Center for Educational Statistics, U.S. Department of Education.

Berryman, S. (1995). Apprenticeship as a paradigm of learning. In W.N. Grubb (ed.), *Education through occupations in American high schools.* Vol. I: *Approaches to integrating academic and vocational education* (pp. 192–214). New York: Teachers College Press.

Berrymen, S., & Bailey, T. (1992). *The double helix of education and the economy.* New York: Institute on Education and the Economy, Teachers College, Columbia University.

Billett, S. (1993) *Learning is working when working is learning: A guide to learning in the workplace.* Queensland, Australia: Griffith University, Centre for Skill Formation Research and Development.

Bishop, J. H. (1989, January–February). Why the apathy in American high schools? *Educational Researcher,* 6–10.

Blau, F., & Ferber, M. (1992). *The economics of men, women, and work.* Englewood Cliffs, NJ: Prentice-Hall.

Boesel, D., & McFarland, L. (1994). *Final Report to Congress, Vol. I: Summary and Recommendations.* National Assessment of Vocational Education. Washington, DC: Office of Educational Research and Improvement, U.S. Department of Education.

Boesel, D. (1994, July). Integration of academic and vocational curricula. In D. Boesel, M. Rahn, and S. Deitch (eds.), *Program Improvement: Education Reform.* pp. 71–104. National Assessment of Vocational Education, Final Report to Congress, Vol. III. Washington, DC: Office of Educational Research and Improvement. U.S. Department of Education.

Boesel, D., and McFarland, L. (1994, July). *Summary and Recommendations.* National Assessment of Vocational Education, Final Report to Congress, Vol. I. Washington, DC: Office of Educational Research and Improvement, U.S. Department of Education.

Bourdieu, P. (1977). *Outline of a theory of practice.* New York: Cambridge University Press.

Bowen, H. (1968). *The finance of higher education.* Berkeley: Carnegie Commission on Higher Education.

Bower, B. (1996, June/July). A Carolina education partnership. *Community College Journal 66* (6), 32–34.

Boyer, E. (1989). *The condition of the professoriate: Attitudes and trends.* Princeton, NJ: Carnegie Foundation for the Advancement of Teaching.

Boyer, E. (1990). *Scholarship reconsidered: Priorities of the professoriate.* Princeton, NJ: Carnegie Foundation for the Advancement of Teaching.

Bragg, D., Hamm, R., & Trinkle, K. (1995). *Work-based learning in two-year colleges in the United States.* Berkeley, CA: National Center for Research in Vocational Education.

Brewer, D., and Gray, M. (1997). *Connecting college and community in the new economy? An analysis of community college faculty-labor market linkages.* MDS-1084. Berkeley: National Center for Research in Vocational Education. RAND/RP-663, Institute on Education and Training. Santa Monica, CA: RAND.

Brewer, J. A. (1995). Integrating academics and vocational education: An investigation of attitudes and curricular values of administrators and faculty in the Wisconsin technical college system. Unpublished manuscript. La Crosse, WI: Western Wisconsin Technical College.

Brint, S., & Karabel, J. (1989). *The diverted dream*. New York: Oxford University Press.

Brown, A., & Palincsar, A. (1989). Guided, co-operative learning and individual knowledge acquisition. In Lauren Resnick (ed.), *Knowing, learning, and instruction: Essays in honor of Robert Glaser*. Hillsdale, NJ: Lawrence Erlbaum.

Brown, A., & Campione, J. (1994). Guided discovery in a community of learners. In K. McGilly (ed.), *Classroom lessons: Integrating cognitive theory and classroom practice*. Cambridge, MA: MIT Press/Bradford Books.

Bruner J. (1990). *Acts of meaning*. Cambridge, MA: Harvard University Press.

Bruner, J. (1996). *The culture of education*. Cambridge, MA: Harvard University Press.

Butler, J., and Evans, G. (1992). Expert models and feedback processes in developing competence in industrial areas. *Australian Journal of TAFE Research and Development*, 8 (1), 13–31.

Callahan, R. (1967). *Education and the cult of efficiency*. Chicago: University of Chicago Press.

Cazden, C. (1996, April). The "mentor paper" writing assignment in one community college Puente class: Preliminary report from a participant observer. Paper presented at the annual meeting of the American Educational Research Assocation, New York.

Chickering, A. W., & Gamson, Z. F. (1987). Seven principles for good practice in undergraduate education. *AAHE Bulletin*, *39* (7), 3–7.

Chickering, A. W., & Gamson, Z. F. (1991). *Applying the seven principles for good practice in undergraduate education*. San Francisco: Jossey-Bass Publishers.

Clark, B. (1960a). *The open door college: a case study*. New York: McGraw-Hill.

Clark, B. R. (1960b, May). The "cooling-out" function in higher education. *American Journal of Sociology*, *65*, 560–576.

Cohen, A. (1990, April 24). Counting the Transfers: Pick a Number. *Community, Technical, and Junior College Times*.

Cohen, A. M., & Brawer, F. B. (1989). *The American community college*. (2nd ed.). San Francisco: Jossey-Bass.

Cohen, D., McLaughlin, M. W., & Talbert, J. E. (1993). *Teaching for understanding: Challenges for policy and practice*. San Francisco: Jossey-Bass Publishers.

Cole, M. (1997). *Cultural psychology: A once and future discipline*. Cambridge, MA: Harvard University Press.

Collins, A., Brown, J., & Newman, S. (1989). Cognitive apprenticeship: Teaching the craft of reading, writing, and mathematics. In L. Resnick (ed.), *Knowing, learning, and instruction: Essays in honor of Robert Glaser* (pp. 453–94). Hillsdale, NJ: Lawrence Erlbaum.

Commission on the Future of Community Colleges. (1988). *Building communities: A vision for a new century*. Washington, DC: American Association of Community and Junior Colleges.

Cook-Gumperz, J. (1986). Literacy and schooling: An unchanging equation? In *The Social Construction of Literacy*. New York: Cambridge University Press.

Cremin, L. A. (1965). *The genius of American education*. Pittsburgh: University of Pittsburgh Press.

Cross, K. P., & Angelo, T. (1993). *Classroom assessment techniques: A handbook for college teachers* (2nd ed.). Ann Arbor, MI: National Center for Research to Improve Postsecondary Teaching and Learning.

Cross, K. P., & Steadman, M. H. (1996). *Classroom research: Implementing the scholarship of teaching*. San Francisco: Jossey-Bass Publishers.

Cuban, L. (1986). *Teachers and machines: The classroom use of technology since 1920*. New York: Teachers College Press.

Cuban, L. (1988). *The managerial imperative and the practice of leadership in schools.* Albany, NY: State University of New York Press.

Cuban, L. (1990, January). Reforming again, again, and again. *Educational Researcher, 19* (1), 3–13.

Cuban, L. (1993). *How teachers taught: Constancy and change in American classrooms, 1890–1990.* New York: Teachers College, Columbia University.

Cuban, L., and Tyack, D. (1989, April). Mismatch: Historical perspectives on schools and students who don't fit them. Unpublished paper. Stanford: Stanford University, School of Education.

Curzon, L. B. (1980). *Teaching in Further Education* (2nd ed.). London: Cassell Ltd.

Darling-Hammond, L. (1994, September). Who will speak for the children? How "Teach for America" hurts urban schools and students. *Phi Delta Kappan 76* (1), 21–34.

Darling-Hammond. L. (1996, November). What matters most: A competent teacher for every child. *Phi Delta Kappan 78* (3), 193–201.

Darling-Hammond, L., & McLaughlin, M. (1995, April). Policies that support professional development in an era of reform. *Phi Delta Kappan 76* (8), 597–604.

DeBard, R. (1995, Summer). Preferred education and experience of community college English faculty: Twenty years later. *Community College Review, 23* (1), 33–50.

Delpit, L. (1986). Skills and other dilemmas of a progressive black educator. *Harvard Educational Review, 56* (4), 379–85.

Dewey, J. (1916). *Democracy and education.* New York: Macmillan.

Dewey, J. (1938). *Experience and Education.* New York: Collier Books.

Dewey, J., & Dewey, E. (1915). *Schools of tomorrow.* New York: E. P. Dutton.

Dill, D., Massy, W., Williams, P, & Cook, C. (1996, Sept./Oct.). Academic quality assurance: Can we get there from here? *Change, 28* (5), 16–25.

Doucette, D., (1994). Transforming teaching and learning through technology. In T. O'Banion & associates, *Teaching and learning in the community college* (pp. 201–22). Washington, DC: American Association of Community Colleges.

Dressel, P. L., & Marcus, D. (1982). *On teaching and learning in college: Reemphasizing the roles of learners and the disciplines.* San Francisco: Jossey-Bass.

Dunkin, M., & Barnes, J. (1986). Research on teaching in higher education. In M. Wittrock (ed.), *Handbook of research on teaching* (3rd ed). New York: Macmillan.

Easton, J. Q., Forrest, E. P., Goldman, R. E., & Ludwig, L. M. (1985). National study of effective community college teachers. *Community/Junior College Quarterly, 9* (2), 153–63.

Eaton, J. (1994). *Strengthening collegiate education in community colleges.* San Francisco: Jossey-Bass.

Edelsky, C. (1990, November). Whose agenda is this anyway? A response to McKenna. *Educational Researcher, 9* (8), 7–11.

Fenstermacher, G. D., & Soltis, J. F. (1992). *Approaches to teaching.* New York: Teachers College Press.

Fingeret, A., & Jurmo, P. (1989). *Participatory literacy education.* San Francisco: Jossey-Bass.

Fischer, F. (1987). Graduation-contingent student aid. *Change* 19(5): 40–47.

Floden, R., Goertz, M., & O'Day, J. (1995, September). Capacity-building in systemic reform. *Phi Delta Kappan,* 77(1), 19–21.

Forman, S., & Steen, L. (1995). Mathematics for work and life. In *Prospects for School Mathematics.* Reston, VA: National Council of Teachers of Mathematics.

Fountain, B. E., & Tollefson, T. A. (1989). *Community colleges in the United States: Forty-nine state systems.* Washington, DC: American Association of Community and Junior Colleges.

Fueyo, J. (1988). Technical literacy versus critical literacy in adult basic education. *Journal of Education, 170* (1), 107–17.

Glaser, R. (1984). Education and thinking: The role of knowledge. *American Psychologist, 39,* 93–104.

Glazer, J. (1983). *A teaching doctorate: The doctor of arts degree, then and now.* Washington, DC: AAHE (American Association of Higher Education).

Goodlad, J. (1984). *A place called school: Prospects for the future.* New York: McGraw-Hill.

Goto, S. (1995, October). The evolving paradigms of developmental/remedial instruction in the community college. Berkeley: Graduate School of Education, University of California.

Goto, S. (1999). The threshold: Basic writers and the open door college. Ph.D. dissertation, School of Education, University of California, Berkeley.

Goto, S., & Masuda, W. (1994). Case study: Remedial writing course at Contra Costa College. Unpublished paper. Berkeley, CA: Graduate School of Education.

Gott, S. (1988). Apprenticeship instruction for real-world tasks: The coordination of procedures, mental models, and strategies. In E. Rothkopf (ed.), *Review of Research in Education, 1988–89,* pp. 97–170. Washington, D.C.: American Educational Research Association.

Gott, S. (1995). Rediscovering learning: Acquiring expertise in real-world problem-solving tasks. *Australian and New Zealand Journal of Vocational Education Research* 3(1): 30–68.

Griffith, M., & Conner, A. (1994). *Democracy's open door: The community college in America's future.* Portsmouth, NH: Boynton/Cook.

Griffith, M., Jacobs, B., Wilson, S., & Dashiell, M. (1988). Changing the model: Working with underprepared students. *Community/Junior College Quarterly, 12,* 287–303.

Grubb, W. N. (1989). Dropouts, spells of time, and credits in postsecondary education: Evidence from longitudinal surveys. *Economics of Education Review, 8* (1), 49–68.

Grubb, W. N. (1991, March/April). The decline of community college transfer rates: Evidence from national longitudinal surveys. *Journal of Higher Education, 62* (2), 194–222.

Grubb, W. N. (1992). Finding an equilibrium: Enhancing transfer rates while strengthening the comprehensive community college. Working Papers 3(6). Washington, DC: National Center for Academic Achievement and Transfer.

Grubb, W. N. (1995a). The old problem of "new students": Purpose, content and pedagogy. In E. Flaxman & A. H. Passow (eds.), *Changing populations, changing schools: 94th yearbook of the National Society for the Study of Education* (pp. 4–29). Chicago: University of Chicago Press.

Grubb, W. N. (1995b). *Education through occupations in American high schools.* Vol. I: *Approaches to integrating academic and vocational education.* Vol. II: *The challenges of implementing curriculum integration.* New York: Teachers College Press.

Grubb, W. N. (1996a). *Learning to work: The case for re-integrating job training and education.* New York: Russell Sage Foundation.

Grubb, W. N. (1996b). *Working in the middle: Strengthening education and training for the mid-skilled labor force.* San Francisco: Jossey-Bass.

Grubb, W. N. (1997, June). The returns to education in the sub-baccalaureate labor market, 1984–1990. *Economics of Education Review, 16* (3), 231–46.

Grubb, W. N. (1998a, January). From black box to Pandora's box: Evaluating remedial/developmental education. Paper presented at the Conference on Replacing Remediation in Higher Education, National Center for Postsecondary Improvement, Stanford University.

Grubb, W. N. (1998b, April). Opening classrooms and improving schools: Lessons from inspection systems in England. Paper presented at the annual meeting of the American Educational Research Association, San Diego.

Grubb, W. N. (1998c, May). Making lifelong learning a reality: Capitalizing on America's community colleges. Berkeley: School of Education, University of California.

Grubb, W. N., & Badway, N. (1998, March). *Linking school-based and work-based learning: The implications of LaGuardia's co-op seminars for school-to-work programs.* MDS-1046. Berkeley, CA: National Center for Research in Vocational Education.

Grubb, W. N., Badway, N., Bell, D., & Kraskouskas, E. (1996). *Community college innovations in workforce preparation: Curriculum integration and tech-prep.* Mission Viejo, CA: League for Innovation in the Community College.

Grubb, W. N., Badway, N., Bell, D., Bragg, D., & Russman, M. (1997). *Workforce, economic, and community development: The changing landscape of the entrepreneurial community college.* Mission Viejo, CA: League for Innovation in the Community College.

Grubb, W. N., Badway, N., Bell, D., King, C., Herr, J., Prince, H., Kazis, R., Hicks, L., & Taylor, J. (1999). *Toward order from chaos: State efforts to reform workforce development "systems."* Berkeley, CA: National Center for Research in Vocational Education.

Grubb, W. N., & Kalman, J. (1994, November). Relearning to earn: The role of remediation in vocational education and job training. *American Journal of Education, 103* (1), 54–93.

Grubb, W. N., & Kraskouskas, E. (1992). *A time to every purpose: Integrating academic and occupational education in community colleges and technical institutes.* Berkeley: National Center for Research in Vocational Education, University of California at Berkeley.

Grubb, W. N., & McDonnell, L. (1995). Combating program fragmentation: Local systems of vocational education and job training. *Journal of Policy Analysis and Management* 15(2): 252–70.

Grubb, W. N., & Stasz, C. (1993). *Integrating academic and vocational education: Progress under the Carl Perkins Amendments of 1990.* Berkeley: National Center for Research in Vocational Education, for the National Assessment of Vocational Education, U.S. Department of Education.

Grubb, W. N., & Stern, D. (1989, January). *Long time a'comin': Options for federal financing of postsecondary vocational education.* Berkeley: MPR Associates for the National Assessment of Vocational Education.

Gudan, S., Clack, D., Tang, K., & Dixon, S. (1991). *Paired classes for success.* Livonia, MI: Schoolcraft College.

Guyton, E., and Farokhi, E. (1987). Relationships among academic performance, basic skills, subject matter knowledge, and teaching skills of teacher education graduates. *Journal of Teacher Education* 38(5):37–42.

Hanushek, E. A. (1986, September). The economics of schooling: Production and efficiency in public schools. *Journal of Economic Literature, 24*, 1141–77.

Hanushek, E. (1989, Fall). The impact of differential expenditures on school performance. *Educational Researcher 18* (4), 45–65.

Hanushek, E. A. (1994, May). Money might matter somewhere: A response to Hedges, Laine, and Greenwald. *Educational Researcher, 23* (4), 5–8.

Hanushek, E. (1996, Fall). Measuring investment in education. *Journal of Economic Perspectives, 10* (4), 9–30.

Hanushek, E. A., & others. (1994). *Making schools work: Improving performance and controlling costs.* Washington, DC: Brookings Institution.

Harkin, J., & Davis, P. (1996a, Spring). The communications styles of teachers in post-compulsory education. *Journal of Further and Higher Education, 20* (1), 25–34.

Harkin, J., & Davis, P. (1996b). The impact of GNVQs on the communications styles of teachers. *Research in Post-Compulsory Education, 1* (1), 97–107.

Harris, L., and Volet, S. (1997). *Developing a learning culture in the workplace.* Murdoch, Western Australia: Murdoch University.

Heath, S. B. (1983). *Ways with words: Language, life and work in communities and classrooms.* New York: Cambridge University Press.

Hedges, L. V., Laine, R. D., & Greenwald, R. (1994, April). Does money matter? A meta-analysis of studies of the effects of differential school inputs on student outcomes. *Educational Researcher, 23* (3), 5–14.

Heinemann, H. (1983). Toward a pedagogy for co-operative education. *Journal of Cooperative Education, 19* (3), 14–26.

Hershey, A., Silverberg, M., Haimson, J., Hudis, P., & Jackson, R. (1998, September). *Expanding options for students: Report to Congress on the national evaluation of school-to-work implementation.* Princeton: Mathematica Policy Research.

Hillocks, G. (1986). *Research on written composition: New directions for teaching.* Urbana, IL: ERIC Clearinghouse on Reading and Communications Skills and National Conference on Research in English.

Hirsch, E. D. (1987). *Cultural literacy: What every American needs to know.* Boston: Houghton Mifflin.

Hofstetter, C. H. (1998, June). Toward an equitable NAEP for English language learners: What contextual factors affect math performance? Ph.D. dissertation. School of Education, University of California, Los Angeles.

Hofstetter, C. H., Lord, C., Abedi, J., & Dietal, R. (1998, April). Language background effects on NAEP math performance. Paper presented at the annual meeting of the American Educational Research Association, San Diego.

Honeyman, D., Williamson, M. L., & Wattenbarger, J. L. (1991). *Community college financing 1990.* New York: American Association of Community and Junior Colleges.

Hughes, J. A. (1992). Approaches to teaching in the community college: What do faculty seek to accomplish? *Community/Junior College Quarterly, 16*, 189–97.

Hull, G. (1993a, Spring). Hearing other voices: A critical assessment of popular views on literacy and work. *Harvard Educational Review, 6* (3), 20–49.

Hull, G. (1993b). Critical literacy and beyond: Lessons learned from students and workers in a vocational program and on the job. *Anthropology and Educational Quarterly, 24* (4), 373–96.

Hull, G. (undated). *Alternative to remedial writing: Lessons from theory, from history, and a case in point.* Paper prepared for the Conference on Replacing Remediation in Higher Education, January 1998, National Center for Postsecondary Improvement, Stanford University.

Hull, G., Jury, M., Ziv, O., & Shultz, K. (1994, December). *Changing work, changing literacy? A study of skill requirements and development in a traditional and restructured workplace.* Interim report 2. Berkeley: National Center for the Study of Writing and Literacy and National Center for Research in Vocational Education.

Hull, G., & Rose M. (1989, April). Rethinking remediation: Toward a social-cognitive understanding of problematic reading and writing. *Written Communication, 6* (2), 138–54.

Hutchings, P. (1994, November). Peer review of teaching: From idea to prototype. *AAHE Bulletin, 47* (3), 3–7.

Hutchings, P. (1995). *From Idea to Prototype: The Peer Review of Teaching. A Project Workbook.* Washington, DC: American Association for Higher Education.

Hutchins, E. (1995). *Cognition in the wild.* Cambridge, MA: MIT Press.

Iowa Board of Education Examiners. (1991, July). *A study of the practitioners licensing standards for instructional personnel teaching at the community colleges.* Des Moines: Iowa Board of Education Examiners.

Jackson, P. (1986). *The practice of teaching.* New York: Teachers College Press.

Kazemek, F. (1988, November). Necessary changes: Professional involvement in adult literacy programs. *Harvard Educational Review, 58*(4), 464–87.

Kerry, T., & Tollitt-Evans, J. (1992). *Teaching in further education.* Oxford: Blackwell Publishers.

Kirshstein, R., Matheson, N., Jing, Z., and Pelavin Research Institute. (1997, September). *Instructional Faculty and Staff in Higher Education Institutions: Fall 1987 and Fall 1992.* NCES 97-470. Office of Educational Research and Improvement, U.S. Department of Education. Washington, DC: U.S. Government Printing Office.

Knapp, M., & Associates. (1995). *Teaching for meaning in high-poverty classrooms.* New York: Teachers College Press.

Knapp, M., Shields, P., & Turnbull, B. (1992). *Academic challenge for the children of poverty.* Volume 1: *Findings and conclusions.* Washington, DC: U.S. Department of Education.

Knapp, M. S., & Turnbull, B. J. (1990, January). *Better schooling for the children of poverty: Alternatives to conventional wisdom.* Volume I: *Summary.* Washington, DC: U.S. Department of Education.

Knowles, M., and Associates (1984). *Andragogy in action: Applying modern principles of adult learning.* San Francisco: Jossey-Bass.

Kohn, A. (1994, December). The truth about self-esteem. *Phi Delta Kappan 76* (4): 272–83.

Kozol, J. (1985). *Illiterate America.* Garden City, N.Y.: Anchor Press/Doubleday.

Kramsch, C. (1993). *Context and culture in language teaching.* Oxford, UK: Oxford University Press.

Kulik, J. A., Kulik, C.-L. C., & Cohen, P. A. (1980). Effectiveness of computer-based college teaching. *Review of Educational Research, 50,* 525–44.

Labaree, D. (1997, Spring). Private goods, public goods: The American struggle over educational goals. *American Educational Research Journal 34*(1): 39–81.

Lakes, R. D. (Ed.). (1994). *Critical education for work: Multidisciplinary approaches.* Norwood, NJ: Ablex Publishing Corporation.

Lauridsen, K. (1994). A contemporary view of teaching and learning centers for faculty. In T. O'Banion & associates, *Teaching and learning in the community college* (pp. 229–44). Washington, DC: American Association of Community Colleges.

Lever-Duffy, J. M., Lemke, R. A., & Johnson, L. (Eds.). (1996). *Learning without limits: Model distance education programs in community colleges.* Mission Viejo, CA: The League for Innovation in the Community College and the Miami-Dade Community College District.

Lieberman, A. (1995, April). Policies that support professional development: Transforming conceptions of professional learning. *Phi Delta Kappan 76* (8), 591–97.

Linn, M. (1996, March). *Cognition and distance learning.* Berkeley: School of Education, University of California.

Little, J. W. (1987). Teachers as colleagues. In V. Richardson-Roehler (ed.), *Educators handbook: A research perspective* (pp. 491–518). New York: Longman.

Little, J. W. (1996, May). Organizing school for teacher learning. Paper prepared for the AERA Invitational Conference on Teacher Development and School Reform, School of Education, University of California, Berkeley.

London, H. B. (1978). *The culture of a community college.* New York: Praeger.

Luria, A. R. (1969). Speech development and the formation of mental processes. In M. Cole and I. Maltzman (eds.), *A handbook of contemporary Soviet psychology* (pp. 121–62). New York: Basic Books.

Lytle, J. H. (1996, June). The inquiring manager: Developing new leadership structures to support reform. *Phi Delta Kappan 77* (10), 664–66.

MacGregor, J. (1991, Fall). What differences do learning communities make? *Washington Center News, 6* (1), 4–9.

Mansfield, W, & Farris, E. (1991, May). *College-level remediation in the fall of 1989.* NCES 91-191. Washington, D.C.: Office of Educational Research and Improvement, U.S. Department of Education.

Manski, C. (1989). Schooling as experimentation: A reappraisal of the college dropout phenomenon. *Economics of Education Review, 8* (4), 305–12.

Marcus, D., Cobb, E., and Shoenberg, R. (1993). *Lessons learned from FIPSE projects II.* Washington, DC: Fund for the Improvement of Postsecondary Education, U.S. Dept. of Education.

Marcus, D., Cobb, E., and Shoenberg, R. (1996). *Lessons learned from FIPSE projects III.* Washington, DC: Fund for the Improvement of Postsecondary Education, U.S. Dept. of Education.

Matthews, R. S. (1994a, Spring). *Notes from the field: Reflections on collaborative learning at LaGuardia.* Long Island City, NY: Office of the Associate Dean for Academic Affairs, LaGuardia Community College.

Matthews, R. S. (1994b). Enriching teaching and learning through learning communities. In T. O'Banion and associates, *Teaching and learning in the community college* (pp. 179–200). Washington, DC: American Association of Community Colleges.

McDonnell, L., & Grubb, W. N. (1991, April). *Education and training for work: The policy instruments and the institutions.* Berkeley and Santa Monica: National Center for Research in Vocational Education and the RAND Corporation.

McDonnell, L. M., & Zellman, G. L. (1993). *Education and training for work in the fifty states: A compendium of state policies.* N-3560-NCRVE/UCB. Berkeley: National Center for Research in Vocational Education, University of California.

McDonnell, L., Burstein, L., Ormseth, T., Catterall, J., & Moody, D. (1990, June). *Discovering what schools teally teach: Designing improved coursework indicators.* JR-02. Santa Monica: RAND Corporation.

McGrath, D., & Spear, M. B. (1991). *The academic crisis of the community college.* Albany, NY: State University of New York Press.

McKenna, M. C., Miller, J. W., & Robinson, R. D. (1990, November). Whole language: A research agenda for the nineties. *Educational Researcher, 19* (8), 3–6.

Mitchell, G. N., & Grafton, C. L. (1985). Comparative study of reverse transfer, lateral transfer, and first-time community college students. *Community/Junior College Quarterly, 9* (3), 73–80.

Moore, D. T. (1981). Discovering the pedagogy of experience. *Harvard Educational Review* 51(2):286–300.

Morris, C. (1994, November). *Success of students who needed and completed college preparatory instruction.* Research Report No. 94-19R. Miami: Institutional Research, Miami-Dade Community College.

Mosteller, F., Light, R., and Sachs, J. (1996, Winter). Sustained inquiry in education: Lessons from skill grouping and class size. *Harvard Educational Review* 66 (4): 797–842.

Murnane, R. J. (1984). *The rhetoric and reality of merit pay: Why are they different?* Report no. 81-1502. Cambridge, MA: Harvard University, Graduate School of Education.

Myers, M. (1996). *Changing our minds: Negotiating English and literacy.* Urbana, IL: National Council of Teachers of English.

NCES (National Center for Educational Statistics, U. S. Department of Education. (1997). *Digest of educational statistics 1997.* NCES 98-015. Washington, DC: U.S. Government Printing Office.

NCRVE (National Center for Research in Vocational Education). (1995, March). *Legislative principles for career-related education and training: What research supports.* MDS-900. Berkeley, CA: NCRVE.

NCTM (National Council of Teachers of Mathematics). (1989, March). *Curriculum and evaluation standards for school mathematics.* Reston, VA: NCTM.

Noddings, N. (1992). *The challenge to care in schools: An alternative approach to education.* New York: Teachers College Press.

O'Banion, T., & Associates. (1994). *Teaching and learning in the community college.* Washington, DC: American Association of Community Colleges.

Oakes, J. (1985). *Keeping track: How schools structure inequality.* New Haven: Yale University Press.

Ogbu, J. (1978). *Minority education and caste: The American system in cross-cultural perspective.* New York: Academic Press.

Ong, W. J. (1982). *Orality and literacy: The technologizing of the word.* New York: Routledge.

Osterman, P. (1994). How common is workplace transformation and who adopts it? *Industrial and Labor Relations Review, 47* (2), 173–88.

Palincsar, A. S., & Brown, A. L. (1984). Reciprocal teaching of comprehension-fostering and monitoring strategies. *Cognition and Instruction, 1,* 117–75.

Palmer, J. (1986–87, Winter). Bolstering the community college transfer function: An ERIC review. *Community College Review, 14* (3), 53–63.

Palmer, P. (1993, November/December). Good talk about good teaching: Improving teaching through conversation and community. *Change* 25 (6), 8–13.

Panel on Educational Technology. (1997). *Report to the president on the use of technology to strengthen K–12 education in the United States.* Washington, DC: Executive Office of the President, President's Committee of Advisors on Science and Technology.

Pascarella, E., Bohr, L., Nora, A., & Terenzini, P. (1995, Spring). Cognitive effects of 2-year and 4-year colleges: New evidence. *Educational Evaluation and Policy Analysis, 17* (1), 83–96.

Perez, R. (1991). A view from troubleshooting. In M. Smith, ed., *Toward a unified theory of problem solving: Views from the content domains* (pp. 115–153.) Hillsdale, NJ: Lawrence Erlbaum Associates.

Pincus, F. L. (1980, August). The false promises of community colleges: Class conflict and vocational education. *Harvard Educational Review, 50* (3), 332–61.

Porter, J. R., Jr. (1995). The roles of administrators. In W. N. Grubb, (ed.). *Education through occupations in American high schools,* Vol. 2 (pp. 102–14). New York: Teachers College Press.

Powell, A. G., Farrar, E., & Cohen, D. K. (1985). *The shopping mall high school: Winners and losers in the educational marketplace.* Boston, MA: Houghton Mifflin.

Puente: Creating leaders for California's future. (Undated). Oakland: Office of the President, University of California.

Quint, J., Musick, J. S., & Ladner, J. A. (1994). *Lives of promise, lives of pain*. New York: Manpower Demonstration Research Corporation.

Quint, J., & Bos, J. (Forthcoming). *The challenge of making a difference: Lessons from a program for disadvantaged mothers and their families*. New York: Russell Sage Foundation.

Raisman, N. (1998, May 19). Equal to any: Community colleges can compete with Ivy League. *Community College Times*, p. 3.

Resnick, L. (Ed.) (1989). *Knowing, learning, and instruction: Essays in honor of Robert Glaser*. Hillsdale, NJ: Lawrence Erlbaum.

Resnick, L. (1987). *Education and learning to think*. Washington, DC: National Academy Press.

Richardson, R. C., & Elliot, D. B. (1994). Improving opportunities for underrepresented students. In T. O'Banion & Associates, *Teaching and learning in the community college* (pp. 97–115). Washington, DC: American Association of Community Colleges.

Richardson, R. C., Jr., Fisk, E. C., & Okun, M. A. (1983). *Literacy in the open-access college*. San Francisco: Jossey-Bass.

Riggs, R., Davis, T., & Wilson, O. (1990, January). Impact of Tennessee's remedial/developmental studies program on the academic progress of minority students. *Community/Junior College Quarterly of Research and Practice, 14* (1), 1–11.

Rose, M. (1989). *Lives on the boundary: The struggle to achieve of America's underprepared*. New York: Free Press.

Roueche, S. D., & Roueche, J. E. (1989). Innovations in teaching: The past as prologue. In T. O'Banion (ed.), *Innovation in the community college* (pp. 46–69). New York: Macmillan.

Roueche, J. E., & Baker, G. A., III. (1987). *Access and excellence: The open door college*. Washington, DC: The Community College Press.

Roueche, J. E., & Roueche, S. D. (1993). *Between a rock and a hard place: The at-risk student in the open-door college*. Washington, DC: American Association of Community Colleges.

Roueche, J. E., & Comstock, U. N. (1981). *A report on theory and methods for the study of literacy development in community colleges*. Report to the National Institute of Education. Austin: University of Texas at Austin. ERIC Document ED 211 161.

Salvatori, M., & Hull, G. (1990). Literacy theory and basic writing. In M. G. Moran & M. J. Jacobi (eds.), *Research in basic writing: A bibliographic sourcebook* (pp. 49–74). New York: Greenwood Press.

SCANS (Secretary's Commission on Achieving Necessary Skills). (1991). *What work requires of schools: A SCANS report for America 2000*. Washington, DC: U.S. Department of Labor.

Scribner, S. (1984). Vygotsky's use of history. In J. V. Wertsch (ed.), *Culture, communication, and cognition: Vygotskyan perspectives*. Cambridge: Cambridge University Press.

Scribner, S., & Cole, M. (1981). *The psychology of literacy*. Cambridge, MA: Harvard University Press.

Seidman, E. (1985). *In the words of the faculty: Perspectives on improving teaching and educational quality in community colleges*. San Francisco: Jossey-Bass.

Sessions, R., & Wortman, J. (1992). *Working in America: A humanities reader*. South Bend, IN: University of Notre Dame Press.

Shaunessey, M. (1977). *Errors and expectations: A guide for the teacher of basic writing*. New York: Oxford University Press.

Shaw, K. (1997, Fall). Remedial education as ideological batttleground: Emerging remedial education policies in the community college. *Educational Evaluation and Policy Analysis, 19* (3), 284–96.

Shulman, L. (1995, May). The pedagogical colloquium: Three models. *AAHE Bulletin 47* (9), 6–10.

Silverman, J., Hughes, E., & Wienbroer, D. R. (1990). *Rules of thumb: A guide for writers.* New York: McGraw-Hill.

Simon, R. I., Dippo, D., & Schenke, A. (1991). *Learning work: A critical pedagogy of work education.* New York: Bergin and Garvey.

Sirotnik, K. (1983, February). What you see is what you get: Consistency, persistency, and mediocrity in classrooms. *Harvard Educational Review, 53,* 16–31.

Sizer, T. R. (1984). *Horace's compromise: The dilemma of the American high school.* Boston, MA: Houghton Mifflin.

Slavin, R. (1980). Cooperative learning. *Review of Educational Research, 50,* 315–42.

Smith, B. (1991, March/April). Taking structure seriously: The learning community model. *Liberal Education, 77* (2), 42–48.

Smith, V. (1993, June). Phantom students: Student mobility and general education. *AAHE Bulletin, 45* (10), 10–13, 7.

Snow, C., Burns, M. S., & Griffin, P. (1998). *Preventing reading difficulties in young children.* Washington, DC: National Academy Press.

Solorzano, R., Stecher, B., & Perez, M. (1989). *Reducing illiteracy in California: Review of effective practices in adult literacy programs.* Report for the California State Department of Education, Adult Education Division. Pasadena, CA: Educational Testing Service.

Spring, J. (1986). *The American school, 1642–1985.* New York: Longman.

Stanley, L., & Ambron, J. (Eds.). (1991, Spring). *Writing across the curriculum in community colleges.* New Directions in Community Colleges, Vol. 73. San Francisco: Jossey-Bass.

Stasz, C., Ramsey, K. Eden, R., DeVanzo, J., Farris, H., & Lewis, M. (1993). *Classrooms that work: Teaching generic skills in academic and vocational settings.* Berkeley, CA: National Center for Research in Vocational Education.

Stasz, C., and Kaganoff, T. (1997, August). *Learning how to learn at work: Lessons from three high school programs.* DRU-1697-NCRVE/UCB. Santa Monica: RAND Corporation, Institute on Education and Training.

Stern, D., Finkelstein, N., Stone, J., Latting, J., & Dornsife, C. (1995). *School-to-work: Research on programs in the United States.* Bristol, PA: Falmer.

Stern, D., Stone, J., Hopkins, C., McMillion, M., & Crain, R. (1994). *School-based enterprise: Productive learning in American high schools.* San Francisco: Jossey-Bass Publisher.

Sternberg, R. J. (1988a, July/August). Mental self-government: A theory of intellectual styles and their development. *Human Development, 31,* 197–224.

Sternberg, R. J. (1988b). *The triarchic mind: A new theory of human intelligence.* New York: Viking.

Sternberg, R. J. (1990, January). Thinking styles: Keys to understanding student performance. *Phi Delta Kappan, 71* (5), 366–71.

Sticht, T. (1988). Adult literacy education. In E. Rothkopf (ed.), *Review of research in education,* Vol. 15 (pp. 59–96). Washington, DC: American Educational Research Association.

Street, B.V. (1984). *Literacy in theory and practice.* Cambridge: Cambridge University Press.

Tanner, D., & Tanner, L. (1990). *History of the school curriculum.* New York: Macmillan.

Tharp, R., & Gallimore, R. (1988). *Rousing minds to life: Teaching, learning, and schooling in social context.* New York: Cambridge University Press.

Tinto, V. (1987). *Leaving college.* (2nd ed.). Chicago: University of Chicago Press.

Tinto, V., & Goodsell-Love. (1995). *A longitudinal study of learning communities at LaGuardia Community College.* ERIC Document ED 380 178. Washington, DC: National Center on

Postsecondary Teaching, Learning, and Assessment, Office of Educational Research and Improvement, U.S. Department of Education.

Tinto, V., Goodsell-Love, A., & Russo, P. (1994). *Building learning communities for new college students: A summary of research findings of the Collaborative Learning Project.* Washington, DC: National Center on Postsecondary Teaching, Learning, and Assessment, Office of Educational Research and Improvement, U.S. Department of Education.

Tinto, V., Russo, P., & Kadel, S. (1994, February/March). Constructing educational communities: Increasing retention in challenging circumstances. *AACC Journal, 64* (4), 26–29.

Tokina, K. (1993). Long-term and recent student outcomes of freshman interest groups. *Journal of the Freshman Year Experience, 5* (2), 7–28.

Tokina, K., & Campbell, F. (1992). Freshman interest groups at the University of Washington: Effects on retention and scholarship. *Journal of the Freshman Year Experience, 4* (1), 7–22.

Tomlinson, L. (1989). *Postsecondary developmental programs: A traditional agenda with new imperatives.* ASHE-ERIC Higher Education Report 3. Washington, DC: George Washington University.

Traub, J. (1994a). *City on a hill: Testing the American dream at City College.* New York: Addison-Wesley.

Traub, J. (1994b, September 19). Class struggle. *New Yorker,* pp. 76–90.

Tuma, J. (1993, April). *Patterns of enrollment in postsecondary vocational and academic education.* Prepared for the National Assessment of Vocational Education. Berkeley, CA: MPR Associates, Inc.

Tyack, D, & Cuban, L. (1995). *Tinkering toward utopia: A century of public school reform.* Cambridge, MA: Harvard University Press.

Van Horn, C. E. (1995). *Enhancing the connection between higher education and the workplace: A survey of employers.* Denver, CO: State Higher Education Executive Officers and the Education Commission of the States.

Villeneuve, J. C., & Grubb, W. N. (1996). *Indigenous school-to-work programs: Lessons from Cincinnati's co-op education.* Berkeley, CA: National Center for Research in Vocational Education.

Walberg, H. (1986). Syntheses of research in teaching. In M. Wittrock (ed.), *Handbook of research on teaching* (3rd ed.). New York: Macmillan.

Weis, L. (1985). *Between two worlds: Black students in an urban community college.* Boston: Routledge and Kegan Paul.

Weisberg, A. (1988). Computers, basic skills, and job training programs: Advice for policymakers and practitioners. New York: Manpower Demonstration Research Corporation.

Willett, L.H. (1980, October–December). Instructional effectiveness of full- and part-time faculty. *Community/Junior College Quarterly of Research and Practice 5* (1), 23–30.

Wills, J. L., & Lurie, I. (1993). *Industry driven skill standards systems in the United States.* Vol. III. Washington, DC: Institute for Educational Leadership, Center for Workforce Development.

Willis, P. (1977). *Learning to labour: how working class kids get working class jobs.* Farnborough, U.K.: Saxon House.

Wilson, S. (1994). What happened to Darleen? Reconstructing the life and schooling of an underprepared learner. In Mark Reynolds (ed.), *Two-year college English: Essays for a new century.* Urbana, IL: National Council of Teachers of English.

Worthen, H. (1997). Signs and wonders: The negotiation of literacy in commmunity college classrooms. Ph.D. dissertation. School of Education, University of California, Berkeley.

Worthen, H. (1998). The problem of the majority part-time faculty in the community colleges. In B. Alford and K. Kroll (eds.), *Two-year colleges and the politics of writing instruction.* Westport, CT: Heinemann.

Zwerling, L. S. (1976). *Second best: The crisis of the community college.* New York: McGraw-Hill.

Zwerling, L. S. (1989). *The community college and its critics.* New Directions for Community Colleges, no. 54. San Francisco: Jossey-Bass.

APPENDIX

Table A-1

**Numbers of Community College Administrators
and Instructors Observed and Interviewed**

Name	Administrators	Academic Instructors	Occupational Instructors	Remedial/ developmental Instructors
College of Alameda, CA	1	3	10	2
Bunker Hill, MA	1			4
Chabot, CA		3		4
Chemeketa, OR	2	3	5	
CC of San Francisco, CA	1	3	3	
Contra Costa, CA	4	3	7	1
CC of Denver, CO	3	3	1	
Fresno, CA			1	
Diablo Valley, CA	2	9	3	2
Indian Hills, IA	3	2	9	1
LaGuardia, NY	6	5	14	1
Laney, CA		1	8	1
L.A. Mission, CA	2	4		1
Madison Area Tech. College, WI	2	4	5	
Marshalltown, IA	2	6	4	
Minneapolis CC, MN	1	6		
Minneapolis Technical College, MN	1		4	1
Merced, CA		Group Interview		
North Harris, TX	7	1	3	7
Northeast Iowa, IA	2	3	10	
Palomar, CA	1	2	1	1
San Diego City, CA		2		
Santa Barbara, CA	2	7	5	2
San Joaquin Delta, CA	1		7	
Seattle Central, WA	3	7		2
Seattle North, WA	5	10	3	1
Skyline, CA	1		3	
Solano, CA	3	5	3	4
Vista, CA		4		
Wayne County, MI		4	2	
West Valley, CA		1		
Western Iowa Technical CC, IA	3	2	4	2
Total	**57**	**101**	**114**	**42**

Table A-2

Instructors observed and interviewed by field of study

	Number
Academic Subjects	*101*
English	27
Math	7
Science	11
Social science	36
Other	20
Occupational Subjects	*114*
Agriculture	4
Business	24
Computers	13
Construction	13
Drafting (CAD) and graphic design	12
Auto	14
Electronics	6
Early childhood education	5
Health occupations	4
Other	19
Remedial/developmental and ESL	*42*
Total	**257**

Other academic subjects include ethnic studies, film, architectural history, and interdisciplinary studies.

Other occupational subjects include aviation airframe and mechanics, band instrument repair, commercial baking, cosmetology, electron microscopy, upholstery, refrigeration and air-conditioning, and machine trades.

INDEX